Chile

Chile

THE LEGACY OF HISPANIC CAPITALISM

BRIAN LOVEMAN

New York · Oxford University Press · 1979

Copyright © 1979 by Oxford University Press, Inc.

Library of Congress Cataloging in Publication Data

Loveman, Brian.
  Chile.

  (Latin American histories)
  Bibliography: p.
  Includes index.
  1. Chile—History. I. Title.
F3081.L68   983'.064   78-13965
ISBN 0-19-502518-0
ISBN 0-19-502520-2 pbk.

Printed in the United States of America

Preface

Chile is a nation where historians and social theorists have participated actively in public life as well as in scholarship. Presidents, mínisters of state, legislators, and party leaders have contributed to Chile's historical tradition, to its literature, and to its art. No historian, Chilean or foreign, can undertake a new look at Chilean history without returning, first, to the great intellectual contributions of Chile's national writers. While this book departs in some important ways from conventional interpretations of Chile's past, it owes much to the insight and thorough research of generations of Chilean writers.

To the intellectual debt I owe to Chilean writers must be added the use I have made of the studies of hundreds of non-Chilean "Chileanists" who have dedicated their attention to Chilean history. As the format of this book generally precluded systematic footnote citations, I have attempted to note appropriately those works upon which I relied extensively in the selective bibliography at the end of this volume.

As I wrote this study, my friend, teacher, and general editor of Oxford University Press' Latin American Histories Series, James Scobie, offered his advice, encouragement, and critical reviews of the manuscript for which I am extremely grateful. The manuscript has also benefitted from the comments and suggestions made by Jacques Barbier, Harold Blakemore, Simon Collier, Thomas M. Davies, Jr., Philip Flemion, Henry Landsberger, Sharon Loveman, Vincent Padgett, William Sater, William Sherman, and John Whaley. Larry Stickell generously allowed me to read chapter drafts of his doctoral dissertation on the development of the nitrate industry in Chile and to use data from his research in the present volume. While the insights of these scholars have greatly improved the present book, I am, of course, responsible for any errors of fact or interpretation that remain in the volume.

I have been fortunate to have help from a number of people in the preparation of the manuscript. Special thanks go to Veva Link, Helen Triller, Jeri Haddon and Paula Forrester, and to Phoebe Hoss for her careful copy-editing. Nancy Ferris provided invaluable assistance in preparation of the bibliography as did Michael Arguello in construction of the index.

A final thank you must also go to my friends in Trovolhue who taught me the political meaning of life's daily struggle against the legacy of four centuries of Hispanic Capitalism.

B.L.

San Diego
August 1978

Contents

Maps

Tables

Chile

Introduction

Harsh exploitation of the labor force in mines, farms, and industry has been the most persistent characteristic of Chilean society since the arrival of European conquerors in the sixteenth century. Despite the recurrent efforts by progressive Church officials or government reformers to improve the lot, first, of Chile's indigenous population and, then, of the ethnically mixed working classes, the Chilean economy continued to rely upon forced labor, agricultural service tenants, and then a highly mobile but miserable wage proletariat. From the first years of conquest and into the 1970s Chilean society and culture reflected the tensions between attempts to better the living and working conditions of the majority of the Chilean people and the realities of an economic and political order resting upon the foundation of conquest, subjugation, and coercion of labor.

In 1620, more than eighty years after the first Spanish expedition to Chile, the king of Spain ordered Chilean encomenderos and settlers to end compulsory labor and to pay farm workers a minimum daily wage. Resistance by the propertied classes and lack of enforcement efforts by public officials prevented implementation of this legislation. More than three centuries later (1953) a Chilean national

3

government enacted a minimum wage for agricultural workers and sought to regulate rural labor conditions. Landowners successfully resisted the feeble enforcement efforts of the Ministry of Labor.

In 1620 Indian and mestizo laborers living on the haciendas of Spaniards were required to work 160 days a year. In 1953 Chilean rural tenants and laborers typically worked well over 200 days a year and provided landowners not only their own labor but also that of family members or other hired hands.

The quest for liberty, justice, and human dignity is a recurrent theme in Chilean history. But in the era of the conquistadors as in modern Chile, the quest has been subordinated inevitably to the requirements of order and material gain for a small privileged minority. Whether the conflict joined Jesuits and encomenderos, or Marxists, reformers, and conservatives, the outcome has repeatedly been a return to pragmatic repression to uphold the economic, social, and political foundations of the Chilean version of Hispanic capitalism— a complex adaptation of neofeudal political and economic institutions to the New World. Relying initially upon slave or forced labor, Hispanic capitalism represented a unique response of the Spanish colonial elite to the expansion of European capitalism.

Some Spaniards called out for social justice almost from the outset of colonization. Clerical and secular precursors of twentieth-century reformers and revolutionaries opposed decimation and abuse of the native population. If the conqueror Pedro de Valdivia came to subjugate and exploit the Indians, the Jesuit Luis de Valdivia urged peaceful conquest and abolition of slavery and compulsory labor. But in a frontier region at perpetual war, efforts by the crown and some churchmen to ameliorate the conditions of the Indians through protective legislation met consistent failure. Governors, soldiers, encomenderos, and even some religious leaders built a Chilean economy from the sweat and suffering of the Indian work force.

For the conquistadors Chile was not the prize of Mexico or Peru. Instead of the vast wealth of the Aztecs and Incas, the Chilean conquerors encountered a people with little more to defend than their land and liberty. Between 1598 and 1612, after more than half a century of warfare and settlement, the Araucanians forced the Spanish to abandon the principal towns south of the Bío Bío River. In 1655 another Indian uprising again destroyed almost all the new and re-established Spanish outposts in Araucania. To survive, to establish a semblance of order, and to achieve some economic returns the Spaniards adopted a de facto policy of pragmatic repression. Ignoring or circumventing royal edicts or colonial legislation designed to protect the Indians, the colonial bureaucracy, soldiers, and encomenderos prevailed. In the words of an Indian cacique: "The King is good and he legislates justly, but your governors and captains do not comply and there is no justice for the Indians."

Thus the struggle between parchment justice and the realities of Chilean society offers a permanent tension in the historical development of the Chilean nation. A war for independence against Spain carried out in the name of liberty, culminated in the establishment of an autocratic order inspired by a merchant deprived of his government-authorized tobacco monopoly. In the tradition of the Spanish governors and captains, Diego Portales used fear and repression to establish political order.

The creation of the Portalian state after 1830 spared Chile the destructive anarchy experienced by most of South America in the first half of the nineteenth century. Portales accomplished this task through harsh, authoritarian treatment of any political opposition. An aphorism attributed to Portales set the tone for the struggle between liberty and autocracy that characterized Chilean development in the nineteenth and twentieth centuries: "The stick and the cake, justly and opportunely administered, are the remedies with which any nation can be cured, however inveterate its bad habits may be." As Portales observed, the social order in Chile was preserved by the "weight of the night . . . the masses' near universal tendency to repose was the guarantee of public tranquility." In case the "weight of the night" should lighten, Portales and his successors never hesitated to use "the stick" to secure that tranquility.

The second half of the nineteenth century brought modernization to Chile as it did in varying degrees to most of Latin America. The steamship, telegraph, railroad, increased labor mobility, and urbanization, as well as expansion of commerce and industry, altered the socio-economic institutions of the nation. Political parties played the game of liberal democracy and mouthed the rhetoric of social justice. Eloquent speeches in the Chilean congress promised relief to the working classes, while laborers and rural workers organized to challenge the propertied interests. New laws guaranteed justice and equality. By the end of the nineteenth century the old order seemed to be coming apart. Growing awareness by the working classes of alternatives to their poverty and misery threatened to end the era of the stick and the cake.

Then in the period 1924-31, in the name of order and justice, a new class of conquistador sought to re-establish authority and to re-impose the "weight of the night" on the Chilean masses. In the tradition of Portales, government-stimulated economic growth accompanied repression of all who voiced opposition to the incumbent regime.

A few years later Chile nevertheless was acclaimed a democracy. Along with Uruguay and Costa Rica, Chile escaped the coups, rebellions, and revolutions that afflicted most of Latin America after the Great Depression. After 1932 the military did not overtly intervene in Chilean politics. Elections took place as scheduled, and votes were fairly counted. Freedom of the press brought a wide range of viewpoints to the Chilean population and spared the incumbent government no criticism. In contrast to the authoritarian pattern of the Portalian state, Chilean presidents failed to control their own political parties, let alone congressional elections or deliberations. No Chilean president in the period 1932-70 could name his own successor. Great legislative strides were made in the direction of popular participation, social justice, and democratization. But the tension persisted between legislative proclamations and the traditional foundations of Chilean society—autocracy, social stratification, and repression of popular activism. The tension gave a special character to Chilean democracy.

In the early 1960s a Chilean president initiated a "revolution in liberty." Priority was given to increased participation of the popular classes, to removing social and economic inequality, and to stimulating the Chilean economy. It soon became evident that removing the "weight of the night" from the Chilean working classes could not be reconciled with maintenance of the existing socio-economic order. Chilean democracy had concealed but not eliminated the conflicts between liberty and participation and the authoritarian tenets of conquerors and twentieth-century capitalists.

By 1970 the struggle was explicit. Revolutionaries and reformers joined in an effort to destroy the institutions and values of the old order. Ironically, but not surprisingly, the principal vehicle they chose to carry out this radical transformation of Chilean society was an updated model of that employed by conquistadors and Portales: a centralized bureaucracy imbued with the prejudices and defects of Hispanic viceroys, governors, and notaries. The attempt did not prosper. Landlords, capitalists, bureaucrats, and soldiers stifled the "revolution" as they had implementation of the king's mandate in 1620.

In 1973 a military coup terminated a three-year effort to restructure Chilean society. Again owing to pragmatic repression in support of Hispanic capitalism, opponents of the incumbent regime lived in an atmosphere of fear. The new military government proclaimed: "In every soldier there is a Chilean; in every Chilean a soldier." In answer to this apparent return to the spirit of conquest, a Christian Democratic politician seemed to echo the Jesuit Luis de Valdivia: "We are convinced that it is not possible to build a lasting order on repression."

From the time of the conquest Chile has been distinctive in Spanish America. Chileans avoided the anarchy and dislocation common to the new nations of Latin America in the early nineteenth century. They have believed themselves to be unique, even referring to themselves as the English of South America. The visitor to Chile has repeatedly heard this theme, summed up in the phrase *No somos tropicales* ("We aren't like those other Latin Americans"). Yet the motto on the national emblem, *Por la razón o la fuerza* ("By reason or by force"), has served as a reminder that the present has not escaped the past. It proclaims that national objectives will be attained "by reason or by force."

For the present generation of Chileans, as for their ancestors, the basic dilemmas persist: how to make Chile a land of liberty while maintaining political order; how to achieve economic progress without exploitation of the working classes; how to maintain social order and create social justice without imposing the terrible "weight of the night" on the Chilean people. This is the historical legacy and current challenge of Chile.

Chapter 1 • Land and Society

The territory occupied by the Chilean nation is the prize of military conquest. From Copiapó south to the Bío Bío River, Spanish conquistadors took the land from a variety of indigenous peoples in the sixteenth century. From an undefined point somewhat north of Copiapó (lat. 27° 22′ S), nineteenth-century Chilean armies extended the national domain by defeating Bolivian and Peruvian forces in the War of the Pacific (1879-83). The territory Chile acquired then has remained a source of friction and potential conflict among the three countries. South of the Bío Bío River the Araucanian Indians successfully impeded consolidation of Spanish and then Chilean rule until after 1880, when modern weaponry finally overcame the descendants of the Indian groups that had offered the most determined resistance to the Spanish conquistadors. Only at the end of the nineteenth century, therefore, did the political unit that is now Chile effectively achieve its present boundaries, extending some 2600 miles from the northernmost city of Arica (lat. 18° 28′ S) past the Strait of Magellan to latitude 56° S. Chile also claims substantial portions of Antarctica (lat. 53° W-90° W).

For most of its history Chile did not include the great northern

9

desert containing the vast mineral wealth for which the country became known around the world. Nor did the territory south of the Bío Bío River form an integral part of European settlement. In colonial times (1535-1810) Chile meant a small number of semi-urban places, from La Serena through the central valley (see Map 3), in addition to the precarious frontier fort towns south of the Bío Bío River which Araucanian Indians periodically destroyed. Bounded on the east by the Andes Mountains, on the west by the coastal mountain range and the Pacific Ocean, and on the north by one of the world's driest deserts, the Chilean colony was little more than a backwater of the Spanish Empire.

Between Copiapó and the Bío Bío River the Andes chain occupies from one-third to one-half of the width of present-day Chile (though certain areas in what is now western Argentina—Tucumán in the early colonial period and Cuyo until the late eighteenth century—also belonged to Chile). Moving south from Copiapó, the Andes narrow and become a single dominant cordillera, with some of the highest peaks in South America. In Argentina at the headwaters of the Aconcagua River, Mt. Aconcagua, the loftiest peak in the western hemisphere, rises some 22,835 feet (7000 meters). In Chilean territory in the same Andean region, Mt. Salado reaches over 22,500 feet (6900 meters). The Andean passes as far south as the central valley town of Curicó (lat. 35° S) are typically found at more than 10,000 feet. Los Leones, Lagarto, and Casa de Piedra are located at more than 13,000 feet, and less than ideal weather makes passage extremely difficult. Near Aconcagua, the pass at Los Patos (4,720 meters) served as a conduit for the liberating army of the independence movement led by General San Martín in 1817. Through the gap at Juncal, almost due east of the city of Los Andes, lies the railroad between Chile and the Argentine city of Mendoza. In general, however, the Andes represent a significant barrier to transport and communication, thereby isolating Chile from eastern South America and Europe.

South of the Bío Bío River, the Andes lose height and passes are found at lower elevations. Permanent snow levels are also lower, so that inland from the city of Valdivia (lat. 40° S) snow persists above

5000 feet year round. In this area beautiful yet treacherously active snow-capped volcanoes edge magnificent lakes. Southern Chile is a region of cereal production, diversified agriculture, cattle raising, and dairies set within the forested cordilleras, islands, and fjords. At the southern extreme are the inhospitable Patagonian plains and Tierra del Fuego, where the Strait of Magellan affords a perilous transit around the tip of South America. Before the opening of the Panama Canal in 1914, this southern passage made Valparaíso a commercial competitor of Lima-Callao for the Pacific shipping trade.

In the late nineteenth century Chile incorporated much of the Atacama desert into the national domain and consolidated control over the provinces south of the Bío Bío River. This gave the country more territory with great natural resources, but these northern and southern territories remained sparsely inhabited. To this day some 70 percent of Chile's population resides between Aconcagua and the Bío Bío River. On a map the nation that emerged in the twentieth century looks like a long, irregularly scalloped ribbon trimming southwestern South America. Seen from the air the country is an indentation of varying depths between the Andes on the east and the coastal mountains to the west.

Chile's major cities—Copiapó, La Serena, Valparaíso, Santiago, Talca, Chillán, Concepción, Valdivia—are situated in one of the world's most geologically active regions and over the centuries they have been repeatedly damaged or destroyed by earthquakes and tidal waves; while floods and droughts make agriculture risky in the south as well as in the north and the central valley. Landslides, volcanic eruptions, and avalanches add to the natural violence that persistently threatens Chilean lives and property.

Nature provides Chile not only a continual challenge but also an incredible variety of landscapes, climates, and natural ecologies, ranging from the arid northern deserts to the Chilean antarctic in the south. This diversity is tied together by the Pan American Highway running through the middle of the country some two thousand miles from Arica to Puerto Montt. For most of the distance the highway runs parallel to the longitudinal railroad, much of which the national

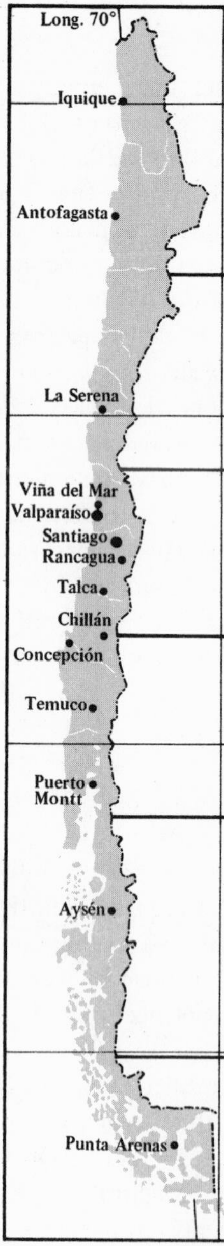

Long. 70° (map)	Lat.	Mean Annual Temperature (C.)	Rainfall in Millimeters	Major Economic Activities
Iquique	20°	18.3	25	
Antofagasta				Oasis cultivation, mining, nitrate, fishing and limited industry.
La Serena	30°	14.4	114	Early vegetables, _fruit,_ limited vines and cereals, goats, sheep, limited cattle, mining, fishing.
Viña del Mar Valparaíso Santiago Rancagua Talca Chillán		13.9	359	Central valley agriculture, _fruits, vines,_ wheat, corn, hemp, tobacco, vegetable oils, diversified livestock —70% of all Chilean industry.
Concepción		13.5	1319	
Temuco	40°	11.8	2511	Coal, steel, petro-chemicals, forest products, cereals, potatoes, dairy and cattle, limited vegetables, _orchards and vineyards._
Puerto Montt				
Aysén	50°	8.9	2865	Forest industries, livestock, subsistence agriculture, fishing, sheep.
Punta Arenas		6.2	2754	Sheep and livestock, wool, oil, and natural gas.

CHILE:
Climate and Major Economic Activities

MAP 1: Chile: Climate and Major Economic Activities

government built and has operated since the late nineteenth century. The Chilean National Airline (LAN) also connects most major cities, though on a reduced scale after 1973 as part of an economy move by the military government.

From north to south the variety of Chilean landscapes may be illustrated by comparing its several natural divisions with the strip of land running from the desert of Baja California to the Yukon and Alaska: the deserts of the Chilean "great north" or *norte grande* (provinces of Tarapacá, Antofogasta, and part of Atacama—Map 2); the transitional steppes and transversal river valleys of the "little north" or *norte chico* (part of Atacama province, Coquimbo, and part of Aconcagua province—Map 2); the fertile central valley (part of Aconcagua province south to the transitional region between the Itata and Bío Bío rivers—Map 3); the "frontier" region of cereal production and forests south of the major industrial center of Concepción (province of Arauco, Bío Bío, Malleco, and Cautín—Map 3); the lake region (provinces of Valdivia, Osorno, Llanquihue—Map 4); and the sparsely settled region of southern continental Chile (provinces of Chiloé, including the island, Aysén, and Magallanes—Map 4).

The Chilean *norte grande* is part of South America's western coastal desert which extends northward through Peru and into Ecuador. In much of this region the coastal range amounts only to rounded hills which drop sharply to the Pacific. From the Loa River south, the first major surface water to reach the Pacific flows in the Copiapó. The major urban concentration and farming belt around Copiapó (almost ninety miles long) is often taken as the southern limit of the Atacama desert. At the time of the initial Spanish expedition of conquest from Peru into Chile (1535), Copiapó marked the northern boundary of the territory that became Chile.

This northern region is a vast desert. Scattered oases and river valleys provide slight relief from the barren landscape. Charles Darwin's description of a part of this region near Santa Rosa and Huantajaya as a "complete and utter desert," in which he saw only cacti and lichen, matches that of Preston James in the twentieth century: "No

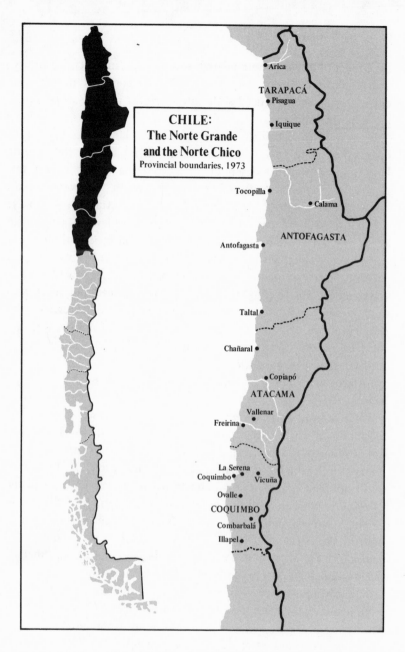

MAP 2: Chile: The *Norte Grande* and the *Norte Chico*

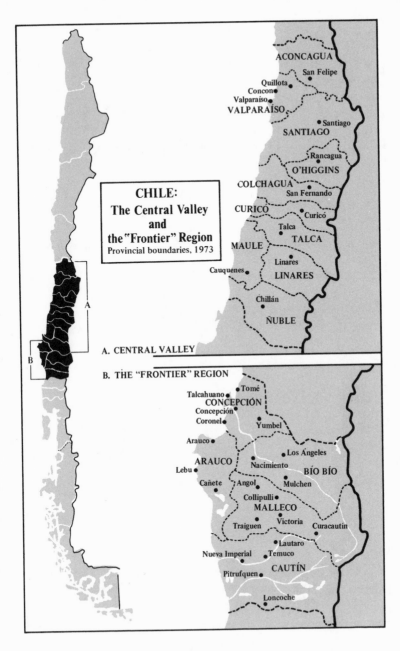

MAP 3: Central Chile and the Frontier Region

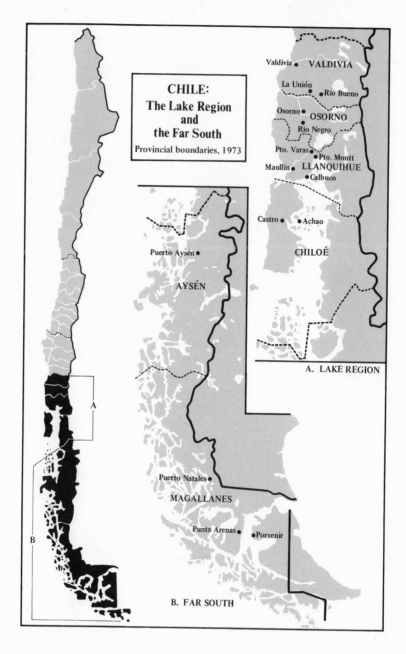

MAP 4: Chile: The Lake Region and the Far South

part of the west coast of South America is more forbidding, more utterly desert-like in aspect than the stretch of about six hundred miles between Arica and Caldera." Despite the fact that weather stations in some parts of the *norte grande* have never recorded rainfall, there are noticeable differences in climate between the coastal and the interior regions. The coast experiences much greater relative humidity and often cloudiness, due to the cooling effects of the Humboldt Current. Inland, skies are cloudless and humidity much less. For example, humidity in the coastal city of Iquique averages about 81 percent, while in Calama, to the southeast, it averages about 48 percent.

For thousands of years small groups of people lived as fishermen along the coast or took advantage of the limited water resources in this region for oasis valley agriculture, especially in the fertile valleys of Azapa and Lluta. Available evidence suggests that the site of Chile's northernmost city, Arica, supported small population clusters many centuries before the Spanish conquistadors came south from Cuzco. In the mid 1960s the entire *norte grande* had only about 11,000 hectares* under cultivation of a total territory of almost 18,000,000 hectares (Tarapacá, 5,528,700 hectares; Antofagasta, 12,-306,300 hectares). Of these, 1200 hectares were in the valley of Azapa, east of Arica, and another 1000 at Calama, southwest of the port of Tocopilla (lat. 22° 5' S).

Many of the population centers in the *norte grande* owe their origins to the mining activity made possible by the great mineral wealth of the desert. The major ports—Iquique, Antofagasta, Tocopilla—as well as minor ports and interior cities arose, and prospered or declined with mineral finds (silver, gold, nitrates, copper, iron). Iquique owed its colonial significance to silver strikes at Huantajaya and its nineteenth-century boom to nitrates. In 1870 a silver strike at what came to be called Caracoles, two hundred kilometers northeast of Antofagasta, attracted some ten thousand miners in its glory days and transformed Antofagasta into an urban and commercial center. Tocopilla and Antofagasta both prospered from copper mining, and

* One hectare equals approximately 2.47 acres.

then from nitrates in the nineteenth and twentieth centuries. Other settlements briefly flourished and then died when the mineral deposits to which they owed their existence were exhausted. The remains of mining camps and settlements that litter the desert are reminiscent of the ghost towns of the western United States in an even bleaker setting.

In the late nineteenth century the ports of the *norte grande* served as service centers and transshipment outlets for the nitrate works (*oficinas*) and copper mines. At the time these ports seemed more like overgrown villages than real cities, though in several, particularly Iquique and Antofogasta, luxurious mansions and new public services gave the wealthy a sense of living in modern comfort. This was made possible by importing fuel, food, and even topsoil for plazas while piping water over great distances. An early twentieth-century description of these mining ports tells us that they were sometimes "mere collections of tin shanties crowded at the base of cliffs . . . connected by little lines of railways with the mines in the interior."

The nitrate deposits themselves occur at elevations between 3000 and 9000 feet above sea level, at distances varying from 10 to 80 miles from the Pacific coast. Layers of *caliche* or raw nitrate sometimes lie on the surface of the earth; at other times they are found 20 to 30 feet below the surface. In addition to the nitrate itself, important byproducts of processing include iodine, salt, sulphur, and sulphuric acid.

Though the *norte grande* occupies about one-third of the national territory (Antofogasta is as large as the territory from Santiago to the Bío Bío River), it contains less than 8 percent of the country's population. Despite its sparse population, the region has played an extraordinary role in determining Chilean economic development since the nineteenth century. The extraction of silver, nitrates, nitrate by-products, and copper allowed foreign investors and Chilean capitalists to accumulate incredible wealth. It also allowed Chilean politicians and governments to avoid fundamental political and institutional issues well into the twentieth century, as they could depend upon revenues from the desert to finance public services and projects instead of devising rational and equitable systems of internal taxation and public finance.

While the desert was yielding wealth to foreign investors and a Chilean elite in the nineteenth and the early twentieth centuries, its ports, rail lines, and mining camps were the principal battleground of class struggle for Chile's emergent proletariat. Both the wealth of the desert and the experience of working-class organization and struggle came south to influence the rest of Chile. Nitrate revenues and the earnings from copper financed the public sector of the Chilean economy, providing funds for public works and government services. Peasant workers returning south with the new experience of class organization, strikes, blacklists, and sometimes massacres by police or military, brought a new consciousness to the wheat fields of the frontier or the grape harvest of the central valley. Union organizers in the north became national leaders of the Chilean working classes and spread their message from the deserts to the centers of economic and political power in the cities and countryside of the "real" Chile to the south.

Even with the decline of the nitrate industry after World War I, and the depression of the 1930s, the minerals (especially copper) of the *norte grande* still constituted the principal basis of Chilean economic performance. Much of the copper also came from the *norte grande*, though to the south there are significant deposits in the coastal cordillera and the lower elevations of the Andes. The largest open-pit copper mine in the world, Chuquicamata, is located inland almost due east from Tocopilla and slightly north of Calama. Until the early 1970s, when the leftist coalition government of President Salvador Allende nationalized the largest copper operations, this mine, like most of Chile's largest copper mines, was controlled by United States companies. Copper in the 1960s and 1970s accounted for 70 to 80 percent of the value of Chilean exports, making the economy highly sensitive to small changes in the international price of this commodity. In 1974-77 drastic declines in copper prices played a significant role in exacerbating the substantial economic depression Chile experienced under the military government headed by General Augusto Pinochet.

The extensive coastline of the *norte grande* makes fishing and fish-related industries of great potential importance. In the early 1960s fish meal production rapidly expanded, only to decline after 1965 as the *anchovetas*, the small fish whose processing induced large investments in plants at Iquique and Arica, seemed to disappear. Other efforts to industrialize the *norte grande* included installation of vehicle assembly plants in Arica, expansion of copper refineries, smelters, and other mineral-related industries, and the processing of agricultural commodities. Above all, however, the *norte grande* remains a copper-mining region which, in the words of ex-President Salvador Allende, provides the "salary of Chile."

South of the *norte grande*, part of the province of Atacama, Coquimbo, and part of Aconcagua form a transition from desert to steppes and then to the fertile central valley. Here, in the *norte chico*, the desert gives way to scrub and brush vegetation which increases toward the south. The transitional character of this region is well illustrated by the average rainfall for selected stations from Arica in the *norte grande* to Quillota at the southern margin of the *norte chico*. Average annual rainfall increases from 1 to 2 millimeters in Arica or Iquique to 28 millimeters at Copiapó. It is 65 millimeters at Vallenar and 133 millimeters in La Serena. Copiapó and the surrounding region are a transition between the arid desert and the semiarid *norte chico*. At the Aconcagua Valley around Quillota, where average annual rainfall exceeds 400 millimeters, there is another transition to the temperate climate of central Chile (see Map 3).

Once called the "region of ten thousand mines," the *norte chico*, like the desert to the north, contains great mineral wealth. In 1811 silver discovered near Vallenar, inland from Huasco, led to the opening of some 150 mines. From 1830 to 1850 mining activity in the region reached a peak with new silver strikes at Chañarcillo, south of Copiapó. Production continued here until the 1890s. In this region, in July 1851, Chile inaugurated one of the first three railroads in South America, to transfer ore from the inland mines to the port at Caldera.

While not as large as the Chuquicamata deposits, copper from Potrerillos and then El Salvador has contributed significantly to Chilean copper production. The smelter at Paipote, just south of Copiapó, serves what is called the small and medium copper sector, which gives employment to thousands of Chileans though it accounts for only 15 to 20 percent of total copper production (see Map 5).

In the *norte chico*, unlike the *norte grande*, a number of rivers cross the otherwise arid region, making possible important agricultural activities and the existence of a number of important interior urban concentrations. Still, this region contains only 3 percent of Chile's arable land. During the colonial period, tiny coastal settlements served as collection points for gold or silver brought down from the cordillera and the inland valleys for shipment to Lima and Spain. English, French, and Dutch buccaneers repeatedly menaced these towns and occasionally sacked them, terrorizing their inhabitants.

Initially agriculture in the *norte chico* met the needs of a limited local market and of the workers in nearby mines. Only later did agriculture expand to supply wheat, specialty crops, and fruits to southern and foreign markets. Always, however, the interdependence of agriculture and mining persisted and has dominated the economy of the *norte chico* to the present.

Like the *norte grande*, although to a lesser extent, the *norte chico* has played a disproportionate role in shaping the class consciousness of Chilean workers while at the same time exporting its products to support the Chilean economy. Owing to the tendency of many rural laborers and peasants in this region to work alternately in agriculture and mining, depending upon weather conditions and access to cultivable land, the militancy of the mine workers spread to the rural regions. In the valley of Choapa, southeast of Illapel, and in much of Aconcagua, the natural ecology and political economy of the region

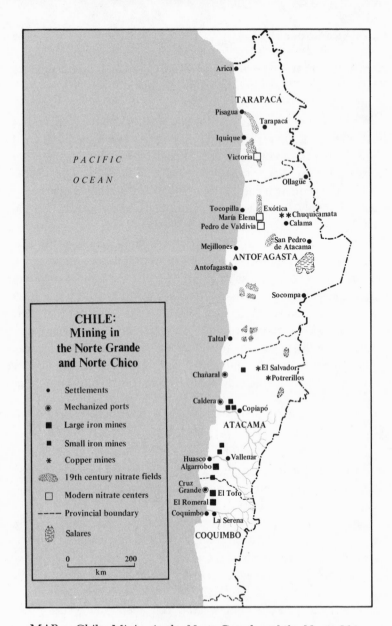

MAP 5: Chile: Mining in the *Norte Grande* and the *Norte Chico*

(Source: Harold Blakemore, "Chile" in *Latin America: Geographical Perspectives*, Metheun & Co. Ltd., London, 1971.)

forged a rural working-class militancy in the early twentieth century; it spread to the rest of rural Chile only after the 1930s.

Agriculture in the *norte chico* combines pastoral activities (goats and sheep especially) in the cordillera with intensive cultivation of vegetables and fruit like tomatoes and melons. These products command excellent prices in urban centers, particularly Santiago, because they arrive before the harvests in the central valley. Cereal crops are also cultivated, but the region's susceptibility to periodic droughts makes all agriculture risky. Experiments with drought-resistant pastures in recent years have given good results in some areas for sheep and goat forage. After the mid-1960s expanded plantings of fruit orchards increased production of apricots, peaches, avocados, and walnuts in selected areas of Coquimbo to complement chirimoya, papaya, and olive production.

Also in the *norte chico,* especially Coquimbo, there prevails a distinctive pattern of partially communal land tenure called *comunidades.* Many of the *comunidades* originated in colonial times with mining concessions. Depletion of minerals or failure to strike pay dirt turned the laborers' attention to agriculture and animal husbandry. Today the limited land of the *comunidades* forces young adults to migrate in search of better opportunities. Thus the *comunidades* have a disproportionate number of the very young and of older adults. Studies estimate the number of these *comunidades* in Coquimbo at slightly more than one hundred, occupying somewhere between 590,000 and 737,000 hectares. Population estimates vary from a low of 53,000 to a high of 88,000. The *comunidades* typically contain large extensions of dry, hilly or cordillera land which the members, called *comuneros,* use as a common pasture. In addition, the *comuneros* have small amounts of permanently or seasonally irrigated land divided into parcels which they work individually. Wheat, barley, potatoes, corn, and beans are cultivated, and in the higher valleys (Limarí, Hurtado, Rio Grande, Rapel) fruits and vineyards play an important part in the *comunero* economy.

Goats constitute the main animal resource, providing dairy products, hides, and meat to the *comuneros* along with some cash income.

Intensified goat husbandry has produced significant erosion of soils in the common pasture lands. In the years 1968-71 serious droughts in this region reduced goat herds by more than 75 percent and drastically decreased yields of wheat, thereby impoverishing the region's rural population. Since in all of Coquimbo and Aconcagua there are little more than 100,000 hectares of irrigable land, agriculture in and out of the *comunidades* remains at the mercy of variations in annual rainfall. Irrigation, where practiced, requires heavy investments in water works and dams. The average *comunero* family in Coquimbo (of whose area *comunidades* occupy about 17 percent) in the early 1970s had access to nearly 60 hectares of dry land and only 1/5 hectare of irrigated land.

As in the rest of Chile before 1964, large rural estates called haciendas or fundos controlled most of the region's agricultural land outside the *comunidades*. These estates usually controlled access to irrigation water and competed with the *comunidades* or with the smallholders for this scarce resource. In most cases the *comuneros* or other smallholders obtained only the water not used by the haciendas, which made small-scale agriculture even more precarious and difficult. Agrarian reforms after 1964 altered the distribution of land and water rights, but the counterreforms under way in the mid-1970s left unclear the future of both the *comunidades* and the agrarian reform cooperatives on the large estates expropriated from 1964 to 1973.

The circumstances of the small and medium-size mining operations and of agriculture in the *norte chico* make stable employment a considerable problem for its population. In the dry years *comuneros* seek work in the nitrate fields, copper, or iron mines in order to support their families who remain on the land. The variety of minerals in the *norte chico* has allowed small enterprises and individual miners to develop beside the giant firms that historically have dominated the nitrate and copper industries. Numerous small and medium-size firms participate in mining activities supported in part by a national government agency called Empresa Nacional de Minería (ENAMI). Despite their poverty, the desperate hope of striking it rich holds many peasant-prospectors in the region. From the exploitation of iron, however, the small miners are essentially excluded. Large foreign interests (Bethlehem Steel) have dominated ore production at El Tofo and El Romeral; from those sites the ore is sent south to the steel mill at Huachipato near Concepción for processing, or is exported.

Apart from the processing of agricultural commodities, pisco* production, fruit drying, and mining, the *norte chico* lacks significant industrial establishments. In the early 1970s droughts intensified rural poverty in the region, and many peasants depended for survival upon government make-work projects and food distribution. Extremely large investments in irrigation, crop development, and agricultural extension are necessary before the *norte chico* can overcome the obstacles to economic development imposed by nature.

At the southern extremity of Aconcagua province, the fertile region known as the "Vale of Chile" marks the northern boundary of Chile's heartland (Map 3). The central valley of Chile contains some 70 percent of Chile's population, provides more than 70 percent of industrial employment, and even accounts for 20 percent of copper production from mines in Santiago, Valparaíso, and especially O'Higgins province. Within a 100-mile radius of Santiago lives more than 50 percent of Chile's population. At its widest the central valley measures some 45 miles between the Andes and the coastal mountains or the sea, and only along the Bío Bío River at its southernmost boundary does the flat valley floor extend all the way to the Pacific. Valparaíso, the only major port in the region, is the primary doorway for imports to the Santiago market. To the south, Chile possesses only two other major ports—Talcahuano (Concepción) and Valdivia.

The Chilean central valley has a mediterranean climate with rainfall increasing gradually toward the south. The climate and the fertility of the soil, reminiscent of central California, are ideal for intensive truck farming, orchards, and vineyards in addition to cereal

* A clear South American brandy made out of grapes.

crops and livestock. With the advantage of a harvest season that occurs during Europe's and North America's winter months, the central valley offers Chile a potential source of foreign exchange through export of high-quality fruits, vegetables, wines, dairy products, and specialty crops.

Despite this potential, extensive wheat cultivation and cattle operations, along with vineyards located in a relatively small number of large estates, have dominated the valley's agricultural history. Into the mid-1960s only a minority of these estates had moved to more modern agricultural practices, making the backwardness of Chilean agriculture a critical obstacle to economic development. After 1964 massive agrarian reform programs disrupted traditional agricultural and land tenure patterns by creating agrarian cooperatives operated by campesinos under the not always benevolent tutelage of government administrators. After the military coup of 1973, former owners recovered many of the large farms (perhaps 30 percent of those expropriated from 1964 to 1973), and the new government made efforts to break up the production cooperatives into individual family farms. Nevertheless, the reforms often altered old production patterns by emphasizing higher-value crops for export. From 1973 to 1978 this policy resulted in expanded exports of table grapes, fruits, and vegetables to Europe and the United States, offsetting somewhat the continued need to import cereals—especially wheat.

The large rural estates in Chile's central valley have influenced much more than agricultural production. Historically, they constitute the single most important political and social institution in Chile. Their owners belong to a small social elite that has controlled most of Chile's best agricultural land as well as its political institutions. As late as 1930, from 60 to 75 percent of Chile's rural population resided on the haciendas. The tremendous power exercised by landowners or proprietors over the rural labor force made each rural estate a quasi-political unit. The landowner controlled access to land, housing, and employment. The resident rural laborer who disobeyed the landlord's orders risked being fined, whipped, dispossessed, or otherwise punished. In the mid-twentieth century the service-tenant, or *inquilino,* worked the landlord's land in exchange for access to perhaps half an acre or an acre of land, a house and garden plot, and various in-kind payments or perquisites, such as food rations, firewood, or permission to graze a designated number of animals on the fundo's pasture.

After adoption of minimum wage legislation for agriculture in 1953, landowners theoretically paid these workers a minimum wage established by the government, provided minimally decent housing, and obeyed a number of labor laws intended to protect the workers. In practice, landowners successfully ignored or evaded the minimum wage legislation as they had previously evaded other labor laws; workers who complained or registered protests with the Labor Department faced reprisals or dismissals. In 1952 an inspector of the Chilean Labor Department reported:

> In the fundo Las Pataguas, owened by the Archbishop of San-tiago but rented to Mr. Dario Pavez, the administrator Ramiro Ramírez, aided by the foreman [*mayordomo*], applied about 100 lashes to the worker [*voluntario*], Roberto González. The same administrator has also whipped other workers [four named] and for this has been nicknamed "The Lash" [*El Azotador*]. In fundo La Carlina, owned by Carlos Aspillaga Sotomayor, and adminis-tered by Vicente Salazar, if workers ask for their social security booklets so they can go to the health service, they are insulted and offered a kick in the ass. . . .

Families who had lived for generations on a fundo could be fired and evicted at the landowner's whim, with no compensation for im-provements they had made to their residence or to the land by way of fences, fruit trees, or outbuildings.

The dependence of the central valley's agriculture upon a rigidly stratified social system and the economically inefficient fundos per-meated Chilean society and made relations between the upper classes and working classes authoritarian, patronizing, and exploitative. This situation prevailed after 1932 as the Chilean political system appar-ently developed into a functioning formal democracy. The inherent contradictions between a truly democratic political and economic system and maintenance of the centuries-old hacienda system generated intense political conflict in Chile in the years 1964-73, leading to profound agrarian reforms and then to renewed, if modified, subjugation of the rural working classes after 1973.

It is difficult to understand the pervasive influence of the haciendas of the central valley on Chile's politics, economy, and social relations unless one has witnessed the ritual subservience of the campesino listening to his landlord's orders—the bowed head, eyes toward the ground, hat held over the genital area—all symbolic admissions of the huge gap separating the hacendado from "his" workers. It is also difficult to understand the deceptive calm of rural Chile in the mid-1970s unless one has witnessed the joy and energy of liberation expressed by campesinos from 1964 to 1973. In those years the hacienda system seemed destined for the scrapheap of Chilean history, and the future of Chilean agriculture appeared tied to thousands of newly formed peasant organizations. Then, in a manner typical of Chilean history, the struggle for social change and justice confronted the reality of naked force defending the interests of the landowners and their allies. While this defeat of the campesinos left unclear the future structure of central valley agriculture, it reconfirmed and perpetuated the essential character of the struggle for the land and subjugation of the labor force initiated in 1535 by the Spanish conquistadors against the native Chilean peoples.

Lack of opportunities in the countryside, and the stifling hacienda system in the central valley in the mid-nineteenth century, pushed rural workers to northern mining camps, railroad construction gangs, and the cities in search of employment and a better life. The rural to urban trend has continued throughout the twentieth century. By the mid 1970s Santiago accounted for about one-third of all Chile's population, while over 70 percent of all Chileans lived in cities with over 20,000 inhabitants—most of these in the central valley (see Table 1).

Not only have agriculture and the hacienda system made the central valley the political, economic, and social heartland of Chile, but historically, industrial activities (other than the mines) have been

TABLE 1. POPULATION OF MAJOR CITIES AND METROPOLITAN AREAS
OF THE CENTRAL VALLEY, 1970

Santiago (metropolitan area)	2,861,900
Valparaíso–Viña del Mar	453,000
Rancagua	95,000
San Fernando	44,500
Curicó	60,000
Talca	103,000
Chillán	103,000
Concepción	190,000
Talcahuano	152,000

concentrated in Santiago, Valparaíso, and Concepción. Modern industry in Chile resulted largely from import-substitution through World War II, but later expanded considerably into secondary products, heavy industrial products, and capital goods. In the mid 1950s over 70 percent of all manufacturing centered in Santiago (51%) and Valparaíso (20%). Since that time planned decentralization has resulted in the emergence of a major steel and petrochemical complex in Concepción-Talcahuano, at the southern extreme of the central valley.

Industrialization has not been able to provide employment for all of the thousands of migrants to the urban areas. Squatter settlements, called *callampas* ("mushroom" settlements) or *campamentos*, surround the major cities of the central valley and house large numbers of Chile's urban poor in dwellings constructed of tin, cardboard, and wood, shelters which barely protect their inhabitants from the whims of nature. These settlements often lack such urban services as electricity, potable water, and sewers. They constitute, in this respect, a massive urban village rather than an integrated part of an urban community. As more and more Chileans move to the cities of the central valley, the strains of hyperurbanization increase, presenting a problem yet to be solved by any Chilean national government.

At the Bío Bío River the central valley gives way to the frontier region (see Map 3), marked by year-round rainfall. Instead of the central valley's irrigated fields on alluvial fans sloping toward the sea, the cereal and pasture lands of the frontier region still bear the scars of forest clearing, which makes cultivation possible. From Arauco to Cautín, the overgrazed, overutilized land of the Mapuche Indians and other smallholders present a red-brown image of eroded soil on the increasingly denuded coastal mountains and the valley floor. To the east the Andes continue to dominate but are not as high as they are north of the Bío Bío River. The climate in this region is comparable with the Pacific Northwest of the United States, with stormy wet winters and cool, less damp summers. The region takes its name from the historical role it played in the struggle between the Spanish invaders and the indigenous Indian population. Until late in the nineteenth century the Bío Bío River marked the limits of Spanish and then Chilean control (see Chapter 2). In a social and economic sense it also remained a frontier region with very limited urban population, agricultural production or industry into the late nineteenth century.

Concepción dominated the development of the frontier provinces from the time of the conquest, serving first as the main base of the frontier garrison and later as the Bío Bío region's commercial center. Livestock and cereal production, which supplied the raw materials for mills and other processing industries, paced economic development. Mining activities, principally coal, also played a role, and the mines around Lota remain in the 1970s important economically.

Agriculture in the frontier region depends much less on irrigation than is the case in the central valley of Chile with its mediterranean climate. The farms of the frontier provinces account for about 25 percent of Chile's wheat production and for 40 percent of the cattle, while an often backward timber industry provides seasonal employment for numerous rural workers and raw material for Chile's expanding paper and cellulose manufacturers.

Also found in the frontier provinces are the remaining communal landholdings (*reducciones*) of the Araucanian (Mapuche) Indians. Deprived of much of their land by the Spanish conquest, and further despoiled by speculators and politicians in the nineteenth century, many Mapuche continue to eke out a livelihood through pastoral, agricultural, and artisan activities. Estimates of the number of Mapuche in the *reducciones* vary considerably, but there are probably between 300,000 and 500,000. Some *reducciones* are located in Valdivia, but most are in the provinces of Bío Bío, Arauco, Malleco, and Cautín—the latter alone accounts for almost 200,000 Mapuche. In Cautín the *reducciones* contain some 343,000 hectares, accounting for 22 percent of the agricultural land in the province, and 86 percent of all agricultural units.

The Mapuche on the *reducciones*—or sometimes "ex-*reducciones*," or *comunidades* without legal title—are family groups that exploit the land, both in common and on individual parcels. Data from an investigation carried out in 1966 by the Dirección de Asuntos Indígenas on 493 *reducciones* indicated that the average *reducción* amounted to 290 hectares with a population of 83 persons. Economic activity in the *reducciones* includes fishing and seaweed collection along the coast, lumbering, charcoal making, and extensive production of pigs, sheep, chickens, and cattle, as well as crops. Household manufactures include basketmaking, weaving, and metal working.

The Mapuche are a poor people subjugated by outsiders after a four-century struggle to maintain their independence. The bravery of the Mapuche, celebrated in Alonso de Ercilla's epic poem *La Araucana*, may afford a source of national pride for educated Chileans, but the persisting poverty of these Indians seems to have little effect on the national conscience. Chileans adore Indian heroes such as Lautauro and Caupolicán who defeated the conquistadors but, like their North American counterparts, ignore the present-day plight of the Mapuche. The most recent study of the Mapuche concluded: "The Mapuche works his depleted lands and waits. For a long time he has lived . . . in a world not under his control. He has lost his land. . . . He lives exploited, submerged in poverty." From 1965 to 1973 agrarian reform programs mobilized many Mapuche for land occupations or "recuperations." Since 1973 the return of land to former owners and repression of organized rural militancy has restored "calm" to the region, but at the cost of the assassinations of Mapuche leaders and the deaths of Indian farmers.

Often little better off than the Mapuche, thousands of campesinos work their small parcels throughout the frontier provinces, barely scratching out a subsistence from depleted soil. During the winter rains long periods of relative idleness are spent around wood-burning stoves in small houses built from the native trees of the region. Larger farms also exist, but they lack the large resident populations characteristic of the central valley.

While most of the frontier region is rural and agricultural, more than 50 percent of the population resides in urban places—with Concepción-Talcahuano and the capital of Cautín province, Temuco, being the most important. Significant industrial activities of the region include Chile's steel industry at Huachipato, paper and cellulose manufacture, textiles, coal mines, petrochemicals, and processing of lumber, flour, beet sugar, matches, cooking oil, cheese, and butter. The coal mined in Arauco and Concepción is of poor quality, necessitating its mixture with imported coal for use in the steel complex. Like the nitrate fields, in the twentieth century the coal mines have been the scene of many labor conflicts that forged working-class consciousness among the Chilean proletariat. They also are the setting for Chilean author Baldomiro Lillo's stories (*Subterra*, 1904) of social protest, describing the lives and suffering of the coal miners.

The lake region—the provinces of Valdivia, Osorno, and Llanquihue—begins south of the Toltén River and is an extension of the frontier provinces (Map 4). Storminess increases as one moves south and is greater, latitude for latitude, in Chile than in North America. Valdivia (lat. 39° 48′ S) receives almost three times the annual rainfall of Tacoma, Washington. Founded by Pedro de Valdivia in 1552, the city of Valdivia witnessed one of the most memorable amphibious military operations in South American history when, in 1820, Lord Cochrane led a seemingly suicidal assault against Spanish fortifications to capture the port for the independence movement.

Renowned for its natural beauty, the lake region contains numerous snow-capped volcanoes; the tourists it draws supplement agricultural activities. Valuable natural hardwood forests as well as plantations of Monterrey pines are the basis for a developing timber industry. Depletion of the natural forests, however, meant that by 1965 some 40 percent of all lumber came from the pine plantations. Dairy farms, beef cattle, and other livestock dominate the agrarian economy, though cereals and diversified small-scale farming also contribute. Together with the frontier provinces the lake region supplies over half of the country's cereal production, over 90 percent of the oats, and 50 percent of the potatoes.

Valdivia, Osorno, and Puerto Montt are the most important urban centers in this region, where almost half of the population still lives in the rural sector. Most of the industries, like that in the frontier provinces, depend upon agrarian production—lumber, wood products, flour mills, textiles, canneries, beer, beet sugar, leather products —or else upon the harvest of the sea. Many industries owe their existence to the influence of German immigrants enticed to Chile in the mid-nineteenth century. When the newly formed Society for Industrial Development (Sociedad de Fomento Fabril, 1883) published a preliminary list of industries in Valdivia and Osorno in 1884, all the breweries, tanneries, brick factories, bakeries, machine shops, furniture manufacturers, and mills (except one) belonged to persons with non-Spanish (mostly German) surnames. While this was the principal region of Chile in which the national government actively intervened to promote colonization in the nineteenth century, the relatively small number of immigrants (perhaps 3000) heavily influenced the economic and cultural development of the provinces from Cautín south, and especially Osorno, Valdivia, and Llanquihue. For example, in 1902 a list of the rural estates in the commune of Valdivia valued at over 40,000 pesos contained not a single Spanish surname. The descendants of these immigrants who cleared dense forest land and prospered through their toil and intellect are still a dominant force in the economy of the lake region.

The territory south from the Gulf of Reloncaví, comprising almost a third of continental Chile, contains no more than 3 percent of the nation's population. This is a region of cold driving winds, great storminess and rainfall, and rough seas. In places rainfall exceeds 200 inches a year. Between Puerto Montt and about latitute 44° S the main structural features of central Chile continue—though the coastal mountain range now runs partly beneath the sea or becomes a chain of forested islands. The snowfall in the eastern cordillera descends to only 2300 feet above sea level at Tierra del Fuego.

The island of Chiloé (lat. 42° S), in a geographical position similar to Vancouver Island in North America, is a densely forested territory where smallholders and a small number of indigenous peoples engage in subsistence agriculture, sheep raising, lumbering, fishing, and potato cultivation. Chiloé makes no great economic contribution to the national economy. Its main town is Ancud (pop. 11,900 [1970]).

Aysén province is made up of canals, lakes, islands, and mountains, though grasslands and plains support thousands of sheep. Aysén, along with Magallanes, is Chile's last frontier. Punta Arenas, located on the Strait of Magellan, is Chile's most southernly city (pop. 61,000 [1970]). It supports a number of industries based on the thousands of sheep raised on the Patagonian plains. Oil wells and natural gas exploration have increased the economic importance of Magallanes in recent years. Most of the petroleum is shipped to Concón, near Valparaíso, or to Concepción for refining, though a topping plant at Manantiales supplies Magallanes with gasoline, kerosene, and diesel fuel. Chile still produces only a fraction of the oil its economy requires. In the mid-1970s the country imported fuel and lubricants valued at over $300 million (20 to 35 percent of the value of copper exports) despite exports of natural gas to Argentina. The substantial increase in oil prices in the 1970s seriously exacerbated Chile's balance of payment difficulties and intensified the economic depression after 1973. Lack of significant fossil fuel supplies seems destined to be a long-term constraint on Chilean economic development.

The vast majority of Chileans descend from the European invaders of the sixteenth and seventeenth centuries and the Indian peoples resident in Chile at the time of Spanish conquest. Africans and non-

Iberian Europeans contributed much less to the formation of the Chilean nationality. As elsewhere in Spanish America, Spanish racism and social prejudices have generally reserved the highest social and political positions for those who claimed "purity of blood" (*limpieza de sangre*), thereby creating caste-class stratifications that distinguished Spaniards from "white" mestizos, "Indian" mestizos, Indians, blacks, mulattoes, and *zambos* (offspring of Indian and black). From generation to generation stratification could become quite complex within the *castas* (racially mixed peoples), but customs and legal practices sought to ensure the "integrity" of the ruling class, especially after the massive miscegenation of the sixteenth and seventeenth centuries.

Legal suits filed in the late eighteenth century by family members who feared that a proposed marriage might put a stain on the family honor, reveal the fundamental racial and social biases of colonial society. Royal officials were asked to prohibit marriages on the legal grounds of "inequality of castes." An irate mother could "charge" a would-be son-in-law with being the grandson and great-grandson of blacks, "mulatto-colored," or "a pure mulatto" with "obviously Negro hair." While official Spanish policy declared that "being an Indian is not a rational or just motive for denial of parental consent," Chilean colonists looked with disfavor upon "staining the family honor" with marriage to Indians or "Indian mestizos." But these attitudes no more prevented widespread concubinage and miscegenation in the later colonial period than they had in the formation of Chilean nationality in the *mestizaje* of the first century and a half of conquest.

While Chilean national mythology claims descendancy from Spaniards and Araucanians, the Indian component of Chilean racial stock was somewhat more varied than this simple union of the heroic Araucanian Indians with their European enemies. About the indigenous population in Chile at the time of the conquest much less is known than about the Indians of Mexico, Central America, and Peru. Some investigators believe all originated in a single racial stock, differentiated in customs, language, and organization over time in response

to local conditions. Other researchers affirm the diversity of the indigenous groups in Chile, noting differences in language, culture,
farming implements, weapons, and political organization. The no-
menclature adopted to describe Indian groups often referred merely
to their location—for example, *puelches* (people of the east, eastern
cordillera down to Mendoza); *picunches* (people of the north—
though those south of the *puelches* called them *picunches*). Less
gradually the Spaniards came to refer to *los pencos, los quillotanos,
los mapochos,* and so on, but again these names simply denote Indians of Penco, Quillota, and Mapocho.

As there are neither important archaeological sites south of Copiapó, nor a written language, nor any large territorial political units,
we are unlikely to have any great clarification of the evolution of
pre-Hispanic Indian cultures in Chile except in the north, where the
desert has preserved artifacts and cemeteries thousands of years old.
Conventional designations of major Indian groups in Chile at the
time of the conquest depend upon the work of a limited number of
scholars, most notably Ricardo Latcham. Latcham adopted the ge-
neric terms *Diaguitas* (valley of Copiapó to the Choapa River), Mapuche or Araucanian (Itata River to Toltén River), and *Huilliches*
(south of Toltén River). In reality no such clear-cut divisions are
possible since Araucanian is an independent linguistic family, and
each region or tribal group in Chile apparently had only small differences of dialect. The authoritative *Handbook of South American
Indians* divides the Araucanians into the following main groups:
Picunche, Mapuche, Huilliche, and Cunco (west of the Andes),
Pehuenche (Andean Highlands), Argentine Araucanians (east of the
Andes). Present-day usage in Chile refers to the major Indian groups
south of the River Itata as Araucanos or, more frequently, simply
Mapuche. Estimates of the Araucanian population at the time of
the Spanish conquest range from 500,000 to 1,500,000.

Prior to the arrival of the Spanish, Inca influence and tribute collection extended as far south as the Itata River or perhaps the Bío
Bío River, but gradually diminished toward the south. Despite initial
resistance and occasional revolts, by the mid-seventeenth century the

Spaniards had pacified, enslaved, or exploited most of the Indian groups north of the Maule River, exacting tribute and recruiting military auxiliaries, as had the Incas. From the River Maule south and into what became the frontier provinces (south of the Bío Bío River), the Araucanians effectively resisted Spanish domination, as they had that of the Incas. By 1568 the Araucanians were making significant use of cavalry in battle against the Spaniards, and well before the end of the sixteenth century they had adopted Spanish firearms, swords, armor, and any other armaments they could capture. By 1600 the Indian stock of horses, estimated at over 10,000, greatly exceeded the horses available to the Spanish settlers and frontier garrisons. Though a simple people with limited handicrafts, a subsistence agriculture, and highly dispersed settlement patterns with no centralized political authority, the Araucanians developed a complex system for organizing large-scale military forces to defend their territory. Indeed, their very dispersion and lack of centralized political structure made virtually impossible either a definitive "victory" or the administration of a Spanish conquest on a scale like that of Peru.

Though they attained no definitive military victory, the Spanish did subjugate thousands of Indians to work in mines, fields, or households. In addition, many Spaniards transferred "their" Indians (Huarpes) from Cuyo (including the towns of present-day Mendoza, San Juan, and San Luis in Argentina) to Santiago or La Serena. Miscegenation and the gradual reduction in the number of "pacified" Indians meant that by the mid-seventeenth century mestizos constituted a majority of the rural population. Population data on Chile in the colonial period must be viewed with great caution since contemporary writers provided widely disparate estimates. Chilean historian Francisco Encina estimated that at the end of the seventeenth century the population of Chile, north of the Bío Bío River, consisted of 110,000 Spanish and "mestizos classified as such," 20,000 Indians and "Indian" mestizos, 15,000 blacks, mulattoes and *zambos*, and 7000 pacified Indians in Chiloé. Most Chileans lived in rural districts on the vast haciendas or encomiendas. According to the educated estimate of Chilean researcher Rolando Mellafe, as early as 1620 "white" mestizos already outnumbered European and *criollo* settlers by a ratio of some four to one.

As in the rest of Spanish America, the total population of Chile was substantially reduced due to the effects of the conquest on the native peoples. Mortality among the Spaniards was also high; at the close of the sixteenth century 20 to 25 percent of the Spanish population was killed in the Indian uprising which liquidated eight of the twelve "cities" then in existence. Disease and natural disasters, including earthquakes and floods, also contributed to the losses. Only in the mid-nineteenth century (1843) did the population of Chile (including the unconquered Indians south of the Bío Bío River) approximate what it had been in 1540—about one million! Of these, historian Luis Galdames has estimated that no more than 40 percent were of European descent and the remainder were Indian and *castas*, including several thousand Negro slaves.

From the outset the towns were the centers of European civilization in Chile, but none could really be called cities until the eighteenth century. When the colonial period ended (1810), Chile contained thirty or more so-called cities; Santiago had some 40,000 inhabitants, and the next largest town, Concepción, some 5000 to 6000. Increasingly, however, the population of Chile moved to towns and cities, so that by 1875 over 25 percent of the population could be found in "urban" places; by 1907 this had increased to 43 percent. According to the most recent census (1970), some 75 percent of all Chileans live in cities of over 20,000 people.

Unlike Argentina and Brazil, Chilean population growth in the nineteenth and twentieth centuries depended little upon the waves of European immigration that also greatly changed the composition of the United States's population during these years. In 1895 only 2.9 percent of Chile's 2,687,985 inhabitants were foreign born, and in 1907 this had increased but to 4 percent of a total population of 3,114,755. While by the early 1900s hundreds of thousands of Italians had become agricultural laborers or tenant farmers or had settled in urban areas in Argentina, from 1889 until 1914 total net immigration to Chile reached only about 55,000. The largest foreign contingents arrived from Peru, Bolivia, and Spain. Despite their small numbers, however, European immigrants owned nearly one-third of Chile's commercial companies (1907), 20 percent of the 554 most valuable rural estates (1908), and, by 1914, 49 percent of all industrial establishments. European, Syrian, and Lebanese immigrants to Chile rarely became rural laborers or urban workers, as in Argentina, but instead formed an upper-middle-class commercial element which often intermarried with Chilean social elites.

The role of the immigrants was most apparent in the mining districts of the north, in the major cities of Antofogasta, Santiago, Valparaíso, Concepción, and Valdivia, and in the farming regions of the south, heavily influenced by Germans. The immigrants' role in Chilean urban society continued into the 1960s, when estimates indicated that three-fourths of Santiago's major industrial establishments were owned by immigrants or their offspring. Emigration to Chile, consequently, little affected the race and class stratifications that grew out of the miscegenation and politics of conquest, and only served to insert a small, heterogeneous, non-Hispanic, upper- and upper-middle-class group between the upper castes of Hispanic society and the mass of Indian, mestizo, and *casta* laborers in the fields, mines, docks, and factories.

Class and caste stratifications have also produced certain Chilean stereotypes which serve both as national symbols and pejorative epithets, particularly the *roto* and the *huaso*. The *huaso* is the Chilean cowboy but connotes much more. The flesh and blood *huaso* is a campesino on horseback or in the fields, who works from sunup to sundown, frequently barefoot or in crude sandals called *ojotas*, and wearing an apron or a flour sack around his waist. When not at work he sports a jacket inherited from his father or older brother and a well-worn hat. There is also the tourist's *huaso*, dressed for the rodeo in a three-colored *manta* and a sash around his waist (red, white, and blue like the Chilean flag). He rides a strong, well-kept horse which he prods with silver spurs. This is the hacendado, or his hireling, dressed in his best *huaso* outfit to visit the countryside at the harvest or to make sure the campesinos attend to their labors. The first *huaso*, the rural worker, bears the brunt of hundreds of country bumpkin jokes. The latter, the postcard *huaso*, typifies the historic rural basis of the wealth and power of many of Chile's leading families. Together they are the story of Chile—a national symbol which denotes hard work, sacrifice, and struggle to the campesino, and power, leisure, and privilege to the hacendado.

The *roto* is the urban counterpart of the *huaso*. The *roto* is the Chilean worker, courageous, strong, persistent, quick to take advantage of a favorable opportunity (V*ivo!*). But *roto* also means "broken one." The command ¡No sea roto! lets one know that he is lacking in social graces, that his behavior is out of line. Perhaps only the typically southern Chilean insult ¡No sea indio! ("don't act like an Indian") is as denigrating a way to put someone "in his place" as to call him *roto*. Yet used among family and friends, with the right tone of voice, with the appropriate adjective—*roto chorro*—*roto* becomes a compliment, even a sign of affection.

Joaquín Edwards Bello, a leading twentieth-century Chilean novelist, published *El Roto Chileno* just after World War I. It depicts the underworld of Santiago society—the brothel, the gambling den, the police station . . . the Senate. There was a bit of the *roto* at all levels of Chilean society, but while the working-class *roto* languished in prison or died in the streets, the upper-class *roto*, the Senator and his collaborators at the police station, lived the good life. Edwards Bello's *El Roto* makes clear that the good life of these latter depended upon the exploitation and suffering of the former. Like the *huaso* then, the *roto* is a complex symbol of *chilenidad* ("Chilean nationality") which signifies both the misery of the poverty-stricken worker and the *viveza* ("opportunism") of those who benefit from the sweat of his toil.

Since the conquest this tension between the powerful minority and the Indian, the miner, the farm worker, the fisherman, the factory worker has been at the core of Chilean history. It is a history that began with the Spanish expeditions of conquest and the subjugation, enslavement, and decimation of the Indian peoples despite their heroic resistance. It is a history that continued after independence with the violent repression of rural laborers, port and rail workers, miners, and nitrate workers who resisted the exploitation of nineteenth-century capitalism. And it is a history whose most recent chapter involves the "reconquest" of Chile's working classes in the 1970s by a military government proclaiming its loyalty to Christianity and the Hispanic tradition. In the more than four centuries between the Spanish conquest of Chile and this most recent reaffirmation of Hispanic capitalism by the Chilean military, the majority of the Chilean people have been engaged in a daily struggle to achieve a better life for themselves and to overcome the dominance of a small elite which has controlled the territory's political and economic life.

Chapter 2 • The Politics of Conquest

In the sixteenth century Spanish soldiers, ecclesiastics, and administrators created a vast colonial empire in North and South America. Moving from their initial bases in the Caribbean—Haiti, Santo Domingo, Cuba—the Spanish and their Indian allies conquered and despoiled the major indigenous civilizations of Mexico, Central America, and the west coast of South America. In the name of the monarchy and the Church they sought to Christianize the native peoples of America while exploiting their labor in the mines and on the land of the "new world" they called *las indias*. Shiploads of treasure came back to the Iberian peninsula as the Spanish exacted tribute from the new subjects of the king of Spain. After each new conquest, groups of Spaniards who failed to make their fortunes, or who lost the booty acquired, or who dreamed of obtaining even greater wealth and power in new expeditions, sought to extend the empire still farther to as yet unknown lands. From Cuba to Mexico, to Central America, and then to Peru, the Spanish conquistadors reaped the spoils of the conquest as rewards for their daring and their brutality.

As a political and economic venture the Spanish conquest initially combined national-imperial aggrandizement with a semifeudal form of private enterprise. Individual conquistadors raised armies and financed their own expeditions by authority of the Spanish monarch. In exchange for authorization to collect tribute from the subjugated natives, to operate mines, to use the land for crops or livestock, or to engage in commerce, the king claimed for the royal coffers a share of all the spoils of conquest and of the production of colonial enterprises. In Mexico, Peru, and parts of Central America booty from the accumulated wealth of sophisticated indigenous civilizations constituted a source of quick fortunes for the first Spanish expeditions. Afterward, however, the accumulation of wealth and capital depended upon large-scale exploitation of labor in mining, agriculture, and commercial enterprises.

Social attitudes of fifteenth- and sixteenth-century Spain reserved manual labor and even craftsmanship to the "lower orders." As the Spanish invaders had no intention of working either the mines or the land themselves, this made control over or access to Indian laborers critical for any productive endeavor. Where the Indians had no tradition of daily work obligations or, still less, of contractual or wage labor, the success of conquest as an economic enterprise turned upon somehow mobilizing Indian labor or importing African slaves to work the mines, tend livestock, and cultivate the land. Consequently, despite the flow of bullion and commodities from the colonies into intercolonial and international markets, and the predominance of "private" enterprise in the conquest economy, the earliest modes of production in Spanish America, including Chile, were less capitalistic (in the sense of relying upon wage labor) than they were bastardized or transitional forms of feudal labor dues, fixed-term labor contracts for "indentured" servants (*asientos de trabajo*), forced labor, or slavery.

Over time Spain created an elaborate administrative apparatus to direct the conquest and the government of *las indias*. All authority emanated from the Spanish monarch who claimed a divine right to rule. From 1524 the crown governed the new territories through the Supreme Council of the Indies, which began as a handful of officials and expanded to about twenty under the Hapsburg monarchs. The Council of the Indies legislated for the colonies and supervised administration. The royal *patronato* extended by the Pope granted the Spanish kings the right to name religious functionaries in the New World, thereby extending the authority of the Council of the Indies to matters of religious concern.

In practice the great distances between Spain and the New World left daily or, more accurately, yearly governance of the colonies in the hands of appointed officials. To govern the largest administrative units, the viceroyalties, the king named viceroys, and to lesser territories, captains-general or governors. In addition, a royal judicial council or *audiencia*, composed of judges called *oidores*, and ecclesiastical authorities shared and to some extent checked the power of viceroy or governor. Local officers responsible to the viceroy or governor—or, in their absence, to the *audiencia*—governed smaller jurisdictions or Indian districts. In the towns and cities, municipal councils called *cabildos* legislated and administered regulations of local concern, including fixing prices of commodities, granting licenses to engage in business, and regulating the activity of artisans. Wealthy colonial-born Spaniards (*criollos*) tended to dominate the cabildos, while the higher administrative posts usually were reserved for native-born Spaniards or *peninsulares*. Some peninsular officials, however, established local roots, founded prominent *criollo* families, and acquired interests that conflicted with their bureaucratic duties. From the late seventeenth century onward, sale of offices to *criollos* accentuated tensions between royal policies and their implementation in the colonies. Moreover, in some cases the cabildos sought to extend their authority and frequently found themselves in conflict with royal officials. Eventually the cabildos would become a rallying point for national independence movements in the nineteenth century.

On paper the government of the empire resembled a strictly hierarchical, neatly arranged chain of command. In reality overlapping authority and conflict between the Council of the Indies, viceroys, governors, ecclesiastical officials, and the cabildos made for continual bureaucratic maneuvering, evasion of royal decrees, and corruption. Though justified by the "donation" to the Spanish monarchy of most of the so-called New World by Pope Alexander VI—in his role as Vicar of Christ—in order to expand the realm of Christendom, the Spanish conquest gave rise to numerous doctrinal and theological conflicts over appropriate treatment of the indigenous peoples. Did the Indians have souls? Could they achieve salvation? If so, could they be forced to accept Christianity, or should conversion be accomplished only through persuasion? Could the Indians be enslaved? Could they be forced to pay tribute? If so, could tribute take the form of forced labor? Everywhere in Spanish America, Church officials and theoreticians debated these questions. In every colony and administrative subunit the conquistadors and those who came after them resisted efforts by royal officials and certain churchmen to regulate the exploitation of the conquered peoples. Nowhere did the idealism of the reformers effectively prevent the abuse and eventual decimation of the native American peoples, as economic realities won out over spiritual and humanitarian objections to the exploitation of Indian labor.

By the time Pedro de Valdivia undertook the conquest of Chile (1540) the formal resolution of numerous doctrinal questions had already resulted in official policies prohibiting many of the early abuses of the Indian peoples by the Spanish. For example, a decree signed by Charles V in 1528 prohibited enslavement of the Indians as well as the widespread practice of using the Indians as pack animals or for other "personal services." It also required that the conquerors provide Indians laboring in the mines with religious instruction, including Mass on Sundays and feast days. Later ordinances outlawed the removal of Indians from cold climates to work in hot climates, and vice versa, as well as the "renting out" of Indians by those commended to supervise their care and religious instruction. But the Spanish colonials evaded or violated these restrictions and the hundreds of others adopted in the protolabor codes contained in the royal decrees and ordinances that regulated taxation or tribute paid by the Indians to Spanish officials. Thus, the history of the

Spanish conquest in Chile and elsewhere must be seen on three levels: Church doctrine and official policy, administrative implementation or nonimplementation, and the reality of everyday life—or death—for the native population.

As a primary institution of conquest and colonial economy in Chile as throughout the Spanish empire, the *encomienda*, with all its variations, illustrates the tremendous gap between Church doctrine or official policy and its implementation upon the subjugated peoples of America. As a reward for military service, and with the obligation to provide for Christianization of the Indians, the crown or its representative "commended" the care of groups of Indians for a specified time—for example, two or three generations—to selected Spaniards and their heirs. The crown insisted that the Indians were free peoples, not to be enslaved except as punishment for rebellion or for resisting Spanish authority. As free vassals, however, the Indians were subject to tribute or taxation. This gave rise to the questions of the form of the tribute and how it could be collected. Concessionary, rather than proprietary, rights to Indian tribute or labor provided incentives to exact *quickly* whatever profits could be made from Indian labor. A new governor might give the encomienda to someone else; a court proceeding could alter the terms of the grant; a new decree might effectively limit the tribute or restrict forced labor. Quick profits through intensive exploitation of the labor force became the main endeavor of individual conquistadors.

A year after the foundation of Chile's first settlement at Santiago in 1541, the New Laws, issued by the Spanish king to control the ambitions of the encomenderos in the American dominions, prohibited enslavement of Indians even as punishment. They also forbade the granting of new encomiendas and ordered ecclesiastics and royal officials to give up any encomiendas they held. Existing encomiendas could be retained but not passed on to heirs; tribute was to be strictly fixed and regulated by crown officials to avoid abuses by the encomenderos. The encomenderos rebelled against these laws in Peru and other parts of the empire, defending the spoils of conquest. Although the crown partially repealed these laws, it subsequently enacted a succession of legal codes and ordinances that specifically defined the obligations of encomenderos and limited demands upon the Indians.

The history of Chile for its first two centuries as a Spanish colony centered upon the implacable resistance of the encomenderos to regulation of their exploitation of the native Chilean peoples and the never-ending struggle of these peoples to maintain their freedom against the Spanish invaders. This struggle shaped the social and economic structure of colonial Chile and its development within the Spanish Empire. Formation of the Chilean ethnic stock, race relations, social stratification, and economic development depended upon the ebb and flow of warfare. No other Amerindian peoples resisted Spanish conquest as did the Araucanians. No other Spanish colony drained the royal treasury and expended the lives of thousands of Spanish and mestizo troops for more than two centuries after initial contact with indigenous peoples. Nowhere else in the Spanish Empire did warfare or the threat of warfare so significantly shape the development of the colonial economy or influence the fate of Spanish towns. Only in Chile did pillage and slave raids, or *malocas*, constitute an important source of wealth for colonial administrators and military personnel into the mid-seventeenth century. In Chile alone among the South American colonies did provisioning a standing army become a principal stimulus to colonial production and internal commerce, buttressed continually by a military subsidy, the *situado*, from Peru and Spain.

Perpetual warfare and the periodic destruction of Spanish settlements gave a unique character to the Chilean colony. Plunder, illegal trade with the Indians, slave raids, and profiteering from the military budget provided unique opportunities for social and economic mobility, at the same time that the risks of an uprising or reprisal raid made economic enterprises in the southern regions insecure. The insecurity of the southern territory encouraged concentration of the Spanish population in the central valley, thereby promoting the development of a relatively homogeneous, geographically integrated society to the north of the Maule River.

Episodic warfare also perpetuated Indian slave labor and the encomiendas in Chile long after these institutions had declined in the rest of Spanish America. In contrast to the more established colonies, Chilean military leaders and soldiers in the seventeenth and eighteenth centuries could still obtain booty, privileges, and rewards from the king for their efforts to subjugate the indigenous population. In a sense, the prolonged resort to violence as a means of acquiring fame, position, and wealth made physical brutality and coercion an integral part of daily life on the Chilean frontier among Spaniards, mestizos, and the subject Indian peoples. This coercion, or threat of coercion, carried over into the encomiendas and haciendas and became the principal mechanism governing relations between the workers and their masters. The inability to enforce the royal decrees regulating these relationships merely added disrespect for law, evasion, and cynicism to the other legacies of the Chilean colonial experience.

The conquest of Chile was an extension of the Spanish victory, led by Francisco Pizarro and Diego de Almagro, over the Inca empire in Peru. In 1534 the Spanish crown divided the land south of Ecuador into four political units (*gobernaciones*): Nueva Castilla, assigned to Pizarro; Nueva Toledo, 200 leagues from Ica to latitude 25° 31′ S, assigned to Almagro; and two others assigned to Pedro de Mendoza and Simón de Alcazaba. Mendoza sold his claim to Almagro, and Alcazaba led a disastrous expedition, which was to go by sea to the Strait of Magellan and from there overland to the north but only reached Puerto de los Leones on the east coast. Almagro contested Pizarro's control of Cuzco but agreed to lead an expedition south to explore the rest of Nueva Toledo while awaiting the king's resolution of the conflicting claims.

The Peruvian Indians, who were plotting a rebellion against the conquering Spaniards, had told exaggerated tales of the wealth of the land to the south. These tales, along with Pizarro's prodding, had persuaded Almagro. In organizing the expedition to Chile, he rapidly depleted the fortune he had acquired in the Peruvian conquest. He assembled a force of more than five hundred Spaniards (almost half cavalry)—a larger army than Cortés had led into Mexico or Pizarro into Peru. Many of these Spaniards had participated in earlier expeditions to Mexico, Guatemala, and, of course, Peru. According to various estimates, ten to fifteen thousand Indian auxiliaries and a small number of Negro slaves accompanied the Spaniards on the first expedition to Chile.

After sending out advance parties—including Inca emissaries to collect tribute from the Indian subjects to the south—as well as some forces by sea, Almagro left Cuzco in July 1535. The main expeditionary force, more than two hundred Spaniards and thousands of Indian auxiliaries, crossed the Bolivian plateau through the Andes range bordering Lake Titicaca. After much privation the expedition reached Tupiza, where it rested for about two months. Here Almagro received a message informing him of the arrival in Cuzco of an emissary from Spain authorized to settle the dispute with Pizarro. The message urged Almagro to return to Cuzco to defend his interests, but he decided to go on to Chile. He led his forces on to Chicoana, near the present Argentine city of Salta; there they encountered hostile Indian activity while reprovisioning themselves and preparing for the Andes crossing.

Upon leaving Chicoana, many of the Indian bearers fled. Rivers flooded from the melting snow, and summer rains drowned numerous llamas, used as pack animals, and destroyed provisions, so food had to be rationed. Almagro's force crossed the Campo del Arenal desert and pushed into the cordillera at the San Francisco pass. In this part of the cordillera the Andes average more than thirteen thousand feet. There was no pasture for the animals, and often no firewood could be found. *Soroche* or *puna*—a condition of nausea, headaches, and sometimes convulsions produced by the altitude—and frostbite added to the misery of the expedition. Many of the scantily clad Indians froze to death, as did horses—to be "defrosted" and eaten five months later by other Spaniards coming to join Almagro in Chile.

Almagro's forces stayed in Chile until the end of 1536, exploring as far south as the Maule River or perhaps the Itata. Periodic skir-

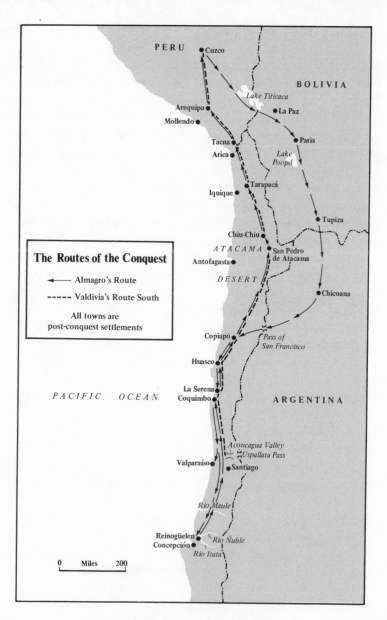

MAP 6: The Routes of the Conquest

(Source: H. R. S. Pocock, *The Conquest of Chile*, Stein and Day, New York, 1967.)

mishes with hostile Indians, as well as the Indians' strategy of hiding food and possessions, hindered Almagro's efforts to establish control. Exploratory expeditions found no gold, no silver, no cities. Failure to find a new Peru, combined with news that Cuzco apparently fell into the jurisdiction of Nueva Toledo, persuaded Almagro and his lieutenants to return to Peru. At the end of 1536 they joined forces at Copiapó, and then crossed the desert in small groups, from water hole to water hole, as a ship followed them up the coast.

Upon arrival in Peru, Almagro found the Indians in rebellion and Cuzco under control of Pizarro's brothers. Almagro liberated the city but proved unable to resolve the conflict with the Pizarros. Civil war ensued. At the battle of Las Salinas in 1538, Almagro was taken prisoner and executed by the Pizarros.

The tales of Almagro's men discouraged further expeditions to Chile for nearly five years. As the historian Barros Arana wrote, "After the return of Almagro this country [Chile] was the most discredited of the Indies in the minds of the conquistadors . . . a cursed land without gold . . . inhabited by savages of the worst kind and incapable of repaying the costs occasioned by the conquest." The failure of Almagro's expedition also meant that Chile's Indians could not again be surprised or intimidated. They now knew that the Spanish were human, not gods, that they could be barbaric and treacherous, and that their horses could be killed or captured.

It therefore came as somewhat of a surprise to the Spanish elite in Peru when the commander of Pizarro's forces at the battle of Las Salinas, Pedro de Valdivia, gave up his valuable encomienda and a silver mine at Porco in exchange for permission to explore and conquer Chile. Valdivia's motivation cannot be known with certainty, but it seems clear that it went beyond mere wealth, as he sacrificed an immense fortune to organize his Chilean expedition.

In 1540 Valdivia left Cuzco with a few Spanish soldiers (from 5 to 20 according to various estimates), his mistress, Inés de Suárez, and perhaps one thousand Indian auxiliaries. Along the way from Cuzco to Arequipa other Spaniards joined him, among them some former members of the Almagro expedition. At Tarapacá, Valdivia waited for reinforcements, but when the army set out across the Atacama desert, it numbered fewer than 110 Spaniards including two priests. After eleven months of hardship, skirmishes with Indians, and internal conflicts Valdivia's forces arrived in the valley of the Mapocho. Almost immediately they were attacked by an Indian army led by the local chief Michimalongo. The Spaniards eventually drove off the Indian warriors and soon thereafter convinced the local Indians to aid in the construction of Chile's first "city"—Santiago— founded in February 1541. Less than a month later Valdivia created a cabildo, which, in turn, called upon Valdivia to make himself governor of Chile in the name of the king of Spain rather than as Pizarro's lieutenant. After appropriate objections Valdivia acquiesced. Seven months later (September 11, 1541) the Indians of the region attacked Santiago, burned the straw-roofed houses to the ground, and left the Spaniards little more than grain for seed and some livestock. The battle for Chile had begun in earnest.

From 1541 until 1553, Valdivia's forces pushed south from Santiago, warring against the Indians and establishing a number of fort towns. These included Concepción, La Imperial (at the site of present-day Carahue), Valdivia, and Villarica. In addition, on the other side of the Andes, Francisco de Aguirre governed Santiago del Estero. With the foundation of each "city," Valdivia handed out encomiendas to selected conquistadors, thereby granting them authority to collect tribute from the Indians in their jurisdiction and take charge of the Indians' Christianization. Since the Chilean Indians had little accumulated wealth, tribute typically took the form of forced labor in the mines or gold washings that the Spaniards "discovered." Of course, if the Indians were to be forced to work, they had first to be subjugated; and south of the Maule River this proved no easy task. Instead of a unified Spanish army, each encomendero had to pacify the Indians in his own grant, and his fortunes depended upon his success at this, not upon a salary from a government treasury.

On Christmas day 1553, the Araucanians, led by the cacique Lautaro—who, in his earlier service as Valdivia's groom, had acquired knowledge of Spanish tactics and limitations—lured the Spanish leader into a trap and obliterated his force of about fifty men at the still smoldering ruins of Tucapel. There were no survivors. Although a legend has the Indians capturing Valdivia and pouring molten gold—the metal so sought after by the Spaniards—down his throat, it is more likely that his decapitated head ended up on the point of an Araucanian lance, the Indians' customary treatment of conquered enemies. Following up the victory at Tucapel, the Indians defeated an army led by Francisco de Villagra at Marigüeñu, despite Villagra's use of six small cannon and thirty harquebuses.* The defeated survivors abandoned Concepción. After twelve years of "conquest," a fearful group of Spanish at Santiago welcomed the refugees from the southern towns fleeing the Araucanian armies.

The Spanish, under Pedro de Villagra, maintained a presence in the south only at Valdivia. Between 1555 and 1557 efforts to resettle the other southern towns met with further defeats at the hands of the Indians, and were complicated by a struggle for power among Valdivia's lieutenants. At first the *audiencia* at Lima left matters in the hands of the local cabildos, but the ensuing chaos led to the appointment of Francisco de Villagra as the ranking officer in Chile. As Lautaro marched toward Santiago, Villagra's forces and Indian auxiliaries surprised the Araucanians at Peteroa, killed Lautaro, and after a gruesome battle, emerged triumphant. This victory avoided total liquidation of the Chilean colony, just as a new governor, García Hurtado de Mendoza, the twenty-one-year-old son of the Peruvian viceroy, arrived at La Serena with five hundred soldiers. This was only the first installment in the continuing and costly flow to Chile of reinforcements and war materiel from Peru and Spain.

By authorizing the expenditure of funds from the royal treasury at Lima, the viceroy also recognized the inadequacy of the private seignioral model of conquest in Chile. Despite the crown's general policy of relying upon private financing of the conquest, by the mid-1560s Chilean governors expended small sums from the royal treasury to help feed and equip soldiers on the Indian frontier. And while Philip

* A harquebus was an early type of fuse-fired gun.

II continued to insist upon the traditional policy of avoiding crown expenditures for the conquest of new territories, by 1572 he had authorized the viceroy at Lima to spend moderate sums from the royal coffers to support the war effort in Chile. Until 1600 most financing for the Chilean venture came from the private fortunes of royal officials, encomenderos, and merchants; but the crown gradually moved toward assuming financial responsibility as it became clear that private resources could not pay for the armaments and soldiers necessary to maintain Chile and Peru secure against the threat of Spain's European rivals and the Araucanians.

Shortly after his arrival, Hurtado de Mendoza arrested Aguirre and Francisco de Villagra in order to assert his own control, and then continued the war against the Araucanians. Numerous brutalities followed, including the torture of the cacique Galvarino, immortalized in Alonso de Ercilla's epic *La Araucana*. In 1558 Mendoza ordered the resettlement of Concepción, for the third time. Ensuing military engagements reestablished a line of southern forts. Just as Mendoza believed he had pacified Araucania, the king decreed his dismissal at the same time his father was removed as viceroy of Peru. Powerful conquistadors had complained that Mendoza was rewarding his own followers and, more important, was enforcing measures devised by his legal adviser to regulate forced Indian labor.

Replaced by Francisco de Villagra, García Hurtado de Mendoza would return to the colonies as viceroy of Peru some twenty years later. But Mendoza's hope that the Araucanians had been pacified proved illusory, though a terrible smallpox epidemic from 1561 to 1563 certainly reduced their war-making capability. The best estimates available suggest that 20-25 percent of the Indian population perished, though reliable data do not exist. Renewed warfare and persistent conflict among the conquistadors and royal officials led the king to decree the establishment of a royal *audiencia* in Chile in August 1565. The *audiencia* failed to resolve either the internal political or the military problems of the colony. While the encomenderos resisted any restriction on their exploitation of the Indians, and refused to subordinate private interests to public necessities, the Araucanians renewed their struggle against the European invaders.

The Araucanians' relative success against the Spanish invaders resulted largely from their adaptability and ingenuity in warfare. When the Spaniards arrived, Araucanian armaments consisted of bows and stone-tipped arrows, hardened wooden spears or lances, clubs, and slings. For protection they wore helmets and coats of sealskin or whalebone and carried thick skin shields. Like other Amerindians their initial encounters with horses and the Spaniards' killer dogs provoked panic and dismay. The Araucanians, however, quickly modified their weapons and their tactics. They constructed new weapons to fight the Spanish cavalry, including lances tipped with pieces of Spanish swords and nooses to yank the Spanish from their mounts. By the late 1560s the Indians frequently used horses and were improving as cavalrymen. A system of double-mounting allowed a lancer and an archer to ride a single horse. Near the end of the sixteenth century the Araucanians even occasionally utilized captured harquebuses, though having learned the limitations of the fuse-fired weapons they attempted to confront the Spaniards when rain or surprise prevented the lighting of fuses.

To avoid the Spaniards' scorched earth tactics, the Indians began to sow hidden fields and to retaliate in kind—waiting until the harvests of the fort towns reached maturity and then trampling the fields at night in cavalry raids. By the end of the sixteenth century the Araucanians had become accomplished guerrilla fighters, effectively harassing the cumbersome Spanish armies, in which each soldier traveled with several Indian servants to do his cooking, bear his weapons, and wait upon him in the fashion of a medieval lord. Lack of mobility combined with scarcity of munitions and artillery to assist Indian resistance. At the time of the general uprising at the end of the sixteenth century, Chilean historian Crescente Errázuriz claimed that in Chillán, Concepción, Angol, Arauco, and Santa Cruz the Spaniards had only 282 harquebuses, 44 muskets, and 26 cannon and lacked sufficient powder and fuses for even these. But above all, the

Indians' determination, inventiveness, and courage stifled the enterprise of conquest.

Half a century after Pedro de Valdivia's forces entered Chile, the colony remained a frontier, governed by military officers who repeatedly took to the field against the Araucanians. The population resided in dispersed fort towns that increased or decreased in number according to the vicissitudes of warfare. Initially, the only significant source of wealth for the conquerors other than crafts in the towns, consisted of limited placer gold mines and the exploitation of Indian labor. Control of the mines and Indians or permission to engage in industry or commerce stemmed from rights vested in the conquistadors by the governor or the cabildos as the reward for military service or simply as personal patronage. Whether in the form of an encomienda grant or a concession for a flour mill, economic opportunity and wealth originated in the manipulation and control of the law and of political authorities. If Indian labor made possible agricultural production, manufacturing, and mining activities, only "politics" determined the distribution of the booty—including the Indian workers themselves. Valdivia granted encomiendas to his followers shortly after founding Santiago and rewarded other conquistadors as well as religious orders with encomienda grants of Indians surrounding all the towns and forts founded between 1541 and his death in 1553. In contrast to the more established colonies such as Mexico or Peru, his successors continued to grant encomiendas until almost the end of the eighteenth century—though by that time their importance had greatly diminished in relation to the large rural estates employing tenant labor.

The perpetual state of war in Chile led the crown to put the Chilean Indians in a "special" category which, through contorted legal and doctrinal reasoning, made them subject after 1608 to legal enslavement as well as to the usual abuses of the conquistadors. This eventually made war not only a fact of life in Chile but a great business venture—based on raids of pillage or "slave hunts" called *campeadas* or *malocas*. Before such slave hunts became legal, however, over half a century of warfare had led the Spanish monarch to establish a permanent Chilean garrison and a yearly budget to sustain the war against the Araucanians. The Chilean encomenderos, the royal officials stationed in Chile and Peru, and the small merchant class would soon owe a portion of their wealth and power to the Araucanian war and the budget associated with maintenance of the Chilean garrison. Thus the war that periodically devastated the Concepción-southern region, made livestock and agricultural enterprise insecure, and deprived the colony of its richest gold mines, enriched royal officials and merchants in Santiago, La Serena, and Lima.

Following continued defeats at the hands of the Araucanians, despite more reinforcements from Peru, and an earthquake that destroyed Concepción in 1570, King Philip II abolished the *audiencia* in Chile in 1573 and named a veteran conquistador, Rodrigo de Quiroga, as governor of the territory. Quiroga, a lieutenant for both Valdivia and García Hurtado de Mendoza, actually assumed office in late January 1575. Two months later another earthquake destroyed La Imperial, Villa Rica, Osorno, Castro, and Valdivia and also affected Santiago and Valparaíso. Nevertheless, Quiroga pressed forward with a brutal campaign of terror against the Indians in order to end the war. Supported by the viceroy of Peru, Quiroga executed captured caciques and deported prisoners to the north to work the mines in Coquimbo. In order to prevent their escape, Quiroga ordered that their feet be mutilated with a machete or a chisel; to avoid loss of blood and subsequent death, each stump was thrust into a pot of boiling tallow. The governor's concern with the lawfulness of this policy is enlightening. Legal proceedings against the Indians, in their absence, had condemned them to death for rebellion against the empire—and then Quiroga generously reduced the sentence to mutilation and forced labor. The king also instructed Quiroga to ship rebellious Indians to Peru, but the latter replied, on behalf of Chile's encomenderos, that the Indians would survive neither the trip nor the change in climate. The king reconsidered his decree and thus saved most of the human booty for the Chilean conquerors. In the meantime the English corsair Francis Drake sacked Valparaíso and attacked La Serena, thus increasing the military pressure upon the colony. Despite Quiroga's victories against Indian armies, conflict continued to rage.

Between 1580, when Quiroga died, and 1598 three more governors sought to combine warfare and conciliation in order to pacify Araucania. The last of these three, García Oñez de Loyola, was a nephew of the Peruvian viceroy and also a relative of Ignatius de Loyola, founder of the Jesuit order. When Oñez de Loyola arrived in Chile, a major economic activity of the southern-based army garrisons consisted of hunting down Indians for personal use or for sale. Since the soldiers found it easier to capture Indians from pacified tribes, many more of them were seized and sold into slavery than rebel Indians captured in war. Despite the new governor's decrees outlawing such practices, Chilean historian Domingo Amunátegui Solar wrote that the whole territory of the Bishopric of Imperial "had been converted into an immense human 'meat market,'" where the soldiers enriched themselves through the sale of Araucanians, and where the encomenderos and wealthy residents of Santiago and Serena found their domestic servants or replaced the personnel of their encomiendas as the local natives died off from overwork or disease. In January 1598, Oñez de Loyola wrote to the king that throughout the country one saw multitudes of lame or mutilated Indians, Indians without hands, noses, or ears, and blind Indians whose tragic condition "incites the others to die rather than surrender."

Ironically, García Oñez de Loyola attempted to end deportation of Indian prisoners beyond the Maule River and otherwise to moderate the abuses of the encomenderos, yet he ended up like Pedro de Valdivia, decapitated after the massacre of his soldiers at the battle of Curalaba in 1598. The defeat at Curalaba marked the beginning of a general uprising by the Araucanians. All major Spanish settlements south of the Bío Bío River were destroyed or abandoned: Santa Cruz and Valdivia in 1599; La Imperial and Angol in 1600: Villarica in 1602; Osorno and Arauco in 1604. At about the same time Dutch pirates attacked Valparaíso and Chiloé. Four governors succeeded one another in rapid succession, and the efforts to subdue the Araucanians continued to no avail.

In 1600 the king of Spain established a permanent military subsidy, or *situado*, for Chile, and war in Chile became a permanent, institutionalized business of the Lima merchants and shippers until almost the end of the seventeenth century. The *situado*, a symbol of the poverty of the Chilean colony, also freed the encomenderos from most financial and military obligations of the war. Conquest and pacification thus became largely a public venture instead of a private semifeudal imitation of the Spanish reconquest of their homeland from the Moors.

Exasperated by the loss of all the towns and mines of southern Chile after 1598 and the continued fighting, including the loss of more than one hundred Spanish soldiers at Boroa in 1606, the Council of the Indies proposed the *legal* enslavement of all captured Indian males over ten and one-half years old and females older than nine and one-half years; captured children would be commended to "virtuous" Spaniards to serve them and to be instructed in the Faith until the age of twenty. On May 26, 1608, the Spanish king signed a royal decree that legalized, indeed encouraged, the enslavement of "rebellious" Indians in Chile. Though in practice, enslavement of Indian captives was common from 1570 onward, this royal decree legitimated slave raids and pillage by the Chilean garrisons. Interim governor and *audiencia* judge, Luis Merlo de la Fuente, promulgated the decree in Santiago in August 1610, and then led a force to the south which took nearly one thousand Indian prisoners.

By 1610, seventy years after Valdivia's entry into the country, Chile boasted five "cities": La Serena, with 46 adobe houses, 11 with tile roofs and the rest of straw; Santiago, 200 houses; Chillán, 52, 8 with tile roofs, 39 with straw, and 5 *ranchos* of wood and thatch roofs; Concepción, 76 houses, 36 wooden with straw roofs; and Castro, on Chiloé, with 12 straw-covered houses. The rest of the Chilean population resided in the countryside on the immense territories of the encomiendas* where subjugated Indians panned gold, tended flocks of sheep and cattle, and cultivated the land. With the loss of the encomiendas south of the Bío Bío River, gold mining near La Serena, Santiago, and Concepción took second place to agriculture and livestock as the major source of occupation for the Chilean work force.

Accustomed by the Inca conquest to the idea of tribute long before the arrival of the Spanish, many of the Indians of northern Chile (Copiapó to Maule) gradually submitted to Spanish domination. They provided the labor that produced gold, food, hides, and tallow—the major exports to Peru—to enrich the encomenderos. As forced labor, mistreatment, and disease (especially smallpox) decimated the encomienda Indians, their periodic replacement was necessary in order to maintain the conquest economy. The war against the Araucanians, as well as the capture of the Huarpe peoples in the eastern cordillera, provided the main source of this replenishment and of concubines for Spanish males; it also supplied Indian labor to Peru. The cruel treatment of captured Indians, in "peacetime" or in war, reinforced their will to resist. The Spaniards used the struggle of the Indians to justify their enslavement, mutilation, "commendation," or "deposit" for use by the encomenderos. Even as the war persisted, so did the never-ending succession of decrees, taxes, and ordinances, which the Chileans applied, appealed, or ignored as suited their convenience.

From 1558 until the general uprising after 1598, the crown's major representatives enacted numerous tribute regulations aimed at controlling the encomenderos and protecting the Indian laborers. In each case Catholic clerics influenced adoption of these codes. But in each case Chilean encomenderos subverted or prevented their implementation.

In 1557, Hernando de Santillán, an adviser to Governor García Hurtado de Mendoza, promulgated in Chile the royal decrees that

---

* Strictly speaking, the encomienda grant did not involve title to land; it merely conveyed the right to exact tribute from the Indians. Nevertheless, encomenderos in Chile often exercised a patrimonial authority within the territory of a grant.

prohibited using Indians as pack animals, forbade the encomenderos to employ more than one-fifth of "their" Indians in the gold washings or mines, and ordered them to pay the Indians one-sixth of the gold they mined. In addition, they were to free pacified Indian servants and, if these Indians voluntarily worked the mines, to give them one-fourth of the ore extracted as well as adequate food and tools. Further decrees sought to regulate the conditions of the Indians laboring in the fields, the vineyards, the artisan industries, and even in households. A similar tribute was promulgated in mid-1558 for the region of Concepción and the south.

Taking account of the recent rebellions in Peru, Santillán did not seek to abolish the encomiendas themselves. Nevertheless, the Spanish settlers had no intention of ameliorating the lot of the subjugated Indians and thereby decreasing their own income. In a communication to the Council of the Indies after his departure from Chile in 1560, Santillán described the brutality of conquest from the first entry of the Spanish: "[They] killed, maimed and set dogs upon the Indians, cut off feet, hands, noses and teats, stole their lands, raped their women and daughters, chained them up and used them as beasts of burden, burned their houses and settlements and layed waste their fields." In La Serena in 1557, Santillán had reported that the encomenderos sent the Indians to the mines as pack animals, as well as employing them in other personal services, leaving them not an hour to rest.

In the tradition of Bartolomé de Las Casas, the best-known clerical defender of the New World Indians against the abuses of conquest, another Dominican, Fray Gil de San Nicolás, provided more ammunition for the growing "black legend" of Spanish barbarism:

> They take the Indian men and women prisoners in chains and use them for "dog bait," watching the dogs tear them apart for sport.
> They destroy the crops, burn the houses and villages full of Indians, shutting the doorways [of the houses] so none can escape.

Describing the mines, he wrote that at first the Indians were to receive a sixth part of the gold they extracted and then an eighth part, but they often received nothing at all. In any case, the regulations obligated the Indians to pay the salary of their "protector" from their "earnings." Either purchased in Spain or acquired from a royal official, the post of "protector" allowed venturesome Spaniards to make their fortunes in the New World by mediating between the encomendero and the native peoples. From limited evidence it appears that the gold earned by the Indians was often actually a source of risk capital for Spanish pastoral and commercial enterprises as the "protectors" and encomenderos colluded in defrauding the Indians.

In 1563 Pedro de Villagra promulgated a dozen new tribute ordinances, including provisions that limited the work period in the placer mines to six months, reaffirmed payment of one-sixth of the gold mined to the Indians, prohibited use of Negro taskmasters, and required the "protectors" of the Indians to buy sheep for them with their gold. The new ordinances also split the obligation of the protector's salary between the Indians and the encomendero and increased the number of "protectors." Once again, the encomenderos largely evaded the new regulations. However, the recently created posts did provide a source of income for the new "protectors" authorized to defend the Indians' rights.

Another major reform of the tribute system in 1580 was the *tasa* of Gamboa, which also failed to halt the encomendero's abuse of Indian labor. The *tasa* of Gamboa sought to substitute a fixed money or commodity tax for forced labor. The encomenderos and even some churchmen opposed the new tax as "prejudicial to the colony and the Indians." Its principal innovation consisted of a commutation of labor tribute for a money or commodity tribute. This innovation in no way benefited the encomenderos since it fixed the tribute at seven to nine pesos a year—one-fourth to one-twelfth the value that an Indian could produce in a normal work cycle of eight to twelve months.

Despite the resistance of the encomenderos, the *tasa* of Gamboa merely appeared benign in contrast to previous policies. Illustrative is the tribute owed by the Indians to Luis Jufré, who inherited from his father the encomiendas of Macul near Santiago, Peteroa and Mataquito in Curicó, and Pocoa north of the Maule River. The Macul grant contained 22 tributary Indians; Mataquito, 142; and Pocoa, 57. These Indians owed collectively to their encomendero the following monies and commodities each year.

Macul: 110 gold pesos plus 2 gold pesos to pay the priest, corregidor,* and the administrator of the encomienda; 30 fanegas† of wheat, 20 fanegas of barley, and 20 fanegas of maize delivered to the house of the encomendero; sufficient fish, chickens, or sheep necessary to equal 44 pesos. In addition, the Indians of Macul were to supply 9 household servants who would receive a salary and not pay tribute.

Peteroa: In addition to 2 gold pesos for administrative costs, 985 gold pesos; 394 pesos worth of fish and agricultural commodities, including 200 fanegas of wheat, 100 of barley, 120 of corn, and 6 of beans; 11 household servants to the encomendero.

Mataquito: 2 pesos each for administrative costs; 710 gold pesos; 284 pesos in foodstuffs: 150 fanegas of wheat, 80 of barley, 5 of maize, 4 of beans, and sufficient quantity of fish, tools, sheep, vegetables, or other commodities to complete the tribute; 10 servants for the encomendero's household.

Pocoa: In addition to 2 gold pesos for administrative costs, 285 gold pesos; 4 domestic servants; 114 pesos in commodities, including 80 fanegas of wheat, 40 of barley, and 50 of maize.

Gamboa prohibited any tribute beyond that specified, but allowed the encomenderos to purchase, at a "just price," commodities to eat and drink or other necessities. In order to avoid abuses, copies of the tribute regulations were given to the encomenderos and the Indian caciques; and to ensure compliance, Gamboa appointed new officials to inspect the mines of Coquimbo and Quillota. The Indians could, of course, choose "personal service" instead of paying the tribute.

---

* The corregidors were representatives of royal authority in towns and rural districts. *Corregidores de Indios* were responsible in particular for Indian settlements or areas of Indian population.
† A fanega is approximately equivalent to 1½ bushels.

Around La Imperial continual war made enforcement of tribute largely academic, but north of Maule initial implementation of the tribute aroused the animosity of the encomenderos.

The encomenderos emerged again victorious when the king sent a new military expedition and a new governor, Alonso de Sotomayor, with the charge to defend the colony and the wealth of Peru against the attacks of English pirates and to pacify the Araucanians. Sotomayor reinstated forced labor, thereby gaining the encomenderos' cooperation for a new campaign to the south. In this campaign he ordered that the hands and noses of Indian prisoners be cut off before they were released, in order to terrorize their fellows. Terror again failed to intimidate the Araucanians, who fought back with vigor. According to García Oñez de Loyola some years later, Sotomayor's policies forced the Indians to produce more than 100 pesos in goods and services in exchange for garments worth at most 3 to 4 pesos. Sotomayor also appointed to the Indian districts new corregidores whose salaries consisted of one-fourth of the grain and livestock raised by the natives, and approved a work cycle or *demora* of eight months instead of the six established by Pedro de Villagra. To "benefit" the Indians, the governor named clerics to the rural districts; their salaries also came out of the Indians' sweat and blood in the fields and the mines.

Although encomenderos continued to evade the regulations intended to improve the conditions of the Indians, the periodic rebellions, and then the disaster following the defeat of the Spaniards at Curalaba in 1598, gave increased credibility to the voices of those few clerics who sought "justice" for the Indian peoples. The best known of these, the Jesuit Luis de Valdivia, finally persuaded the Spanish monarch to introduce a policy of "defensive warfare," which had been suggested earlier by officials in Lima. After 1612 official policy forbade sorties or settlements across the Bío Bío River—except by Jesuit missionaries. Luis de Valdivia returned to Chile with a new military governor, Alonso de Ribera, and with comprehensive authority to impose the policy of defensive warfare. This included pardons for rebellious Indians, suspension of the decree permitting slavery of captured Indians, prohibitions on selling outside of Chile those previously captured, dismantling the forts of Angol and Paicaivi, and a recommendation to the *audiencia* to suspend the labor obligations of the Indians and replace them with money and commodity tribute.

Frontier garrisons resisted defensive warfare for both professional and economic reasons. Encomenderos and most other colonials also sought to reverse governmental policy. Governor Ribera openly violated his charge, while other Spanish violations made a mockery of the defensive warfare policy. New instructions from the king, at the insistence of Luis de Valdivia, reaffirmed this policy, but Alonso de Ribera had died by the time these arrived in Chile (1617).

His interim successor received explicit instructions to comply in all respects with the defensive warfare policy; but when the next governor arrived in Concepción, he wrote to the king that forced Indian labor still had not been eliminated from Chile. At the instruction of the viceroy of Peru, still another tribute regulation, the *tasa* of Esquilache, attempted to limit the encomenderos' abuse of the Indians, while officials also suggested that the importation of one thousand black slaves to be sold "at cost" would help to liberate the Indians from *their* slavery. The *tasa* of Esquilache prohibited *any Indian*, whether peaceful or not, from providing "personal service"; it specified a new formula for taxation or tribute, it limited the percentage of encomienda Indians obligated to work to one-third each year; and it freed the others to sell their labor if they desired. If the encomendero did not need all his laborers, he could rent them to other encomenderos or deserving Spaniards.

The encomenderos, nevertheless, resisted all prohibitions against Indian slavery or forced labor in the mines, and any limit on the number of days that Indians could be forced to work. Luis de Valdivia's departure for Spain in 1619, along with the deaths of the Chilean governor and King Philip III, soon eliminated even the pretense of defensive warfare. Chile's governor from 1625 to 1629, Luis Fernández de Córdoba y Arce, boasted to King Philip IV that he had captured more than 250 Indians in fighting near Imperial in 1627 and had killed or captured more than 2500 in Yumbel and Arauco. According to this governor:

> I entered in the province of Imperial and thereabouts, where Spanish have not trod since the uprising twenty-eight years ago, with such good results that I burned many houses and more than 14 or 15 thousand fanegas of food of all sorts, and destroyed 4 or 5 thousand head of livestock. . . . Despite the obstinate resistance of the enemy we have only lost thirty Spanish dead and some hundred Indian allies. . . .

Still, the governor attempted to ameliorate somewhat the condition of nonhostile Indians—by prohibiting the branding of Indians who were not, within three months of their capture in war, registered in the appropriate government office! Araucanian counteroffensives, led by the cacique Lientur, inflicted important defeats on the Spanish in the La Imperial region, including a total rout of Spanish forces at Las Cangrejeras. The Indians killed seventy Spaniards or mestizos and took thirty-six Spanish prisoners, including Francisco Nuñez de Pineda y Bascuñan, who later described the battle and his long captivity in a diary of his life with the Indians called *Cautiverio Feliz* ("Happy Captivity").

The long history of war, brutality, pillage, and unenforced decrees "protecting" the Indians continued as Governor Laso de la Vega (1629-39) persisted in the offensive in Araucania. An initial Spanish victory at Albarrada in 1633 ended with butchery or enslavement of the routed Indians—812 dead and some 600 prisoners—and halted the Indian advance into the central valley, blunting yet another threat to Concepción and Santiago. The new governor also faced a new royal order abolishing "personal service" or forced labor "wherever and in whatever form." Despite the determined resistance of the cabildos of Santiago and Concepción, this reform and others emerged in yet another decree—the *tasa* of Laso de la Vega in 1635.

The new *tasa* consisted of sixteen regulations, including the elimination of "personal service," although the Indians still were to pay tribute to the encomenderos in money or commodities each year in the presence of the "protector" and the priest in the encomiendas, or of the administrator and priest in the Indian villages. In general, this new legislation was meant to complement, not replace, the *tasa* of Esquilache by giving the Indians a choice of paying tribute with either labor or commodities and by adding more paternalistic supervision and enforcement. The Indians could pay tribute in labor if they so informed the corregidor, who would also evaluate the commodities delivered by the Indians to the encomendero. In addition, the Indians were authorized to "rent" themselves, with preference to their own encomendero during the time necessary to pay the tribute, and after that to anyone whose property was located within four leagues of the town or hacienda where they resided.

The new restrictions on the encomenderos met with resistance and were little enforced. In 1639 a judge of the *audiencia* of Chile reported to the crown that while some of the poorer Spaniards observed the *tasa*, the rich and powerful continued as always "using the natives as if they were slaves, treating them harshly, without paying them the small wage of their sweat and labor . . . bringing them from as far as Tucumán and Rio de la Plata . . . and working them day and night in the copper mines at La Serena or . . . to mine gold at Andacallo." The judge also noted that due to the brutality of the soldiers and the venality of the corregidors and priests, as well as to the exploitation of the encomenderos, most of the Indian villages had been depopulated and the lands gradually appropriated by Spaniards. In a classic understatement concerning the judges' report, Chilean historian Amunátegui Solar suggested:

> From this exposition, it can be deduced that the *tasa* of Laso de la Vega was as inefficacious as those of Santillán, Ruiz de Gamboa, Sotomayor, Ribera and Esquilache; and that at the end of his [Laso de la Vega's] government the Chilean natives were subjugated to forced labor with the same harshness as in the times of Pedro de Valdivia. The orders of the king and the ordinances signed by viceroys and governors came to nothing.

In 1639 another professional soldier—Francisco López de Zúñiga, who had fifteen years' experience in Flanders and Germany—replaced

Laso de la Vega as governor. Faced with continued Indian resistance, the new governor attempted to carry out a modified policy of defensive warfare by arranging the Pact of Quillín, in which Spaniards and Mapuche celebrated a "peace treaty." The Spanish formally recognized Indian sovereignty south of the Bío Bío River with the exception of the fort at Arauco and the region thereabouts. In all the enterprise of conquest since 1492, Spain had never before recognized the sovereignty of an Indian people. The Spanish also agreed to discontinue the slave hunts and forced labor. In exchange the Indians agreed to return Spanish captives, to allow missionaries to preach in Indian territory, and to ally themselves with the Spanish against English and Dutch corsairs. King Philip IV approved the pact in 1643. But despite the governor's half-hearted efforts, the frontier garrisons as well as other royal officials and encomendero-commercial interests refused both to observe the *tasas* and to comply with the terms of the Pact of Quillín. Indian labor was too valuable to give up merely because of a peace treaty or official policies.

The soldiers on the frontier continued slave hunts and pillage as their principal source of enrichment. Events slowly led to still another general uprising on the scale of the butchery between 1598 and 1606, as Araucanian resistance to "Christianization," especially to the ban on polygamy, frustrated clerics and governors alike.

Despite reaffirmation of the Pact of Quillín in March 1651, Indians in the region of Cunco killed the shipwrecked survivors of the Spanish vessel bringing the military subsidy to Chile. A punitive expedition slaughtered a number of Indians and sent many women and children north as slaves. Then a series of raids led by the governor's two brothers-in-law provoked increasing Indian retaliation.

The governor and his brothers-in-law took over provisioning of the troops, stole supplies, and launched a large-scale commerce in Indian slaves, with the Boroa fort town serving as a clearing house. The 1608 decree allowing enslavement of rebellious Indians provided the basis for a lucrative "certification" business, in which frontier officials certified that the Indians were captured in battles with rebellious tribes.

In February 1655, a mestizo called Alejo, an ex-soldier in the Spanish garrison, led an Indian uprising and at the same time inspired rebellion by the prisoner-slaves still in the frontier region. The Indians again destroyed the towns and forts south of the Bío Bío River and forced the abandonment of towns as far north as Chillán. According to the historian Carvallo y Goyeneche in the years following the uprising, the Indians captured 1300 Spaniards, sacked 396 estates, took over 400,000 head of cattle, horses, and sheep, and caused property damage estimated at 8 million pesos. The Spanish lost Arauco, San Pedro, Colcura, Buena Esperanza, Nacimiento, Talcamávida, San Rosendo, Boroa, and Chillán, along with over half the armaments in the region. An angry mob in Concepción—shouting, "Long live the king! Death to the bad governor!"—temporarily deposed the corrupt governor, and he was officially replaced in 1656. By then the Spanish held only the town of Concepción in all the Bishopric of Imperial, and communication with Santiago was possible only by military patrols. For all practical purposes Chile consisted of the towns of La Serena, Santiago, and Concepción, along with the encomiendas, mines, and rural estates from the valley of Coquimbo to the Maule River.

From 1657 to 1662 Spanish and Indian soldiers battled each other without resolution, until a Spanish army of six hundred soldiers surprised and defeated fifteen hundred Indians led by the cacique Misqui near Curanilahue. Soon thereafter the interim governor ordered the resettlement of Chillán and requested still more troop reinforcements to press the war against the Araucanians. In the meantime the king named a new royal governor and, in order to secure another force of one thousand soldiers in Spain, promised the recruits for Chile the same benefits enjoyed by soldiers who served in Flanders.

Governor Francisco de Meneses came to Chile in 1664 and ruled it as a Hispanic robber baron until 1668. Taking full advantage of the warfare economy, the governor demanded heavy bribes for renewal of encomienda grants, sold military and civilian government posts, and made those he promoted pay him in gold; he taxed ships carrying on commerce between Valparaíso and Callao before they left port—unless they carried his merchandise; and he appropriated for sale in his own retail outlet a large part of the goods arriving as part of the military subsidy. Supported by the Peruvian viceroy's desire to increase the flow of Indian slaves to the mines and fields of Peru, Meneses renewed expeditions to the south, especially against the pacified tribes, where it was easier to obtain human merchandise. In a single raid around Paicavi, Cayucupal, and Tucapel, the Spaniards obtained 400 *piezas* (a weighted equivalent of four hundred Indians, allowing for the lesser value of the labor of children or the old) and assassinated twenty chiefs who spoke out against these "military" operations. Meneses' arbitrary, corrupt rule also adversely affected the interests of important Chilean colonists. Eventually he was replaced owing to their letters of protest and after an unsuccessful attempt on his life.

With a permanent force of some 2500 soldiers, Meneses' successor Juan Henríquez vigorously carried the war into Araucanian territory and also withstood attacks by English Corsairs, including Bartholomew Sharp's sack and burning of La Serena in 1680. He also accumulated vast wealth from slaving, despite the royal decree of 1674 prohibiting Indian slavery. Chilean historian Luis Galdames claims that during his tenure Governor Henríquez took prisoner some 800 Indians and sold them as slaves. The governor set the price at 500 fanegas of wheat for each Indian, with the fanega valued at 50 centavos (in the mid-seventeenth century a first-class Indian, *pieza de lei*, sold for 200-300 pesos and lesser valued Indians, *piezas de servidumbre*, for 150-200 pesos). When he had accumulated 400,000 fanegas of wheat, he sold the grain to the contractors of his own army at 2 pesos a fanega and was paid from the royal treasury. War was good business! Henríquez left office after almost twelve years (1682) with a fortune estimated at close to one million pesos.

In 1674 and 1679, during Governor Henríquez's tenure, new decrees abolishing Indian slavery challenged the ingenuity of Chilean encomendero and business interests. In response the Chileans adopted a legal device called the *depósito*, which placed captured Indians in the custody of encomenderos or landowners who agreed to supervise them in exchange for the right to use their labor. An

Indian under the *depósito* did not legally "belong to" a particular Spaniard as did a slave, but in practice he might as well have. The Chilean economy continued to depend upon warfare, slave hunts, pillage and exploitation of the rural labor force.

At the end of the seventeenth century, not only the Indians, but also the Spanish-mestizo troops manning the frontier outposts, suffered the consequences of government corruption. As Chilean author Benjamín Vicuña Mackenna noted, the military subsidy became "an open bag of money into which everybody dug with both hands, except those [the soldiers] for whom the subsidy had originally been established." The war budget profited Lima merchants, royal officials, and Chilean colonials, while the human booty of the continual raids "stocked" the mines, farms, and *obrajes*. Until 1685 the *situado* consisted largely of commodities, many of which were of no use at all to frontier garrisons which lacked shoes, clothing, and munitions. Moreover, the purchase of oil, salt, and soap in Lima for shipment to Chile benefited only the Lima military contractors, since these commodities were generally available in Chile. The shipwreck of the *San Juan de Díos*, which was bringing the *situado* to Chile, provided the pretext for a request by Chile's governor that the subsidy be sent overland from Potosí—in coin of the realm—thereby avoiding the risks of loss at sea and attack by pirates. The approval of this request in 1685 meant that the soldiers were to be paid in cash and buy their supplies at lower costs in Chile. Unfortunately, however, from the mid-1680s onward the subsidy often arrived late if at all.

An earthquake which shattered Lima-Callao and led to the loss of the Peruvian wheat crop in 1687 induced a temporary boom in Chilean wheat exports and also a considerable increase in prices (see Chapter 3). This made it difficult to buy the needed provisions for the Chilean garrison within the constraints of the military budget. By the time the last seventeenth-century governor of Chile (1692-1700) took over, the Chilean frontier army could not depend upon the annual subsidy as a sure source of support. From 1692 to 1697 the export boom allowed the governor to maintain the army with loans from colonial merchants. But with the military subsidy almost seven years in arrears, Chile's governor wrote the king in August 1697 that the soldiers were not only unclothed, but in debt for what they had purchased or borrowed in recent years; and "what never before has occurred, now is happening, the captains and the corporals of the army leave their posts, as they find themselves in the same misery as the soldiers . . . going to the rural estates to feed and clothe themselves . . . [destroying] order and military discipline."

In the first years of the eighteenth century, the Wars of the Spanish Succession in Europe intensified difficulties in the Spanish-American colonies. When in 1702 the new Chilean governor, Francisco Ibáñez de Peralta, received a payment of 292,000 pesos—against a debt of over 2 million pesos, he made sure that his own salary and certain other obligations were paid in full, leaving little for the garrison. (Ibáñez had already opened a butcher shop, sold a number of official positions, and collected payments for renewal of the encomiendas.) This situation provoked a military uprising that led to serious internal disorders. The governor ordered rebellious soldiers tried by military tribunals, and executed a number of the revolt's leaders, despite an earlier promise of pardon if they surrendered. In 1704 the military subsidy was eight years in arrears, and the army lacked armaments and munitions. In these conditions official policy sought to avoid provocation of the Araucanians by soldiers or missionaries.

By the last two decades of the seventeenth century, the effects of the 1655 uprising had been largely overcome north of the Bío Bío River. To the south the Araucanians remained in control. The degeneration of Spanish military capabilities from the Homeric exploits of the sixteenth century to the professional rabble-garrisons sent from Lima in the seventeenth left the conquest incomplete. Corruption, war-profiteering, and insufficient troops combined with the fierce resistance of the Araucanian and allied Indian armies to prevent Spanish control of the regions most coveted by Pedro de Valdivia and his followers.

In the first decades of the eighteenth century, tentative initiatives to renew the conquest and establish settlements in Araucania met with another general uprising (1723). In response, Governor Gabriel Cano y Aponte (1717-33) ordered the dismantling of the forts of Colcura, Arauco, and Tucapel and the erection in their stead of forts with similar names north of the Bío Bío River. Apparently the Indians did not share Francisco Encina's judgment that "contrary to the fantasies and neurotic mysticism of the Jesuits and the nineteenth century historians, the Indians' condition when left to themselves was much worse than the harshest servitude imposed by the Spanish." A new agreement, celebrated at Negrete in 1726, established the usual obligations of the Indians to receive Christian missions and to ally themselves against enemies of the king; it restored "peace" temporarily, until the next major conflict later in the century (1766).

In 1700 some 100,000-150,000 Spanish, mestizos, Indians, mulattoes, and Negroes lived in Spanish Chile. From 1541 until 1664, 20,000-30,000 Chilean soldiers and settlers had died fighting the Mapuche at an official cost of 17 million pesos—though the Jesuit Rosales estimates the toll from 1545 to 1674 at 42,000 Spaniards, including deaths from accidents and epidemics, and a military subsidy of 40 million pesos from the Peruvian and Spanish treasuries. This does not include the vast personal fortunes expended in sixteenth-century enterprises of conquest. Estimates of Indian losses are too varied to be relied upon, but there can be no doubt they amounted to many times those of the European invaders, especially taking into account death through epidemic diseases. The material losses of the indigenous peoples of Chile likewise cannot be accurately measured— for they had no great stores of wealth but rather lost their autonomy, their land, and ultimately their cultural integrity.

The uncompleted military conquest would be resolved only late in the nineteenth century, but the authoritarian politics of conquest had already created in Chile the foundations of a highly stratified class society in which labor was denigrated and laborers were exploited. The politics of conquest also institutionalized political corruption, arbitrary use of government authority, disrespect for and evasion of law, and the social and economic institutions of Hispanic capitalism that would condition Chilean development into the twentieth century.

These latter characteristics Chile shared with most of the Spanish colonies. Unlike the principal colonial centers, however, relative geographical isolation, poverty, and lack of significant gold and silver mines contributed to the development of an agrarian-based economy in Chile. Relative ease of communication and concentration of population in the central valley, along with the constant threat and challenge of the Indian frontier, forged a colonial elite with strong localistic orientations, a fortress mentality, and a significant military tradition. An impressive ability to coopt royal officials through business or marital ties and to absorb new wealth and successful immigrants created an integrated political, economic, and social elite with interests in agriculture, commerce, and mining. Intermarriage, shared social values, and dependence for economic well-being upon the exploitation of the rural labor force unified the Chilean upper classes and helped forge a unique variant of Hispanic capitalism on the periphery of the Spanish Empire.

Chapter 3 • Hispanic Capitalism

The colonial experience in Chile drastically reduced the indigenous population of the territory between Copiapó and the Strait of Magellan and resulted in a deterioration in the quality of life for the overwhelming majority of the territory's population. Disease, warfare, and exploitation destroyed the fabric of Indian life. At the same time miscegenation gave rise to a new people descended from the conquistadors and their Indian or Negro slaves and servants, or from Indians and their Spanish captives. Accustomed to polygamy, Indian women adapted to Iberian promiscuity if they were not forcefully subjected to it, and bore increasing numbers of "Spanish" children. To a lesser extent Spanish women gave birth to the children of their Indian captors or lovers. Though by 1810 the entire population of Chile had probably not reached the size of the indigenous population at the time of conquest, its character testified to the profound ethnic transformation that accompanied the social and economic evolution of colonial Chile.

If, in retrospect, the most important product of colonialism in Chile is the mestizo, the Spanish had not come to Chile with that intention. They came to take mineral wealth and the booty from

TABLE 2. ESTIMATED POPULATION OF CHILE, 1540-1620

	Spanish and European Creoles	"White" Mestizos	Negros and "Non-white" Mestizos	Encomienda and Peaceful Indians	Unpacified Indians	Total
1540	154		10		1,000,000	1,000,164
1570	7000	10,000	7000	450,000	150,000	624,000
1590	9000	17,000	16,000	420,000	120,000	582,000
1600	10,000	20,000	19,000	230,000	270,000	549,000
1620	15,000	40,000	22,000	230,000	250,000	557,000

(After Rolando Mellafe, La introducción de la esclavitud negra en Chile, 1959, p. 226.)

Indian empires—as they had done previously in Mexico, Central America, and Peru. Shortly after the founding of Santiago in 1541, gold from the mines at Marga Marga and other gold washings in the northern and southern districts seemed to justify the prospect of a profitable extractive economy based upon the forced labor of subjugated indigenous peoples. But by 1600 the relative poverty of easily worked gold mines in Chile became evident, and when the Spanish lost all the southern settlements (1598-1604), the products of the countryside came to dominate the colonial economy. Rapid proliferation of livestock soon made tallow and hides Chile's most important exports.

Both in the export of gold and tallow, Chile's Spanish settlers operated from the outset in the intercolonial and international market. The essentially commercial motivation of the Chilean conquest and the distinctly export orientation of the colony's leaders contradict the common characterization of the early colonial economy as feudal, autarkic, or merely subsistence. Yet caution must be exercised in labeling this colonial economy capitalist merely because of its participation in international commerce. The colonial economy functioned within a Hispanic, absolutist juridical order that had more in common with a bastardized Iberian feudalism than with nineteenth-century liberal capitalism. Spanish imperial theory, property institutions, and commercial policy, as well as the economic enterprises of the religious orders and the Araucanian war, combined to give a distinctive character to colonial economy and society. If it was capitalist, then it was a special sort of capitalism, modified by the unique milieu of colonial Chile—a miserably poor backwater of the Spanish Empire. The colonial economy of Chile produced a surplus for export, but it did not do so under the fundamental conditions of capitalist production—the sale by free workers of their labor to the possessors of money and the means of production.

In principle, every economic enterprise in colonial Chile operated only with the permission of the royal authorities or the cabildo, which fixed by decree the price for commodities, labor, and services. Spanish imperial policy sought to limit trade among the colonies to approved channels and to direct the economic surplus to Spain. In turn the colonies were expected to import goods carried from Spain in Spanish vessels. The high cost of transport made many colonial agricultural products noncompetitive when moved great distances from the point of production, but the necessities of frontier life often led local artisans and landlords to ignore prohibitions on local industries or limitations on the cultivation of particular crops such as grapes. Almost from the outset smuggling played an important role in commerce both among the colonies and between the colonies and non-Spanish merchants. Chile could trade legally with Spain only via the merchant fleet that came to Panama once a year or, sometimes, less often. After sailing to Panama via Peru, Chilean merchants had to cross the isthmus on mules to obtain merchandise from the annual fairs where Spanish merchants dictated the prices. The Spanish merchants greatly overvalued their own merchandise. While they sought profit margins that often reached over 500 percent, they paid poorly for colonial commodities. The rigors of travel, the rigged markets, and the capital required severely limited the access of Chileans to this commerce, and left most legal Chilean commerce in Peruvian hands.

Resource allocation within the colonial economy did not occur as a result of the functioning of a capitalist market. Official policy dis-

couraged economic competition, established publicly authorized monopolies, and, by the seventeenth century, created a number of
publicly owned haciendas and industries intended to supply food,
clothing, shoes, and materiel to the Chilean frontier garrison. For all
these economic activities, the labor force consisted largely of slaves,
subjugated or tributary Indians, fixed-term "indentured" laborers
(*asientos de trabajo*), and agricultural tenants until well into the
eighteenth century. Even then the development of a wage proletariat came slowly as class relations in the countryside moved toward
tenant labor.

Three primary bases of wealth initially underlay the colonial economy: land, Indian or Negro labor, and the authority to exploit
them. To these were added commerce and artisanship and, after
1600, the military *situado*. Always, however, the most important
"commodity" remained political authority: from government concessions, licenses, grants, or official positions stemmed all economic opportunity, including land grants (*mercedes*), mining concessions, and
the right to exact tribute or exploit Indian labor.

In the early years of the colony, gold mining took first place in the
incipient economy. The most fortunate of the conquistadors appropriated the mines and washings worked by the Indians prior to the
arrival of the Spanish, and obtained respectable quantities of the
yellow metal. At Marga Marga, near Valparaíso, mines that had supplied the natives with the tribute for the Incas now passed into the
hands of Pedro de Valdivia and several of his companions. With the
relatively simple techniques employed, gold production required
large numbers of laborers. Estimates of the number of Indians forced
to work in the mines and gold washings are neither systematic nor
reliable, but the contemporary chronicler Pedro Mariño de Lobera
claimed that in 1553 more than twenty thousand Indians worked
the mines of Quilacoya alone. While this figure is probably exaggerated, there can be no doubt that thousands of Indians were
forced to extract gold for the Spanish from La Serena in the north
to the southern mines in Osorno and Valdivia.

Work in the mines was strenuous. The Indian labor force detested their virtual enslavement, the separation from their families, and the harsh working conditions. As disease and overwork killed off Indian laborers, the Spaniards sought to replenish the labor supply from the encomienda Indians (Huarpes) transported across the Andes and with the captives from the war to the south.

In the mining process itself, groups of Indians dug the earth and put the excavated material into tubs, or *bateas*. Other Indians then carried the dirt-filled tubs to the water's edge. Still other laborers, usually Indian women or Negro slaves, spent almost entire days in water up to their knees washing the dirt in a procession of *bateas* until only gold remained at the bottom. Along the streams and rivers the laborers also employed techniques similar to the gold-panning methods of the California gold rush. Thanks to Indian and Negro labor, a few of the earliest conquistadors managed to turn the dream of gold into reality in the Chilean colony.

Owing to the frontier conditions on the Chilean periphery of the Spanish Empire, it is impossible to make accurate estimates of the quantity or the value of the gold extracted in the sixteenth century. As 20 percent of all gold mined (the *quinto*) belonged legally to the royal treasury, there was, of course, no incentive for precise accounting by the conquistadors. During the first few months following the settlement of Santiago, the Spanish obtained some 7000 pesos' worth of gold at Marga Marga, and in 1547 Pedro de Valdivia sent a large gold shipment to Peru. Royal officials estimated that to that time the *quintos* equaled approximately 40,000 gold pesos. Taking into account the inevitable losses to corruption and unreported gold, the Indians produced well over 200,000 gold pesos for the Spaniards at the mines from 1541 to 1547. While this was not an inconsiderable sum, the Chilean mines could not compare with the incredible wealth of the silver mines at Potosí in what is now Bolivia or with the mines of Mexico later in the sixteenth and seventeenth centuries.

In 1552 the most important mines were located at Quilacoya near the Bío Bío River. The defeat at Tucapel (1553), where Valdivia died, took these riches from the Spaniards, but new mines were discovered shortly thereafter at Osorno and Valdivia. The Jesuit chronicler Diego de Rosales tells us, with obvious exaggeration, that in 1561 the Indians' labor produced some 1.2 million pesos at the Madre de Dios mines near Valdivia and in the mines at Choapa in Coquimbo. About Osorno, Father Rosales reported that "the land has gold and silver mines, and it is taken in such abundance that with one or two days' work the Indians mine enough to fill their quota for the week; mining stones so large that they break them into pieces and give them to the encomenderos [to pay off their obligations]." A less poetic account by Juan López de Velasco suggests that from 1542 to 1560 gold output in Chile reached more than 7 million pesos.

As the sixteenth century progressed, gold production dramatically declined. The royal *quintos* went from 35,000-40,000 pesos in 1568 to 32,000 pesos in 1571 and 22,000 in 1583. By way of contrast, Potosí produced 170,000 pesos in *quintos* in 1570. Chronic warfare in the southern territories limited output, and at the height of the Indian uprising in 1600 total royal income from Chile, including the *quintos*, amounted to only 3000 pesos. A royal official reported that "this is all the royal income there is here for now, because the whole territory is so afflicted with war that the pacified Indians cannot mine gold, because they are all employed in making supplies for the war." Even before the uprising another report to the king (1594) had noted that "the Indians serving in the cities of La Serena, Santiago, Concepción, and the others have so diminished in number that gold is hardly mined in all the kingdom and their number [the Indians'] is barely sufficient to sustain the cultivation of the haciendas and tend to the cattle of the encomenderos." Thus, with the possible exception of the mines at Andacollo, gold mining had dropped off sharply by the last decade of the sixteenth century.

In spite of this decline, the location of the mines had influenced substantially the sites the Spaniards chose for the towns that were to become the cradles of European culture in Chile. Though all of the first settlements were destroyed at least once by Indian attack or by pirates and several times by earthquakes, tidal waves, or floods, each was refounded. Their names can be found on modern maps of Chile:

La Serena, Santiago, Concepción, Imperial (now Carahue, to the west of Nueva Imperial), Villa Rica, and Valdivia. In each town the settlers looked to the municipal council, or cabildo, to order urban economic activity and also, initially, to establish regulations governing exploitation of the mines, agricultural lands, and the cottage industries created in the towns and encomiendas. These towns, however, remained little more than struggling villages with one-story adobe or wooden houses roofed with tiles or straw. Only an occasional two-story building or the larger constructions of the religious orders even hinted at the skyscrapers of later years. In Santiago most of the houses were built around patios—many planted in gardens or fruit trees. Through the middle of the cobbled or dirt streets of the town ran open sewers. The other towns were much smaller and even less prosperous.

In these towns soldiers with seignioral aspirations formed households with Indian women and servants. As the colony grew, the number of domestic servants increased; the more held by a household, the higher its social status. As few skilled artisans came to Chile in the early years, these households developed a sort of pioneer self-sufficiency, until increased population permitted more economic specialization. For those artisans who did set up shop in Santiago, the cabildo attempted, with little success, to replicate the guild system of Spain. The cabildo regulated the quality and price of almost all manufacturing services, and commodities, including such items as bread, tools, clothing, and fish. As soon as brickmaking took on a commercial character, the cabildo decreed official prices and established a fine of ten pesos in addition to forfeiture of goods sold in excess of these prices. To establish a brickyard required an official permit, and at times a permit was denied if the proposed location posed environmental hazards to the town. As early as 1548 the cabildo approved official prices for different types of clothing made by tailors and for the products of armorers, smiths, and carpenters. Adjustments took place as business interests or consumers pressured the municipal officers. Public policy in colonial Chile left no room for the "free competitive marketplace," and the tradition of government responsibility for regulating industry and ensuring availability of basic commodities at reasonable prices survived even the superficial imposition of liberal capitalist ideology in the nineteenth century. In at least one case the cabildo even prevented a settler from leaving town lest Santiago lose its only blacksmith.

The earliest colonial manufacturers met demands for food, shelter, clothing, and armaments. The first recorded flour mills were established at the foot of Santa Lucía by Rodrigo de Araya and Bartolomé Flores (Blumenthal). Other early enterprises include shoemakers, smiths, armorers, tanners, and saddle makers. Pottery, textiles, and cordage became important cottage industries. In the manufacture of textiles the Spanish took advantage of the developed Indian traditions in weaving. Boatbuilding also gained importance around Valdivia, Osorno, Concepción, and Valparaíso-Concón.

Some of the early manufactures testify to the entrepreneurial skill of the conquistadors. For example, Antonio Nuñez arrived in Chile shortly after Pedro de Valdivia and acquired large rural estates near Santiago and Valparaíso. Nuñez built the first warehouses at Valparaíso, engaged in commerce between Peru and Santiago in his own ships captained by his sons-in-law, established the boatbuilding works at Concón, and negotiated a fishing concession with the cabildo at Santiago (1579). In a business transaction that could be understood by any modern Chilean capitalist, Nuñez offered to bring fish to Santiago *if the cabildo would fix a convenient price for a period of three years.* The cabildo agreed, but Nuñez recalculated his costs and, before delivering a single fish, petitioned for an increase in price "due to the high costs of boats and nets, which will be at least 500 pesos, and since seven or eight workers will be required to cast the nets, in addition to three or four Indians. . . ." Colonial entrepreneurs, like their modern counterparts, sought monopoly market positions, guaranteed prices, captive markets, and cheap labor in collusion with government officials. This tradition of Hispanic capitalist enterprise carried over from the conquest to become the prevailing spirit of the colonial economy.

Whereas Spanish colonial towns were the centers of political authority and the beginnings of urban culture and industry, most of the population lived in the countryside, and the agricultural encomiendas, mines, and rural industries produced the bulk of colonial commodities. The encomenderos and hacendados created textile sweatshops, oil presses, wineries, tanneries, mills, rope and tool manufacturers and even, briefly, sugar mills in Copiapó and Aconcagua, to process the produce of the land. At the end of the sixteenth century Chile paid for its imports of European and Peruvian merchandise with exports of tallow, hides and leather goods, sheepskins, wine, wood, apples, hemp, salted meat, olives and olive oil, and copper. Despite recurrent warfare, the Chilean economy produced a considerable surplus of food and agrarian products. Excellent yields in the territory's virgin soil converted the river valleys into gardens, while the proliferation of livestock made meat available to all classes. In 1565 shippers charged 46 gold pesos a head to transport cattle from Callao to Valparaíso. The success of the Chilean livestock industry meant that thirty years later 300 head of cattle sold for 450 pesos (1.50 pesos per head) in Santiago. Due to the unending Araucanian war, however, the encomenderos preferred to raise mules for trans-Andean transport, which the royal governors would not requisition as they would horses. At the end of the century a horse brought 150 pesos or more as compared to 1.50 pesos for a cow. A shortage of horses led Governor García Ramón to prohibit further mule breeding (1607); and when this measure failed, Governor Jaraquemada (1611) ordered the gelding of all jackasses within twenty days, subject to a fine of 100 gold pesos per animal for noncompliance. The extensiveness of the Chilean countryside and the value of mules for transport and as export commodities to Potosí made this measure as unsuccessful as the one decreed by García Ramón.

With the loss of all the southern towns and mines at the end of the sixteenth century, the Chilean economy was reduced to several regional economies centered upon the small towns of La Serena (46 houses), Santiago (200 houses), Concepción (66 houses), and Chillán (52 houses). Gradually the trans-Andean settlements of Cuyo were incorporated de facto into the economy of Río de la Plata, though Santiago continued to import Huarpe Indian laborers from the encomiendas across the Andes. The varied natural ecologies of these regions and their location with respect to the battlefields contested by Spanish and Araucanians led to distinctive patterns of social and economic development, though the foundation for wealth and power throughout the colony remained land, exploitation of Indian, Negro and, later, mestizo labor along with the economic opportunities derived from the influence of government decision makers.

In 1544 Pedro de Valdivia ordered Juan Bohon to found a city somewhere in the valley of Elqui or Coquimbo as a way station between Peru and Santiago. After four years as little more than an encampment, an Indian attack destroyed the settlement entirely. With the arrival of reinforcements at Santiago from Peru, Valdivia sent Francisco de Aguirre to refound La Serena. Aguirre chose the modern site some two thousand meters from the sea. Valdivia gave all the land and Indians from the valley of Choapa to the valley of Copiapó to only eight *vecinos*.* Unlike the rapid turnover among most of the Chilean encomiendas and land grants in the early years, the northern encomienda grants often remained in the same family for many generations. No better example of this could be found than the Aguirre family whose descendants retained the encomiendas of Copiapó and Coquimbo until the abolition of all encomiendas in Chile in the late eighteenth century (1791), and remained important landowners in the region into the twentieth century.

The town of La Serena grew slowly. By 1610 nine square blocks contained a church, Augustinian and Franciscan convents, and government buildings, surrounded by fields and orchards. No more than one hundred Spaniards and mestizos and some eight hundred tributary Indians resided in or about the town. Growth continued slowly until 1680 when pirates led by Bartholomew Sharp sacked and burned the settlement. Many of the principal *vecinos* abandoned the town and fled to their rural estates. After another pirate attack in

* A *vecino* was a principal citizen in an urban center, a tax-paying property owner with a "voice" in the cabildo; he was also often an encomendero.

1686 the cabildo attempted to prevent total abandonment of the city by decreeing heavy fines for those leaving without permission. Increased wheat exports and mining activity in the last decade of the seventeenth century brought renewed vitality to La Serena, while its port at Coquimbo became an important point of transshipment of copper to Peru. Copper smelters near Coquimbo sent the elaborated red metal to Callao, and artisans sent their copper wares south to Santiago as well as north to Lima. Nonetheless, in the first decades of the eighteenth century the French engineer Frezier still remarked on the "scarcity of population, the rudeness of the streets without pavement, the poverty of the houses built of mud and roofed with straw, which gives La Serena the aspect of a country village [campo]."

In the first decades of the seventeenth century the major export commodities from the *norte chico* included, along with copper, the livestock products of tallow, hides, lard, and sheepskins. Small amounts of wheat also went from the northern valleys to Peru or Potosí. Although data on agricultural production and exports for the seventeenth century are incomplete, recent studies suggest that between 1620 and 1690 agriculture gained in importance relative to livestock, and the *norte chico* became an important source of hemp, cordage, aguardiente, pisco, wine, and wheat for the Peruvian market. By the beginning of the eighteenth century the present-day agriculture-livestock-mining triad had already emerged, along with the accompanying cycles of mining booms and depressions.

The regional economies of the *norte chico* between Copiapó and Quillota, furthest removed from the Araucanian wars and closest to Peru, developed within a far more stable environment than did the regions south of Santiago. Indians imported from across the cordillera along with Araucanian captives worked the gold mines, planted, tended, and harvested crops, and labored in the limited number of artisan industries, or *obrajes*, and mills. But the limited grain exports to Peru belied the delicate balance between population, agricultural potential, and food supply throughout the region. As population increased in the late seventeenth century, hints of future regional grain deficits were evident. In 1695, in response to expanded Chilean wheat exports to Peru and the accompanying rise in local prices, the cabildo in La Serena ordered producers to sell one-tenth of their output at a fixed price to the town's bakers in order to ensure availability of flour and bread below market prices. By 1724 more drastic measures prohibited export of grain or flour outside the region, even to Copiapó or Illapel. These measures, adopted also in modified form in central Chile, sought to guarantee local consumption at reasonable prices. The need for these measures and others like them from 1692 to 1750 pointed to a basic conflict between participation in the international economy and the provisioning of local markets at regulated prices. This conflict, which reappeared frequently in the history of Chilean agriculture, inspired the age-old responses of smuggling, black market trading, and hoarding of commodities until more favorable prices could be obtained. Thus, in 1747 the cabildo in Copiapó authorized the corregidor to regulate producers in order to assure adequate supplies. Later it noted that a number of *vecinos* had violated the decree, which established a maximum price for wheat and flour, and had hidden away the wheat. As late as 1798 the cabildo complained about "manipulation of grain prices by a small number of persons in times of scarcity."

In the middle of the eighteenth century the region around Copiapó still was essentially a mining district, producing silver, gold, and copper. The region imported foodstuffs, such as wheat, jerked beef, lard, and livestock products, to support the mining population, though it exported wine to Peru. This situation changed little in the rest of the century. La Serena also experienced a renaissance of mining after 1735-40 but barely produced enough wheat to supply its own needs. Like Copiapó, the La Serena district imported tallow, lard, flour, and livestock, in contrast to its relative self-sufficiency in these products earlier in the century.

These economic changes in the *norte chico* were accompanied by an alteration in the composition of the population and the work force. The decline of encomienda Indians throughout the seventeenth century coincided with an increase in mestizos, mulattoes, and other ethnic mixtures or *castas*, as the offspring of conquistadors,

Indians, and Negroes made the population more heterogeneous. Miscegenation and the urban population increased more in the *norte chico* than farther south—in large part because the north avoided the costs and scars of the Araucanian wars which devastated the Concepción-Bío Bío region. By the mid-eighteenth century the attraction of work in the mines contributed to the growth of urban centers in the *norte chico*; between 1755 and 1778 Copiapó expanded from a settlement of 2900 to a small city of 5300, with a rate of increase in excess of 3.5 percent per year.

Both natural increase and migration to the mineral districts added population to the *norte chico*. Still, the encomenderos resisted employing mestizo, Indian, or *casta* free laborers, preferring to rely on traditional labor arrangements with "their" encomienda Indians. The mestizos, free Indians, and *castas* thus became a sort of underclass, prohibited from occupying official posts, joining the priesthood, or obtaining the status of master artisan. As the encomienda system declined, this underclass found its way into the mines and haciendas as labor-rent tenants, renters, sharecroppers, or peons. Others took up the life of a vagabond or a criminal. Cattle rustling was so serious by the middle of the eighteenth century that the hacendados received judicial authority within their estates, which often covered entire regions; and punishments for robbery increased in severity from floggings or banishment to prison sentences or, when a theft involved more than five cows, death. In addition, the authorities attempted to force transients into productive work. Local registers kept track of all those living within a district and required "all *vecinos* to report vagabonds and all those entering or leaving the district to present themselves to the corregidor." Those who could not prove they had jobs were assigned to public works.

The existence of a growing and mobile proletariat did not suit the needs and expectations of colonial elites and threatened to "corrupt" the sedentary labor force. The concentration of agricultural lands into vast estates along with the political limitations on creation of private enterprises prevented absorption of this underclass into the economy as small farmers, artisans, or merchants. Many could find no employment or could do so only seasonally in the mines or at harvest time. In a report on the state of Chilean agriculture, industry, and commerce at the end of the eighteenth century, a royal official commented that "this lack of employment makes common the lamentable use of certain modes of forgetting their plight, of removing the weight of such a sad, languid existence; of those beverages with which the unfortunate, with the pretext of enjoying their afflictions, seek a cure for living." In the same report Manuel de Salas noted the tendency of these vagabonds to remain single, to be promiscuous, and to avoid the responsibilities of a family, thereby "becoming the fathers of a new generation of the underclass [*miserables*], vagabonds like their fathers, without homes and with little more possessions than those sufficient to cover their bodies." By the end of the colonial period, the conditions leading to intergenerational "inheritance" of misery had already taken shape in the *norte chico*.

From these transients or drifters sprang also in the period 1690-1750 an incipient wage labor force of peons, or *gañanes*, in the mines of the northern district. Often, however, an advance loan of food, clothing, or tools reduced the peon to a sort of debt-servitude, even though decrees at the end of the century prohibited advance payment of more than one month's salary to single workers or two months' to married workers. To obtain employment in the mines, workers had to have a paper, or *boleta*, in which the last employer confirmed that the worker owed no further debt. This system of internal passports served to monitor the movements of thieves or other "undesirables" as well as of indebted laborers who sought entry into a new mining camp. If an Indian, a mulatto, or a Negro fled from the mines while he owed money, he could be punished by a fine and by flogging "to serve as an example to the others." Even the worker with a *boleta* could not legally leave the mine without giving notice to his employer. In this manner debt-peonage and mining on shares replaced the encomienda. In both cases Hispanic capitalism depended still upon an exploited but essentially preproletarian labor force, though by the middle of the eighteenth century a true wage proletariat was beginning to emerge in the mining districts of the north. Gradually this mestizo and *casta* labor force replaced the dwindling numbers of encomienda Indians.

The miner worked from sunup to sundown with a noonday meal and rest period of two hours. He received jerked beef and bread as food rations. With his earnings and perhaps some minerals "stolen" from the mine owners, the miner could enjoy Sundays or holidays at the combination store-saloons, or *pulperías* and *bodegones*, of the nearby camps or villages. These *pulperías* served as social centers, gambling dens, dance halls, and houses of prostitution. In 1781 fifty-two such *pulperías* could be found in Copiapó and ten at the small settlement at Huasco.

Despite the increase in population in the *norte chico*, until the end of the seventeenth century not a single new major city was founded— only a large number of mining camps, trading centers, and small settlements. Indeed, at the end of the colonial period La Serena with five to six thousand residents still ranked as the largest urban center in the north. Throughout the region the population was concentrated in the river valleys—Elqui, Sotaqui, Salsipuedes, Andacollo, Limari, Quillota, Aconcagua—and the mining camps, as it is to this day. At the end of the colonial period the *norte chico* remained a sparsely settled, agro-mining region which sent copper, silver, gold, and livestock products, especially goatskins, to international and intercolonial markets.

In the early years Santiago and the central region served as a base camp for the enterprise of conquest. Rebuilt after an Indian attack that left the town in ashes a mere seven months after its foundation, Santiago grew slowly during the first half-century of its existence. It suffered, nevertheless, from some problems common to most urban places. In 1551, taking note of the frequent disorders and robberies at night, Lieutenant Governor Rodrigo de Quiroga and the cabildo decreed that no one could go out of his house at night after curfew under penalty—for Spaniards, of losing their weapons and being arrested, and for the Indians or Negroes, of one hundred lashes.

In addition to dealing with law and order, the cabildo had to provide essential public works. The Mapocho River periodically inundated the town. Residents needed a safe supply of potable water. Lack of bridges across the river impeded communications and commerce. Dusty or muddy streets required cobbling. During the sixteenth century the cabildo began to deal with the physical needs of the city. For example, in 1578 water was brought from the cordillera to the central plaza, but the service could not be maintained, and in 1588 Santiago residents again turned to water from the Mapocho. In 1578 the cabildo also cobbled a number of streets. By the first decade of the seventeenth century, after a flood had destroyed the Hermitage of Saturnino and part of the lower sections of the town, construction began on the flood-control works. Notwithstanding these improvements, the town continued to have a rural flavor: the cabildo prohibited pigs from slogging around the water in the plaza and, while the public waterworks underwent rehabilitation (1613), prohibited washing of clothes at certain points on the river bank, under penalty of two hundred lashes.

At the turn of the century 500-700 Spanish and mestizos and several thousand Indians resided in this village capital. Despite the frontier simplicity of the physical environment, the wealthiest residents imported luxury goods from Europe and China via Peru. Merchants brought velvet, silk, and damask to a colony that often lacked munitions, horses, and military supplies and whose very existence remained in jeopardy. In the midst of frontier warfare a would-be aristocracy clung to its pretensions. According to one chronicler, "every Spanish woman wanted thirty Indian servants to do her washing and sewing as if she were a princess." Even in the face of the loss of the most prosperous colonial towns (those south of the Bío Bío River) after 1598 and the threat to Santiago itself, the conquistadors and their successors maintained the superficial forms of a European nobility they wished to emulate.

The elite of the new-society-in-formation consisted of encomenderos, public officials, including religious functionaries, and merchants. After Pedro de Valdivia's initial generosity, the relative scar-

city of sedentary Indians in Chile forced the first governor to reduce
the number of encomiendas granted to the *vecinos* of Santiago from
sixty to approximately thirty between Copiapó and Maule. When
Valdivia died in 1553, a very small number of encomenderos, including his mistress, Inés de Suarez, had been granted the natives in
most of the territory of Chile. These grants served as the basis of
wealth and power over generations for certain of Chile's colonial
elite.

The abbreviated case history of the encomienda of the German-
born conquistador Bartolomé Flores is illustrative. To Flores, Valdivia commended "all the caciques and principals, with their Indians, named below, to wit, Talagante, Mavellangai, Codamolcalebi,
Upiro, Lebalo, Guarcamilla, Acai, Nabalquivi, Conquemangui and
Namarongo, with all their Indians and subjects in the valley of Mapocho." Flores consolidated these grants into the two estates of Talagante and Putugan (Linares), where he raised horses, chickens, and
pigs and cultivated wheat, barley, beans, and corn. On these estates
Flores built the first oxcarts in Chile and taught the Indians certain
manual skills. Flores married the daughter of the cacique Talagante,
and his heir from this union, Doña Argueda, married another Ger-
man-born conquistador, Pedro de Lisperguer, who had arrived in
Chile with Governor García Hurtado de Mendoza (1557). Two
other children born in Peru also came to Chile and obtained encomienda grants through marriage. These lands, and others conceded
throughout the seventeenth century, remained in the hands of Flores'
descendants until 1721-24. Many of the Indians from the southern
grant were transferred to the Santiago region, but as was typical of
the encomiendas during this period, decimation or flight reduced
radically the number of tributary peoples. In 1721 the Talagante
grant had a mere fourteen tributary Indians. Nevertheless, these estates and those of the other encomenderos played a significant role
in the economic development of the central region during the colonial period. At least twenty of the original grants persisted intact until the final abolition of the encomienda in Chile in 1791.

In Santiago and central Chile there was a rapid growth of livestock

and agricultural production, centered in the vast estates of the encomenderos and the hacendados. By 1571-74, according to a nineteenth-century historian, the Santiago regional economy produced "a
great quantity of wheat and barley, much wine, and all the other
commodities, fruits, and livestock of Spain; there are also many orchards and gardens within and without the city. . . ." Commerce
with Peru developed immediately, with the arrival in 1543 of reinforcements for Valdivia and goods sent in exchange for the gold dust
collected by the settlers. The extent of this trade can be judged by
the loot taken by Sir Francis Drake when he sacked Valparaíso in
1578: 2500-3000 jugs of wine, salted meat, flour, agricultural and
livestock products ready for shipment to Lima and Potosí.

In the first years a sea trip from Callao to Chile could take over
a month. Maritime communication, therefore, was irregular; only
twenty-four ships arrived from Peru between 1543 and 1556; and
seventeen sailed from Valparaíso to Callao-Lima, a trip that took
three to four months due to the southerly winds and the Humboldt
Current. Six others were lost at sea. A trip from Santiago to Madrid
could easily take a year. Despite the difficulties and perils of communication, the export economy developed steadily, and Valparaíso,
with only a handful of residents, began to serve as a port of commerce.

While the countryside produced most of the colony's wealth, the
principal beneficiaries were colonial administrators and merchants in
the towns. The colonial merchants, who took great risks to bring
goods to Chile and to send them from Chile to Lima or Spain,
charged prices that yielded enormous profits. A study of the wealthy
residents in Santiago and La Serena from 1567 to 1577 shows that
only fifteen to twenty-five years after the conquest, merchants paid
almost as much into the royal treasury on the gold registered for payment of the *quintos* as did the encomenderos. The amount of smug-
gled or unregistered gold acquired by merchants in urban shops or
through trade with the Indians cannot be estimated. Some encomenderos also invested the gold "their" Indians mined in commodities
or merchant ventures; from the outset, merchant capital and en-

comendero interests formed an interrelated elite, rather than two distinct social groups. Thus, trade and commerce took their place as integral elements in the colonial economy even under the harsh conditions of sixteenth-century conquest.

Unlike the La Serena region, however, the *vecinos* of Santiago bore a heavy burden in the Araucanian war. The military disasters of the sixteenth century threatened the very existence of the regional economy as well as the maintenance of the Chilean colony itself. The development and character of the economy of the central region at that time depended substantially, therefore, upon the vicissitudes of warfare.

The monarchy's response to the colony's distress after the fiasco at Curalaba at the turn of the century created a new source of wealth, which relieved the colonials of much of the economic burden of warfare and also allowed them to pay greater attention to their economic enterprises. By decree of March 21, 1600, the Spanish monarch authorized a yearly subsidy, or *situado*, of 60,000 ducats, or 82,500 pesos, from the royal treasury in Peru for three years to assist the Chilean colony in its struggle to survive. The new Chilean governor, Alonso de Ribera, received most of this subsidy in the form of clothing and supplies for the troops en route to Chile. Ribera's reports to the king on the desperate conditions of the Chilean garrisons—"so poorly disciplined that their style of warfare seems more like confusion and barbarism than like Spanish militia"—persuaded the crown to create a permanent military establishment of 1500 soldiers whose salary would be paid by the viceroy of Peru. Later this number was increased to 2000. In 1603 the crown raised the military budget to 140,000 ducats; and in 1606, to 212,000 ducats, or 293,000 pesos.

Thus to secure its Chilean outpost, the Spanish state took over the administration and the financing of conquest, for which it utilized the wealth of the mines at Potosí and the income of Peru. Ribera added to this subsidy the revenues obtained through taxes on the sale of captive Indians, and also organized royal estates to provision the troops with grain, beef, and livestock products. At Melipilla the governor established royal textile workshops to supply clothing, blankets, and other goods to the garrisons. These estates—Loyola, between Chillán and Concepción; Catentoa, between Maule and Chillán; and Quillota—harvested 7,410 fanegas of wheat, 500 of barley, and 200 of potatoes in 1604. Large herds of sheep and cattle as well as hemp plantations at Quillota provided part of the basic necessities for the army. In 1607 the Loyola estate earned slightly more than 53,000 pesos, and the Catentoa estate, some 75,000 pesos. Ribera also created a tannery in Santiago and a number of artisan industries in Concepción. Following Ribera's example, his successor established a cordage industry at Quillota and constructed a large number of oxcarts as baggage wagons for the military.

The military subsidy stimulated the colonial economy by increasing demand for supplies and by largely freeing the settlers from the obligations of annual military campaigns. It also brought a continual flow of Spaniards and mestizos as troops, especially to the Concepción region. But the purchase of many supplies for the army in Lima limited the beneficial effects on the Chilean economy; and owing to the institutionalized corruption at Lima, the Chilean army received silk stockings, damask, and honey as well as a number of commodities available in Chile such as soap and oil. The luxury items profited Chilean officials and merchants but did little to help the war effort. The Peruvian viceroys insisted that the major share of the subsidy be spent in Peru, which benefited Peruvian producers and merchants much more than the Chileans. Not until 1685 did Governor José de Garro get authorization to have the subsidy sent in money from Potosí. But, as noted in Chapter 2, at the end of the seventeenth century the subsidy arrived late or not at all.

Throughout this century the royal *situado* and warfare against the Indians reinforced the agro-commercial economy of the Santiago-central region. Loss of the agricultural and livestock output between the Itata and Maule rivers after the uprising of 1655 forced the central district to supply most of the needs of the entire colony; and as the century progressed, it had to respond to demands for grain from Peru, though the quantities of grain sent to Lima remained paltry

(9000 to 12,000 fanegas per year) until late in the seventeenth century.

The Santiago-central region provided most of the wheat needed by the colony until the 1680s without pushing prices over 3 pesos per fanega. Except under the extreme conditions of warfare or siege, even the poorest Chilean produced enough to eat or could purchase food at reasonably low prices, while animal products in particular were available in abundance. Existing external markets did not permit a significant expansion of commercial agricultural production. In contrast, livestock products, such as tallow, salted beef, lard, hides, and sheepskins, as well as wine could compete favorably in the Lima-Potosí markets. At midcentury (1647) Martín de Mugica wrote to the king that Chile exported 20,000 quintals of tallow to Peru (and internal consumption amounted to about the same).

The livestock economy fitted nicely with the social attitudes of the encomenderos and hacendados who preferred the prestige of horses, cattle, or sheep to the plebeian tasks of farming. As the livestock economy also required considerably less labor than cereal production, there was also less need for Indian laborers whose numbers were declining in the encomiendas.

The perilous state of the Chilean colony at the end of the sixteenth century had induced the viceroy to exempt Chilean products from the traditional import duties, or *almojarifazgo*. From this time the number of land grants, or *mercedes de tierra*, around Santiago greatly increased in number; by 1604 most of the territory of modern Valparaíso and Santiago provinces had been legally granted to Spanish owners. Important factors in the rush for *land*, in contrast to the earlier desire for grants of Indians, included the Peruvian demand for Chilean livestock products, the need for sheepskins used to transport quicksilver from Huancavelica to Potosí, and the needs of the army to the south.

Land grants varied considerably in size, but some exceeded 5000 hectares. Sometimes grantees sold portions of the land in order to obtain capital to purchase livestock and initiate an agrarian enterprise; or the land grants emerged indirectly from previous encomienda grants. In either case the land became valuable as the livestock-export economy opened up business opportunities. Most of the large land-owners or encomenderos were *vecinos* of Santiago, even when they held rural estates located in Cuyo, La Serena, or Chillán. According to the *audiencia* in 1647, Santiago had 516 established households with a total of almost 5000 residents. At least one-third of the *vecinos* held encomiendas. Of a list of 164 encomenderos called upon by the governor for aid in putting down the Indian rebellion of 1655, over one-third (59) were royal officials or descendants of sixteenth-century encomenderos. The remaining two-thirds (105) came from families that arrived in Chile in the seventeenth century or that had not earlier obtained encomiendas. Increased land values, participation in commerce, and the casualties of war made entry into the small Chilean elite relatively open for the able or for those with "good" family connections.

In 1604, to safeguard their investments, and supposedly to protect the remaining Indian villages, the cabildo of Santiago commissioned a land survey and boundary markings by Gines de Lillo. Lillo's survey became the basis for the boundaries of many of the Santiago region's most important estates in the following centuries. From 1604 to 1620 *merced* holders attempted to acquire unclaimed lands near their properties through grants of *demasia* which added "leftover" land to existing estates. By the middle of the seventeenth century the legal basis for the Santiago region's vast haciendas was firmly established. Indeed, fewer people owned more land than at any time in Chile's history in the period from 1670 to 1680. The extensive seignorial estates precluded formation of a large class of small independent farmers.

An earthquake at Lima in 1687 produced a crisis in the agricultural valleys that supplied wheat to the Lima market. Destruction of irrigation systems left the lands "infertile" for a number of years. Prices for wheat soared as high as 25-30 pesos per fanega, ten times the normal price. Chilean and Peruvian merchants took advantage of the catastrophe and Chilean wheat was shipped to Lima. In the *norte chico* the Peruvian crisis intensified already existing patterns of trade; for the Santiago region the opening of the Lima market offered the chance for a radical transformation of its pastoral economy. At first, the limited grain surplus produced in the region permitted only a weak response; soon thereafter the valleys of Aconcagua, Mapocho, and regions to the south were planted in wheat, and 150,000-200,000 fanegas were exported annually. In 1712, though prices had returned to 2-3 pesos per fanega, the Santiago-central region sent some 180,000 fanegas of wheat to the Peruvian market.

Land values increased with the expanding demand for wheat. Wheat cultivation also required greater labor input than the livestock enterprise. In order to attract tenants, the landowners offered rentals, or *prestamos*—land "loaned" with only a token rent. As the encomienda Indians died off or fled, mestizo, *casta*, or even poor Spanish workers replaced them as peons or tenants. Indians, slaves, indentured labor, "free" laborers, and tenants all played a role in the expanding agrarian economy. Even the indentured or "free" laborer rarely obtained a money wage but rather received the equivalent of 5 to 7 pesos a month (1685-1707) in food, clothing, and other payments in kind. As these arrangements excluded from the money economy the great mass of Chileans who worked in the countryside, the internal markets for manufactures were exceedingly small.

As the eighteenth century progressed, the role of the encomienda Indians drastically declined, while coincidentally tenancies and the system of *inquilinaje* became more important. The origin of the *inquilino* laborer, who became the backbone of the rural labor force in Chile, still stirs controversy among Chilean historians. A traditional interpretation has the encomienda Indian as the forerunner of the *inquilino*. More recent studies of several regions in the central valley point to the *arrendatario* and the worker receiving *préstamos de tierra* from the early eighteenth century onward. Of course, as wheat cultivation expanded, many of the remaining encomienda Indians fled to other farms and/or took on mestizo culture and were incorporated as peons or *arrendatarios* in the rural economy. Thus, the institutions of tenancy, as they evolved, allowed for absorption of the Indian laborer, as well as the rural *casta* and mestizo, as *inquilinos*, while encomenderos continued to exploit tributary Indians as long as possible.

In the large estates more tenants could be absorbed without seriously disrupting the livestock economy, and the tenants produced an increasingly larger share of the wheat of the central region. The *préstamos de tierra*, or rentals, consisted of variously sized parcels, but as land increased in value, the token rental fees and commodity rents often became labor rents, or the landlords required labor services in addition to commodity rents. As land became scarcer and its value increased, the hacendados required more service from the tenants. Soon the landlords required individual *inquilinos* to provide a worker year round for the agricultural labors of the *estancia* or hacienda. They also demanded additional labor at peak agricultural periods, such as planting, round up, or harvest. In the later years of the eighteenth century, the term *arrendatario* was less used and thereafter replaced by *inquilino*—the service tenant who predominated until the mid-1960s in Chilean agriculture.

Lack of land outside the large estates made possible establishment of a service tenantry, and labor-rent obligations multiplied as internal and external demand for wheat increased. However, if *inquilinaje* in Chile bore some resemblance to *colono* or service-tenant labor systems in other Latin American nations, its origins and the predominantly mestizo composition of its work force distinguished it from the harsher arrangements involving Indian labor in Peru, Bolivia, and Ecuador. Even when economic conditions worsened, Chilean *inquilinos* as a class did not experience systematic cultural and ethnic repression on the scale of the rural labor force in the Andes, nor did debt-peonage typically restrict their mobility.

Neither external nor internal markets placed great demands on the Chilean landlords in relation to the territory's agricultural potential. By mid-eighteenth century Chile produced perhaps 400,000 quintals* of wheat on less than 50,000 hectares. Even the largest rural estates rarely cultivated more than 100 hectares of wheat. Commercial ex-

* One metric quintal equals 100 kilograms.

pansion of agriculture enriched a number of landowners and provided considerable opportunities for improvement to a relatively small portion of the rural labor force who succeeded at crop farming or stock raising as tenants. But even the "boom" after 1687 and continued expansion in the eighteenth century did not absorb the growing numbers of floating population which squatted on "vacant" land, took up banditry, or served the landlords as a pool of seasonal laborers. Labor surpluses made debt-peonage unnecessary and, therefore, relatively rare.

The sharp increase in demand and massive exports of wheat to Peru (1687-1700) not only influenced rural land-tenure and labor systems but also created serious problems for local consumers. The Santiago cabildo first attempted to monitor the harvests and retain a fixed proportion in the region in order to avoid scarcity or excessive increases in price. Landowners registered only a fraction of the harvested grain to circumvent the cabildo's regulations. In response the cabildo in 1695 urged the governor to prohibit wheat exports. With the *audiencia's* approval the governor revoked all licenses for export of wheat. Opposition from landowners and merchants included the clever request by the Jesuits—who owned many of the most important rural estates in Chile—for permission to "transfer" 1000 fanegas of wheat from their storehouses in Chile to their college in Lima. The governor rejected this request and even forced a merchant ship at Valparaíso to unload wheat already in the ship's hold.

In the following years the tension continued between the need to provision the local market at reasonable prices and the economic opportunities of the Peruvian market. Dual pricing schemes attempted to limit the price of wheat sold locally, but the rapid expansion of commerce made effective regulation practically impossible. Increased production, however, lowered prices substantially. In 1713 over 140,-000 fanegas of wheat left Chile for Peru in thirty ships; two-thirds of these embarked from Valparaíso with wheat from the central region, seven from Penco-Concepción, and two or three from Coquimbo.

The wheat trade also promoted the commercial and physical growth of Valparaíso. A small group of merchants and warehouse owners soon controlled the wheat market in the port. Despite the efforts of the cabildo to limit commercial corruption, this group often defrauded producers with discounts for spoilage. As the years went by, the Lima shippers also conspired to depress the price paid to Chilean wheat producers. The wheat trade epitomized commerce in the context of Hispanic capitalism: a monopoly or a small clique of suppliers colluded with government officials to fix prices and restrict supplies of basic commodities in order to guarantee "reasonable" profits.

The end of the seventeenth century saw not only the transformation of agriculture in the Santiago-central region but also a significant increase in contraband trade with European powers. The succession to the Spanish throne of the French Duke of Anjou, who governed Spain as Philip V, placed Spain alongside France in a long war against England, Austria, Portugal, Savoy, and Holland. Unable to defend or supply its overseas empire, Spain authorized French vessels to maintain communications with its colonies. Contraband trade mushroomed, and Chilean governors profited enormously from new commercial ventures. When the French engineer Frezier arrived in Valparaíso in 1713, he commented on "the abundance of merchandise in the country when we arrived and the low prices." The limited market for European goods in Chile ruined many merchants in Lima who could not compete with French manufacturers. The contraband trade also brought a reversal in trade patterns as merchandise arrived in Concepción and Valparaíso from Europe and then was shipped to Lima. On a lesser scale, merchandise also arrived via Buenos Aires and the base for contraband at the Portuguese settlement of Colônia do Sacramento. In 1712 the Spanish crown worked out an arrangement with the French king, Louis XIV, to halt the contraband trade. However, it had become so excessive that the Spanish waited seven years to re-establish the fleets bringing merchandise to the "annual" fairs at Portobello (Panama) in order to allow the surpluses from contraband merchandise to be absorbed. In 1724 the French expeditions temporarily ended, but British merchants had by then replaced them.

The Treaty of Utrecht (1713) ending the War of the Spanish Succession gave the English a thirty-year monopoly on the slave trade with the Spanish American colonies; during this time the English were to bring 144,000 Negroes to the Atlantic ports. Of this quantity, 400 could come yearly to Peru and Chile. Queen Anne of England granted the slave monopoly to the South Seas Company, which established itself in Buenos Aires. From 1715 to 1739, 61 ships brought over to Buenos Aires 18,000 Negroes, nearly 4000 of whom were shipped on to Chile and Peru. Since they were not as successful at slaving as they had anticipated, the English turned to smuggling. On the pretext of transporting necessities for the Negroes, all sorts of merchandise came into Buenos Aires and from there via Mendoza to Chile. In return, the English took silver or gold in payment. Traders loaded merchandise into oxcarts for the trip across the pampas and in Mendoza transferred their goods to mules for the Andes crossing. Mendoza's merchants and cabildo identified so closely with the contraband trade that they banished the new corregidor who had been sent from Santiago to stifle it.

By 1722 commercial reform allowed greater shipping activity through the so-called "registered ships," or *navíos de registro*. Direct trade between Europe and Buenos Aires was extended overland to Chile. Protesting Lima merchants urged an end to this link, but the Spanish fleets could no longer compete with the French and the English. In 1735 the merchants of Cádiz and Peru requested that no further fleets come to Panama until they could dispose of the merchandise on hand. Nevertheless, a fleet arrived in 1739, only to be rerouted to Cartagena due to the destruction of Portobello by an English squadron under Edward Vernon. This marked the end of the fleet system and forced the crown to open a new Pacific route for the *navíos de registro*.

After two hundred years as a colony Chile could finally trade with Spain by sea, although Callao remained an intermediary port of call. Due to the war with England, however, French vessels contracted by merchants at Cádiz, carried out the first legal trade between Chile and Spain. In the following three decades the Chilean market never lacked for European manufactures; indeed the market was so glutted that prices declined considerably for most imported merchandise, and many merchants, unable to sell their goods, went bankrupt.

In the last quarter of the eighteenth century, new reforms further reduced commercial restrictions. Prohibitions on much intercolonial trade disappeared in 1774; and with the creation in 1776 of a new viceroyalty centered in Buenos Aires, trade restrictions were eliminated between Chile and Río de la Plata. Despite protests regarding the coincident separation of the western Argentine province of Cuyo from Chile, the creation of the Río de la Plata viceroyalty benefited the Chilean economy. The initial measures of the viceroy, Ceballos, encouraged Chilean commerce by opening the ports to European goods destined for Cuyo. Lastly, the crown also removed Callao as a mandatory stop. Between them these measures eroded Peruvian domination of Chile's commerce.

Yet with all the commercial restrictions of the colonial period, it is difficult to point to any that fundamentally impeded development of Chile's agrarian economy. Inconveniences for merchants or small groups of elite consumers resulted from prohibitions on bringing sugar from Mexico or trading directly with Buenos Aires and Potosí. But Lima was the logical market for most Chilean products. In 1650, and even by 1800, there was little European or North American demand for the commodities of Chile's agrarian economy, as there came to be in the middle of the nineteenth century. In 1788 the value of all (official) Chilean exports (676,222.50 pesos) did not pay for Chilean imports of sugar and yerba mate (684,617.04 pesos); total imports exceeded 2 million pesos.

Efforts by Ambrosio O'Higgins (1788-96) to stimulate expansion of production, in part through import substitution, and to open new markets for Chilean commodities met with little success. Sugar, cotton, and other tropical products, even when the crops survived in Chile, could not compete with Peru or Mexico. Likewise, Chilean industries could not compete with European or North American manufactures. Imports of luxury goods—fine textiles, furniture, jewels— could only be paid for by minting coins from the gold, silver, and

copper taken from the earth and exporting money to maintain the
pretensions of the colonial aristocracy. European merchants brought
manufactured goods to the Chilean market and took gold, silver, or
livestock products in return, but offered no great prospect, at the
time, of absorbing significant amounts of rural Chile's products.
Chile's economic development, given its agro-mineral output, depended upon fluctuations in the international economy's demand for
a range of primary or semi-elaborated products. This remained the
case long after the end of Spanish colonial domination. Mining
booms in the *norte chico* in the eighteenth century increased import
capacity, but the concentration of wealth and the inability to compete with imported manufactures stifled internal industrial development.

European manufactures entered Chilean markets throughout the
late seventeenth and the eighteenth centuries. At the end of the
eighteenth century import duties amounted to one-third those
charged by the first national government after 1810. The textile
"factories" in Chile declined after 1650, as did the sugar mills. The
only surviving industries were shipbuilding, cordage, foundries, and
those processing products of the agrarian economy such as tanneries,
wineries, and flour mills. Perhaps more extensive commerce in mineral products with British and French merchants might have allowed even greater imports of European manufactures, but this
could not have benefited colonial industrial development or altered
the institutional structure of the agrarian economy. Unlike the Spanish prohibitions on direct trade with Buenos Aires prior to 1778 and
the demands for "free trade" which inspired Argentine independence,
freer trade offered little benefit to overall Chilean economic development in the seventeenth and eighteenth centuries.

If Spanish commercial policy did less to shape Chilean development than is often supposed, the internal dynamics and customs of
Hispanic capitalism left an indelible mark on Chilean society. It
molded economic and social practices and expectations so as to create numerous institutional obstacles to political and economic advancement for the colony and the future Chilean nation. Much more

important than the often-evaded commercial regulations, the factors
that impeded social and economic development were the authoritarian, arbitrary processes of policy making, the bureaucratic modes of
implementation or circumvention, the use of public resources for private profit, the mingling of public and "private" enterprise, the denigration of labor, and the exploitation of the labor force. More important than any Spanish mercantile restrictions as impediments to
Chilean development were the institutions of enterprise which condemned the vast majority of laborers to a subsistence existence outside the money economy. The encomienda system in Chile practically made slaves of the Indians. Extreme concentration of land in
the large estates condemned the mestizo rural laborers to generations
of exploitation. State-supported monoplies on commerce and the artisan trades limited opportunities for the evolution of a prosperous
middle class. The royal bureaucracy's comprehensive regulation of
prices and economic activity ensured that private enterprise was never
really a private matter—that public policy inhibited operation of any-
think like a market economy. The combination of Spanish seignioral
institutions, neofeudal labor systems, and monopolistic commercial
enterprises created a highly stratified society in the Santiago-central
region, and the lack of effective internal demand inhibited the development of domestic industry. Chilean elites maintained this legacy
of colonialism long after they had rejected Spanish imperial domination.

At the end of the eighteenth century the Santiago-central region
was still an essentially rural society. Only Santiago, of all the urban
places, looked like a city. With a population of 25,000 in 1780, Santiago grew to an urban center of 34,000 to 40,000 in the first decade
of the nineteenth century. In a territory with between 500,000 and
750,000 inhabitants outside of Indian territory, the urban centers contained barely 10 percent of the population. While this was similar to
general trends of urbanization in the Western World, it means that
the daily existence of most Chileans consisted of toil from sun up to
sun down in the countryside or mines.

Between 1740 and 1754 governors Manso de Velasco and Ortiz de

Rozas organized and partially financed the foundation of new towns in the central region: San Felipe, Los Angeles, Cauquenes, Talca, San Fernando, Melipilla, Rancagua, Curicó, Copiapó, Florida, Casablanca, Petorca, Ligua. These towns, which would later become important urban centers in the region, were still, in the words of Amunátegui Solar, "miserable villages" at the end of the eighteenth century. Valparaíso, despite its importance as the major port for the commerce of the central region, had a population of only 4500 as late as 1808.

The relative smallness of the urban population belied the overriding concentration of political and economic power in Santiago and Valparaíso. In the capital the cabildo and royal officials determined the regulations that would affect the economic interests of the colonial elites and granted the concessions, monopolies, and privileges that were the source of economic opportunity. Hispanic capitalism linked urban elites to the landowners, miners, and merchants when they were not one and the same. Despite the rural base of economic production, family connections, business partnerships, and the politics of colonial society knit together the economic life of the colony in the major urban centers. Unlike the dispersion of economic power and decision making characteristic of European feudalism, Hispanic capitalism in Chile concentrated wealth and decision making in urban centers even while feudal-like production generated the economic surplus.

In the last quarter of the eighteenth century important public works enhanced the city of Santiago. Under direction of the architect Joaquín Toesca, the city rebuilt the dikes destroyed by the floods of 1783, and work on the new mint, La Moneda, was intensified. In 1795 George Vancouver admiringly called the Santiago mint the "best building in all the Spanish colonies." Roads between Santiago and Valparaíso also received attention made necessary by the expansion of commerce. Sidewalks on major streets and beautification projects testified to the fact that the town had become a city. Here lived the colonial aristocracy, a mixture of landowners, merchants, and the growing number of royal officials brought to the colony as a result of administrative and commercial reforms implemented by the Bourbons in the late eighteenth century. A number of elite *criollo* families intermarried with the colonial administrators and the new arrivals from Spain. Between 1701 and 1810 some 24,000 immigrants came to Chile from Spain, including numerous Basques. Arrival of these Basques at a time of commercial expansion altered the composition of the Chilean elite. The Basques succeeded in commerce, bought rural estates (including some of the estates confiscated from the Jesuits expelled from Chile in 1767), and soon occupied official positions in the colonial administration.

Marriage of royal officials with the daughters of *criollo* elites, a violation of royal policy, created significant conflicts of interest. These led frequently to complaints by those negatively affected as well as to injury to the public interest: "By their [the *oidores*] marriages here, infinite [numbers] of relatives, the connections and haciendas that they have, and by their maximum opposition to that which is . . . advantageous to royal finances, all is reduced to becoming a [victim] of their passions." Not only intermarriage but also expanding opportunity for *criollos* in the royal service created problems for the crown. In 1759 six of the eight members of the *audiencia* were *criollos* and in 1776 all the *oidores* had been born in the colonies. This contrasted markedly with general patterns of peninsular dominance of high administrative and judicial offices throughout the Spanish Empire. Though decrees in 1776 purged *criollos* and their peninsular relations from the *audiencia* to overcome their supposed opposition to fiscal reforms, in the last decade of the eighteenth century *criollos* and *peninsulares* related to Chileans reassumed influence in the *audiencia* and in other official positions. Jacques Barbier's study of colonial elites in Chile confirms that from 1796 to 1810 there were always at least two Chilean *oidores* in the audiencia. Still, tension existed between the aspirations of the colonial aristocracy for control of the local society and the efforts of the crown to limit the corrupting influence of family ties and local loyalties. Above all, however, the efforts by the Chilean elites to influence or control royal officials merely point again to their own awareness that in the context of His-

panic capitalism all wealth, economic opportunity, and status were
ultimately linked to politics.

By the beginning of the nineteenth century the institutions of Hispanic capitalism had shaped the Santiago-central region into a highly
stratified socio-economic system. A small elite lived well—if not as
splendidly as the upper classes in Peru or Mexico—from the returns
on colonial commerce, the salaries of official position, and the corruption linking politics and business. Landowners reaped profits from
agriculture and livestock. Rural workers and tenants suffered from
hunger and lived in misery. The economy grew, and the living conditions of much of the rural population and the emergent proletariat
worsened. Economic growth within the context of Hispanic capitalism led to the development of a society in which, as one royal official
said, "nothing was more common in the countryside, where harvests
had recently been taken in and sold for the lowest of prices, than to
see the hands that had recently harvested the crops extended for
alms." In Santiago the same official reported that he continually saw
"similar conditions in regard to the public works of the capital, where
numbers of the unfortunate present themselves seeking jobs, beg-
ging for admittance to work."

The internal contradictions of Hispanic capitalism already con-
strained Chilean development. In the words of Manuel de Salas, "the
decadence of this kingdom was a necessary result of its economic
structure."

Of all the Chilean territory, the Concepción-southern region offered the brightest prospects to the conquistadors with Valdivia in
the first years of conquest. Here could be found gold mines, good
land for livestock and agriculture, and large numbers of Indians for
a potential work force. Some of the conquistadors gave up encomiendas in the Santiago region in exchange for grants south of the Bío
Bío River. But the defeat at Tucapel (1553) marked the first of
many military disasters that thwarted Spanish dreams of enrichment
in what appeared to be the most attractive region of Chile. For the
entire colonial period this southern region was an open wound—an

insecure frontier where Spanish economic enterprise and urban culture barely managed to survive against the Indians and the calamities
of nature.

Valdivia's forces first established the city of Concepción in 1550
near the site of present-day Penco. The town was destroyed in 1554,
symbolically refounded in 1555 and abandoned, then re-established
again in 1558 when Hurtado de Mendoza arrived with reinforcements from Peru. In recognition of the town's role as the principal
fort on the Indian frontier, the crown created Chile's first *audiencia*
at Concepción in 1565. But in the words of Carvallo y Goyeneche,
"This had no purpose: all were military men and a *consejo de guerra*
would have been more appropriate than a legislature; pens were as
useless then as swords were necessary." When an earthquake and
tidal wave destroyed the town again in 1570, a chronicler tells us that
the residents "didn't know what to do, believing that the world was
coming to an end, because they saw black water gush up from the
cracks in the earth, and a smell of sulphur that seemed like the in-
ferno. . . ." To the end of the sixteenth century Concepción remained a small military camp; only after 1603 did it begin to take
shape as a permanent city with the stationing there of the large permanent military garrison.

The other settlements founded south of the Bío Bío River in the
sixteenth century constituted no more than small fortified encamp-
ments. Mining activity around Imperial (present day Carahue),
Osorno, and Valdivia made them relatively prosperous, though they
were always menaced by the threat of Indian attack. In 1575 an
earthquake damaged all the southern settlements, but the settlers rebuilt them; and in 1580 Governor Martín Ruiz de Gamboa founded
the city of Chillán during the annual military campaign. These
southern settlements developed around the prosperous livestock and
agricultural estates of the encomenderos as well as around gold mines.

The dispersion of the Spanish forces among so many small settlements left each town extremely vulnerable to any large-scale Indian
attack. Had enmity not existed among various Indian groups, these
southern outposts could not have survived at all. For most of the last

decade of the sixteenth century the Spanish lived as prisoners in their own forts.

Despite its insecurity, the southern territory developed important agrarian enterprises and sent large quantities of gold north to Santiago and Peru. The rural estates produced wheat, barley, oats, vegetables, and great quantities of apples, which in later years became a major Chilean export. Abundance kept prices low. Livestock multiplied rapidly among the Spanish and also the Indians, who soon had large herds of sheep and horses as well as lesser amounts of cattle. Southern industries included the well-known textile workshops, or *obrajes*, at Osorno as well as mills, tanneries, crafts, and the mines. The Osorno *obrajes*, utilizing local Indian labor, produced cloth that the chronicler Mariño de Lobera compared favorably with the textiles of Flanders. Much of this production found its way to Santiago, Lima, and even Europe. Indeed, Osorno, Valdivia, and Imperial were the most prosperous settlements in Chile—until the military disasters after 1598. In 1598 the town of Valdivia had six hundred Spanish and mestizo residents, and over 60 percent of all Spanish and mestizo settlers in Chile lived south of the Bío Bío River. By 1600, 90 percent of all Chilean Indians also lived south of the Bío Bío, as disease, enslavement, and warfare radically reduced their population in the north.

In the years 1598 to 1604 the Araucanians erased all Spanish settlements south of the Bío Bío River. Chile thus lost all the wealth of its southern economy. Unsuccessful military campaigns (1603-12) followed by a policy of "defensive warfare" (1612-26) left this territory in the hands of the Indians. After 1626 the crown ordered a return to active efforts to reconquer the lands south of Concepción, but these efforts degenerated into periodic pillage and slave hunts and proved ineffective. The only "products" harvested by the Spanish in these years were Indian slaves and concubines. Though able to send military expeditions through Indian territory, the Spanish could not guarantee the safety of permanent settlements. After years of raids, pillage, and occasional battles the Chilean governor ordered resettlement of Angol in 1637. A fire reduced the fort to ashes in 1638, and in the peace of Quillín (1641) the Spanish agreed to abandon Angol and to establish the Bío Bío River as a frontier between the sovereign Indian people and the Chilean colony.

In order to defend the Chilean colony against Indian and European adversaries, the viceroy of Peru committed a large expeditionary force (12 ships, 1800 men, 188 artillery pieces, as well as artisans) to the resettlement of Valdivia in 1645-46. For some years to come Valdivia depended directly upon the viceroyalty instead of on the Chilean authorities. It served as an isolated outpost in Indian territory, strongly defended and communicating only by sea with Peru or Santiago.

North of the Bío Bío River, between the Maule and Itata rivers, the Spanish maintained ongoing rural enterprises even after the loss of the southern towns. This district became the granary for the limited Concepción region; its wheat and livestock products fed the frontier garrisons and even provided a surplus for export. But the Spanish slave raids and pillaging finally provoked the Indians into another large-scale uprising in 1655, in which the Spanish lost the forts and fort towns of Arauco, San Pedro, Colcura, Buena Esperanza, Nacimiento, Talcamávida, San Rosendo, Boroa, and Chillán. As a measure of the impressive economic growth that had occurred in this region, Carvallo y Goyeneche estimated that in sacking 396 rural estates, the Indians took 400,000 head of livestock and occasioned losses amounting to over 8 million pesos—in addition to capturing some 1300 Spaniards and over half the colony's armaments. Also destroyed were the entire farm infrastructure and small manufacturing enterprises such as mills and tanneries, which had been established between 1603 and 1654, along with crops in the cultivated fields and vineyards. The Spanish army lost some 900 men—over half its effective strength—and the surviving settlers retreated to Concepción or dispersed across the Maule River.

Two years later (March 15, 1657), with the Indian rebellion uncontained, an earthquake and tidal wave again utterly destroyed Concepción, the only remaining town in the southern region. Casualties amounted to forty dead; the survivors faced a winter without supplies or shelter. This tragedy, combined with the Indian threat, prompted an official of the *audiencia* at Santiago to propose moving the frontier north to the Maule River. Instead, the new governor, Porter Casanate, led a successful campaign against the advancing Indians, pushing them back across the Bío Bío. Slowly the Spanish rebuilt Concepción, and by the 1670s the Maule-Concepción triangle regained self-sufficiency in basic foodstuffs. By the end of the century both wheat and wine production had recovered to pre-1655 levels, and the region again sent livestock products, wine, and wheat to Lima. The opening of the Lima market to Chilean wheat in the 1680s stimulated the rural economy of the Concepción region as it had the central valley, but the direct export trade remained relatively small; an average of only two to three ships a year trafficked between Concepción and Callao during the last two decades of the seventeenth century.

Delays in the arrival of the military subsidy between 1700 and 1717 seriously injured the southern economy and debilitated the frontier garrisons. The crown reduced the annual *situado* to 100,000 pesos after 1705; it actually arrived only in 1706 and 1717. By the early 1720s the effective garrison consisted of about 700 soldiers instead of the authorized 1500 to 2000. The reduced garrison found itself dispersed in a number of small forts, including some south of the Bío Bío River. These served as centers of trade with the Indians, but the abuses of soldiers and traders also provoked the Indians' anger.

The Indians took advantage of the decline in colonial military capabilities and in a general uprising in 1723 besieged and forced abandonment of the southern forts at Tucapel, Arauco, Colcura, and Purén. Raiding the haciendas between Laja and Chillán the Araucanians took thousands of cattle (40,000 according to one estimate) and again disrupted the rural economy. In a midcentury report to the king, a Jesuit urged a new frontier policy. He also conveys an idea of the character of the forts destroyed in the 1723-26 uprisings: "If the forts don't defend us nor scare the enemy, what good are they? They serve merely to conserve a few 'ranchos' covered with straw, for—with the exception of Arauco, that is all they amounted to, in an area with few Spanish families. . . . To defend so little did not justify provoking the Indians' hostility." An indication of the economic effects of this uprising was that the tithes, or *diezmos*, collected by the Bishopric of Concepción declined from 18,000 pesos in 1717 to 7000 pesos in 1724. The same report tells us "in the year of 1738, the *diezmos* did not exceed 11,000 [pesos] because the Indians took over 100,000 head of cattle and again as much of smaller livestock from 1724."

Despite the intermittent warfare, cattle rustling, and minor incidents, the pastoral-agricultural economy in the Maule-Concepción region survived. Some settlers, called *conchabistas*, even carried out a good amount of trade with the Indians, exchanging wine, hardware, and trinkets for Indian ponchos, textiles, and livestock.

Just as Concepción was recovering from military disasters and natural calamities, still another earthquake and tidal wave (July 8, 1730) leveled most of the city. The bishop wrote to the king that two-thirds of the principal buildings and houses of the city, along with granaries, storehouses, and shops, had been destroyed. Emergency relief and military supplies arrived from Santiago to avoid a military disaster while the city recovered from the earthquake. The viceroy at Lima advanced 50 percent of the next year's subsidy, and the governor in Santiago contributed over 10,000 pesos to the churches and residents. Twenty-one years later (1751) an even worse earthquake entirely destroyed the settlement again; after struggles between the bishop and those wishing to relocate the town, Concepción was officially refounded in 1764 in the valley of Mocha, between the Andalien and Bío Bío rivers.

Apart from Concepción, a city of perhaps 6000 residents by 1800, few significant urban centers grew up in the southern district. At the end of the eighteenth century Carvallo y Goyeneche reported 449 families at Chillán (also destroyed by the earthquake of 1751) living in small adobe houses. The plaza "which is 150 varas square lacks the adornment of impressive buildings, with the exception of the house of the priest . . . built in the style of the capital." Other towns of the region, founded in the 1740s and 1750s by administrative order of the governor, included Quirihue (1741) which "merits not even the name of village with its five families"; Gaulqui, in the district of Puchacai, where 14 families resided; San Luis Gonzaga (1766), in the district of Rere, with 40 *vecinos* and a total population of 201; Los Ángeles (1741), the most important town in Rere with 159 *vecinos* (less than 800 total residents). In a number of small forts handfuls of soldiers also formed "urban" nuclei on the frontier. Farther south the colonial authorities in Lima and Santiago financed the refounding of Osorno, in the last decade of the century, with expenditures of over 30,000 pesos; in 1796 some 1,012 settlers (170 families) had established themselves in a region lost to the Spanish for many years. In all, however, if we accept the estimates of Marcello Carmagnani, fewer than 8 percent of the population in the southern region lived in "urban" situations near the end of the eighteenth century, and most of these resided in Concepción.

Social structure and land-tenure patterns in this region differed from those in the central valley and to the north of Santiago. Lack of security made maintenance of large estates extremely difficult. Most of the Spanish and mestizos who wanted to farm had access to parcels and could provide for their own sustenance. With a population composed largely of soldiers, ex-soldiers, and the families of soldiers, racial and social stratification was much less rigid than in other parts of the Chilean colony. Most of the inhabitants led a life of subsistence scratched from the soil, or from the low military pay, small mines, trade with the Indians, livestock and related manufactures, or pillage. In the last decade of the eighteenth century Carvallo y Goyeneche accurately described the region's pathetic state:

> Almost all of its inhabitants are laborers, the only work available. With this they do not want for food but they live a miserable life. Those who do not want to believe this need merely enter the houses (or I should say, huts) and observe the rustic clothing, food, and manners of the men, the weariness of the women and the nudity of the children. . . . It is a cause for tears that a reigon so potentially rich, does not produce for itself or for the peninsula Spain the immense wealth [which it could].

In the last half of the eighteenth century the rural economy of the region grew—but not dramatically. From 1750 to 1778 no more than seven ships a year departed from Concepción harbor with the tallow, hides, sheepskins, fruits, and wine from the rural estates. In the last decades of that century and the first decade of the nineteenth, commerce and contraband increased with the appearance of whaling ships and smugglers from the United States, Great Britain, and elsewhere. Nevertheless, the southern region remained a real frontier, with the unconquered Indians south of the Bío Bío still outside effective jurisdiction of colonial political authorities. Not until the 1880s did an independent Chilean nation definitively incorporate this southern zone.

With regional variations Hispanic capitalism shaped colonial Chile into a highly stratified caste-class society whose political and economic institutions survived long after imperial rule. The sparsely settled northern agro-mining district, the dominant Santiago-central region, and the Concepción frontier territory had impressed upon them a common juridical mold, altered in practice by local conditions, but uniform in its formalism and its flexibility of application— at the discretion of government officials. Overt deference to authority combined with systematic evasion of the law became the norm. Intermingling of private and public business blurred the distinctions between corruption, "conflict of interest," and routine public administration. The war against the Araucanians conditioned economic development while offering royal officials, soldiers, and merchants enormous opportunities for profit, promotions, and patronage. Centralized, authoritarian, and often arbitrary policymaking became the expected, accepted pattern of government. Concentration of wealth, status, and real estate in the hands of a privileged few, denigration of work, and exploitation of labor were all essential ingredients in the socio-economic structure of the colony.

As long as the legitimating symbol of empire—the monarchy—remained intact, there was only minor resistance to the institutions and processes of Hispanic capitalism in Chile. Colonial elites made no significant attack on the legitimacy or fundamental character of Spanish rule prior to 1810. And even when events in Europe precipitated independence movements in Spanish America, Chilean leaders ultimately re-established political order by reaffirming the basic assumptions and institutions of the colonial era, with the exception of submission to Spain and European monarchism. The Spanish crown might lose its dominions in America, but Chile would retain the indelible markings of Hispanic capitalism.

Chapter 4 • Independence and the Autocratic Republic

In the last decades of the eighteenth century administrative reorganization of the Spanish Empire left Chile an autonomous captaincy-general, no longer subject directly to the viceroy of Peru. Until 1808 the colony was governed by a succession of capable, professional administrators; its gradual material progress and the public sentiment of the leading *criollos* gave little premonition of the violent movement for political independence that occurred after 1810. Perhaps overstating the case, Manuel de Salas, the well-known colonial administrator and intellectual precursor of independence, claimed that Chileans "desired only to be good Catholics and good Spaniards, which they regarded as the two inseparable conditions of their happiness."

The last royal governors administered Chile with vigor and correctness. Ambrosio O' Higgins—whose illegitimate son, Bernardo O'Higgins, would become the George Washington of Chile—began his term of office (1787-96) with an extended tour on horseback of the northern regions, visiting the towns and mining districts. Intent on stimulating the Chilean economy and reducing its dependence upon imported commodities, O'Higgins attempted to introduce new crops and to reestablish colonial plantations such as sugar, cotton, and rice as well as to encourage increased exports of mineral products, hides, and wool to Spain. He also sought to establish direct trade between Chile, Guayaquil, Central America, and Mexico. To revive old trade patterns between Chile and Charcas, O'Higgins helped form a commercial enterprise with an eight-year monopoly to promote exports of copper, aguardiente, wine and other products of the northern districts.

Though well-intentioned, this economic program, which anticipated to some extent the policy of import-substitution by Chilean governments after 1930, brought very limited results. The tropical and plantation crops failed to survive in the difficult conditions of northern Chile; the colony continued to import large amounts of sugar, cotton, and rice from Peru or elsewhere in the empire. Exports expanded slowly, and local industry did not develop to provision local markets with substitutes for the luxury goods imported from Europe, Lima, and Buenos Aires. Many of the structural constraints on economic development that plague Chile today were already evident in the obstacles facing Ambrosio O'Higgins' economic program during the last decade of the eighteenth century.

In the last days of O'Higgins' administration the crown established a *tribunal de consulado* in Chile. This was both a commercial court and an agency to promote economic development. The royal decree creating the *consulado* assigned it responsibility for "protection and stimulation of commerce . . . the advancement of agriculture, improvement in crops and commercialization of the fruits of the land, introduction of beneficial machinery and implements. . . ." Whatever the limitations imposed by colonial status, the establishment of the consulado indicated that Spain was not entirely ignoring the problems or the needs of the Chilean economy.

O'Higgins' achievements and his rectitude as governor of Chile earned him promotion to the Viceroyalty at Lima. His successor, Gabriel de Aviles y del Fierro, had lengthy experience in the colonial bureaucracy and military establishment. Aviles continued in the footsteps of O'Higgins and supported public projects such as dikes, cobbling of streets, and beautification of Santiago. In cooperation with Manuel de Salas, the syndic of the *consulado*, Aviles provided competent administration of the Chilean colony during his short tenure (in 1799 he was promoted to the Viceroyalty at Buenos Aires).

As the eighteenth century ended, Chile received a new governor with all the pomp and ceremony that it could marshal, including bullfights, feasts, theatrical presentations, and other public festivities. Far from hinting at any desire for independence from Spain, Santiago society welcomed the new governor with subservient splendor.

When the last of the royal governors assumed office in 1802, the colony remained loyal to Spanish authority. A long-standing dream came to fruition with initiation of work on the canal from the Maipo River to irrigate the land in the valley and augment the water in the Mapocho. Public works in Santiago continued with the completion of dikes and, also, after fifteen years, of the future presidential palace, La Moneda. When the governor died at the age of seventy-three in February 1808, few Chileans could have anticipated the juntas that would soon spring up throughout Spanish America to cut the bonds linking it to Spain. Notwithstanding Bourbon efforts to implement administrative reforms, no great change in internal administration or unusual abuses occurred to anger the colonials; there was in Chile nothing like the Stamp Act or the tea tax that incited the North American colonies to rebellion.

Though the colonials remained loyal to Spain, certain persistent complaints or dissatisfactions did exist. The *criollos* resented the preference given to native-born Spaniards in royal appointments and also the condescending treatment they themselves frequently received from Spanish officials or merchants. They also disliked certain of the commercial regulations and taxes that burdened Chilean commerce, and the lack of educational opportunities in Chile which necessitated travel to Lima or Spain for professional training. A belief of many Chileans that Peru maintained a privileged position vis-à-vis Chile—despite the favorable impact on Chile of certain of the Bourbon reforms—contributed to a resentment of royal policy. Geographical isolation and the evolution of a distinctive Chilean culture had also eroded the allegiance of some colonial elites to Spain. Finally, a very small minority of intellectuals, attracted by liberal, republican ideology and propaganda, had come to blame Chile's backwardness on Spanish imperial rule.

Even taken all together, however, these criticisms of the imperial system proved mild in comparison with those in Buenos Aires, Guayaquil, and Mexico City. In the words of Chile's well-known nineteenth-century historian, Barros Arana, "the most advanced men were persuaded that the reform of a few laws, the growth of population, and the diffusion of useful knowledge would make Chile a region privileged by her products and by the virile and enterprising character of her people." Most elites opposed protestant or liberal doctrines imported from Europe, Britain, and the United States in the increasing number of foreign ships in Chilean ports after 1790 (when the Convention of San Lorenzo opened the South Pacific to European and North American shipping). Deliberate ideological subversion of Spanish rule was clearly the goal of a small number of North American merchants and seamen. Some of the 257 North American ships that plied Chilean coastal waters between 1788 and 1810 carried copies of the Declaration of Independence and the Federal Constitution. Nevertheless, while most Latin American republics can point to at least one or two prerevolutionary conspiracies of some import, no serious anti-Spanish conspiracies occurred in Chile prior to 1810.

Just as the conquest of Chile was an extension of the Pizarro-Almagro venture in Peru, so the Chilean independence movement depended on events in Europe and other parts of Spanish America. The movement for Chilean independence, like that of most other Spanish American republics, originated in European politics and warfare. Napoleon Bonaparte, in an effort to impose French hegemony in Europe, took his armies into Portugal and Spain in 1807. Charles IV and his son, Ferdinard VII, yielded the Spanish throne to Joseph Bonaparte. Spanish insurgents resisted this usurpation of the Spanish crown: in the name of Ferdinand VII, a junta at Seville directed the struggle against the Napoleonic armies; and in the Spanish American colonies, local juntas organized to defend the legitimate king of Spain.

News of Napoleon's invasion of Spain arrived in Santiago via Buenos Aires in mid-1808. The French usurpation of the Spanish crown raised the issue of how best to administer the colony on behalf of the legitimate monarch and what to do if the French occupation should become permanent. For a small minority of Chilean leaders this political dilemma provided an ideal context for pursuing complete independence from colonial rule. The majority of Chileans, however, saw the events in Europe as a temporary interruption of legitimate Spanish domination. Nevertheless, confrontations occurred between those professing to favor the temporary "nationalization" of authority in a local junta and those favoring continued submissiveness to French authorities in Spain. The former group found its principal leadership in the cabildo of Santiago, and the latter in the governor, Francisco Antonio García Carrasco and the *audiencia*.

Unlike the seasoned colonial administrators who had governed Chile ably in the late eighteenth and early nineteenth centuries, García Carrasco lacked administrative experience and political skills. He had assumed the governorship due to a reform that left the office in the hands of the highest military official above the rank of colonel in the case of the incumbent's death. With the continual arrival of disturbing news from Buenos Aires—especially reports of the revolt of May 22-25, 1810—the governor decided to take repressive measures. His inept actions, including the arrest and deportation to Lima of three prominent *criollos* on charge of subversion, increased the tensions in Santiago. The *audiencia* attempted to restore calm by announcing García Carrasco's resignation and his replacement by the aged Conde de la Conquista, Mateo de Toro Zambrano, whose rank as brigadier of the royal armies gave him rightful claim to the office. But this desperate effort to maintain legitimacy failed; and on September 18, 1810, a *cabildo abierto*, or "town meeting," convened in the *tribunal de consulado* in Santiago, accepted the resignation of the governor, and proclaimed the creation of a national junta.

For the next two decades a dizzy succession of juntas, assemblies, congresses, military dictatorships, and supreme directors sought to impose their authority in Chile—with a three-year interlude (1814-17) when Spanish royal authority reasserted itself. At first the contending factions all proclaimed their loyalty to King Ferdinand VII or to Spain. The national junta set up September 18, 1810, swore "to govern and to protect the rights of the king during his captivity." A leader of the Chilean independence movement, José Miguel Infante, even justified establishment of the junta by citing Spanish legislation in the principal preconquest codification of Spanish law, the venerable *Siete Partidas*. If, as was probably the case, a minority of Chileans who were bent upon independence from the outset hid their motives behind the mask of loyalty to the king, this mask was enough to gain recognition for the junta from the council of the regency in Spain, making the Chilean junta the only one ever recognized by that body.

The political history of these two decades (1810-30) is conveniently divided into four main periods: (1) four years of civil war and uncertain advance toward independence, 1810-14 (called the *patria vieja*, or "old fatherland"); (2) reimposition of Spanish authority by the viceroy at Lima through force of arms, 1814-17 (called the *reconquista*, or "reconquest"); (3) dictatorship of Bernardo O'Higgins, 1817-23; (4) a chaotic succession of governments proclaiming liberalism, federalism, and republicanism, 1823-30.

After 1830 the internal strife was ended by a coalition of conservative business interests, the clergy, and the landowner class—led by a businessman named Diego Portales—which installed a unique political regime. Republican in form and authoritarian in practice (thus the epithet "autocratic republic" some Chilean historians have given to this regime), the new political order reconsolidated the Hispanic ideal of a strong, centralized executive who imposed order through decrees and the necessary coercion to ensure their implementation. A man who openly claimed he would have shot his father if it were necessary for public order, Portales wrote bluntly: "Democracy, which self-deceived men proclaim so much, is an absurdity in countries like those of America. . . ." Agreeing with the *criollo* intellectual Mariano Egaña that liberal principles were "the greatest enemies of America and would eventually bring her down to total ruin," Portales and his colleagues brooked no opposition to their programs and spared no effort to save Chile from the perils of imported liberal ideology. A great irony of Chilean independence was that the political order devised by Portales, Egaña, and the three presidents who served from 1831 to 1861 exhibited more than a passing similarity to the autocratic tradition of colonial rule.

Independence liberated elite *criollos* from the restraints of Spanish authority and left them free to exploit rural labor, miners, and urban shanty dwellers. It also opened Chile to British, North American, and European merchants along with a few European settlers. It did not mean political, social, or economic improvement for the vast majority of Chileans.

In the process of establishing the postcolonial order, political and constitutional conflicts developed which would recur often during the nineteenth and twentieth centuries. These included disputes over the basic character of the constitution, especially the balance of power between executive and legislature; over the relationship between Church and State; over the inclusiveness of citizenship and civic participation, at first limited to a small minority of wealthy Chileans; and over the scope of the state's authority to confiscate or expropriate private property in the public interest. This latter issue emerged with particular intensity in political maneuvering over abolition of slavery (1811-24) and elimination of titles of nobility and entailed estates (*mayorazgos*).

In the social and economic realm, the chaos of the years 1810-30 also raised critical policy issues that would endure in Chilean national life. Domination of mining output and commerce by foreign (mostly British) merchants and the Chilean government's dependence upon foreign loans, ships, armaments, and technicians to pursue the internal war of liberation against the royalists and carry out the naval expedition to Peru, made clear that shedding the colonialism of Spain would bring a more subtle economic exploitation by the stronger European nations and by North Americans. Lack of efficient internal taxing mechanisms and reliance upon revenues from foreign trade, particularly import-export duties, made public finance highly vulnerable to fluctuations in international trade and to the extensive smuggling and corruption at the ports. Attempts to raise revenues through authorizations of exclusive commercial monopolies and special concessions continued colonial practices and set precedents for policies that later surrendered Chile's most important economic resources, especially mineral wealth, to foreigners. Opening the ports to international shipping—but with significant import duties—generated debates between free trade advocates and early proponents of protection for Chilean industries. These debates set the tone for a persistent conflict over this issue which carried over into the twentieth century—and dramatically re-emerged in the 1970s.

The independence decades also saw an initial statement by a handful of Chilean elites of the need to attract immigrants from Europe in order to populate the country with peoples they considered racially superior to the predominantly mestizo and *casta* work force in the mines, countryside, and towns. The tendency for the most radical *criollo* leaders to blame Spain for Chile's backwardness added to the desire for Europeanization (especially immigrants from England, Ireland, and northern Europe) of the Chilean ethnic stock as well as for the Anglicization of Chilean institutions. This propensity to disparage the mental and technical capabilities of the working classes endured into the twentieth century; it reached its maximum expression in Francisco Encina's twenty-volume *History of Chile to 1891*. Over and over again Encina bemoaned the debilitating effects of mestization. Critical of the economic effects of free trade, Encina nevertheless emphasized the "precious gift of European blood" which the resident foreign merchants contributed to the "Chilean race."

The independence movement used Negro and *casta* troops to expel the Spanish, and decreed emancipation of the *offspring* of the approximately four thousand remaining slaves as a wartime expedient; but it ended by reinforcing the tremendous social gap between Chil-

ean elites and the common folk. These class divisions would be the
basis for bitter confrontations later in the nineteenth century, even
as the newly formed Sociedad de Fomento Fabril (Society for Industrial Development, 1883) repeatedly called for European immigrants
to replace the "lazy, shiftless, mongrel" Chilean laborers.

Independence brought a change in political form but not in social
structure. While the English and French displacement of Spanish or
Peruvian merchants in Valparaíso and Santiago after 1817 influenced
furniture and architectural styles in the homes of the wealthy, the
dwellings of the rural tenant laborers typically remained little more
than straw-covered huts or, at best, small adobe *ranchos*. In the towns
and cities, lower-class residents could spend their leisure hours in the
chinganas (these were a combination of bar, dance hall, and brothel),
which were increasing in number, or at horse races, but they continued to live in "suburban" huts ringing the solid homes and commercial centers spreading out from the central plazas. As the towns
and cities grew and became more affluent in the later part of the nineteenth century, the fusion of liberal political ideology with social
Darwinism would both recall the racist sentiments of the early proponents of European immigration in the independence decades and
"justify" the misery that modernization and "progress" brought to a
growing proletariat after 1850.

From 1810 to 1814—a period labeled *patria vieja*, or "old fatherland"—by Chilean historians, the personalities and ambitions of
those later enshrined in the pantheon of the independence movement's heroes determined the politics of Santiago and Concepción.
The national junta formed on September 18, 1810, largely dominated
by Juan Martínez de Rozas, was followed by experiments with a national congress and then gave way to the dictatorship of José Miguel
Carrera and his two brothers. Feuds between Carrera, the prominent
Larraín family, and Bernardo O'Higgins created an environment of
intrigue and uncertainty. Jealousies between Santiago and the provincial junta at Concepción further confused and debilitated political
authority. In the meantime the United States consul, Joel Poinsett,

allied himself with the Carreras and promoted Chilean independence. Mindful that, despite protestations of loyalty, the Chilean situation was developing into a full-blown separatist movement (as had already occurred in Venezuela in 1811 and in New Granada and Mexico shortly thereafter), the viceroy of Peru sent a military expedition to restore order in Chile. The military force disembarked at the island of Chiloé, which was still directly dependent upon the viceroyalty, and, after gathering new recruits, proceeded to Valdivia, where royalists had already gained control. From there the expedition went by sea to Talcahuano and captured Concepción, where a great part of the garrison also took up the royalist cause. These events induced the major southern cities to swear again their allegiance to Ferdinand VII.

Early in 1814 a second royalist expedition commanded by General Gavino Gainza entered Chile. After a number of encounters with the military forces led by Carrera, O'Higgins, and Juan Mackenna, the royalist armies captured Chillán and Talca in the southern part of the central valley. Thereafter a stalemate occurred between the opposing movements. In 1814 British commodore James Hillyar mediated a treaty agreement (Treaty of Lircay) that ended hostilities with Chile's recognition of Ferdinand VII, an exchange of prisoners, suppression of the Chilean national flag introduced in 1812, and a promise by the Spanish-Peruvian forces to leave Chile within a month.

This treaty proved unacceptable to both the viceroy and prominent *criollo* leaders in Chile. Carrera carried out still another coup in Santiago, banished his personal enemies, and determined to carry on the war against the royalists. O'Higgins refused to recognize Carrera's authority. To complicate matters, the Peruvian viceroy sent a new military expedition to Chile commanded by General Mariano Osorio. Osorio's advance from Talcahuano to Chillán brought Carrera and O'Higgins together again to meet the royalist threat. At the battle of Rancagua (October 1-2, 1814), Carrera failed to reinforce the besieged patriot army, and Osorio defeated O'Higgins. This ended the *patria vieja*. The remnants of O'Higgins' army as well as Carrera's forces fled to Mendoza, accompanied by a mass exodus of prominent *criollos* from Santiago. In Mendoza, José de San Martín, leader of the Argentine independence movement, welcomed O'Higgins; and plotting began for the campaign that would liberate Chile and Peru from Spanish rule (1817-25).

For three years Spanish officials sought to purge Chilean society of separatist sentiments. Secret police, courts-martial, and imprisonment of leading citizens alienated even moderate *criollos* previously uncommitted to independence. Instead of ameliorating *criollo* resentment, the Spanish "reconquest" (1814-17) greatly intensified discrimination against native-born Chileans. Spanish army personnel received salaries up to five times larger than those of *criollos* of the same rank; Chileans were denied government appointments and were refused the economic concessions that stemmed from official largesse. When Chileans complained of these conditions, the governor was reputed to have told his entourage: "I shall not leave to the Chileans even tears with which to weep."

Polarization of sentiment in Chile coincided with San Martín's planning of an expedition to oust the Spanish from all of the southern cone of South America and Peru. While San Martín's agents collected intelligence, and the general prepared his forces in Cuyo, Manuel Rodríguez, former secretary to Carrera, carried out the guerrilla activities against the royalists which made him the hero of the independence movement most acclaimed by leftists and revolutionaries in Chile in the 1960s and 1970s—when guerrilla soldiers sought to liberate Latin America from another imperialism.

Crossing the Andes in early 1817, San Martín defeated the royalist army at Chacabuco to the north of Santiago. Mobs in Santiago ransacked the houses and property of royal officials and wealthy royalists; they also destroyed the portraits of royal governors (back to Pedro de Valdivia) hanging in the government palace. No longer did those bent on independence mask their intentions. On February 14, 1817, San Martín and O'Higgins entered Santiago at the head of the victorious army. After San Martín declined the cabildo's offer to become dictator of Chile, O'Higgins accepted the "supreme directorship" of the colony.

During the ensuing year Spanish victories in the central valley again threatened Santiago until San Martín won the decisive battle on the plains of Maipo (April 5, 1818). By mid-1818, therefore, despite continued royalist resistance in the south, Chilean territory from Copiapó to Concepción was free of Spanish authority. In 1820 the British Lord Cochrane, lending his services to the rebels' cause, returned from an unsuccessful strike at Callao and captured Valdivia in a daring amphibious assault. Attention then turned to the liberation of Peru—though not until 1826 did Chilean soldiers commanded by Ramón Freire wrest control of the island of Chiloé from the Spaniards.

Notwithstanding these military victories, the political chaos and economic costs of more than a decade of civil war, together with continued instability, made political independence cause for less than unconditional jubilation even to the separatists. And like many revolutions, the personal and ideological struggle within the circle of separatist leadership took its toll among most of those later included in the pantheon of revolutionary heroes: José Miguel Carrera, like his brothers earlier, executed in Mendoza; Manuel Rodríguez, assassinated, seemingly with O'Higgins' knowledge; O'Higgins, exiled to Peru (1823), whence he would never return to his native land.

Bernardo O'Higgins, though born in Chile, spent much of his youth in England and Europe. Despite a number of efforts to gain the approval of his father, the former governor of Chile and viceroy of Peru, the latter seems never to have responded to the desire of his illegitimate offspring for formal recognition. In Europe, O'Higgins met Francisco de Miranda, the leading Venezuelan proponent of Latin American independence, and was influenced by Miranda's zeal for liberation of the colonies from Spain. O'Higgins returned to Chile as one of a small minority of *criollos* committed to independence even prior to the Napoleonic invasion of Spain.

After leading separatist troops from 1813 to 1814 and fleeing to Mendoza when defeated by the royalists at Rancagua (1814), O'Higgins returned to Chile as a subordinate of General San Martín in an army aspiring to liberate Chile and Peru from Spanish rule. O'Higgins also belonged to the secret revolutionary group called *logia lautarina*. This lodge, dedicated to independence for the Spanish American colonies, swore its members to secrecy on pain of death and required that members who gained high position in any of the liberated colonies submit for prior approval the names of those they would appoint to military, government, or other positions in the new regimes. The lodge also sought to control government policy. Critics of the lodge saw it as a group of anticlerical, masonic subversives bent on destruction of the old order. A modern biographer of O'Higgins even suggested, with obvious hyperbole, that "the lodge controlled the new Chilean administration as completely as the Party controls the government in a Communist state." Due to his association with the lodge, a segment of Chilean opinion came to see O'Higgins as somewhat less than a truly national leader and blamed him and the lodge for the executions of the three Carrera brothers as well as for the assassination of Manuel Rodríguez.

O'Higgins believed that it was necessary, with a people like the Chileans, "to confer good upon them by force" when other means failed. He promulgated a new constitution in 1818. The document called for a five-man senate with members elected from the provinces. O'Higgins essentially handpicked the membership, as he also did later the delegates to the constitutional convention of 1822.

Despite manipulation of government appointments, the O'Higgins government lacked firm institutional supports. Conflicts with Church leaders over a variety of issues—expulsion of a priest who asked the wife of an O'Higgins supporter to leave a church because she was wearing an inappropriate low-cut dress; establishment of Protestant cemeteries; and introduction of Protestant teachers to develop an anticlerical educational system—weakened O'Higgins' position. Confrontations with certain aristocrats over elimination of titles of nobility, and efforts to abolish the entailed estates, as well as strife with his "own" senate also created problems for O'Higgins. Finally, the implacable resistance of friends and supporters of the Carrera brothers, who never forgave O'Higgins for the Carreras' death, undermined his administration.

Financial difficulties associated with the war effort and corruption also contributed to O'Higgins' failure. Describing the situation in Chile in 1820 a sea captain wrote in his journal:

> No permanent System of Finance had yet been established whereby the Expenses of the Government & of the War might be defrayed and on every emergency Recourse was had to temporary loans and forced contributions. Nothing like a regular appraisement of Land & other Permanent Property had yet been attempted, or any one Species of Regular Taxation resorted to, and when arbitrary contributions were levied the quotas were evidently determined by favoritism or Caprice.

In attempting to raise revenues, O'Higgins re-established the colonial tobacco monopoly, or *estanco*, only to suspend it for two years after protests by foreign merchants. At the same time the Supreme Director's confidant and finance minister and a prominent merchant were apparently speculating in tobacco and other commodities. Furthermore the finance minister, although a Chilean by birth, had sided with the royalists and even accompanied one of the early Spanish expeditions from Peru which sought to reconquer Chile. These circumstances—in addition to the general amnesty for most former royalists who had sworn loyalty to Chile, and the government's attempts to return to the royalists some property confiscated from them—provided effective ammunition for those who wished to discredit O'Higgins. Resistance by merchants to new commercial regulations, political intrigues surrounding a new constitution (1822), a debate concerning a loan secured in London, failure to pay the fleet in Valparaíso, and a threat to replace Ramón Freire, commander of the army at Concepción, all contributed to O'Higgins' downfall.

In 1822 two of the country's five senators left on diplomatic missions. Another expressed a desire to leave public office. O'Higgins then suggested that the senate temporarily suspend its sessions and transfer legislative authority to himself as Supreme Director. The senators met this breach of the principles of liberalism with categorical opposition. Ramón Freire led his forces at Concepción against Talca and threatened to march northward. The city of La Serena followed Concepción's lead, and O'Higgins' opponents in Santiago adhered to the movement to oust him from office. With an emotional farewell speech, O'Higgins surrendered the presidential sash and left for Peruvian exile, never to return to Chile.

Political uncertainty followed O'Higgins' abdication. A barrage of political slogans, ideologies, and personalities accompanied a confusing succession of congresses, assemblies, interim supreme directors, presidents, and military rebellions. Ramón Freire, who had led the Concepción forces, attempted to govern the country from 1823 to 1826 and returned to office several times between 1826 and 1829. Freire later attempted an invasion of Chile from Peru (1836), after being forcibly exiled to the former viceroyalty.

Freire's term in office and his interventions between 1826 and 1830 were associated with superficial experiments with liberalism and federalism in Chilean politics. Exponents of European or North American liberalism sought to impose republican institutions and practices on Chile's traditional administrative, economic, and social structure. To many, liberalism also meant religious toleration or anti-clericalism. Implementation of liberal principles implied confrontation with perhaps the most significant social institution and symbol of Hispanic society: the Catholic Church. This alone assured bitter resistance to liberalism by some prominent *criollo* families.

A small number of influential intellectuals and political leaders also proposed a federalist regime, with considerable regional autonomy, for a new nation lacking strong traditions with local government. The schemes for decentralizing political authority or copying North American federalism appealed to certain regional interests seeking to cast off the economic and political domination of Santiago and Valparaíso as well as to those intellectuals who equated progress and freedom with emulation of the institutions of the United States. But neither liberalism, nor liberal principles and a federalist constitution, corresponded to the socio-economic reality of Hispanic capitalism in Chile after independence.

In 1824 the Freire government confiscated the possessions of the regular clergy. This ruptured Church-State relations, including dismissal of the ex-royalist bishop, Rodríguez Zorilla, whom O'Higgins had re-established in his office in an effort to negotiate diplomatic relations with the Pope. Regional uprisings and Freire's inability to organize effectively the national public administration resulted in continued intrigues, polarization of sentiments by opposing forces, and ruin of the public finances. By 1825, in the words of Chilean author Augustín Edwards, "Freire . . . distracted and impotent, saw his authority being set at naught. Santiago alone recognized the Governing Junta. . . . Meanwhile neither Concepción nor Coquimbo recognized either Freire or the junta. The anarchy into which the country had fallen was reaching a climax; it was under the rule of four governments." Totally frustrated, Freire resigned from office. Personal ambitions combined with rabid commitments to misunderstood slogans threatened to dismember the new nation.

After an enthusiastic speech by federalism's most avid supporter, José Miguel Infante, in July of 1826, Congress formally approved a federal system for Chile. The legislature then embarked upon a piecemeal program designed to define the nature of Chilean federalism. Congress divided Chile into eight provinces, each of which would have a provincial assembly and its own constitution. In addition, local government would continue to exercise a broad range of authority in the *municipios*. In a country lacking provincial political and administrative machinery, let alone provincial constitutions, federalist ideology did not correspond to political reality, but it did intensify regional conflicts that made effective national government illusory.

Meanwhile the army went unpaid, the public treasury remained empty, and president succeeded president. Civil strife reached such a level that Congress requested Freire to reassume the presidency and impose order. After winning several battles against opposing forces, Freire again resigned, to be followed in office by the Vice-President,

Francisco Antonio Pinto. In August 1827 the country reverted to a unitary form of government, ending its imitation of North American federalist principles.

Pinto's administration adopted a new liberal constitution in 1828 that pleased neither ardent federalists nor important liberal factions. Conservatives viewed the constitution as an unrealistic document inspired by imported utopian ideology. By abolishing the *mayorazgos*, the constitution generated opposition in the old aristocracy, while President Pinto's anticlericalism disturbed a broader segment of "public opinion." Conflict degenerated again into civil war.

Led by the personalities who would dominate Chilean politics for the next two decades—Diego Portales, Manuel Rengifo, Joaquín Prieto, and Manuel Bulnes—conservative forces defeated the remnants of the liberal army, commanded by Ramón Freire, at the battle of Lircay in April 1830. The new government banished Freire to Peru—just as Freire had earlier done to Bernardo O'Higgins.

Political activity in the post-independence decades took place within very restricted social circles. Intellectuals wrote constitutions and liberal legislation for a country unfamiliar with the practical meaning of federalism, inalienable rights, or effective limits on government authority. Chileans understood the idea of benevolent despotism and the practice of pragmatic despotism. Royal officials had implemented well-intentioned decrees as their consciences, local interests, "reality," or corruption determined. Involvement of "the people" in legislation or administration conformed neither to the theory nor to the practice of Hispanic politics. It proved no surprise, therefore, that after independence the emergence within elite circles of overlapping ideological factions and personalist movements, such as those of O'Higgins, the Carreras, and Freire, anticipated the multiparty politics of later years without involving the masses except as cannon fodder. Those who supported liberal and/or federalist principles were known as *pipiolos* ("upstarts" or "novices"), and those defending more traditional principles, including the existing privileges of the Church, as *pelucones* ("bigwigs"). But within these two camps, factional disputes and personal loyalties prevented the development of unified political movements, let alone political parties in the modern sense. The highly partisan tabloid newspapers slandered the opposition at will. Political factions and various governments stretched freedom of the press to its limits. No end seemed in sight to the quick succession of presidents and constitutions which accompanied the movement of armies, rebellions, and bandits across the country.

In these conditions public finance fell into a dreadful state. Tax farming on the colonial model continued with respect to the tithes (*diezmos*) and the tolls paid by muleteers and carters on the principal roads. Lack of respect for shifting government authorities and knowledge that the tax farmers retained 30 to 40 percent of the taxes levied increased still further the propensity to evade payment. This held true especially in the case of the *diezmos* paid in kind by the peasantry. Corrupt administration of the customs houses also kept needed revenues from the government. The observations of John Miers, an English businessman more than disenchanted with Chile, summarize the deplorable state of affairs:

> I have elsewhere alluded to the mode in which the duties upon the custom-house were paid, and to the great extent of the contraband introduction of foreign goods. It now remains to say a few words upon the mode of levying the customs. The duties are always, after the Spanish system, estimated and levied at so much percent upon a valuation, not determined by the market price of the articles, but by the arbitrary valuation of the vistas, or custom-house searchers: it is, therefore, impossible for a merchant to calculate upon the actual cost of introduction of foreign goods; but, as the government of Chile does not allow their officers a sufficient salary, they are obliged to connive with the merchants, both in smuggling and in fixing undervaluations, receiving from the latter a proportionate bribe. Similar parcels of goods may at one time be valued in the custom-house at 1000 dollars, at another 100 dollars, and the usual tariff duties paid thereon accordingly; the difference is a robbery to the state, no advantage whatever results to the foreign manufactures, but goes entirely into the pockets of the custom-house officers, merchants, and agents.

Miers concluded that "the foreign trade of Chile, like all matters in state, justice and police, is maintained by empino [sic] influence, intrigue and bribery."

Ironically, however, it was the chaos of public finance that brought to the fore the businessmen and military leaders who ended two decades of near anarchy with a conservative restoration. Led by Diego Portales, a merchant who had remained aloof from the independence struggle, an alliance of the Concepción military elite, merchants, prominent *pelucón* families, and the Church hierarchy established— at bayonet point—a unique political regime in Chile. This regime set it apart from its sister republics as a model of political stability and economic growth in the nineteenth century.

Diego Portales was born in 1793 in Santiago, the son of an influential royal official who served as superintendent of the mint. Distantly related to two colonial governors, his ancestry linked him to Chile's Basque-Castilian aristocracy. After giving up his own position at the mint, Portales formed a commercial partnership with Manuel Cea in the export-import trade, and moved to Lima. Failure of the joint enterprise brought both partners back to Chile where in mid-1824 they contracted with the Freire government to take over the state monopoly (*estanco*) on tobacco and certain other commodities in exchange for servicing the loan contracted by Chilean agents in London in 1822.

The Portales-Cea Company obtained the *estanco* contract amidst rumors of improprieties in the bidding process, including an allegation that a rival firm lost the contract despite its higher bid. If these allegations were true, it proved fortunate for those who lost the contract. Contraband imports of goods subject to the *estanco*, illegal tobacco plantations, and the high price paid for the contract contributed to the enterprise's commercial failure. Portales and his partner attempted to enforce their monopoly rights by destroying illegal tobacco plantations and seeking stronger intervention by government authorities to stop the contraband trade. While personal enemies of the partners and opponents of the government accused the firm

of fraud and bribery, it struggled unsuccessfully to meet its obligations on the British loan. In September 1826 Congress voted to liqui-
date the *estanco* concession and return the monopoly to the government. Though Portales bitterly resented the government's failure to
negotiate new terms or even to allow his firm to administer the government monopoly on a fee basis, the equitable manner in which
Manuel Rengifo liquidated the *estanco* contract formed the basis for
the future cooperation between those two hard-headed businessmen
who would dominate Chilean political economy after 1830.

Many people believed Portales' participation in politics stemmed
from a desire for revenge against those who had deprived him of the
estanco contract. Others saw Portales' motivation in his distaste for
liberalism and the continual disorder following independence. Whatever the motivation, Portales' solution for political disorder, imposed
in cooperation with conservative interests, the higher clergy, and the
military forces of Prieto and Bulnes, emphasized *restoration* of legitimacy, law and order, and fiscal integrity. Implementation of this program required a strong, centralized government which did not tolerate opposition or even criticism. Acting as President Prieto's chief
minister and then as "informal" adviser, Portales cashiered the liberal officers of the army, many of them "heroes" of the independence
period, persecuted the opposition press, and controlled elections to
ensure the victory of government candidates. This was the beginning
of the "autocratic republic" which one Chilean historian described
as "the last and most beautiful chapter of Spanish colonial history."
Less romantically, an English historian suggests that "the atmosphere in Chile after 1830 was one of fear and trembling."

Portales' style and beliefs left little room for constitutions or formal principles. He favored decisive, pragmatic action unconstrained
by legal obstacles or constitutional limits. While Portales concerned
himself with action, however, other conservative leaders and intellectuals felt the need for a constitution to define the nature of the
new regime, to formalize its structure, and to legitimize its practices.
Ironically, then, Portales played almost no official role in elaborating
the Constitution of 1833 which institutionalized what historians

have called the "Portalian state." Nevertheless, the centralized, authoritarian character of the constitution owed as much to Portales as to its principal author, Mariano Egaña.

Both Portales and Egaña sought restoration of legitimacy, law and order, and public morality. They recognized the critical need to build viable national political institutions as instruments through which to govern effectively and stimulate economic recovery. Above all, they sought to provide political stability. Both Portales and Egaña disdained democracy, popular suffrage, and liberalism. Egaña called for establishment of an authoritative centralized regime that did not allow "anarchy in the shadow or name of popular rule, liberal principles, republican government. . . ." Portales urged creation of a "strong, centralizing government, in order to set the citizens on the straight path of order and virtue." The Constitution of 1833 formalized these antidemocratic principles. The new constitution created a strong executive with authority to declare a state of siege in any part of the country when Congress was in recess. Declaration of a state of siege entailed suspension of all constitutional guarantees in the affected territory. In each province and administrative subdivision the president appointed intendants and governors as his direct agents. All pretense of provincial initiative, let alone federalism, disappeared. The power of Congress to approve annually the budget, taxes, and the size of the military provided the basis, later in the century, for bitter executive-legislative confrontations and even civil war (1891). But from 1831 to 1861 three strong presidents each served the two constitutional five-year terms and efficiently suppressed opposition forces.

The 1833 constitution also maintained the Roman Catholic apostolic religion as the state faith and excluded from "public exercise" all other religious doctrines. The founders of the autocratic republic thus sought to transfer the privilege of appointing Church officials, or *patronato*, from the Spanish crown to the new national regime—though the Church did not concede that the republican government had inherited the *patronato* from the empire. Summarizing the intent of the constitution, General Prieto called it "a means of putting an end to the revolutions and disturbances which arose from the confusion in which the triumph of independence left us. For this reason the system of government to which the republic was subjected . . . may be called autocratic in view of the great authority or power . . . concentrated in the hands of the citizen elected as president."

Executive control over distribution of certificates qualifying citizens to vote made effective challenges to the incumbent nearly impossible. This system of executive dominance of elections was adroitly described by Chilean historian Luis Galdames:

> The constitution permitted the re-election of the president to succeed himself for a second period of five years, and while this provision remained in force all the presidents availed themselves of it to have themselves re-elected. This meant, then, ten-year presidential terms. Re-election was achieved without difficulty, owing to the irresistible power placed by the constitution itself in the hands of the chief of state, who named the mayors and members of the municipal councils, the governors, intendants, and judges. . . .
>
> In practice, the intendants and governors controlled the elections of senators and representatives within their own jurisdictions. The chief of state and his ministers made lists of the people who were to make up each chamber for a constitutional period, and the elections were carried out according to these lists. It was rare that more than three or five opposition candidates succeeded in defeating the government candidates in the different departments. The orders of the minister of the interior to the agents of the executive were expressed more or less in these terms: "His Excellency instructs me to make known to you that Señor or Señores [here the names] should be chosen in your department for the post of [here the name of a senator or deputy]." If any candidate of the opposition attempted to electioneer at any point whatever in the country, the respective government agent would receive from the minister of the interior a communication like this: "Manage to prevent Don [name] from coming to your department by advising him to refrain from presenting himself in it. If he insists you can have him arrested as a disturber of the public peace.

Suffrage limitations restricted the vote through property or income qualifications and literacy requirements. But lax enforcement and deliberate delays in implementing the literacy requirement allowed landowners to enroll their tenants as voters and commanders of the militia to do likewise with their troops. After 1840 the Congress allowed those already registered to continue to vote despite efforts to impose the literacy requirement on *new* voters. In this way the votes of the rural work force became a valuable asset of the owners of large rural estates.

Along with electoral manipulation, the alliance of merchants, landowners, clergy, and military officers which restored law and order did not lose sight of Portales' admonition: "The stick and the cake, justly and opportunely administered, are the specifics with which any nation can be cured, however inveterate its bad habits may be." Thus, Chile would largely avoid the chaos and instability of the rest of Latin America, despite rebellions in 1851 and 1859, by imposing a modified version of "benevolent" despotism. Only later would incipient industrial groups and renewed anticlericalism among prominent elite families upset the mutuality of interests shared by members of the relatively small ruling class. The Constitution of 1833 provided a viable instrument for maintaining existing class relations, including restoration of the *mayorazgos* and consolidating the political position of prominent *criollo* families. It also helped create a business climate attractive to foreign capitalists and Chilean merchants alike.

At Portales' urging, Manuel Rengifo served as Minister of the Treasury from 1830 to 1835. Rengifo reorganized the system of public finance, transferred the customs houses to the ports, rationalized regulations and duties on the coastwise trade, and took a number of measures intended to increase fiscal revenues. Though some of Rengifo's tax policies drew criticism, the overall effect of his program was to establish a sound basis for Chilean public finance and to inspire the confidence of domestic and foreign capital. Unfortunately Rengifo's successes made him a likely presidential candidate for an alliance of dissatisfied conservative elements and certain liberal factions. In September 1835, Portales returned from his self-imposed "absence" from politics and assumed the ministries of War and the Interior. Joaquín Tocornal, President Prieto's firm supporter and perhaps the most proclerical member of the government coalition, replaced Rengifo as Minister of the Treasury. Despite Rengifo's successful economic policies, his spirit of political conciliation and his moderation on the politico religious issues of the times lost out to the expediencies of the presidential election of 1835 and Portales' intolerance of any drift toward liberalism. Under Portales' leadership Prieto was re-elected—after the agitation and propaganda of the electoral campaign had led to reimposition of government through "state of siege." Notwithstanding the considerable economic progress and improvement in public finance, when Prieto began his second presidential term (1836-41), institutionalization of the political system detailed in the Constitution of 1833 seemed far from certain.

A new constitution has nowhere guaranteed political stability. This is especially the case in Latin America. It is important therefore to attempt to understand how the repressive policies of the Prieto administration, a fortunate stroke of international politics—that is, a successful war against the Peru-Bolivian confederation—the "martyrdom" of Portales, and the character of Prieto's successor, Manuel Bulnes, solidified the "autocratic republic."

In the wake of civil wars and clashes of personalist factions from 1810, numerous Chilean émigrés found themselves in Peru, while Peruvian exiles went to Chile. Shortly after Prieto's re-election (1836) General Freire sailed from Peru with a military force, landed in Chiloé, and moved to the mainland. Internal dissidents also threatened rebellion. Freire was captured and eventually exiled to Australia. But in response the Prieto government broke relations with Peru.

Relations between Chile and Peru had been tense in any case, due to Peru's failure to repay the loan extended for the San Martín expedition (1820-22) and to disputes over import duties that discriminated against Chilean merchandise as well as over goods deposited in the warehouses at Valparaíso or ships landing in Chilean ports. General Andrés Santa Cruz's efforts to unify Peru and Bolivia and the Peruvian government's support for Freire exacerbated this tension. Portales saw Santa Cruz's policies and armies as a direct threat to

Chile. He sent two ships to Callao, which took the Peruvian navy, such as it was, by surprise. Santa Cruz negotiated a settlement that left the Peruvian ships in Chilean hands, but Portales remained unsatisfied because Santa Cruz refused to apologize for the imprisonment of the Chilean chargé d'affaires. Bent upon war, Portales believed the judgments of the numerous Peruvian exiles in Chile that large-scale rebellion against Santa Cruz would result if a Chilean army merely appeared in Peru.

The Chilean Congress declared war and sent Mariano Egaña to Peru at the head of a small squadron. The Chileans demanded (1) satisfaction for the injuries done to their chargé d'affaires, (2) dissolution of the Peru-Bolivia confederation, (3) an indemnity for the Freire expedition, (4) recognition of liability for the loan extended for the San Martín liberation expedition, and (5) limitations on Peruvian naval forces. When Santa Cruz rejected these humiliating conditions, the Prieto government prepared for war by declaring a state of siege in all of Chile. With Portales exercising extensive emergency powers, those who "disturbed public order" or were "disrespectful toward the government" faced banishment or execution at the hands of military tribunals.

Portales' regime of terror incited rebellion. In June 1837 mutinous troops, led by Colonel José Antonio Vidaurre, assassinated Portales. Government defeat of the rebellious troops was followed by the execution of the assassins. Now Portales became a martyr as the government tried to link his assassins and the rebellion to General Santa Cruz's agents in Chile.

During 1837 Chilean forces under Admiral Blanco Encalada faced defeat in Peru from Santa Cruz's armies. Surrounded and in despair, Blanco Encalada recognized the Peru-Bolivia confederation and returned the ships earlier seized at Callao. The Chilean government rejected these concessions, blockaded Peruvian ports, and dispatched a new force commanded by General Manuel Bulnes, the victor at Lircay and Prieto's nephew. Accompanying this expedition were a number of Peruvian exiles, including ex-President Augustín Gamarra and the future Peruvian caudillo Ramón Castilla. Troop movements by both sides in and out of Lima and the interior culminated in early 1839 at Yungay, where Bulnes decisively defeated Santa Cruz and dissolved the Peru-Bolivia confederation. He returned to Santiago a military hero.

The war against the Peru-Bolivia confederation united Chilean political elites. While defeat, in Encina's words, might have sent "leaders, government and order tumbling to earth," victory contributed to a new national pride. According to Barros Arana, when Bulnes made his triumphal entrance into Santiago, "he was greeted by a fanfare unknown until then in the celebration of public festivities. . . ." For months after the victory, Chile celebrated its new-found "greatness" with public festivities and theater productions that re-enacted the military glories of the Chilean armies.

Bulnes' victory made him the perfect successor to Prieto and at precisely the right time in the five-year electoral cycle. In control of the army, and enjoying popular acclaim, Bulnes then married the daughter of ex-President Francisco Antonio Pinto, his principal opponent in the presidential race. For the first time in Chilean history a peaceful transition to the presidency took place with Bulnes' inauguration in 1841. During the next decade Bulnes' great popularity, his support for the development of legislative and judicial institutions, and his refusal to become a caudillo on the model of contemporary Latin American rulers, all served to solidify the "Portalian state." Thus the fortuitous outcome of Chilean bellicosity provided the basis of solidarity and legitimacy, as well as the leadership that spared Chile the political disorder and *caudillismo* common to Latin America in much of the nineteenth century. It also institutionalized a centralized autocratic regime that discouraged democratization of Chilean politics.

Consolidation of the autocratic republic also depended upon the improved state of public finance and of the economy in Chile after 1830. From 1810 to 1830 loss of perhaps 15 percent of the male population in the 20-to-40 age group, in the military campaigns in Chile, Río de la Plata, and Peru, caused a temporary scarcity of labor in the

TABLE 3. AVERAGE ANNUAL VALUE OF AGRICULTURAL AND
LIVESTOCK PRODUCTION (IN PESOS)

Years	La Serena	Santiago	Concepción
1750-59	44,377	427,084	181,615
1760-69	41,409	461,086	189,530
1770-79	40,055	621,086	262,961
1780-89	33,543	551,441	270,669
1790-99	45,198	556,046	244,242
1800-09	84,296	885,292	425,376
1810-19	80,766	623,877	271,357
1820-29	76,156	824,439	187,740

(Source: M. Carmagnani, *Les mecanismes de la vie économique dans une société coloniale, Le Chili*, pp. 213, 235, 249.)

northern mines and in the countryside. Marauding soldiers and bandits in the rural areas discouraged agricultural production. In addition, Peru's internal strife and financial crisis disrupted Chile's normal export trade in wheat, livestock products, and other agrarian commodities.

Recent estimates for the value of agricultural and livestock production, by region, illustrate the decline in output that accompanied the independence struggle.* Declines in the northern region and even in Santiago were relatively moderate, with recovery beginning after 1820. In the Concepción-southern region continued warfare and Indian problems contributed to a persistent decline in output until 1830; the absolute value of production in 1830 failed to regain the level attained in the decade 1760-69.

The most serious decline in economic activity occurred south of the Maule River where, in any case, Chilean agriculture was least secure due to the Indian frontier. Short-term local food shortages resulted from the seemingly unending civil wars. In 1822 the cabildo at Concepción reported that "eleven years of a ferocious, devastating struggle have reduced the province to the most extreme calamity in its history. Its residents . . . have consumed whatever work animals or

---

* Naturally, given the internal situation, these estimates are more suggestive than definitive—and the price inflation at the time probably leads to an underestimate of the decline in output.

beasts of burden, not taken by their enemies or their defenders, to keep themselves alive."

In the La Serena-northern region the independence movements little affected agricultural production. Free trade meant expanded demand for minerals and stimulation of the northern economy. But migration to the north, due to the war and to the hope for opportunities in the mines, placed increased pressure on the region's limited food-producing capabilities. In 1826 the provincial assembly of Coquimbo lamented that this city "must buy everything, for it produces little but metals. Smaller animals are brought from Chillán, more than six thousand animals come each year from the environs of Santiago; . . . tallow from Maule; flour and grain from Aconcagua, wood from Chiloé, Valdivia, and Concepción."

With the achievement of independence, the northern region's mines provided the primary source of the copper and silver that financed imports of European goods, paid for military supplies, and attracted foreign investment. In the 1820s, however, many foreigners who invested in mining enterprises lost their capital, as the cost of food, fuel, and supplies and the lack of adequate transport undermined these speculative ventures. Indeed, the prospecti of some of these "mining" ventures seem to have deliberately misled British investors. For example, the Chilean Mining Association declared that "few countries are so well watered as Chile, affording means of conveyance by water to the ports of the Pacific. . . ." This was true, of course, but the prospectus failed to mention that there were no navigable rivers in the northern region, no coal, no lumber, and that provisions had to be brought over a considerable distance from the south. Despite the disappointments suffered by many speculative investments, new discoveries of copper and silver augured well for the development of mining in the northern region. Gold production declined, but the mint in Santiago maintained the level of silver coinage achieved in the period 1790-1809, despite increased contraband and the dislocation of war. In 1832 a silver strike at Chañarcillo created boom conditions in the northern territory and brought also some of the earliest significant labor conflicts in Chilean national history. Even at this early date the harsh conditions experienced by the peons spawned an incipient militancy among the growing mining proletariat. A rebellion at Chañarcillo in 1834 foreshadowed hundreds of future confrontations between miners and mine operators in the nineteenth and twentieth centuries.

Though the northern mining districts afforded the most glamorous economic potential and paid for the bulk of Chilean imports, agriculture and livestock remained the foundations of the Chilean economy. Based in the Santiago-central region—especially with the wartime dislocations in the south—agriculture continued to be extensive and backward. Wooden plows pulled by teams of oxen broke the ground for sowing the traditional colonial crops. Productivity declined with the spread of agricultural pests and the reduced fertility of the land. Threshing still depended on horses and was carried on during extended fiestas and accompanied by considerable consumption of wine, *chicha,** or *aguardiente.* As in the rest of Latin America at this time, winnowing with wooden pitchforks evoked images of biblical harvests.

Livestock production also remained primitive. No new breeds were introduced before 1830; animals took five or six years to "fatten" on natural pastures before slaughter. Even then they yielded only 60 to 70 percent of what cattle provided in Europe. Nevertheless, hides and tallow contributed substantially to Chilean exports, as they had since early colonial days. But while the Chilean countryside was admirably suited to dairy production, the output of milk, cheese, and butter was quite low; to 1820, at least, butter cost more in the Concepción region than in the United States. Although the contesting armies of the independence decades provided markets for foodstuffs and drove up prices, they also created conditions of uncertainty or devastation in which Chilean agriculture barely held its own (in the central region) or retrogressed (in the Concepción-southern territory).

Through all the strife, however, the large rural estates continued to dominate in the countryside. Ironically, by 1827 the independent nations of Chile and Peru had re-established the basic structure of colo-

---

* *Chicha* is a hard cider made from grapes or apples.

nial trade. Chile exported over 500,000 pesos of wheat, flour, salted meat, tallow, barley, wood, and other agricultural commodities and minerals to Peru. In exchange, Peru sent back almost 350,000 pesos of goods to Chile—approximately half in sugar. The blood spilled to win political independence consecrated the reconfirmation of colonial patterns of commerce as well as colonial economic institutions in the rural areas.

While internal productive activity stagnated, the arms trade, whaling, and contraband of all sorts made Valparaíso an important Pacific way station to North America as well as to western Spanish America and to British colonies in Asia. The port's strategic location brought increasing numbers of British, North American, and other foreign merchants to Valparaíso, Santiago, and other principal towns. Some of these merchants settled permanently in Chile, founding businesses and families which became fixtures of Chilean high finance and Chilean society—including Waddington, Sewell, Walker, Chadwick, Davies, Bunster, Clark, Gibbs, Lynch, and Eastman. Two future Chilean presidents would descend from an Italian immigrant-merchant, Pedro Alessandri, who arrived in Valparaíso in 1820.

Provisioning the army of liberation provided economic opportunities for colonial merchants and public officials, much as had the royal *situado* in the past. In contrast to Santiago, which changed little from 1810 to 1830, Valparaíso grew rapidly from a town of 5500 to a city of almost 20,000. A floating population of several thousand from the ships in the bay frequented the increasing number of shops, cafés, billiard parlors, bars, and brothels. An underworld of muggers, thieves, and murderers preyed upon drunken sailors and began to make Valparaíso the rough-and-tumble, bawdy Pacific port for which it became famous.

By 1822 foreigners represented nearly one-quarter of the residents of the port and virtually dominated commerce. Establishment of warehouses in which shippers could deposit merchandise for a set fee helped increase mercantile activity. Chile's merchant marine grew from three ships, owned by Spaniards, in 1810 to well over seventy by 1830. Foreigners owned many of these, but native Chileans and naturalized citizens also took part in the shipping trade. The dramatic growth of international trade also reinvigorated the shipbuilding industry. Despite the great increase in shipping, however, port facilities remained exceedingly inadequate. No docks existed. Peons, up to their waists in water, carried ashore heavy bundles on their backs from small boats sent from the anchored wooden sailing vessels. From Valparaíso merchandise went overland on mules to Santiago or to the northern towns and mining districts. Not until several decades later would railroads and steamships dramatically alter colonial modes of transport and communication.

Expansion of commerce confronted Chile's leaders with numerous political issues related to domestic industrial development, public finance, and, in the short run, successful completion of the war against Spain and achievement of diplomatic recognition by England, the United States, the Holy See, and other European powers. Diplomatic efforts by the Chileans to maintain the neutrality of England and, more important of the British Pacific squadron, during the years of war against Spain made Chilean governments cautious in dealing with powerful English merchants. The need to pay for military supplies and to meet salaries of public personnel, along with the ascendancy of English, French, and North American "free trade" doctrines, pushed Chile away from protective tariffs and toward a commercial policy that emphasized revenue-producing export and import duties.*

Chile had opened its major ports to trade with all friendly or neutral nations in 1811. The decree authorized introduction of all commodities except rum, beer, wine, aguardiente, hats, and items subject to the government *estanco* (especially tobacco). Foreign merchants could engage legally only in the wholesale trade; retail trade and coastal navigation were supposedly reserved for Chilean citizens, but violations of these provisions were common. From 1810 to 1830 import duties averaged 35 percent or more *ad valorem*, but contraband or corruption in assessing the value of imported goods significantly

---

* "Free trade" in this context meant opening ports to international commerce—not the elimination of import duties.

reduced government revenues. Export duties varied considerably from product to product, ranging from 6 to nearly 20 percent.

Government policies allowed low-priced imports to eliminate almost entirely the remaining Chilean manufactures save for some household production, food processing, mining and livestock-related artisan activities such as soap, candle making, and tanneries. These developments conflicted directly with the commitment of elites like Manuel de Salas or Rodríguez Aldea to stimulate industrial growth through some form of protection for Chilean enterprises. Efforts to combine limited protective tariffs with revenue-producing duties, and the repression of contraband, which probably accounted for over half of Chile's imports, displeased the merchant community and contributed to O'Higgins' ouster.

The penetration of the economy by foreign interests in the period between 1810 and 1830 paved the way for a much more serious domination of Chile's economic development by British and North American enterprises later in the nineteenth century. By 1849 some fifty British firms controlled most Chilean exports: nearly 50 percent of the value of these exports went to England, and English goods accounted for 30 to 40 percent of the value of Chilean imports. Reacting to these trends more than a century later, historian Francisco Encina declared:

> What resulted in these years was not, as usually suggested, an intensification of international trade. Rather what occurred was an exploitation of the Chilean economy by foreign interests. They traded 60 percent of their goods, at least, for silver, gold, or copper . . . avoiding the customs house. . . . Luxury goods went down in price while the price of articles of primary necessity which the country did not produce went up. . . . Between 1823 and 1830 some three or four thousand foreigners . . . sucked the blood from the Chilean economy . . . while 95 percent of the Chilean people had retrogressed to the life style of the last third of the seventeenth century.

This view perhaps exaggerates the effects on Chile of the replacement of Spanish influence by that of England and North America. Nevertheless, the tightening noose of foreign control over the Chilean economy and the vulnerability of that economy to fluctuations in the international market in the nineteenth century give credence to both Marxist and Hispanicist analyses of economic policy in the early independence era.

When installation of the "Portalian state" brought an end to the political chaos of the independence movements, the Prieto government faced the enormous tasks of reorganizing public finance, rationalizing commercial policy, and determining the direction of economic development. The government fulfilled these tasks by adopting strict internal economies and by accepting Chile's role as a supplier of raw materials to the more developed capitalist economies and importers of manufactured goods. Public personnel were dismissed, government expenditures on frills were reduced, and a good climate was created for business. Emphasis was placed on honesty and efficiency. This meant two things. First, law and order were re-established, and harsh penalties were meted out to common criminals. Second, government sought to encourage private enterprise. As Minister Rengifo put it in his report to Congress in 1835:

> The measures which favorably affect the economy of a State may be reduced to two types: First, . . . laws that remove obstacles to industry, that protect property and its use, that reduce the costs of production, and that open free channels for the export [salida] of national products; second, . . . laws which regulate taxes with moderation and discernment . . . and prevent expenditures from the public treasury for purposes other than those of strict administrative necessity.

To attract foreign trade and shipping, a decree of 1832 established warehouses of deposit (almacenes francos de depósito) in Valparaíso; by 1835 the government was operating sixteen such warehouses and renting out another twenty-seven. Administrative reforms put the public treasury in order and established confidence in public credit. Gradually the government attempted to pay off the public debt.

More than anything else, the political economy of the "Portalian state" aimed at stimulating production of traditional colonial com-

modities and incorporating Chile into the world capitalist econom
Summarizing this strategy, Chilean author Miguel Cruchaga tells us
that "They believed the country was not ready . . . for the development of manufactures, and desiring to give it easy access to articles of
consumption and easy export opportunities for what was produced,
they sought to facilitate commerce with the foreign countries who
could provision us at least cost." This strategy suited the interests of
the major economic groups in Chile, landowners, mine owners, and
merchants, as well as foreign merchants. It allowed the upper classes
to import luxury goods from Europe, live the good life, modernize
the cities, and maintain traditional social relationships and property
institutions in the countryside. But it also contained serious internal
contradictions which would become ever more evident as modernization of transport and communication, along with economic growth
in the nineteenth century, created industrial and working class-inter-
ests for whom liberal political economy meant ruin or deprivation.
In the short run, however, the autocratic republic proved a highly
pragmatic reconciliation of the economic interests of the upper
classes with both the demands of foreign capitalists and the need for
internal order. It preserved the essentials of Hispanic capitalism, restored centralized political authority, and maintained the social stratification of the colony, while allowing "free trade" to cater to the
tastes of the upper classes. This was the fruit of Chilean independence.

Chapter 5 • Modernization and Misery

Consolidation of authoritarian government after 1839 gave Chile a truly national political system with administrative capabilities that paved the way for impressive economic growth during the next three decades. Attracted by the relative political stability, foreign investors brought the wonders of modern technology to Chile. The first railroad, built between 1849 and 1851, connected the mining regions of Copiapó to the port of Caldera; by 1863 another line linked Valparaíso to Santiago and was extended south to San Fernando. The American entrepreneur William Wheelwright, who had introduced steam navigation to Chile in the 1840s, directed construction of the telegraph line between the capital and Valparaíso in 1851-52; twenty-five years later the telegraph provided communication to forty-eight Chilean towns as well as connections to Peru and Argentina. Steamships and railroads permitted increased movement of products from the northern mines and the agricultural hinterlands of the central valley and the Concepción region to the port cities and the exterior. From Talcahuano, Valparaíso, La Serena, Caldera, and other legal and illegal points of departure, Chilean commodities left for North America, Australia, Asia, and Europe. An apparent economic miracle quadrupled the value of Chilean exports between 1845 and 1875, while the number of ships entering Chilean ports more than doubled in the decade of the 1860s alone.

Beginning with the discovery of silver at Chañarcillo in 1832, followed by strikes at Tres Puntas to the north of Copiapó and at other mines in the mid-1840s, silver production increased dramatically. After reaching an official level of 100,000 to 200,000 kilos annually between 1851 and 1856, recorded output hovered in the neighborhood of 100,000 kilos a year until the 1870s, when the Caracoles mine came into production. Copper production likewise expanded from a level of 8,000 to 10,000 kilos a year in the period 1844-50 to almost 35,000 kilos in 1860. In that year the value of copper exports exceeded 14 million pesos—double the national budget and approximately 56 percent by value of all Chilean exports. During the next decade annual average copper production more than doubled again, with the principal center of production remaining at José Tomás Urmeneta's mine at Tamaya (see Map 7).

Agricultural production also grew significantly in the middle years of the nineteenth century. Cereal, livestock, and vineyard output increased to meet the demands of the transitory foreign markets opened with the discovery of gold in California and Australia. The growth of the northern mining economy, and the commercial expansion of the principal towns and cities, further encouraged the agricultural economy. Between 1844 and 1860 the value of agricultural exports—led by wheat, flour, and barley—quintupled; between 1871 and 1876 the value of agricultural exports exceeded by fifteenfold the levels attained in the mid-1840s. In the 1850s, complementing expanded cereal cultivation, North American and British entrepreneurs sparked development of a new flour-milling industry, which soon took second place only to copper as the major industry in the Chilean economy.

Shortly thereafter the first Chilean joint stock companies, banks, and credit institutions took shape, and the *Caja de Crédito Hipotecario*, established in 1855, soon became the most important mortgage bank in South America. The first joint stock companies in commercial banking, which emerged in the early 1850s, allied Chilean, British, and North American capital in insurance and railroad enterprises. Landowners, merchants, and mining interests came together to capitalize new economic activities through the modern financial institutions of Western capitalism—the corporation, or *sociedad anónima*. Significantly, the Chilean government also participated in the financing of railroads, setting an important precedent for "mixed" public-private economic ventures linking an ever more integrated economic elite to the apparatus of the state.

Accompanying these trends came diversification of retail trade and an incredible rise in imports of tropical commodities and manufactured goods by the wealthy residents of Valparaíso, Santiago, Tomé-Concepción, and the northern mining districts. In a study published in 1874, entitled *Our Enemy, Luxury!*, a Chilean author captured both the glitter of a superficial prosperity and the dangers of the preference by national elites and foreigners for imported luxury goods.

Economic expansion created new economic interests, made social stratification somewhat more complex, and exacerbated regional animosities as both the southern and northern provinces sought to keep pace with the progress of Santiago, Valparaíso, and the central valley. With some 115,000 residents, Santiago no longer seemed merely a colonial administrative center. Connected by rail in 1863 to the port of Valparaíso, which was itself a bustling commercial center of over 60,000 people, Santiago was becoming more and more a real urban capital in a growing new nation.

As the towns became cities, there developed an impressive liberal intellectual movement. Its leaders were known as the "Generation of 1842," as the movement's beginnings coincided with the creation of The University of Chile in 1842. Soon after a normal school was established, and in subsequent decades, the system of primary instruction expanded: the 1850s witnessed the creation of more than five hundred public schools. The Montt government (1851-61) also stimulated construction of libraries, technical schools, and even special institutions for the deaf. By 1861 some 45,000 children attended public and private institutions of learning, and several thousand were enrolled in secondary schools. Nevertheless, the vast majority of the population—especially those living in the countryside—still could not obtain even a minimal education for their children. Like the superficial prosperity of the nation, the educational system remained accessible primarily to the privileged few in the principal urban centers.

The intellectual movement of the 1840s combined the talents of Chileans with those of expatriates from Argentina, Venezuela, and Colombia, who found refuge from *caudillismo* and tyranny in an orderly Chile, whose authoritarian regime spared it from the widespread anarchy characteristic of Latin America at the time. Although the movement was made possible by Chile's stability, it soon proved subversive to the incumbent regime. Typifying the anti-Hispanic spirit of this movement was an article by Francisco Bilbao that appeared in 1844 in a periodical called *El Crepúsculo ("The Twilight")*. This article, entitled "Chilean Society," harshly criticized the colonial past, the Church, and most of the country's political institutions. The government ordered the burning of all copies of the periodical in which the article appeared. In September of the same year José Victorino Lastarría delivered the first annual paper on Chilean history at the national university. Lastarría's paper, called "Investigation into the Social Influence of the Conquest and the Spanish Colonial System upon Chile," blamed the Hispanic heritage and the Church for most of the nation's problems. For the next two decades the intellectuals of the "Generation of 1842" could be found at the forefront of social and political movements that opposed the leadership and policies of the autocratic regime.

Despite criticisms by liberal intellectuals, Chile's apparently impressive economic growth and political stability temporarily overshadowed both the vulnerability of its economic system and political frailties. Because it depended upon duties from international trade for most of its revenues, the government tended to centralize power and resources at Santiago and Valparaíso. Even though the northern mining districts and the southern cereal-flour complex produced a disproportionate share of the nation's exports, Chile's political leaders made only marginal budgetary allocations to the northern and southern provinces. As a result, considerable regional opposition arose against the autocratic regime. Reflecting this provincial resentment, an editorial in *El Curicano* in December 1858 decried the fact that

> while the capital absorbs all the income, receives all the material improvements, concentrates all the benefits, the provinces . . . languish in misery and backwardness. . . . Under the Spanish regime the provinces were exploited and paid heavy taxes to support the Spanish court. Now, there is little difference. We pay heavy taxes and are exploited in a thousand ways to beautify the court of Santiago. In our jurisdiction [department] the government does not invest a tenth of the funds we contribute to the national treasury.

The growing ideological, political, and regional fragmentation of the Chilean elite would lead to civil wars in 1851 and 1859 and to a gradual, but fundamental, transformation of the autocratic republic into the quasi-parliamentary, oligarchical system that predominated from the 1890s to the 1920s.

Just as the apparent stability of the political system masked its gradual transformation, so, too, did favorable international economic trends disguise the fragility of the Chilean economy. Temporary markets in California and Australia had stimulated agricultural production, processing industries, and shipping from 1849 until almost 1860. Soon, however, California wheat and flour competed favorably with the Chilean products even at Valparaíso.

Foreign and immigrant-owned commercial firms in Valparaíso controlled much of the country's credit system. Operating under a flexible option-buying scheme, these merchant lenders loaned capital to mining and agricultural interests against future production. They reserved the option to pay for agricultural commodities or minerals at the market price current when credit was extended or at the market price at the time of delivery. Under this system producers bore all the risks of price changes, while lenders benefited from either a decline or a rise in market prices. Foreign investors also gained control over much of Chile's flour-milling industry, mining, shipping, and commerce. Fluctuations in demand and prices for Chilean minerals and agricultural commodities in the international marketplace produced periodic economic crises with serious political implications.

Above all else, the mid-nineteenth-century Chilean economy continued to depend upon mineral exports. Periodic discoveries in Chile's northern provinces stimulated the rise of mining towns and their accompanying ports throughout the *norte chico* from 1832 until the late 1870s. Export duties from the mineral sector provided the national government with over 50 percent of public revenues during the entire period. Continuing essentially colonial politico-economic relations, the central government siphoned off most of the tax revenues from the mines without investing substantial resources in the northern provinces.

The independence period commenced in 1811 with the opening of the Agua Amarga silver mine south of Vallenar (see Map 7). This and other mines helped pay the costs of the war for independence. Establishing a pattern later followed by other northern regions, the area around Vallenar experienced rapid growth in population along with increased cultivation of nearby agricultural land. Then, with exhaustion of the silver veins, population in the zone decreased to perhaps 3500 by the early 1850s. Following the Agua Amarga strike in 1825, the rich Arqueros discovery located inland from Coquimbo seemed so important that the Chilean government established a new mint at La Serena. After Arqueros the next big silver strike occurred at Chañarcillo in 1832. Chañarcillo reportedly yielded more than 12 million pesos worth of silver in less than a decade, and the surrounding region, especially Copiapó, enjoyed boom conditions. New discoveries in the late 1840s, in particular at Tres Puntas between Copiapó and the "port" of Flamenco to the northwest, prolonged the silver fever. In 1843 the government officially proclaimed Copiapó a city; and, graced by this blessing, population in the department of Copiapó mushroomed from 11,300 in 1843 to almost 65,000 in 1865.

Tres Puntas exemplified the difficulties facing the mining industry in Chile's northern provinces: poor roads, lack of water, and scarcity of almost all basic necessities including food, fuel, and implements.

MAP 7: Major Mining Discoveries 1811-1870,
Atacama and Coquimbo

Yet within five years a settlement of some 4000 residents had sprung up around the mines. Despite the high cost of everything needed for survival, Tres Puntas, like the other mining towns, grew and prospered as long as the ore held out. As late as the mid-1860s mining activity persisted at Tres Puntas, and miners still sent ore by mule and wagon to Flamenco over what a contemporary writer called a "tolerable road."

Other less significant silver discoveries kept the miners' hopes alive until the next big strike in 1870 at Caracoles (legally in Bolivia), located on the road between Antofogasta and San Pedro de Atacama. Again the pattern of rapid urbanization occurred; by 1873 Caracoles had become a growing, prosperous town with more than 2500 residents. Commercial houses from the coast established branches, hotels opened, and the usual proliferation of cantinas, houses of prostitution, billiard parlors, and retail shops proclaimed the importance of the new northern mining district. This development took place despite the total lack of nearby water sources, fuel, and local agriculture. Everything had to be brought in from the coast or across the Andes. Carters and muleteers charged twice as much to carry goods between Antofogasta and Caracoles than did shipping companies to bring freight to Antofogasta from Europe. Nonetheless, miners dug out the ore; more than 1200 carters and thousands of mules carried it to Antofogasta—now, due to Caracoles, a growing Bolivian port city.

Located in a region disputed by Chile and Bolivia, the Caracoles minerals renewed a conflict only partially resolved in a treaty of 1866 in which the two nations set Chile's northern boundary at latitude 24° South and specified that the two countries would divide equally revenues from guano and mineral deposits within the territory located between latitudes 23° and 25° South. Bolivia agreed to finance construction of a port at Mejillones and to maintain a customs house with a monopoly for exacting export duties on the minerals of the region. The 1866 treaty also promised Chile one-half the revenue collected at Mejillones from export taxes on guano or other minerals. This stipulation gave Chilean agents the right to audit the accounts of the customs house, a provision the Bolivians bitterly resented as insulting to national sovereignty. In time Bolivia ignored the terms of the treaty by exporting minerals extracted from the shared territory through the more northerly port of Cobija, and refused to pay Chile its share of the custom receipts. In 1871, shortly after the Caracoles silver strike, a new Bolivian government disavowed all international agreements made by the previous administration. Subsequent negotiations and a new treaty in 1874 failed to resolve the fundamental issues. Less than a decade later Bolivia would lose all the territory and riches under dispute, along with its access to the Pacific, when it was defeated by Chile in the War of the Pacific (see Chapter 6).

Despite the great importance of silver to Chile's northern provinces, copper mining proved even more significant. Since colonial times Chilean copper had found its way to Europe, Asia, and North America. In the 1830s British vessels carried the red metal from Chile to India. British capitalists made significant investments in Chilean copper mining from the mid-1830s and early 1840s when Joshua Waddington exploited mines at Chañaral Alto in the department of Combarbalá. By the mid-1860s British interests had invested more than 4.5 million pesos in the Caldera area alone, almost all of which involved copper.

Although British and other foreign interests made substantial investments in the copper industry, a small number of daring, persistent Chilean capitalists and adventurers played a key role in the northern copper business. Suggestive, if untypical, was the eighteen-year quest of José Tomás Urmeneta at Tamaya, northwest of Ovalle (see Map 7): in 1852 he finally hit an incredibly rich vein. During the next eleven years the Tamaya mine reportedly produced copper valued at 5 million pesos. Urmeneta subsequently established foundries at Guayacán and Tongoy on the coast and also contracted with Henry Meiggs to build a rail line from the port at Tongoy to the mines. Urmeneta expanded his investments to coal and railroads in the southern region, a fleet of steamships purchased in Europe and public works in Santiago. He also acquired the important Hacienda Limache near Valparaíso. An unsuccessful candidate for president in 1871, Urmeneta was an extreme example of how the mineral wealth of the northern regions filtered south to Santiago, Valparaíso, and beyond, incorporating a new commercial and mining element into the Chilean agrarian elite. His career epitomized the opportunities available to a favored few in the years from 1835 until the outbreak of the War of the Pacific in 1879.

Copper mines also provided the rationale for the first railroads in Chile, built by William Wheelwright between the copper-rich Copiapó littoral and the port of Caldera to the northwest. Arrival of the railroad converted Caldera from a small settlement of perhaps 50 residents in 1850 into a port town of 2000 by 1853. The number of ships putting in at the port increased from 160 a year in 1850 to more than 600 five years later. In contrast, the previously favored point for copper shipment at Puerto Viejo, to the southwest, was practically abandoned. Writing in the late 1850s, Vicente Pérez Rosales noted that "the railroad to Copiapó brought gas, beautiful buildings, theater, conveniences, luxury, abundance of fuel and food, along with a spirit of enterprise, attracting thereby numerous foreigners and Chileans to the city and the surrounding regions." Extension of the line to the mines near Púquios and around an irregular semicircle to the northern Bay of Chañaral stimulated economic activity throughout the departments of both Chañaral and Copiapó. The region's physical and economic subsistence soon came to depend more upon steamships, steel rails, and locomotives than upon mules, wagons, and the precarious river-valley agriculture of southern Coquimbo.

While copper deposits encouraged investments in modern transportation, the copper mines themselves generally remained technologically backward and almost entirely dependent upon imported fuel. As in the case of silver, Chilean copper miners relied upon technology essentially unchanged from colonial times until the introduction of the reverberatory furnace in the 1860s and 1870s. They extracted only the richest ore and sold the slag to traders for delivery to more modern refineries in Germany, France, and England. The mining industry utilized British coal along with domestic supplies shipped from the Concepción region. Higher-quality British coal made the Chilean coal industry around Lota, Coronel, and Lebu in southern Chile vulnerable to British oversupply of the copper districts. As late as 1862 a large importation of British coal resulted in serious production cutbacks at Lota and Coronel. Fortunately for Chilean producers, a combination of British and Chilean coal proved technically most desirable; and consequently the foundries at Caldera tended to use a 50-50 mixture of Swansea and Chilean coal. The overall share of the coal market in the copper districts going to the British varied year to year from 25 to 50 percent.

In addition to silver and copper, a number of less significant mining activities, along with extraction of guano and nitrates, hinted at Chile's economic future by the end of the 1870s. Like the silver mines and copper discoveries, exploitation of other mineral resources encouraged related agricultural and commercial ventures. In the favored river valleys of Coquimbo and Atacama provinces, crop cultivation and livestock husbandry increased production to meet a part of the growing demand for food and animal products. Towns rose, stagnated, or declined with the fate of the mineral discoveries that had created them.

The sequence of mineral discoveries from the 1830s to the early 1870s brought waves of fortune hunters to the provinces of Atacama and Coquimbo. The former province tripled its population between 1843 and 1875, while the population of Coquimbo province doubled. This contrasted markedly with the relatively stable population of the predominantly rural departments of the middle central valley. By the mid-1870s most of the population of the northern provinces lived in "urban" settlements of more than two thousand people, though overall population density of these provinces was much sparser than those of the less urbanized middle central valley. The overwhelming influence of mining and the lack of large areas of cultivable land concentrated the population of the north into ports, administrative centers, and mining districts.

The obvious physical and economic contrasts between the northern provinces and the central valley lent a distinctive character to life in the north. Higher salaries, higher costs of living, and the concentration of wage workers in isolated production centers gradually forged a militant proletarian labor force. The great power of the mine owners in association with government officials, also often on the payroll of the mining enterprises, and the dramatic ups and downs of the mining ventures encouraged the evolution of a volatile political culture among northern workers. The agricultural export boom of the 1850s, which so greatly benefited Valparaíso merchants and Chilean landowners, meant higher food prices for the northern miners. Demands for higher wages led to strikes, violence, and looting by miners during the civil war of 1851. Miners, artisans, dockworkers, and muleteers in the *norte chico*, especially the region around Copiapó, played an even more significant role in the subsequent civil war of 1859. In the railroad machine shops and foundries of Caldera, workers cast cannon to use against government forces; in Chañarcillo, Copiapó, and other mining centers workers formed battalions that helped make the *norte chico* a temporarily "liberated zone." If the motivation of the mining entrepreneurs for rebellion could be detected in the decrees promulgated during this temporary "liberation"—for example, reduction by 50 percent of export duties on minerals—the experience of armed revolt by thousands of northern workers made the northern labor force more aware that government authority and the interests of the propertied classes conflicted with their own. With the War of the Pacific (1879-83) and the Chileanization of the nitrate fields, the northern work force would expand even more dramatically, class consciousness would become more acute, and class struggle would intensify. Soon thereafter the reality of the "social question" and industrial conflict would sweep southward from the northern provinces into Chile's heartland.

Modernization and material progress in the middle decades of the nineteenth century brought hard times to many of Chile's people in the central valley. While acreage under grain cultivation and production more than tripled between 1850 and 1875, thousands of rural families migrated to Santiago, Valparaíso, or the northern mining districts or looked for work in railway construction and public works projects. Whereas the population for the entire country increased

from about 1,000,000 in 1835 to 2,100,000 (outside of Indian territory) in 1875 and to over 2,700,000 in 1895, that of rural central
Chile had by 1895 barely changed from its 1865 level of 950,000.

Santiago, Valparaíso, and provincial capitals drew substantial
population from the rural areas (see Table 4). Between 1865 and
1875 alone, Santiago's population increased from 115,000 to more
than 150,000, while Valparaíso grew from 70,000 to almost 100,000
(42%). Favored central valley towns such as Curicó also experienced
dramatic growth in the decade 1865-75; this provincial town almost
doubled its population, growing from 5900 to 10,000, while the population of Curicó province remained almost stable at 90,000.

Although immigrants played a relatively minor numerical role in

TABLE 4. COMPARISON OF URBAN AND RURAL POPULATION IN SELECTED
NORTHERN AND CENTRAL VALLEY DEPARTMENTS, 1875

Department, Northern Provinces	Total Population	"Urban" Population as % of Total
Copiapó	31,877	68
Caldera	10,511	78
Vallenar	13,569	51
Freirina	15,541	53
Serena	29,057	67
Coquimbo	12,650	73
Elqui	12,147	52
Ovalle	39,567	32
Combarbalá	14,002	17
Illapel	32,011	41

Department, Middle Central Valley Provinces	Total Population	"Urban" Population as % of Total
Melipilla	32,253	23
Rancagua	98,092	13
Caupolicán	75,186	15
San Fernando	72,668	15
Curicó	57,312	24
Vichuquen	35,546	8
Lontué	19,791	16
Talca	90,597	30
Loncomilla	31,689	21
Linares	53,420	14
Parral	33,652	16

the urbanization process, at Valparaíso and in the northern mining towns a foreign presence was ever more apparent. For the country as a whole, immigrants composed less than 2 percent of the population in 1875; but in the province of Atacama they accounted for 11 percent, and in the department of Copiapó, approximately 20 percent. More important than their numbers was the financial and commercial power wielded by these groups.

The prosperity of foreign merchants at Valparaíso or in the mining districts contrasted sharply with the plight of the mass of rural laborers in the central valley. After 1860 wages in the countryside fell further and further behind the rising cost of food and basic necessities. The conditions of the *inquilinos* worsened as landlords required the service tenants to work more days, provide more family labor, or pay additional peons to fulfill the family's labor obligations. The tenants received ever smaller land allotments and faced restrictions on pasture rights for their animals. By 1858 a Chilean writer told his countrymen to "open your eyes and every day you see families leaving their homes. . . . Their single purpose is to leave the place where they cannot earn a living. . . . Travel our roads and you will see numerous families with all their belongings on their backs moving toward the capital to increase the existing pauperism."

Between 1849 and 1855 Chileans went in search of gold in California or to work on the railway under construction in Panama. The California census of 1852, which probably underestimates the Chilean presence, enumerates over 5500 in California at that date. Railroad gangs constructing the Santiago-Valparaíso line occupied a work force of 9000 to 10,000 a year; railroad projects in Peru (1868-72) directed by American entrepreneur Henry Meiggs, recruited 25,000 to 30,000 Chilean workers. Extension of the Chilean line to San Fernando (1862), Curicó (1868), and Talca (1874) employed thousands more. The Chillán-Talcahuano line (1869-74) provided jobs for over 9000 peons—and yet the army of rural unemployed increased.

Despite complaints by hacendados that construction projects and Meiggs's Peruvian venture created a shortage of hands, Chilean agriculture in the central valley experienced peak performance between 1868 and 1872. More important, except in critical periods of the agricultural cycle such as harvest, wages for rural labor failed to climb above the typical 10 to 25 centavos a day plus meager food rations. Upset at the inconvenience of competing for harvest labor with railroad crews, landowners filled the country's newspapers with exaggerated reports of the awful conditions and epidemics suffered by Chileans in Peru. Meanwhile the tide of migration carried thousands out of the rural districts as the rural poor sought better opportunities elsewhere.

The fact that a promise of a wage of 62 centavos a day plus food rations could move 30,000 Chileans to Peru indicates the plight of the Chilean rural lower classes. Thousands of families endured precarious lives in squatters' huts on marginal land along the coast; thousands more lived an ambulatory existence following the crops from Aconcagua south. Still others turned to banditry and cattle rustling, making some of the rural districts unsafe for travel. Official reports of the 1840s and 1850s contain many references to the large "vagrant" population of the central valley. Under these conditions hacendados in some areas could attract harvest labor by sponsoring a type of harvest fiesta called *mingaco*, thereby "paying" the workers only with food and drink.

With the sweat and blood of these workers and that of their families, a small wealthy elite initiated the physical modernization of Chile in the middle decades of the nineteenth century. Railroads built to carry minerals of the north to Caldera or the cereals of the central valley to Valparaíso permitted Chilean and foreign entrepreneurs to live an extravagant existence in the principal urban areas. Wealth accumulated in mining and commerce bought land and social status. To the list of traditional landed families like the Aguirre, Larraín, or Errázuriz, mining and commercial fortunes added British, French, and German surnames along with those of newly enriched Chileans. The economically integrated upper class that emerged treated the Chilean masses with contempt. Railroad and mining interests bewailed the drunken orgies of their workers, while landowners defended the practice of paying workers in company scrip on the grounds that it spared them the temptation of "foolish" consumption outside the haciendas.

Sumptuous houses and importation of luxurious European furnishings absorbed many of the windfall profits associated with wheat and flour exports, commerce, and mining. Santiago, Valparaíso, and even lesser central valley towns boasted new, lavishly decorated edifices. Upper-class gentlemen emulated the life styles of European capitalists and aristocrats. Prestigious social clubs and the National Agricultural Society (1869) brought together sociopolitical elites to decide matters of state and economy outside the public halls of the Congress. The best-endowed maintained haciendas near Santiago or Valparaíso as recreational retreats with ornamental gardens and well-furnished residences, or *casas de fundo*. With the extension of the railroad south to Talca, lesser properties, located farther from the capital, increased in value and, subsequently, in the ornamentation of the landowner's "big house."

No less impressive than the sumptuous buildings in the cities, the gracious country residences stood in stark contrast to the rude huts of the campesinos whose pitiful wages barely provided subsistence. Low labor costs inhibited the same landowners, so fond of modern urban convenience in their townhouses, from modernizing farm technology. Chilean landowners preferred labor-intensive, sickle-and-scythe harvesting of cereals long after most of North America and Australia had mechanized the wheat harvest. A minority of Chilean landowners adopted machinery, new crops, and new breeds of animals and pastures or began construction of irrigation canals; but the economics of Chilean agriculture—cheap labor and vast rural estates with uncultivated land—did not invite large-scale mechanization prior to the 1880s. The poverty of the Chilean masses limited internal demand for agricultural products; and by the early 1870s Chile's inability to compete with North American and Australian producers restricted expansion of its output despite the importance of the British market. Under these conditions, even without substantial mechanization, Chilean agriculture based upon the large haciendas could

not provide year-round employment to the growing number of root-
less rural laborers.

Industry offered no solution to the employment problem. Modernization and commercial expansion brought little industry to Chile.
An American naval officer visiting the country at midcentury noted
that Chile was "almost without factories of any description . . . dependent on foreign nations for every supply except food." This description ignored the numerous small-scale producers of household
goods, cordage, rigging, tanneries, and the like, but it accurately por-
trayed the lack of any significant manufacturing establishment, apart
from flour mills and breweries established by German immigrants in
the south and the mining enterprises in the north. Major economic
interest groups such as landowners, merchants, and mine owners generally opposed protective tariffs to encourage local industry. Dependent upon the export trade, albeit in different ways, landowners did
not wish to pay taxes on imported European goods; mine interests,
closely linked to British firms, commercial houses, and shippers, supported "free trade"; merchants, like merchants everywhere, defended
the right of the consumer to buy quality goods at low prices. Occasional editorials in Santiago or regional newspapers in the 1860s and
1870s supported, without notable success, some form of protective
tariff to encourage domestic manufacturers. Any tariff the government adopted had as its primary purpose an increase in public revenues; a truly protective tariff would have had just the opposite effect.

In the mid-1870s the overwhelming majority of Chilean manufacturing establishments were quite small, typically artisan producers of
consumer goods or more durable items such as carriages and wagons.
Rarely did firms employ large numbers of workers or operate anything like an industrial assembly process, although by 1874 some of
the Talca flour mills were utilizing imported steam-powered machinery. Even shipbuilding, a likely enterprise given Chilean participation in the Pacific grain trade and the country's extensive mineral
exports, experienced no significant growth. Of 259 Chilean-registered
ships in 1865, only 26 were constructed in Chile, and all but 6 of
these came from boatworks in the southern region. A brief war with

Spain between 1864 and 1866 over supposed insults to Spanish honor resulted in the loss of a number of these ships and a change in the registry of others. The Spanish blockaded Chile's main ports of entry, but lacked sufficient ships and troops to make the blockade effective along Chile's entire coast. Frustrated by the stalemate and Chile's refusal to provide the proper salute to the Spanish flag, the Spanish fleet bombarded Valparaíso, seriously damaging warehouses and port-works. Although the blockade caused temporary disruptions of commerce, it did nothing to stimulate Chilean shipbuilding even in the face of the obvious lesson of the nation's vulnerability to one of Europe's third-rate powers.

With no significant industry to occupy a growing population, the central valley sent its surplus labor into construction projects, the northern mines, or to foreign lands in search of employment. Mining depressions, reduction of public works, or decline in demand for the products of Chilean agriculture meant immediate crisis for the mass of the population, just as it meant bankruptcy for overextended entrepreneurs, landowners, or merchants. According to the census of 1875, more than 60 percent of the enumerated male labor force worked as unskilled laborers (*gañanes*) or "farmers" (*agricultores*). Of the more than 300,000 women reported in the census, approximately 85 percent worked as cooks, servants, washerwomen, seamstresses, or weavers. These figures obviously understate the contribution of women to the economy, especially in agriculture, but do provide a revealing glimpse into the economic opportunities open to most of Chile's female population during these years. More generally, including the data for unskilled and semiskilled laborers in the countryside, construction crews, ports, and railroads, together with miners and various artisans (for example, 14,000 shoemakers, 250 candle and soap makers, etc.), the census suggests that 85 to 90 percent of all actively employed Chilean males corresponded to these working class categories. Even with the most ample interpretation of *comerciantes*, or "merchants," of the professions, of industrialists of various sorts, of white-collar and public employees, and of miscella-

neous non-"working-class" categories, substantially less than 10 percent of the enumerated actively employed corresponded to an emerging "middle" strata or to the numerically tiny economic elite.

Thus the economic progress of the middle decades of the nineteenth century quite narrowly restricted wealth to an upper crust of
society and allowed a thin veneer of ornamentation and physical
modernization to cover the major urban centers. This veneer cracked
with each economic recession or decline in prices for Chile's principal
exports. Loss of the California and Australia markets after 1856, declines in copper prices, and the switch to a gold standard by European nations in 1873 shortly after the rich silver strike at Caracoles
(1870), all drastically affected Chile's prosperity.

The economic recession of 1857-58 brought widespread unemployment and bankruptcies, followed by civil war in 1859. The worldwide
economic depression of 1873 set in motion a train of events that
looked even more disastrous for Chile. The shift to a gold standard
by European powers was followed by a 50 percent drop in copper
prices. Bad weather ruined the Chilean wheat crop of 1876-77. Fam-
ine followed. The economic depression seemed to climax forty years
of economic "development." Government revenues, still dependent
upon the devastated export sector, drastically declined. Budget reductions exacerbated employment problems with a cutback on public works and government personnel. Government borrowing to meet
the crisis increased the fiscal deficit; in desperation President Pinto
proposed direct taxation of income, real estate, and capital. Finally,
as a last resort, the government shifted to paper currency—while the
country now imported wheat to feed itself. Despite a favorable upturn in the balance of trade in 1878, the bubble seemed about to
burst. The limits of the export-oriented economy had apparently
been reached.

But then, much as the victory in the early nineteenth-century war
against the Peru-Bolivia confederation had helped to consolidate the
Chilean polity, another war against the same adversaries would now
provide Chile with a new "golden goose"—the nitrate fields of the

Atacama desert. The nitrate boom would allow the hard economic realities of export-dependent development to be put off for another four decades. As occurred with export booms throughout Latin America in the late nineteenth century—whether they were based upon coffee, sugar, wheat, minerals, or other primary commodities— exploitation of the nitrate fields provided Chile with extensive export revenues which financed public works and modernization without coming to terms with the internal contradictions of the economy or the structural inequalities of Chilean society. At Santiago, Valparaíso, and other central valley cities and in the central valley countryside, landowners could patch the cracked veneer of prosperity and continue the beautification of their urban mansions and country estates while they postponed confrontation with the reality of the country's growing population of urban and rural poor.

The agro-commercial expansion of the mid-nineteenth century took on a special meaning for the population of the Concepción-southern region and the Araucanians to the south. In the southern area traders, farmers, and speculators maintained contact with local chieftains, but farms and settlements in the frontier territory remained subject to periodic raids or even relatively large-scale uprisings that wrought considerable destruction of property and loss of life. Araucania remained outside the Chilean nation.

External demand for wheat, flour, and animal products made southern lands potentially more valuable. Expanded cereal cultivation accompanied by the growth of a prosperous flour-milling industry in the environs of Tomé put renewed pressure on the Indian lands. Partly in response to these pressures, an Indian insurrection from 1859 to 1860 coincided with the civil war that pitted Concepción forces against the central government, and caused much destruction in the areas of Negrete, Nacimiento, and Los Ángeles. In April 1859 the periodical *El Correo del Sur* called in no uncertain terms for violent repression and blamed the Indians and "Indian territory" for numerous real and imagined evils:

>   The necessity, not only to punish the Araucanian race, but also
>   to make it impotent to harm us, is so well recognized that almost
>   everyone desires that such measures be taken as the only way to
>   rid the country of a million evils. It is well understood that they
>   are odious and prejudicial guests in Chile. . . . The thousands
>   of families that today find themselves in misery; the innumerable
>   robberies committed by these savages . . . are clamoring for
>   prompt and extreme measures, since conciliatory measures have
>   accomplished nothing with this stupid race—the infamy and dis-
>   grace of the Chilean nation.

Once again the lure of quick profits and Indian land pitted the Araucanians in a struggle for survival against the superior firepower of
"civilization." Now "odious guests" in their own land, the Indians
faced a last desperate attempt to maintain their land and their autonomy against the encroaching outsiders.

The land rush occasioned by expansion of cereal cultivation—accompanied by government colonization schemes, legal chicanery, and
corruption—necessitated troops to enforce the "property rights" of
Chilean landowners. A new Indian uprising, led by a Frenchman
who proclaimed himself King Aurélie Antoine I and swore to free
the Indians from Chilean tyranny, spurred the government to renewed repression. Reminiscent of the military tactics of many colonial governors, the Chilean leaders established forts at Mulchén and
Angol in 1863 and then "defense lines" near Malleco (1867-68) and
Traiguén (1878-79), as troops drove the Indians farther south
and east. The official frontier shifted to the Malleco River in 1866,
and in 1875 Bío Bío became a new Chilean province (see Map 8).

Chilean squatters, speculators, and would-be hacendados rushed to
gain control of "empty" frontier lands. From 1852 to 1866 the national government attempted unsuccessfully to regulate land transac-
tions in the southern territories. A ban on land deals with Indians in
1858 failed to stem the tide. Legislation defining as "public" all
frontier lands that had not been "continually and effectively occupied for at least one year," set in motion thousands of legal conflicts
between the government, Indians, squatters, and land speculators.
Many of the conflicts were resolved outside the courts by force; oth-

ers were decided by bribes or by influence exercised by powerful economic interests.

Finally in the mid-1870s Congress enacted a law that required public auctioning of all contested lands in a region bounded by the Renaico River to the north, the Malleco to the south, and the Vergara to the west (see Map 8). The down payments required were so high that they practically excluded peasants, workers, and artisans from acquiring these lands; incentives for private colonization companies to bring in "high quality"—that is, northern European—colonists discriminated against Chilean settlers. The government seldom sold properties of less than the legal maximum of 500 hectares. Instead of creating a frontier yeomanry, government policy allowed the frontier territory to become another domain of the large hacienda. In imitation of the central valley model, political and economic elites carved out new manorial possessions upon which ex-squatters, landless peasants, and Indians became *inquilinos* or peons. Between 1850 and 1875 ex-presidents and future presidents of Chile, along with such well-known entrepreneurs as Waddington, Bunster, Cousiño, and Smitmans, acquired large rural estates in the southern provinces.

Passage of the 1874 public lands legislation coincided with the maiden journey of the southern region's new railroad from Concepción to Chillán. Since the 1850s local elites in the frontier territory had struggled to obtain government support for a southern railway. At midcentury the region contained only two important urban centers: Concepción and Chillán. Agriculture and livestock entirely dominated the regional economy, though an incipient coal industry and a few fishing villages along the coast provided a hint of things to come. The gold strikes in California and Australia that stimulated demand for Chilean wheat and flour encouraged the export trade at Concepción-Talcahuano and brought dramatic growth to Tomé. Developing as the center of the milling industry and recipient of foreign investment and technology, Tomé accounted for more than 90 percent of the provinces' reported 842,000 quintals of flour by 1855. Expanded production and commerce also benefited Concepción and Talcahuano, which was the only legal port of entry for the entire

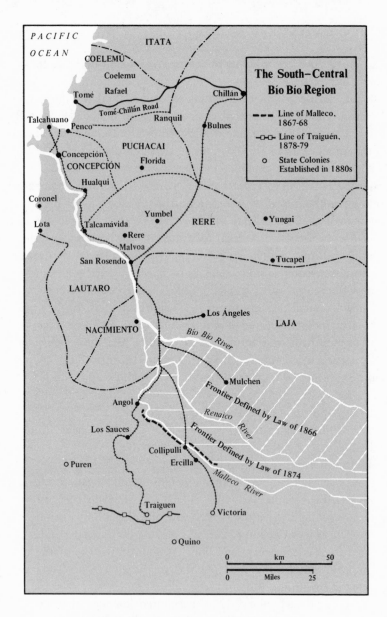

MAP 8: The South-Central Bío Bío Region

(Source: John Whaley, "Transportation in Chile's Bío Bío Region 1850-1915,"
Ph.D. dissertation, Indiana University, 1974.)

southern region. But until railroads began to operate after 1874, high freight rates and the constraints of transport by oxcart seriously disadvantaged the southern region in relation to the central valley.

Loss of the California and Australia markets, economic depression in 1857, the havoc of civil war, and Indian uprisings (1859-63, 1868), all represented setbacks for the frontier provinces. With virtual completion of the Santiago-Valparaíso railroad in the early 1860s and its connection to San Fernando, southern agriculture faced the prospect of being unable to compete with the central valley. Until the early 1860s the southern mill industry supplied most of the flour exported by Chile; thereafter the southern share dropped off to somewhat less than 50 percent of the total, and what had been a modern industry in the 1850s failed to keep pace with rapid technological innovations in flour milling in the United States and Europe. By the late 1870s Chilean millers could not compete effectively in the international market, though trade with Peru, Ecuador, Argentina, and Brazil continued, along with less significant shipments to Europe or North America. Moreover, the share of the export market accounted for by shipments through Valparaíso rose from less than 25 percent between 1846 and 1850 to over 90 percent in 1880. Fortunately, after bumper crops in 1862-63 and a short-term decline in prices, increased Peruvian demand for Chilean wheat and the growing British market rescued the economy of the region from disaster. Over the next ten years British purchases of Chilean wheat increased from approximately 340,000 pesos in 1863 to more than 2 million pesos in 1874— when the railroad connected Talcahuano to Chillán and the wheatlands of the interior.

Southern agriculture expanded by putting more and more land under cultivation by means of slash-and-burn technology. With large tracts of land available, high yields on virgin soil, and relatively cheap labor, southern agriculture could expand output with small amounts of capital investment. Agricultural workers received low wages along with food rations consisting of beans, potatoes, corn, and unleavened bread, or *galleta*. Peons rarely ate meat. Agricultural implements generally remained primitive: wooden plows, and weighted bramblebush harrows. While labor supply remained plentiful and secure, no need to mechanize existed. Into the 1870s most hacendados of the south employed labor crews for the harvest, and paid temporary wages double or triple those paid to the resident labor force. Significent mechanization would come only later in the nineteenth century, when the supply of harvest laborers became less secure and workers less compliant due to the possibility of other employment in railroad and public construction projects or in the nitrate fields taken from Peru and Bolivia in the War of the Pacific.

Foreign markets for southern agriculture and the demand for coal by northern mines also stimulated the growth of some of the cities and towns of the region. Near Concepción the coal-mining enterprise of Matías Cousiño changed Lota from a rustic village into a mining town of some 5000 by the mid-1860s. Shortly thereafter the government extended telegraph service to Lota and from there to Nacimiento on the Araucanian frontier. Copper foundries, a brick factory, and other associated commercial establishments contributed to Lota's expansion. Coal mining also stimulated commercial development around Lebu and Coronel between 1862 and 1874. From 1865 to 1875 the population of Coronel increased from 2,132 to 5,568; by 1875 Lebu's population exceeded 5700.

The mining proletariat created in the 1860s and 1870s would eventually make the coal-mining region one of the most explosive areas of class conflict and union struggle in Chile. In the short run, development of the Chilean coal industry meant that despite the low quality of Chilean coal, the country could supply more than 50 percent of domestic consumption. Perhaps even more significant, the coal trade along with lumber and food exports expanded contacts between the two regions most hostile to policy emanating from Santiago and between workers in the most dynamic sectors of the Chilean economy.

By 1851 flour-milling and shipping activities at Tomé had transformed a tiny settlement of a dozen shacks into a mushrooming town with some 2000 residents. Favored by nearby sources of water power and an oxcart road connecting it to the wheat fields of the interior, the population of Tomé more than doubled in the next decade, reaching some 5300 in 1865. In contrast, Talcahuano's population declined from 2500 to 2000, and Concepción remained more or less stagnant, as Tomé took the fore in the cereal and flour-based commercial boom. After 1877 this situation would reverse itself as the favorable freight rates on the rail line between Talcahuano and Chillán killed off the oxcart traffic between Tomé and the interior.

Intraregional rivalries between Tomé interests and those at Concepción made even more discouraging the central government's neglect of the southern region. Limited economic progress, including the temporary booms of the early 1850s, did not fully incorporate the Concepción-southern region into the incipient process of modernization experienced by the central valley. The Indian frontier continued to limit southern expansion, while Santiago politicians and speculators treated the region as a vast opportunity for economic exploitation. Complicating this situation, some foreign interests even suggested that Chile had no effective control of or legal claim to Araucania. For example, a report by a British representative in Santiago to the Foreign Office in 1875 stated this position explicitly: "It seems to me that the Chilean government cannot claim any legal title to Araucania. It certainly has not had success in the conquest of this territory nor has it acquired rights to this territory through any treaty. . . ."

Only with the War of the Pacific and the nitrate boom of succeeding decades would the full importance of southern agriculture become apparent to the national government. Only then were the Araucanians finally subjugated—though not fully incorporated—into Chilean national life. For the Araucanians and for numerous Chilean landless peasants and squatters, the agro-commercial growth of the south in the mid-nineteenth century meant still another confrontation, and eventual defeat, by the economic and political forces associated with the expansion of Western European and North American capitalism. For the Araucanians it meant a final death struggle to maintain their land and autonomy. For most of the poor mestizo peasants and squatters it meant loss of the last opportunity to escape the poverty and lack of mobility inherent in the social structure of the central valley latifundia.

What most distinguished Chilean political development after 1830 from events in the other Spanish American republics was a remarkable constitutional continuity. Four elected presidents each served two consecutive five-year terms between 1831 and 1871. Congressional elections occurred on schedule with the repeated return of representatives of Chile's elite families to the Senate and Chamber of Deputies. Presidents and legislators of all political persuasions came overwhelmingly from a small number of intermarried, extended kinship groups with well-known surnames.

Oligarchy buttressed by endogamy and *compadrazgo*** preserved the basic solidarity of a ruling elite whose economic interests extended from agriculture to mining, commerce, banking, and, later, industry. The geographical compactness of Chile's central valley—unlike the fragmentation or the greater size of Colombia, Mexico, Peru, or Brazil—facilitated national unity and elite consensus on fundamental social and economic institutions—even when philosophical disagreements or the clash of personalistic factions led to political conflict. To illustrate, a doctoral dissertation by Gabriel Marcella completed in 1973 found that one extended family—the Errázuriz—contributed 4 presidents and 59 parliamentarians from 1831 to 1927. On occasion as many as 6 served in the same legislature. Overall, Marcella reported that among 599 deputies and senators (out of 782 for whom some quantity of kinship data was available) there appeared 98 sets of brothers, 61 sets of father and son, 57 sets of uncle and nephew, 20 of cousins, 12 of father and son-in-law, and 32 of brothers-in-law. Moreover, the influence of kinship in the legislature *increased* rather than decreased between 1834 and 1888. Chilean political stability from 1831 to 1891 depended more than a little upon restricted suf-

---

* *Compadrazgo* is a common form of fictive kinship prevalent throughout Spain and Latin America; literally "godmother" and "godfather" for baptism, marriage, etc.

frage, low levels of political participation, and maintenance of government positions in the hands of a small, intermarried, social, and economic oligarchy. Notwithstanding these oligarchical features and the relative political stability of nineteenth-century Chile when compared with the rest of Latin America, there existed underlying tensions between economic interests in the outlying provinces and Santiago as well as between autocratic and oligarchic tendencies within the Chilean political system. These tensions, along with conflicts over the relationship between Church and State, fragmented the ruling elite. The Hispanic tradition of an authoritarian executive conflicted with the evolving desires of the leading families to rule Chile in their collective interest and to protect themselves from an overzealous president or an administration that took political debate outside the confines of salon, parliament, or the prestigious Club de la Unión.

Application of certain provisions of the 1833 constitution—in particular those requiring annual legislative action on the national budget, periodic approval of tax rates and tax collection, authorizations to maintain military personnel and to station troops within ten leagues of where Congress was in session—led gradually to an erosion of presidential dominance between 1841 and 1891—when a bloody civil war would confirm the victory of Congress over the executive.

The autocratic interpretation and implementation of the 1833 constitution by President Prieto (1831-41) could not eliminate entirely the influence of imported liberalism or the desire of certain Chilean elites to emulate British and Continental parliamentarism. Nevertheless, the presidential regime provided no formal mechanism for changing executive leadership through parliamentary elections or votes of no confidence. Instead, gradually but insistently—using the leverage of Congress' budgetary and tax authority—the foes of presidential dominance imposed constraints upon executive action and established the principle of ministerial responsibility to Congress.

As early as November 1841, Congress agreed to suspend consideration of legislation authorizing tax collection as well as the budget bill until the executive submitted an expanded legislative agenda—including legislation aimed at extending congressional oversight of public expenditures. Executive agreement to these demands meant de facto abrogation of an exclusive constitutional prerogative of the executive: designation of matters to be considered in the extraordinary sessions of the legislature. More important, President Bulnes' acceptance of the congressional demands was an implicit recognition of the legitimacy of legislative checks on government policy.

Influenced by Belgian procedures, legislators intent on asserting congressional authority also introduced the practice of "interpellation"—a questioning period to hold ministers accountable for their acts. Under this procedure individual deputies could request particular ministers to appear in the chamber to explain or justify government policy. Combined with delays on critical legislation, the practice of interpellation moved Chilean politics in the direction of quasi-parliamentarism. Liberal intellectuals such as José Victorino Lastarria argued that interpellation and censure of ministers were rights inherent in the supervisory authority of Congress and served as guarantees against executive irregularities and abuses.

After bitterly contested congressional elections in 1849, during which the Bulnes government mounted a campaign of repression against the liberal forces, dissident conservatives, and the opposition political groups based on family ties or personal friendships, Lastarria submitted reform proposals to the new Congress. These proposals aimed to limit further presidential authority as well as to guarantee freedom of the press and the right of assembly. Though Congress did not approve these reforms, the attacks on executive dominance continued.

In 1850 a new political movement emerged called the Society of Equality. Headed by Francisco Bilbao and a number of personalities like Santiago Arcos and the Matta brothers who would play important roles as political reformers, the society held numerous public meetings and demonstrations against the government. In response, the intendant of Santiago prohibited further meetings and declared the society "dissolved"; all similar organizations were outlawed. Government officials closed opposition newspapers, and many of the leaders of the reform movement fled into exile.

Toward the end of President Bulnes' second term in office (1851), conflict intensified. The government election machine, based upon control of the votes of the militia, provided more than sufficient votes to make Bulnes' chosen successor, Manuel Montt, the next president —despite support by liberals and regional interests in Concepción and La Serena for Bulnes' cousin, José María de la Cruz. Since the president appointed militia officers, and the officers handled distribution of the "certificates of qualification" that allowed the militiamen to vote, presidential intervention in elections generally spelled defeat for the opposition. Officers could also withhold certificates from unreliable militiamen and give them to more "trustworthy" citizens. Although this practice had become more or less expected, the increasing resistance to presidential dominance and the frustration of important economic interests in the provinces made it impossible for Bulnes' opponents to swallow the election results.

Opponents of the regime contested the legitimacy of the rigged elections and broke into armed revolt in Concepción and La Serena. Rebel forces in Coquimbo requisitioned the British ship *Firefly* and extorted contributions from wealthy government supporters. Before the intervention of the British squadron—encouraged by the Montt government—the northern rebel forces occupied the towns of Elqui, Huasco, Ovalle, Combarbalá, and Illapel. Miners from the important El Tamaya mine marched on Ovalle, and other groups occupied haciendas around Illapel. Miners, construction workers, and peasants mobilized to the rebel cause in other northern towns—an event in which some Marxist historians have discerned elements of an armed popular insurrection. Although this interpretation is not entirely inaccurate, the basic struggle in the 1851 revolt pitted the incumbent political machine against regional and liberal forces protesting the outcome of the elections and the more fundamental subordination of the southern and northern provinces to Santiago. Indicative of this underlying source of conflict was the leadership of the Concepción rebel forces in 1851 by would-be railroad entrepreneur, landowner, and liberal politico, Pedro Félix Vicuña. Vicuña's proposal for government subsidies of his project for a southern railroad had fallen upon deaf ears in Santiago shortly before he led the Concepción forces in support of the defeated liberal candidate. Vicuña also owned a major newspaper in the region and had himself named intendant of the province by the rebel forces. Thus the desire for political reform and frustrated economic interest, as well as personal ambition, motivated the rebel leadership in the civil conflict of 1851.

As in the north, the Montt government availed itself of British support to help quell the southern rebellion. In the words of the exiled Argentine Domingo Sarmiento, in a pamphlet he wrote supporting the Montt government, "British capital needs the guarantee of peace . . . to invest millions in the interior and to stimulate the export of cereals. . . . Montt is public tranquility, authority, good faith, and efficient administration." Within three months the Montt government reasserted control in both the northern and southern provinces.

Victory in the civil war in 1851, however, did not end the movement to put legislative checks on the presidency. By 1857 not only government policy but also the very composition of the president's cabinet became hostage to congressional approval. In August 1857 Congress approved an opposition senator's motion to postpone consideration of the budget until the President announced who would be appointed to the new cabinet. President Manuel Montt reluctantly acquiesced and, at congressional insistence, even named members of the liberal opposition to the cabinet. In effect this development put the Congress in control of the cabinet, making the Chilean political system a curious mixture of parliamentary and presidential government. The threat of congressional refusal to approve budget legislation or other critical government programs gradually transformed the autocratic presidential regime envisioned by Portales into a delicately balanced system of negotiation between government and opposition forces. On any particular issue, government supporters could defect and form an opposition majority to complicate further the life of the incumbent executive. Thus, by 1861 the institutional foundations of the multiparty "parliamentarism," for which Chile became well known after 1891, had substantially modified the auto-cratic regime installed by Portales and Prieto.

Erosion of presidentialism could not have occurred without a coin-cident ideological and political fragmentation of the Chilean elite. Introduction of liberalism as a political ideology in early nineteenth-century Chile threatened in two essential ways the hegemony of Iberian autocracy re-established by Portales: (1) rejection of Cathol-icism as the exclusive moral underpinning of the state and (2) ac-ceptance of social pluralism, including freedom of association, free-dom of the press, and the gamut of civil liberties associated with the British liberal tradition.

In the 1840s the "Generation of 1842" had arisen, as previously mentioned, from the new (1842) University of Chile. This liberal movement, headed by José Victorino Lastarria, brought an imme-diate response from the Church, which opposed any hint of religious toleration. Among the partisans of the national coalition surrounding President Bulnes (1841-51) as well as his successor, Manuel Montt (1851-61), were a number of personalities who favored a dilution of the Church's influence or at least a firmer exercise of the *patronato* by the State over the Church. Their efforts, together with liberal at-tacks on the Church and the intervention of foreign governments— especially the British—on behalf of foreign nationals resident in Chile, resulted in a series of laws offensive to the Church and to devout Catholic politicians. Among other provisions, these laws ex-panded the power of civil authorities to supervise the activities of parish priests, and allowed non-Catholics to marry without conform-ing to Catholic ritual.

This politico-religious conflict divided the government coalition. Continued disputes between the Bulnes and Montt governments and the Church gave rise, in 1857, to the Conservative party, which grad-ually became the political voice of the Catholic Church. This meant that an integral part of future electoral battles and parliamentary debates would consist of issues related to the privileges and role of the Church in Chilean society. In addition, the Conservative party, finding itself in opposition to the incumbent executive, now supported the movement to shift the balance of power from the president to party coalitions in the Congress—albeit for different reasons than the liberals.

Approval of certain anticlerical measures by the Bulnes and Montt governments did not mean acceptance of the secular implications of liberalism. In the short run, the secular conservatives now known as the "Montt-Varistas," or the National party, continued to oppose social pluralism, unrestricted civil liberties, freedom of the press, and elections uncontrolled by the national executive machine. The Montt government, in particular, repressed opposition elements after facing civil war in 1851 and 1859.

Despite the outcome of the 1851 civil war, the formation of the Conservative party in 1857 seriously weakened the antiliberal government coalition. Now both Catholics and liberals favored further restriction upon presidential authority and institutionalization of "parliamentary" government. The Catholics desired a stronger Church role in government and society; the liberal program included expansion of the suffrage, prohibition of presidential re-election, and reform of the restrictive press laws. To complicate matters further, many liberals did not share the violently anticlerical positions of Bilbao or Lastarria. Indeed many Conservatives and Liberals came to take a common political stance against the incumbent regime.

Montt's apparent intention to impose the forceful minister of interior, Antonio Varas, as his successor, along with the government's hesitancy in granting a complete amnesty to those involved in the insurrection of 1851, pushed the Conservatives and the majority of Liberals into a "fusion" that sought to prevent Varas' election. A group of intransigent liberal anticlericals rejected this fusion, but nevertheless joined the opposition. Led by the future founders of the Radical party (1863), men like Guillermo Matta and Justo and Domingo Arteaga Alemparte, as well as other opposition forces, launched an antigovernment propaganda campaign across the nation.

The government response—declaration of a state of siege, arrests

of prominent opposition leaders, closure of opposition periodicals—
moved Pedro León Gallo, a rich miner and leader of the opposition
in Copiapó, to send a private army against the government. As in
1851, the rebellion centered in the *norte chico* and spread to Concepción, but outbreaks also occurred in Valparaíso and the central valley.
While the government eventually crushed the rebellion after both
sides had sustained numerous casualties, Varas withdrew his candidacy, and Montt named José Joaquín Pérez as the government-
supported candidate. Neither the moderate liberals nor the clericals
in the Conservative party had any serious objections to Pérez as
Montt's successor.

By 1861, therefore, the ruling elite had fragmented into at least
four major groups: National party, Conservative party, Liberals and
militant liberals, who eventually formed the Radical party in 1863.
The new President formed a cabinet composed of Nationals, Liberals,
and Conservatives. Soon after taking office he approved an amnesty
law for all political exiles. Despite Pérez' effort to conciliate long-
standing animosities, personal and political differences made the
coalition ineffective. Pérez then turned the cabinet over to the
Liberal-Conservative "fusion" which gained a congressional majority
through the expected executive intervention in the 1864 congressional
elections. The National party (the party of Montt) and the Radicals
now formed the opposition. Pérez governed for ten years without
declaring a state of siege; at the end of his term in 1871 a constitutional amendment prohibited immediate presidential re-election.

During the next presidential term (1871-76) further legislative reforms consolidated the congressional-oligarchic system. Control of
elections passed to juntas, or committees of wealthy taxpayers—a
reform that assured significant minority representation in Congress,
as well as the predominance of the landed elite in the central valley.
It did not, however, settle the ongoing "religious question" including
controversies over secularizing cemeteries, civil marriage, public education, and, more generally, separation of Church and State. This
"religious question" remained the most prominent political schism

in Chile until 1891, nearly a decade after the War of the Pacific (1879-83), when efforts by President Manuel Balmaceda (1886-91) to reverse the course of over half a century of political evolution by reasserting executive dominance, led to a bloody civil war. Indeed, the oligarchic "parliamentary" regime that had evolved between 1841 and 1876 and entrenched itself after 1891, would continue to wrangle over the "religious question" into the twentieth century, long after the social and economic issues of industrialization, class conflict, and democratization seemed to portend more profound and radical changes in Chilean politics and society.

In 1876 newly elected President Aníbal Pinto faced not only the "religious question" but also the economic depression that had begun in 1873. Policies suggested to combat the economic situation, such as working on Sundays and fiesta days, antagonized the Church. Government attempts to exert control over public education and proposals to secularize the cemeteries added fuel to the fire. The economic crisis heightened tempers. Clericals promised rebellion if the religious reforms passed; anticlericals accused priests of hoarding food while others starved. The death in 1878 of the conservative archbishop Ramón Valdivieso further divided opposition forces when the President refused to consult with the Church hierarchy before choosing Valdivieso's successor. When President Pinto selected a priest notorious for his illegitimate birth and liberal politics, clerical forces successfully petitioned the Pope to oppose his appointment. The issue remained unresolved for years.

Confronted by the mounting difficulties of the economic situation and the hostility of the ultramontane opposition, Pinto's situation seemed ever more impossible. While prosperity could provide the grease to make the delicately balanced political machine function, an end to the windfalls of the export economy and foreign investment typical since the 1840s spelled disaster. Fortunately for Chile's elites, Bolivia shortly provided the Pinto government with a pretext for declaring war and for the subsequent annexation of the nitrate fields of the Atacama desert. The nitrate fields would provide the means to lubricate the Chilean economy and political apparatus for some years to come. They would also spawn a militant proletariat that would force Chile to confront directly the "social question" and the politics of industrial class conflict.

Chapter 6 • Nitrate

Plagued by economic difficulties and internal political dissensions, Chile faced the possibility of war with Argentina, Bolivia, and Peru. Owing to poorly demarcated boundaries in Patagonia, a territorial dispute with Argentina had simmered since Chile's creation of the Punta Arenas colony in the early 1840s. A flare up of this dispute in the late 1870s menaced peaceful relations between the two nations. To the north, investments of Chilean capital and the migration of thousands of Chilean workers to extract guano, nitrates, copper, and silver from the Bolivian desert of Antofogasta created increasingly tense relations between Bolivia and Chile.

Skillful negotiations avoided war with Argentina, but the vast economic stakes in the north made a peaceful settlement with Bolivia impossible. A new Bolivian government contravened the provisions of the 1874 treaty prohibiting Bolivia from increasing export taxes on the Chilean nitrate operations for a period of twenty-five years, and imposed a surtax on nitrate shipments of ten centavos per metric quintal (100 kg). The Chilean government's support of the Chilean-owned Antofogasta Railroad and the Nitrate Company's refusal to pay the tax led ultimately to war.

In the course of the Chile-Bolivia dispute in the 1870s, Peru entered into a secret alliance with Bolivia in February 1873. The alliance provided for mutual guarantees of independence and territory against aggression by a third party. According to the terms of the alliance, neither nation could conclude a peace, a truce, or an armistice without prior approval of the other; nor could either cede territory or privileges that would reduce or limit independence or sovereignty. Peru's interest in such a treaty stemmed from its almost total economic dependence upon the export of guano and nitrates to Europe. The expansion of European agriculture led to a spectacular increase in demand for fertilizer, which, in turn, stimulated intensive economic activity in Peru's southern provinces, particularly Tarapacá, and in Antofogasta in Bolivia. This activity, on top of the silver strike at Caracoles and the extensive copper mining in the 1870s, made the Peruvian and Bolivian deserts suddenly highly prized economic assets.

Depletion of the guano deposits that had provided Peruvian governments with most of their revenues between 1830 and 1870 led to increased emphasis on nitrates. In contrast to the Peruvian government's monopoly on guano, however, the nitrate industry developed under the control of private capital. Prior to the War of the Pacific (1879-83) foreign interests (Chilean, British, German, and French) acquired almost 50 percent of the productive capacity of the Tarapacá nitrate fields. Perhaps just as important, more than half the population of the province of Tarapacá consisted of foreigners (57%); farther south in the district of Iquique this figure reached almost 70 percent. In the municipality of Antofogasta, Chileans constituted 85 percent of the population. Thus, in the nitrate fields, Peru's principal economic resource, both much of the ownership and the labor force owed their principal allegiance to other nations.

Responding to financial difficulties, the Peruvian government in 1875 decreed "nationalization" of many of the nitrate plants, or *oficinas*, issuing payment certificates redeemable in two years and bearing 8 percent interest. In reality this "nationalization" was a mixed venture associating the Peruvian government and international finance capital in an effort to create a nitrate monopoly. Unable to float bonds to finance payments, the Peruvian government failed to redeem the certificates. Eventually many of the certificates changed hands as speculators in Lima paid from 10 to 60 percent of face value. Mismanagement by the Peruvian government, poor coordination between government and those operating the nitrate plants, coupled with a devastating earthquake in 1877 that destroyed numerous coastal loading platforms, brought a 25 to 30 percent decline in nitrate exports. Peruvian certificate holders and guano creditors put great pressure upon Chile to annex Tarapacá, but the Chilean government made no effort to contest Peru's sovereign right to nationalize property within its territory.

New Bolivian taxes on nitrate exported from the province of Antofagasta proved to be a different matter. Here a treaty protected Chilean economic interests, and most of the population was Chilean. In Antofagasta a Chilean company produced all of the nitrate, and of the port's 8000 inhabitants more than 75 percent were Chilean. When Bolivia ordered enforcement of the new nitrate tax in December 1878, and the Antofagasta company refused to comply, Bolivian officials ordered the arrest of the company's manager and seizure of company property sufficient to cover the debt owed for the new tax. The manager took asylum with Chilean authorities. Relations between the two countries deteriorated rapidly. In February, Bolivian officials notified the company that its confiscated property would be auctioned to pay the nitrate tax; in the meantime the captain of the port prohibited further nitrate exports, causing suspension of operation and unemployment for more than 2000 workers. In response to Chilean protests, Bolivia revoked the company's nitrate concession—putting the company out of business—and then eliminated the nitrate tax.

After Bolivia rejected arbitration, a Chilean military expedition landed at Antofagasta and took control of the city. Chilean forces also occupied Caracoles and Solar del Carmen, while a warship went to Cobija to protect Chilean interests. Bolivia shortly declared war upon Chile, decreed confiscation of all Chilean property, and gave Chilean citizens ten days to leave the country. Peruvian diplomats hurried to Santiago in a final attempt to prevent full-scale war, but public revelation of Peru's secret alliance with Bolivia undermined the Peruvian role as mediator. In early April Chile declared war upon Bolivia and Peru.

None of the belligerent nations were prepared to go to war. The Chilean army, quite small throughout the middle decades of the nineteenth century, numbered less than 2500 men, most of whom were stationed on the Indian frontier. Though somewhat better equipped and provisioned than Bolivia's or Peru's forces, the Chilean army lacked training in modern warfare, had no experience with large-unit maneuvers, and was practically without auxiliary services. The national guard, even more so than the army, had been seriously affected by the government's recent economy moves. Never a well-trained military organization, even the national guard's significant political role seemed threatened when the government in 1878 reduced it to approximately 7000 men—a 70 percent decline. Chilean naval forces, depleted by the sale of a transport and a corvette for economic reasons, consisted of six ships—only two of which the director of arsenals considered seaworthy. Although the addition of the merchant marine and vessels purchased during the war would allow Chile to move troops by sea to the war zone, at the outbreak of hostilities Chile's naval posture was dismaying. Having closed the Naval Academy and School for Mariners in 1876, the Chilean government had to hire foreigners to man its tiny armada.

Peruvian and Bolivian forces, though they outnumbered the Chileans, suffered from the effects of a half-century of political disorganization and internal strife. Neither Bolivia nor Peru were equipped to fight a modern war or to provision a large army over any considerable period of time. Peru's navy, relying upon two sound ironclads and a number of far less seaworthy wooden and iron vessels, appeared to be a worthy match for Chile's anemic fleet. Foreigners also manned the Peruvian navy, though their quality as described by a contemporary—"the offscouring of the foreign merchant and naval services"—left something to be desired.

Notwithstanding their lack of preparedness, both the Chileans and their adversaries mobilized relatively large armies, reaching in Chile's case over 45,000 men by the end of the war. In the first months of the war Chilean forces successfully occupied most of the Bolivian desert. Rugged terrain made it extremely difficult for Bolivia to send troops across the Andes to Antofogasta. Following a series of Chilean-Peruvian naval encounters, Chile dominated the seas by the end of 1879. When its armies took Pisagua and Iquique, the resultant political disorders in Peru and Bolivia ousted the presidents of both these nations. In early 1880 Chilean forces moved into Arica and Tacna. A bloody battle, during which the opposing forces left 5000 casualties on the field, gave Chile control of Tacna in May 1880. Twelve days later the port of Arica also fell to the Chilean invaders.

After efforts by United States diplomats to mediate the conflict in late 1880 failed, Chile sent an army of 25,000 men to Lima. Chilean soldiers crushed the Peruvian defenders in mid-January 1881, and Lima became an occupied city. Though a guerrilla campaign continued until 1883, Chile controlled Lima and Callao, confiscated considerable Peruvian property, and levied taxes to support the army of occupation. The Chileans also imposed port duties and encouraged increased production by the nitrate industry.

The victorious Chileans dictated a harsh settlement to Peru and Bolivia. By virtue of the Treaty of Ancón (October 23, 1883), signed by a president imposed upon Peru by the Chileans, Peru ceded Tarapacá to Chile and agreed to a ten-year Chilean administration of the provinces of Tacna and Arica. A plebiscite, which was never held, was to decide which nation ultimately retained these territories. Of the fourteen articles in the peace treaty, nine referred in some way to guano or nitrates—a clear indication of the underlying issues of the "fertilizer war." Bolivia, though not a party to the treaty, eventually signed a truce with Chile in March 1884; it stipulated that confiscated property be returned to Chilean citizens. Antofogasta passed into Chilean hands, and Bolivia acquired access to the then Chilean-administered port of Arica. Chile conceded to Bolivia 35 percent of the import duties on goods passing through Arica destined for Bolivia. No peace treaty was signed between Bolivia and Chile for

MAP 9: Chilean Expansion Northward

A. Original Chile-Bolivian boundary. B. Claimed by Chile in 1842. a. Established by treaty in 1866, but in A-B nitrate revenues were divided equally. C. Original Peru-Bolivian boundary. D. Boundary of Chile as a result of the War of the Pacific, 1883, with D-E to be occupied by Chile ten years. d. Chile-Peruvian boundary by settlement of 1929.

Source: W. J. Dennis, *Tacna and Arica*, New Haven: Yale University Press, 1931.

twenty years, when Bolivia recognized Chile's absolute and perpetual dominion of Antofogasta.

The terms of the Treaty of Ancón greatly benefited Chile. The victor in the war that was ostensibly fought over a ten-centavo surtax on nitrate exports, took as spoils the single most important source of Peruvian and Bolivian national wealth—the mineral-rich Atacama desert—along with Bolivia's access to the Pacific. For the next century this desert wealth would be the single most important factor in Chilean socio-economic and political development. The manner of its acquisition remains a source of bitter resentment. Neither Peru nor Bolivia has forgotten their loss; they remain unresigned to Chile's "absolute and perpetual dominion" over the conquered territories. Numerous Peruvian generals still desire to recapture the battle monument at the Morro de Arica and redeem Peru's national honor. Similar sentiments in Bolivia have led the three nations to continue one of the most costly arms races in Latin America.

The War of the Pacific enlarged Chilean territory by more than one-third. It also had immediate and profound effects on Chilean national life. The war itself significantly increased demand for foodstuffs and wine, thereby stimulating agriculture and livestock production in the south, the central valley, and the *norte chico*. Coastal shipping dramatically expanded as merchants contracted to supply the army in the north. Industry also responded positively to the war, particularly those firms producing foodstuffs, beverages, tobacco, footwear and leather goods, and other materiel for the military. According to a report of the National Manufacturer's Society (Sociedad de Fomento Fabril), founded in 1883, more factories were founded between 1880 and 1889 than had existed in Chile prior to the war. The enormous quantity of capital investment in the nitrate sector and the gush of tax revenues flowing to the national government from the nitrate companies helped to pull Chile out of the prewar economic stagnation. The merchant marine quintupled in size between 1880 and 1883, and coastal shipping, or *cabotaje*, expanded dramatically, since shipments to Antofogasta or Tarapacá had become domestic commerce.

The Chilean victory not only provided an economic bonanza but added to the pantheon of national heroes military leaders such as Baquedano and Prat. The war also reinforced the prevailing Chilean belief in the nation's racial and cultural superiority over its northern neighbors. Chile *was* special in Latin America, and after the War of the Pacific Chileans of all classes believed more than ever in their national destiny.

With the end of the war a new spirit of nationalism contributed to renewed concern for Chile's lack of significant industry. In the first issue of its *Boletín*, the Sociedad de Fomento Fabril proclaimed that "Chile can and should be an Industrial Nation." The same proclamation went on to say that "only by dedicating its energies to industrialization will Chile achieve the stable base of political and economic equilibrium of the most advanced nations. . . . To contribute to this great objective, to make Chile an industrial nation, the Sociedad de Fomento Fabril has been founded under the protection of the government." Committed to encouragement of Chilean industry through moderate protective tariffs and government subsidies, the SFF represented a potential threat to the economic policies favored by the integrated elite triumvirate of landowners, merchants, and miners. In the short run, however, the fact that the act of foundation of the SFF occurred in the principal salon of the National Agricultural Society, at the behest of a minister of the national government, suggested that the new industrialists would not be far removed from the traditional holders of power. The list of the officers and members of the executive committee of the new industrial society revealed also the disproportionate influence of immigrants and their offspring in Chile's economic elite and its industrial life. Only three Spanish surnames accompanied those of the other members of the directorate: Edwards, Subercasseaux, Hillman, Tupper, Tiffou, Mitchell, Gabler, Lanz, Klein, Muzard, Lyon, Bernstein, Crichton, Osthaus, Stuven.

In addition to stimulating industry, the War of the Pacific also affected labor supply throughout the republic. Military recruitment with appeals to patriotism, bounties, or through impressment depleted the work force in the nitrate fields, the northern mines, and the countryside. As the Chilean army moved north, desertions helped repopulate the nitrate fields, and demobilization after the war let loose thousands of potential laborers for employment in the desert, the *norte chico*, or public works. Mobilization of thousands of Chilean miners, campesinos, and laborers not only disrupted the labor supply but also changed the world view and long-term aspirations of the war veterans. Most had little inclination to return to the subordination of the central valley haciendas. Some acquired land in the southern frontier regions, but those who did not increase the ranks of vagabonds, beggars, and criminals sought their fortunes in the nitrate fields and the booming towns of the conquered territory, or went south to Coquimbo, Valparaíso, and Santiago. Wartime experiences and the opening of the northern desert as a *Chilean* mining region portended a radical transformation in the character of the Chilean work force and the beginnings of a truly industrial wage proletariat.

Rapid military victories against Bolivia and Peru also made available a large army capable of subjugating the people of Araucania. At the onset of the war some Indian groups took advantage of troop movements to the north and carried off a small-scale uprising in the region around Traiguén. In response President Pinto ordered the conquest of the Araucanians and the establishment of a new frontier line at the Cautín River. Closing off the Andean passes that linked the Araucanians to their brethren in Argentina, Chilean troops gained control of Indian territory in a concerted offensive. Simultaneous campaigns against the Indians by Argentine troops, modern weapons, and troop mobility resulting from the newly constructed southern railroad finally integrated the frontier territory into the Chilean nation. Roads, bridges, telegraph lines, and the army brought Carahue, Villa Rica and Temuco—regions lost since the days of Pedro de Valdivia—into the national patrimony. Reduced to wards of the Chilean state on shrinking tribal lands, the Araucanians faced cultural and economic destruction at the hands of corrupt government officials, traders, speculators, and Chilean settlers seeking land to farm.

The national government tried to ensure orderly opment of the frontier territory by claiming the righ the *terrenos baldíos*, or "vacant lands." Influence racial superiority, some Chilean authorities looked rope for colonists to populate the newly opened / More than ten thousand colonists from Germany, France, a... zerland settled at Victoria, Ercilla, Quillen, Temuco, Traiguén, Galvarino, Contulmo, and other frontier outposts in the 1880s. Instead of setting an example of European yeomanry, however, the colonists took quick advantage of Chilean and Indian sharecroppers and rural laborers, adapting thereby to the convenience of Chile's exploitive rural labor systems. The immigrant colonists who prospered in agriculture found *inquilinaje* a useful device to promote their interests, just as did the Chilean landowners in the central valley. Some colonists also contributed greatly by establishing artisan manufactures and even some industry, but most preferred towns or cities to the hardships of peasant pioneer farming in the Chilean south.

In any case, the government was unable to compete with Argentina, Brazil, or Uruguay in attracting the numbers of Europeans it desired to "upgrade" the Chilean race. Instead, it fell back on public auctions to deliver the frontier lands into private hands. Spontaneous colonization, squatting, and speculation continued as the major instruments of settlement in the southern region.

Conquest of the Araucanians ended the most important pre-1879 rationale for maintenance of a standing army in Chile. The frontier had provided a genuine military mission for Chilean armed forces since the time of independence, making them a necessary and valued element of national life. Acquisition through war of the northern territories and the persistent Argentine border dispute now gave a new mission to the Chilean military. The threat of conflict with Peru and Bolivia or with Argentina made military preparedness a national concern. In 1885 the Chilean government contracted the German Lieutenant Colonel Emil Körner to become subdirector of the Escuela Militar and to direct the modernization of Chilean military education. In the same year a military periodical first appeared, and ortly thereafter a military club, the Círculo Militar, was established in Santiago. Both periodical and club received government subsidies.

Under Körner's leadership Chile founded the Academia de Guerra, or War College, in 1886 with the stated purpose of improving the technical and scientific education of army officers. The Academia de Guerra nurtured a new Chilean junior officer military elite; critical of outdated methods, political patronage, and government inefficiency, it would eventually (in the 1920s) challenge the traditional political parties for control of the Chilean state. In the short run, only five years after establishment of the Academia de Guerra, Körner and his small core of followers would play a key role in the Chilean civil war of 1891. From the outset, therefore, the professionalization and modernization of the Chilean military on the Prussian model entailed serious consequences for Chilean politics—just as similar Prussian or French military missions soon affected civil-military relations in Argentina, Bolivia, Peru, and other Latin American nations. The War of the Pacific proved a turning point in Chile's civil-military relations as well as being the most important economic watershed in its history.

A mere seven years after termination of the War of the Pacific, Chile faced its most serious and bloody civil war of the nineteenth century. Chilean historians still debate the causes of this civil war, with explanations ranging from narrowly political interpretations to those that attribute it to President Balmaceda's (1886-91) tragic confrontation with British imperialism and its Chilean lackeys. Events in Chile between 1970 and 1973 led many people to draw analogies between Balmaceda and President Salvador Allende as nationalists and reformers who met defeat at the hands of foreign interests and the Chilean oligarchy. As with most such historical controversies, there is evidence to support all versions of the conflict. No understanding of the civil war of 1891, however, can ignore the complex relationships between the changes in Chile's political economy wrought by the War of the Pacific and the persistence of long-standing political issues, such as the "religious question" and the constant tension between the Congress and the executive.

The nitrate fields of the Atacama desert added an entirely new factor to Chilean political economy. Basic questions had to be answered about how to integrate the wealth of the desert into the economy. Should the state operate the fields as a national industry, as the Peruvians had attempted? Should private capital be allowed to exploit the nitrate deposits and control the transportation networks, especially railroads, that shipped the nitrates to the ports? To what extent should foreign capital be permitted to invest in the nitrate industry?

Imbued with a fundamental commitment to liberal economic ideology, the government of President Pinto set the direction for the next four decades of nitrate policy by imposing an export tax of 40 centavos per metric quintal upon the nitrate company at Antofogasta. After Chilean troops seized Tarapacá, thereby bringing the richest deposits of nitrate also within Chilean control, the government increased the tax to $1.50 pesos. Considering that the original dispute between the Antofogasta company and the Bolivian government— the dispute that precipitated war between Chile, Bolivia, and Peru— had arisen over an additional 10-centavo levy by Bolivia on nitrate exports, President Pinto's policy hardly made the nitrate producers happy.

Meanwhile President Pinto created a commission to consider long-range nitrate policy. This commission recommended return of the nitrate concessions to the holders of the Peruvian certificates, along with an export tax of $2.20 pesos per metric quintal. This recommendation established the basis for Chilean political economy for the next four decades. Private enterprise, foreign and national, would exploit the nitrate fields, and export taxes on nitrate would constitute more than 50 percent of all Chilean government revenue.

The Chilean government's decision to allow substantial foreign participation in the nitrate industry and the sale of certain Chilean-held certificates to foreigners soon placed thousands of Chilean workers in large nitrate complexes, or *oficinas*, controlled by foreign administrators. By 1883 the work force in Tarapacá alone had increased to 7000, with similar increments in the ranks of dock workers, construction and railroad crews, prostitutes, merchants, and industry related to nitrate production. Investments in public services in Iquique and Antofagasta provided jobs for still more, as demobilized troops returned from Peru. Nitrate mining depended upon pick and shovel; as the industry expanded in the last decades of the nineteenth century, it required more and more workers in the *oficinas*.

Caliche, the ore of the nitrate industry, consists of sodium nitrate and varying amounts of potassium nitrate, trace metals, iodine, and insolubles. Variation in nitrate content made some deposits more valuable, but the basic refining process was relatively uniform. Found in deposits up to two meters thick, the ore was blasted from the desert crust, crushed, and boiled in caldrons or dissolving tanks until it formed a solution and precipitated out impurities. When cooled, the evaporation formed *salitre*, or nitrate crystals. In the 1850s and 1860s coal-fueled furnaces that piped steam to dissolving tanks began to replace the fire-heated caldrons, thereby increasing the efficiency and scale of the *oficinas*. Mechanical ore crushers also made their appearance, but the industry remained highly labor-intensive. Laborers blasted the desert crust, crushed the caliche, loaded the ore for hauling, manned the catwalks over the open tanks, cleaned the pipes and machinery, and performed numerous specialized jobs in the production process. Women sewed the bags of fertilizer and served as cooks, laundresses, and seamstresses. Nitrate companies took few safety precautions; workers frequently suffered burns or mutilations by machinery. Amputees and otherwise disabled nitrate workers became a common sight in Iquique, Antofagasta, and other nitrate towns where displaced laborers drifted in search of subsistence.

Though the nitrate industry employed a large number of unskilled workers, the market for nitrates proved extremely volatile. Producers responded to short-term contractions in sales or declines in price by reducing output or laying off workers. Consequently the labor force of the nitrate fields periodically faced unemployment, and the Chilean government's revenues, increasingly dependent on nitrate export duties, could decline or increase precipitately over very short periods of time. In good times the nitrate companies could not always count upon sufficient workers to meet demand; in bad times thousands of displaced workers departed from the nitrate pampa to the northern cities and south to Coquimbo, Valparaíso, and Santiago. Fluctuations in international demand for nitrates, therefore, caused periodic political crises as Chile struggled to manage the consequences of large-scale movements of unemployed workers out of the nitrate fields into the ports, the *norte chico*, and the central valley.

The War of the Pacific also marked the onset of long-term price inflation. Paper money issued to finance the war, and the usual rise in prices associated with the artificial demand of a wartime economy, introduced serious inflation as a permanent facet of Chilean economic life. In the nitrate regions the companies controlled both the workers' income, usually paid in company scrip called *vales* or *fichas*, and the price of consumer goods at the company store, or *pulpería*. Thus, inflation pitted workers against the nitrate capitalists at the most basic level of subsistence. When labor was relatively scarce, the companies could use "low prices" at the *pulpería* to attract workers; when labor was more abundant or demand for nitrate slackened, the workers received less favorable treatment by the companies. Payment in company scrip limited the workers' ability to purchase consumption goods from independent merchants or peddlers. In order to maintain the workers as captive clients of the *pulpería*, the nitrate companies attempted to restrict independent traders from entering the nitrate *oficinas*. If a worker wished to use the company scrip in the "outside" world, storeowners typically discounted the scrip 10 to 30 percent. Under these conditions there emerged among the workers a sense of exploitation and a list of quite concrete demands for improvement of their situation. The militant expression of these demands in a strike in 1890 would play a key role in the civil war of 1891 when nitrate workers joined congressional forces to defeat President Balmaceda.

In the decade after the War of the Pacific these internal contradictions of the nitrate industry and the industry's sensitivity to the international market made themselves felt quite strongly. By 1885 nitrate prices declined from their wartime high of 12 shillings to 5s. 4d. In an effort to control the decline in prices, the major nitrate companies formed a "combination," or cartel, assigning quotas according to installed capacity. This first of several "combinations" (1884-86) over the next thirty years had some success in reversing the price trend; but as conditions improved, the more efficient producers relied on their technological advantage or the richness of the deposits they exploited, and the "combination" disappeared. Rapid increases in output and in exports—1886, 451,000 metric tons; 1887, 713,000 metric tons; 1890, over 1,000,000 metric tons—unaccompanied by a corresponding increase in demand again placed pressure on the companies to control the level of supply. Given the bulky nature of the "ore," storage could quickly become a problem if exports slackened off, leaving production shutdowns as the most obvious instrument for dealing with the fickle market.

Limiting production or exports favored neither the Chilean government nor the labor force. Government revenues were tied to the total tonnage exported—not to price. Production cutbacks or shutdowns meant unemployment for the workers. Complicating this picture further, enterprising British capitalists who had made a financial killing by acquiring the Peruvian nitrate certificates, sought to consolidate control over the industry, including the railroad networks that linked the pampa with the coastal cities. The most ambitious, like John Thomas North, who became known as the "Nitrate King," also invested in related commercial ventures. In North's case investments included a company that controlled the water supply at Antofagasta and the region's principal bank. Competition among foreign capitalists for control of the nitrate railroads, for workers, for nitrate concessions, and for other favors from the Chilean government further enmeshed the evolution of the nitrate industry in Chilean politics. Meanwhile a growing nationalist sentiment in Chile publicly condemned the increasing foreign influence over the nation's new economic resources.

Revenues from the nitrate fields permitted the Chilean government to embark on a most ambitious program of public works, including impressive extension of the rail and telegraph network as well as significant expansion of the educational system. In 1888 a newly created Ministry of Industry and Public Works absorbed more than 20 percent of the national budget, and investments in education accounted for another 15 percent of government expenditures. With increased expenditures came new public jobs, and new opportunities for the national government to distribute patronage positions to its supporters. Personal and party feuds over the spoils of the new wealth, job opportunities, and government contracts made nitrate prosperity almost as much a political liability as an asset for the incumbent administration.

Nor did economic expansion eliminate fundamental conflicts within the Chilean polity. President Domingo Santa María's (1881-86) Liberal government steamrollered anticlerical legislation through a Liberal-dominated Congress. Engineered through the legislature by Minister of Interior José Manuel Balmaceda, laws establishing secular cemeteries, civil marriage, and civil registry of births profoundly offended Conservative interests, now in a decided though still influential minority. The latter, losers in the congressional debates, would not lose the opportunity to avenge themselves when Balmaceda took office as president and faced Chile's worst political crisis of the nineteenth century. Santa María's government also extended the suffrage to all literate, adult males—and then intervened in congressional elections in the most overt fashion to secure a compliant legislature. In power, liberals like Santa María proved just as enamoured of presidential discretion and just as likely to abuse presidential power as any of the Conservative or National party presidents of the mid-nineteenth century. Such inconsistency between action and previously proclaimed principles divided the Liberals into numerous factions and personalist cliques based upon animosity toward Santa María, Balmaceda, or other government ministers, the desire for a public post, or ideological commitment to particular reforms.

Santa María's choice of Balmaceda as his successor—and the

knowledge that through presidential intervention in the elections
Santa María could impose his choice—totally disrupted the Congress.
An alliance of independent Liberals, or *sueltos*, Conservatives, and
Radicals tried to obstruct passage of the tax bill that permitted the
government to collect revenues to carry out its program. The opposition sought in this way to persuade Santa María to withdraw his support for Balmaceda. Though they failed to carry the day, this action
set the tone for Balmaceda's difficulties in his next five years as
Chile's president. If Santa María's own authoritarian bent as president seemed to conflict with his liberal record in Congress, Balmaceda's confrontation with Congress would be even more ironic inasmuch as throughout his long and distinguished public career he had
been a champion of the parliamentary system and especially of congressional checks on the executive.

President Balmaceda took office at a time when public revenues
were increasing dramatically as a result of the nitrate duties. Between
1886 and 1890 government revenues rose from 37 million pesos to
over 58 million. Although Conservatives criticized the government
for its failure to re-establish the convertibility of the Chilean currency, Balmaceda's policy of investing the windfall nitrate revenues
in social and transport infrastructure, public works, and education
produced quite positive results. Despite a general prosperity and visible evidences of the government's progress in realizing its program,
personal rancor and political infighting over ministries and patronage
weakened Balmaceda's coalition. At the same time the President
faced a number of issues concerning the financial manipulations of
John T. North and other entrepreneurs in the northern provinces.

From 1888 on Balmaceda delivered a number of ominous speeches
hinting at an increased state role in the nitrate industry or, at the
least, at an effort to enlarge the role of national producers in the nitrate regions. In March 1889, Balmaceda traveled to the northern
provinces. At Iquique the President publicly blamed foreign monop-
olists in control of the nitrate railroad and nitrate production for
difficulties in the industry. He also stated that the state ought not to
create an industrial monopoly but should prevent private monopolies

from controlling production or restricting output. In short, Balmaceda sought to defend the government's stake in the revenues of the nitrate industry and to encourage further national investment without injuring the rights of foreign investors.

Other voices in Chile called for more radical measures, including complete nationalization of the nitrate industry. But Balmaceda himself never made this proposal or supported it. In his annual address to Congress in June 1889, Balmaceda proposed public auctions of certain state-owned nitrate fields limited to Chilean bidders. The President further recommended that foreign purchase of nitrate properties be limited to one-half of new concessions. Though certainly nationalistic in orientation, this policy proposal—never adopted by Congress—hardly constituted an attack on existing foreign investment in nitrates or exclusion of further foreign participation in the nitrate industry. And though certain historians see in Balmaceda a "decided anti-imperialist," Balmaceda never took actions considered universally hostile to foreign investment in Chile. Indeed, in a manner of questionable propriety, he supported the associations of certain of his congressional adherents with foreign interests. On the other hand, Balmaceda's commitment to a program of internal modernization and national development depended upon a continuous flow of nitrate revenues, and he certainly opposed any private program that might artificially restrict nitrate production and hence decrease the government's ability to finance public programs. In this sense the interests of the large British investors directly conflicted with those of the Chilean state and the policies of the incumbent government. Despite Balmaceda's careful *actions* in regard to foreign investment, his public *statements* made British interests wary, thereby creating powerful potential allies for the president's domestic adversaries.

Toward the end of 1889 the nitrate industry again faced a situation of surplus; stockpiling began, and prices declined. It looked as though another producers' "combination" would form to withhold production until the adverse market reversed itself. Balmaceda's government not only sought to avert this development and prevent layoffs, but also moved against John North's Nitrate Railway Company which monopolized nitrate hauling in Tarapacá. The government correctly recognized the burden on the industry of the monopoly prices charged by the Nitrate Railway, and therefore entered into negotiation with other entrepreneurs for the construction of other nitrate lines. Significantly, the greatest threat to North's railway came from the potential competition of other British investors, including the long-established commercial house of Gibbs and Sons.

When the government canceled the Nitrate Railway's monopoly concession, and entered into negotiations with Campbell, Outram and Company to construct a railroad from the *oficina* of Agua Santa to Caleta Buena, the Nitrate Railway interests appealed the decision in an effort to preserve their economic dominance in the region. President Balmaceda's Council of State ruled against the Nitrate Railway. North's company claimed that the executive had exceeded his constitutional authority, in that appeal of the monopoly concession was a matter for the courts. Influential domestic political opponents of Balmaceda supported North's constitutional arguments as further ammunition in the struggle against the President, though this did not necessarily mean support for the Nitrate Railway's monopoly. Nitrate Railway interests, playing on the executive-legislative tensions to press their claims, sent a memorandum to the Senate calling upon that body to hold Balmaceda accountable for violations of the constitution. Not only did this controversy intensify internal political dissension, but North's allies persuaded the British Foreign Office to raise the matter with the Chilean foreign minister despite objections by competing British companies within Chile. British diplomatic pressure added to Balmaceda's woes.

The complexity of the situation increased still further with the upcoming presidential elections of 1891, the spread of labor conflicts across the nitrate fields, and the deteriorating economic situation. Balmaceda, despite public disclaimers, seemed to favor as his successor a personal friend and wealthy landowner, Enrique Salvador Sanfuentes. Despite election reforms in the 1870s, the overriding influence of the President, in congressional elections as well as presidential elections, continued unabated. This meant that presidential blessing and mobilization of the presidential electoral apparatus generally guaranteed victories at the polls. Illustrative is a letter to Balmaceda in 1890 from a would-be congressional candidate, cited by Harold Blakemore in his brilliant study *British Nitrates and Chilean Politics 1886-1896*:

> I recollect that Your Excellency told me to write to you when I thought it was time for my re-election to the Deputies, and since I think that time has now come, I take the liberty of writing to Your Excellency to say that I wish to continue in my post as Deputy for the next period, with the sole aim of serving Your Excellency's policies at all times and with the same loyalty as always and with the unshakeable resolve of not missing a single day of the sessions.

Once elected, of course, the President could neither control the deputy's actions nor guarantee his loyalty—as Balmaceda discovered. Nevertheless, the President's control over elections through the cabinet, the intendants, and the governors, made selection of ministers and administrative officials prior to elections of primordial political significance. Since Sanfuentes counted numerous personal enemies among his Liberal colleagues, Balmaceda's ministerial appointments from 1889 on were subjected to ever more intense congressional scrutiny.

Partisan politics couched in the rhetoric of fundamental constitutional issues concerning presidential authority polarized the opposing forces. Policy regarding the volatile nitrate economy pushed the opposing factions toward violent confrontation. The President came to view interpellation or censure of his ministers—a practice well-established by this time and strongly supported by Balmaceda during his legislative career—as antipatriotic or "political" attacks on his program for national development. Gradually Balmaceda hardened his position against congressional manipulation, acting ever less diplomatically toward the growing number of congressional critics. In January 1890 the President closed the special session of Congress and appointed a new cabinet without reference to party alignments in the legislature. Contrary to custom, he refused to reconvene the Congress upon the appropriate request by the *Comisión Conservadora* of the legislature. When the next ordinary session of Congress convened in June 1890, Balmaceda's message to it focused mainly upon the need to reverse the trend toward weakening of the executive authority by a "bastard parliamentary system" that led to "the dictatorship of Congress." These remarks and the particulars of the President's reform proposals represented a direct attack upon the very principles liberal politicians, including Balmaceda, had fought for since the 1830s.

Three days later the Senate overwhelmingly censured Balmaceda's cabinet, headed by Enrique Sanfuentes; the Chamber of Deputies took similar action on June 7, 1890. In a move totally without precedent, Balmaceda refused to accept the resignation of his ministers, and Congress countered with the now traditional device of refusing to discuss the law authorizing tax collection until the President had appointed ministers acceptable to the legislature. Balmaceda persisted in his refusal, and tensions mounted. Only mediation by the archbishop of Santiago brought a temporary compromise in August, with the appointment of a Supreme Court judge to head the cabinet.

Precisely as the political crisis heightened, a cyclical downturn in the nitrate industry fueled discontent among workers in the northern provinces. Continued monetary inflation reduced the workers' real income as prices rose, and unemployment even threatened subsistence. Isolated incidents of violence and work stoppages had reflected growing dissatisfaction among the workers between 1884 and 1889. In early July 1890 a strike by dockworkers in Iquique spread to rail and foundry workers, the mines at Huantajaya, throughout the nitrate pampa, north to Pisagua and south to Antofagasta. The workers' petitions varied from one work site to another, but typically they demanded an end to payment in company scrip, monthly cash settlements in silver or the equivalent in currency, freedom of commerce in the nitrate fields and mining camps (an end to monopolies by the company store), and elimination of the arbitrary fines or discounts from their wages which the companies imposed. For the first time in Chilean history workers carried off a "general strike" that threatened production from Tarapacá to the coal fields of Concepción.

Balmaceda received urgent appeals from employers in Tarapacá to use troops to restore order. Initially hesitant to intervene and seemingly supportive of the workers' demands in his public pronouncements, Balmaceda nevertheless dispatched warships with troops to the north. Violence, looting, and repression by company police or soldiers in some *oficinas* left dozens of casualties; at other locations the strike evolved more or less peacefully. Within ten days employers agreed to most of the workers' demands, thereby ending the strike —though in most of the *oficinas* and the cities employers failed to live up to their promises. Having temporarily squelched the strike by agreeing to meet the workers' terms, the employers gained time for the troops to arrive and deploy themselves. The presence of military units discouraged the workers' further efforts to revive the conflict, though it spread as far north as Arica and south to Valparaíso.

In the port of Valparaíso rioting and extensive looting brought harsh reprisals from police and military units sent from Santiago. Other military units arriving from Concepción stifled militancy in the coal mines, but lesser movements or isolated incidents of violence occurred at Quillota, Los Andes, Santiago, and Talca. With the restoration of order employers across the nation fired leaders of the strike movement and reinstituted the traditional practices on the work sites against which the workers had protested. A glut of nitrate stocks in relation to world demand allowed employers to rid themselves of "undesirable" laborers at the same time as negotiations continued to establish another "combination" to depress output until market conditions improved.

The timing of the labor crisis—Chile's first experience with a truly national, if spontaneous, labor movement—coincided exactly with the political crisis between Balmaceda and Congress. According to the 1833 constitution, Congress had to authorize tax collection every eighteen months. Refusal to authorize tax collections left the government, in theory, without revenues to carry on its daily operations.

Instead, Balmaceda responded by notifying banks with government deposits held at thirty days' notice of intended withdrawal, to consider these accounts henceforth as "deposit accounts on call." This measure startled the financial community and escalated further the conflict with Congress. Feelings were so polarized that it became difficult to remember that the supposed issue at stake remained Balmaceda's refusal to accept congressional demands that he appoint a new cabinet.

By this time the opposition attacked Balmaceda's increasingly "dictatorial" and unconstitutional behavior, while Balmaceda reacted with insults in kind concerning the opposition's lack of patriotism and their political motivation. Seeking to create a personalist political machine apart from the old Liberal party upon which he could no longer rely, Balmaceda entangled himself in the jealousies and intrigues of local politics and patronage. Naturally the single most important issue continued to be designation of his successor, and this gave added importance to the distribution of patronage around the country and the appointment of "reliable" administrators in the provinces.

Balmaceda proved unable and unwilling to compromise. Progressively bitter charges of antinationalist, unpatriotic activities punctuated the running battle with the growing legislative opposition. Throughout the entire year of 1890, Congress refused to pass the budget bill or to authorize force levels for the military. Undaunted, the President illegally decreed that the 1890 legislation would remain in effect. In quick response to this overtly unconstitutional act, Congress called upon *capitán de navío* Jorge Montt and the navy to support it against the President's usurpation of power. The fleet sailed north to occupy Iquique and gain control of the nitrate revenues for the congressional insurrectionists. Balmaceda, who had the loyalty of most of the regular army, imposed a state of siege, instituted highly repressive policies against the press, and suspended civil liberties in an effort to suffocate the rebellion.

Civil war continued for seven months with severe losses on both sides. Ultimately, control of the nitrate revenues, financial and mate-

rial support by British and other foreign interests, and the skillful
leadership of Emil Körner left congressional forces victorious. Congressional agents successfully delayed arrival of two new ironclads the
government had ordered from France, and obtained Mannlicher re-
peating rifles which helped carry the day for the congressional army.
Ironically, the nitrate revenues Balmaceda had counted on to carry
out his development program bought arms and equipment abroad for
his enemies. The congressional army, recruited largely among the
nitrate workers, received training under the direction of the Prussian
officer contracted by presidents Santa María and Balmaceda to modernize Chile's army and defend the newly acquired nitrate regions.
Since railroad construction in the north had been dominated by private interests, the civil war found Santiago unconnected to the north
by a longitudinal rail line. Defection of most of the navy, which had
received large amounts of money from the Balmaceda government
for modernization, prevented Balmaceda from transporting sufficient
forces north to overcome the insurgents. After his army was defeated
at Concon and Placilla by an amphibious assault directed by Körner
and a number of Chile's new professional, Prussian-trained officers,
Balmaceda took refuge in the Argentine embassy. He left in charge
in Santiago General Baquedano, the hero of the War of the Pacific,
who had remained neutral in the civil war. The day after his presidential term ended—September 19, 1891—Balmaceda shot himself.
In October, Jorge Montt was elected Balmaceda's successor, and
Chilean politics entered a new era of congressional dominance.

The outcome of the civil war shifted the balance of Chilean politics from the executive to the Congress but did little to change the
nation's dependence on nitrates. Population in the northern provinces more than doubled between 1885 and 1907; workers traveled
from the *norte chico*, the central valley, and even farther south to
seek their fortune in the nitrate fields. Average levels of employment
in the nitrate fields jumped impressively from nearly 6500 in the
1880s to almost 50,000 between 1910 and 1920. Cyclic downturns
continued to inflict periodic depressions, shutdowns, attempts to

form production cartels, and massive unemployment. Economic depression between 1896 and 1897 saw nitrate production reduced to 40
percent of capacity. Large-scale unemployment followed. Financial
panic associated with the government's unsuccessful experiment with
a return to convertible currency (1895-98) and increased defense expenditures—25 percent of the budget—exacerbated the crisis, but still
only provided a relatively mild hint of the more severe crises that
would occur during the next three decades of nitrate dependence.
As the labor force increased, the misery inflicted by the downturns of
the economy became more severe. Instead of 5000 jobless workers,
the nation now periodically faced the desperation of tens of thousands of laborers temporarily without work, means of subsistence, or
domicile. The workers retained by the companies experienced wage
cuts.

The linkage of the nitrate economy to the agriculture of the central valley and the Concepción-frontier region further integrated the
regional economies into a national economy. Downturns in nitrate
affected agriculture, coal mines, commerce, and a slowly growing
industrial sector. Led by food and primary product-processing firms—
canneries, flour mills, breweries, match factories, sugar refineries—
along with foundries, cement, and even a nascent locomotive works,
Chilean industry expanded during the last decade of the nineteenth
century and into the first years of the twentieth. Forty percent of
Chilean factories in 1895 dated from no earlier than 1890—almost
60 percent of these were located in Santiago or Valparaíso. Imported
technologies made some of Chile's new industries—for example, cement—modernized flour mills, and wineries as efficient, by the first
decades of the twentieth century, as any in the world. Increasingly integrated in their economic relationships, domestic firms produced
input—alcohol, wood, paper, containers—for other national industries as well as consumer articles for the growing cities and nitrate
districts. Protective tariffs adopted in the 1890s reflected the effective
lobbying by industrial interests like the SFF and the growing concern of certain Chileans to make Chile an industrial country. The
Errázuriz Echaurren administration (1896-1901) also directed its

ministries to give preference to Chilean manufactures in public projects, so long as domestic manufacturers charged no more than 10 to 15 percent more than foreign competitors.

Urbanization in the years after 1885 increased Valparaíso's population to over 120,000 and that of Santiago to more than 250,000 by the turn of the century. Iquique grew into a bustling nitrate port of 33,000 inhabitants, and Antofogasta's population rose to 14,000. To the south, rural migrants continued their exodus out of the countryside to Concepción, Talcahuano, and Talca. By 1907 the Chilean census classified 43 percent of the population as urban. Though the crude definition of "urban"—as concentrations over 1000—gives a somewhat misleading impression, it cannot be denied that ever more Chileans were potential customers for Chilean agriculture and manufacturers as they left the rural estates and settled in towns, mining camps, or nitrate fields. And it was to this internal market that Chilean manufacturers largely dedicated their attentions. Of the total value of exports in 1900 (162 million pesos), only 3.3 million corresponded to manufactures—less than wealthy Chileans spent on imported perfume, jewelry, liquor, and fine textiles.

If nitrates brought uncertainty to the Chilean economy and much of the labor force, it also brought great wealth to a small number of capitalists and stock speculators. It allowed Chilean governments to avoid serious examination of the internal tax structure and to eliminate taxes on wealth or income. Balmaceda himself proposed abolition of the income and inheritance taxes introduced in the late 1870s. Nitrate financed public works, railroad construction, private mansions, and construction of irrigation canals for Chile's agricultural heartland. The nitrate industry's expansion generated secondary and support industries in the north and in the central valley and also provided a market for Chilean agriculture and coal mines while stimulating coastal shipping. More than anything else, however, the nitrate industry altered the character of the Chilean labor force. The conditions in the nitrate fields spawned an increasingly militant labor movement which carried its struggle against exploitation south to the countryside and the cities. The plight of the northern work force be-

came a platform for political reformers and a school of leadership for
a new generation of labor leaders.

A select group of Chilean intellectuals joined the battle with short
stories, novels, and plays depicting the misery of Chile's masses in
contrast to the decadence and pedantry of the nation's political elite
and the splendor of the manor house on the hacienda or the urban
mansion of the northern mining magnates. Publication of *Casa
Grande* in 1908—by a member of Chile's oligarchy who scathingly
attacked the character of his brethren—and of *Sinceridad: Chile ín-
timo en 1910*—by a schoolteacher writing under the pseudonym Dr.
Julio Valdés Cange—focused attention in Chile upon the reality of
what became known as the "social question."

The "social question" or "workers' question" by any other name
still meant industrial class conflict combined with serious concern
by some Chilean leaders with mass poverty, educational backwardness, and the whole range of issues associated with social and economic development. The War of the Pacific and the nitrate economy
had ushered Chile into the industrial age. Unfortunately the civil
war of 1891 reaffirmed the oligarchic tradition of Chilean politics,
even reinvigorated the power of central valley landowners with legislation granting municipal autonomy and extending responsibility to
local government for administration of congressional and presidential
elections. The contradiction between the politics of parliamentary
stalemate, and the evolution of an industrial labor movement influenced by imported socialist and Marxist ideology, would destroy the
nation's commitment to the 1833 constitution and radically alter
class relations. Finally, in the 1920s this process would culminate
in a military coup d'état when Chilean parliamentary government
would prove unable to confront head on the reality of twentieth-
century industrial society.

Chapter 7 • Politics, Labor, and the Social Question

In 1927, thirty-six years after congressional forces imposed parliamentary government upon Chile, José Manuel Balmaceda's son presented the presidential sash worn by his martyred father to an ambitious military officer named Carlos Ibáñez. Balmaceda's son delivered an emotional speech, claiming that Ibáñez represented the "perfect incarnation" of *Balmacedismo*—the principles for which his father had died.

Whether or not Ibáñez rightfully belonged to the tradition of Balmaceda or sympathized beyond convenient political rhetoric with Balmaceda's programs of the late 1880s, he explicitly rejected the interminable, parliamentary squabbles and the restrictions on executive authority that had frustrated his predecessors. More than had any Chilean president since the era of Portales, Ibáñez returned to Hispanic authoritarianism and condemned the imported liberalism that dominated Chilean political life in the late nineteenth and early twentieth centuries.

A prominent military officer trained in the Prussian tradition established in Chile by Emil Körner, Ibáñez led a new generation of Chilean military officers who despised parliamentary practices, politicians, and, above all else, politics. They blamed politics for Chile's economic problems, for the increasing class conflict, for the corruption and venality of public life, and for all else that ailed the nation. These views were epitomized in 1924 by a Chilean officer writing to a civilian government minister:

> Even though you, at this time and place, represent for us the most disgusting element in our country—politicians—that is, all that is corrupt, the dismal factional disputes, depravities and immoralities, in other words, the causes of our national degeneration, we recognize that you, despite the fact that you must defend sinecures, hand out public posts, and support avaricious ambitions, that you are one of the few honest politicians.

If the sentence was long, the sentiments it expressed reflected the frustration of the professional military with more than three decades of congressional neglect of Chile's most pressing problems. It also expressed the utter contempt for politics and politicians held by the military and by Chile's growing class of technicians and professional people. The professional military nurtured by Balmaceda's successors through the first decade of the twentieth century (and then neglected, to the Congress' ultimate regret) would no longer tolerate the sterile politics of salon, intrigue, and immobility that had both weakened the military institution and made the armed forces shock troops for oligarchical repression.

Whatever the objections to Ibáñez' dictatorial regime, it is easy to understand the disdain of a moralistic professional soldier for the type of political system that functioned in Chile after 1891. Even apart from the immediate issues of 1924 prior to the September 5 coup that brought the military into the government—Congress' decision to pay its representatives a salary contrary to constitutional prohibitions, while salaries due civil servants and military personnel were in arrears; its constant meddling in military personnel matters; its failure to pass social legislation in the midst of growing labor conflict—Ibáñez and his followers could no longer brook the political charade called parliamentary government in Chile.

Manuel Rivas Vicuña, one of the country's most respected politicians—and eventual political enemy of Ibáñez—captured the fundamental character of the Chilean political process during the post-1891 years. He described his "Election Memories of 1918":

> Would I again have a seat in Congress? We could hardly wait for the train to arrive in Curicó.
> What happened here?—I asked the first person I encountered in the station.
> The same as usual, *patrón*, the bosses [*futres*] got together and stole the money sent by the government for the elections.
> Afterward I found out from my friends that an agreement had been reached. My name and that of the Conservative candidate had triumphed without opposition; they had made no use of the blank check that I left in the event of an electoral struggle, and they had made only small payments to the voters.
> The bosses had stolen the money sent by the government for the elections.
> I've been lucky to avoid the necessity of buying votes for my campaigns. I've had no competition the four times I was elected deputy, and my friends generously took care of my electoral expenses.
> The general rule, I've been assured, is the opposite and reveals that from the worker to the great proprietors, all believe that elections are a business that provide those elected not just with honor but also with [material] benefit.
> Vote buying [*cohecho*] is a habit so deeply rooted it will be very difficult to eradicate.

The men who acquired offices in the Congress through vote buying debated interminably while Chilean society underwent profound socio-economic changes. In 1915 an ex-president of the Federation of Chilean University Students gave a funeral oration for the nation's political leaders—at the end of a presidential term in which President Ramón Barros Luco told his compatriots that "there are only two types of problem: those without solution and those that solve themselves." The military intervention of 1924 and Ibáñez' authoritarian regime (1927-31) were reactions to this type of political thinking and to the politics of parliamentary stalemate.

Ibáñez' usurpation of presidential authority and subordination of

Congress also temporarily halted more positive trends during the parliamentary period—institutionalization of respect for civil liberties and political liberalization in the Chilean polity. Whatever the defects of the parliamentary period, however, it had allowed for the evolution of freedom of the press, for a growing, if not complete, recognition of the legitimacy of opposition movements and parties, and for a formal respect for the procedures of liberal democracy. Despite electoral corruption and empty political rhetoric, along with Congress' failure to deal with pressing social issues, the country's political institutions permitted expanded suffrage and a more open pattern of recruitment to public office. The military intervention of 1924 and the subsequent Ibáñez administration not only ended, temporarily, this trend toward political liberalization, but it represented a resurgence of the traditional Hispanic intolerance for liberalism, intensified by a military ideology of national regeneration.

In 1887 the recently organized Partido Demócrata brought a new political ideology and style into Chilean politics. Led by Malaquías Concha, the party proclaimed as its objectives "political, economic, and social liberation of the people [*pueblo*]" and proposed numerous reforms, including direct election of the president, municipal administration of the departments (eliminating the presidentially appointed governors), taxes on land and capital, compulsory public education, and support for industrialization through protective tariffs. Appealing especially to artisans and the lower middle class, the party also promoted policies designed to improve the lot of the urban poor.

The Partido Demócrata evolved as Chile's first populist political party, electing its first deputy to Congress in 1894. By 1903, it had obtained representation from Valparaíso, Santiago, and Concepción. The most progressive elements within the Partido Demócrata later emerged as leaders of the ever more militant labor organizations of the cities, the nitrate and mining camps, and the southern coal mines, as well as of the Socialist Workers Party (POS) formed in 1912. The party sponsored mass rallies, supported the workers' press and cultural centers, and generally provided a legitimate voice of political opposition on behalf of the working classes. Though it never became a truly proletarian-based organization and continued to recruit its leadership from artisans and the middle class, the Partido Demócrata nevertheless challenged the assumptions and policies of the landowning, commercial, and industrial interests that dominated Chilean politics.

The hypocrisy and the contradictions of the parliamentary era permitted greater latitude for political and social organization by workers and the urban poor than could have occurred under a more authoritarian civilian regime or a military government. Chilean elites believed themselves to be progressive. With the exception of the Conservatives who insisted still on the prerogatives of the Church or opposed universal education, they identified with the civil libertarian tradition of Britain. After all, Congress had only recently won a victory for liberty against the threat of executive tyranny! The constant changeovers of cabinets, punctuated by acrimonious debates in the legislature and the press, provided a milieu in which the political system could usually tolerate the worker press and even moderate representatives of the working class. This did not mean acceptance of all elected representatives of the working class. The Congress refused to seat Luis Emilio Recabarren, the most important labor leader in the country, after his electoral victory in 1906, on the pretext that he refused to swear the customary oath. One deputy commented that "even if it were not strictly in accord with justice to expel Mr. Recabarren from the Chamber, it would be necessary to do so for social morality . . . since it is not tolerable that the ideas of social dissolution sustained by Mr. Recabarren be represented in the Chamber." Nevertheless, the parliamentary system did allow increased political influence for middle class and provincial interests. Before the parliamentary era ended (1924), Recabarren and other self-declared revolutionaries had also gained seats in the Congress.

Parliamentary politics tended to diffuse and weaken governmental authority. The multiplicity of political parties and factions and the electoral reforms that placed supervision of elections and registration in the hands of 267 "autonomous" municipal administrations, decentralized national politics. The Congress became a creature of local political machines which were frequently dominated by landowners, mining interests, or industrialists in accord with the economy of each congressional district. Executive intervention through use of the police or military could still influence electoral outcomes, but generally money to buy votes became much more important than naked force. In these respects the Chilean political system shared the corruption that accompanied expansion of the suffrage and democratization throughout most of the Western world. Dishonesty in public life and patronage as a principal instrument of assembling and maintaining local political machines reached no more distressing levels in Chile than it did in the United States or Argentina during the same period.

Unlike the United States, in Chile no wave of immigrants served the elite as urban "voting cattle"; government remained largely in the hands of a small clique of "political families" with aristocratic pretensions and a political base in the countryside—in an increasingly complex urbanizing society. Overt military intervention in Chilean politics in 1924 and the subsequent Ibáñez dictatorship (1927-31) meant, above all else, an end of an era in Chilean national life when socioeconomic changes moved the country rapidly into the twentieth century, yet political leaders clung to a bastardized version of imported nineteenth-century liberalism.

No other problem so dominated Chilean development after 1891 —and received so little meaningful attention by Chilean political leaders—than the continued growth of the urban and industrial proletariat and the intensified struggle between labor and capital called the "social question." Modest but persistent industrial growth in Chile from the 1890s until the world depression of the 1930s gradually increased the number of workers employed in factories, workshops, construction industries, and other urban manual jobs. This urban working class remained unprotected by social legislation or a strong labor movement.

Liberal philosophical and economic doctrine current in Europe and transplanted to Chile condemned associations of workingmen that attempted to negotiate collective agreements with employers as contrary to "liberty" and the "right to work." In England, where the Industrial Revolution first made itself felt and gave rise to the social question, laws against workers' "combinations" and repression of labor organizations were the common reaction by government and employers to labor activism. Only after years of organized struggle, protests, violence, and the resultant political reform did the English working classes obtain legislation that limited the duration of the work day, protected child labor, set minimum wages, or guaranteed the right of organization.

As the industrial age advanced, the same type of struggle eventually developed in the rest of Europe, the United States, and Latin America. Thus the social question in Chile, as in the rest of the Western world, consisted of political, social, and economic issues derived from the technological and demographic effects of industrialization during the nineteenth and early twentieth centuries.

Prior to 1924 Chilean laws provided no institutionalized procedure for dealing with conflicts between worker and employer. In theory a worker sought employment from an individual employer and came to an agreement concerning wages, conditions of work, and length of employment. Each worker had to reach his or her own agreement with the employer. No collective agreement or written contract existed, and prevailing custom defined as subversive strikes or work stoppages. According to this classic liberal interpretation of the worker-employer relation, the worker could freely come and go as he or she pleased, and could work or not work, depending upon the attractiveness of the employment offered. Likewise employers, competing for workers in the free labor market, would offer conditions of work and sufficient pay to attract and retain workers.

In reality, of course, this highly idealized conception of the labor market—imbued with the legitimacy of prevailing law and enforced as necessary by the police or the military from country to country— ignored the tendency for industrial ownership to become gradually more concentrated, for owners of factories to cooperate in holding down wages, and for the threat of unemployment in the cities to pose a life-and-death dilemma for the growing proletariat.

This liberal formulation also failed to recognize that the extensive political influence of the propertied classes had shaped the laws restricting labor organization but allowing employers' associations that effectively lobbied legislatures and administrators in their own behalf. For example, the Sociedad de Fomento Fabril (SFF) in Chile, which opposed labor organizations and collective labor agreements, attempted to protect its own interests with constant lobbying for protective tariffs. Its members also were sent to Congress, staffed government bureaucracies, or acted as ministers of state. Between 1883 and 1930, 36 percent of the association's executive council members served as congressmen, senators, or ministers of state. During the same period the monopolistic or oligopolistic structure characteristic of Chilean industry in the 1970s had begun to emerge. By 1918, 3.3 percent of all manufacturing firms employed 43.2 percent of manual workers in industry. A small number of firms dominated most of the important manufacturing sectors, including textiles, sugar, breweries, wineries, foundries, tobacco, cement, paper, glass and bottles, chemicals, vegetable oils, and coal. Collusive marketing and supply agreements reinforced the lack of competition as the larger firms attempted to freeze potential competitors out of the market. In a fashion compatible with both Hispanic and the liberal capitalism of the late nineteenth century, Chilean entrepreneurs sought to eliminate competition throughout the economy except in the labor market. Here they enthusiastically accepted the principles of British liberalism long after the advent of labor legislation and the recognition of the legitimacy of labor organizations in Britain. Although the industrialists strongly supported protective tariffs, government subsidies, monopoly profits, and influential industrial associations working closely with the government, they staunchly opposed organized collective action on the part of workers to improve their living conditions or to demand higher wages.

Likewise, Chile's wealthiest landowners, organized in the National Agricultural Society (SNA) since 1869, actively lobbied to restrict the negative effects of "free trade" on cattle interests. Highly influential in Chilean politics—from 1873 to 1901, 25 to 33 percent of the members of Congress belonged to the SNA—the landowners sponsored legislation in 1888 to establish a protective tariff on imported cattle. Landowners thus hoped to insulate Chilean cattle producers against the more modern cattle industry of Argentina. The proposed legislation indirectly provided incentives for landowners to revert land to pasture, even as the country proved unable to supply sufficient foodstuffs at reasonable prices to feed the growing cities and northern mining districts.

The cattle tax issue infuriated the leadership of the newly formed Partido Demócrata and became a symbolic rallying point for lower-class protests against the general inflation which was eroding an already precarious standard of living. Landowners responded that the lower classes ate little meat anyway and that in any case beans were healthier. A wave of protests and strikes in Santiago and the provinces, along with the other issues facing the Balmaceda government in 1888-89, led to withdrawal of the proposed cattle tax by its sponsors. A decade later, however, the landowners successfully put through legislation that imposed a duty on imported cattle in conjunction with the protective tariffs supported by the SFF for manufactured goods. Meat prices rose considerably from 1897 to 1902 amidst continual political conflict over a "tax on poor peoples' stomachs." Finally, in late October 1905, urban unrest related to the spiraling inflation culminated in two days of mob violence, looting, and destruction. This period, known since then as the "Red Week," found the army out of Santiago on maneuvers. To put down the violence the government and private groups distributed arms to members of Chile's most prestigious social club, the Club de la Unión, and to youths from elite families. These white guards massacred hundreds of people in the streets of Santiago. The SNA and other social leaders blamed the riots on agitators "stirring up class hatred." In reality, as the movement developed, usurious merchants, retail shops, and other symbols of the exploitation and deprivation of the poor all felt the spontaneous wrath of the urban underclass.

Despite the events of October 1905, the cattle tax remained in effect until the economic crisis of 1907, when the government "suspended" its operation for two years. Congress reinstituted the cattle tax in December 1909, and it remained in effect until 1918—when almost 50 percent of all congressmen owned large haciendas. Whatever the real contribution of the cattle tax to increasing food prices and the widespread nutritional deficiencies among the urban poor, its survival until the end of World War I reflected the influence of the SNA and the ambiguity of the Chilean elite's commitment to the "free market" of liberal doctrine. Though seasonal competition between agriculture, public works, and the nitrate producers sometimes forced employers to sweeten the pot, only the labor force was truly expected to compete in the "free" market—for jobs!

By 1920 more Chileans worked in manufacturing than in the mining sector. Other urban employment, in construction, commerce, services, on the docks, and in transport, further enlarged the nonrural work force. It also added to the number of Chileans out of the immediate influence of the owners of large rural estates. Manufacturing itself had achieved moderate diversification, though it still lacked heavy industry and a significant capital goods sector. Diversification meant specialization of the work force and a growing pool of skilled laborers. Urban life for these workers pitted them against the continual inflation and periodic recessions generated in great part by the country's vulnerability to fluctuations in the nitrate market. These business cycles subjected much of the labor force to a grinding poverty that contrasted markedly with the prosperity and economic modernization that surrounded them.

Workers saw the palatial mansions of Santiago politicians and their extended families, along with the evident affluence of the new industrial elites. Technological innovations brought streetcars, automobiles, electric lights—even airplanes—to a nation where the best urban transport only a decade earlier consisted of elegant horse-drawn carriages. Workers could also not fail to notice the overwhelming influence of immigrants and their offspring in the nation's new factories, for by the outbreak of World War I foreign-born industrialists owned slightly more than half of all the country's manufacturing establishments, and foreigners filled more than half of the technical positions in industry.

Unlike the situation in neighboring Argentina, European immigrants did not swell the ranks of Chile's working classes. Whereas by 1914, 40 percent of Argentina's agricultural labor force and 60 percent of the urban proletariat had been born abroad, in 1907 only 1 percent of Chile's rural labor force and fewer than 4 percent of industrial workers were foreigners. This meant that before World War I the labor movement in Chile was influenced far less by immigrant leadership and imported ideology than its counterpart across the Andes. Chilean authorities and political leaders did sometimes blame the labor agitation prior to the 1920's upon "waves of human scum thrown upon our beaches by other countries," but such hyperbole could not deceive government officials and employers who knew that the flow of immigrants to Chile hardly reached "wave" proportions. Only after the Russian Revolution of 1917 did Chile pass a Residence Law allowing the government to forbid entry into the country or to deport "foreigners who preached violent change in the social or political order." In contrast, Argentina passed much harsher legislation in 1902 in response to a more serious participation by immigrants in a growing labor movement. Even in 1918, however, Chilean leaders, who wanted to use the immigrants as scapegoats for mounting social tensions, had to admit that the leadership and the rank and file of the Chilean labor movement, as well as of the socialist-oriented political movements, consisted overwhelmingly of Chileans.

Historical treatments of the origins, character, and evolution of the Chilean labor movement in the early nineteenth century remain extremely fragmentary. Lack of source material means that efforts to identify the first strike by Chilean workers face insurmountable obstacles. Chilean historians often cite the rebellion of miners at Chañarcillo in 1834 as a starting point in the story of the Chilean labor movement, but this rebellion certainly had antecedents in the northern mining camps of colonial times and the early national period. Whatever the specific chronology of significant events in labor history, the sporadic, spontaneous protests, rebellions, or strikes prior to the 1880s clearly preceded the more integrated, politically significant movements of the parliamentary era. A study published in 1971 by Manuel Barrera documented 299 strikes in Chile's first century (1810-1910) in addition to numerous other "movements, rebellions and incidents." Of the 299 strikes, only 42 occurred before 1890, while the remainder took place between 1901 and 1910. Even if this study underestimates the number of strikes before 1890, the Chilean labor movement as an organized, militant, *national* socio-political forces dates essentially from the last decade of the nineteenth century.

Beginning with the general strike of 1890, described in Chapter 6, the Chilean labor movement developed impressively, if unevenly, until World War I. A heterogeneous collection of mutual aid societies, cooperatives, anarchist-oriented resistance societies, and brotherhoods, or *mancomunales*, of the nitrate regions brought together thousands of workers in a struggle to better living conditions, to provide minimal levels of security, or to petition Congress for legislation improving their lot. Tactics and objectives varied from one organization to another. Many of the mutual aid societies limited their attention to self-help efforts, such as burial expenses, and temporary relief in time of unemployment, sickness, or disability. Sometimes, however, an organization that began as a mutual aid society or a cultural group evolved into a more militant labor organization or engaged in explicitly political activities. In this sense, workers' organizations constituted an extremely diversified agglomeration conforming to no unified ideological, political, or social pattern. Paternalistic Conservative politicians, following in the steps of the earlier Catholic workers' circles of the 1870s, patronized the formation of Catholic workers' clubs while anarchists, socialists, and Democrats spread contradictory reformist and revolutionary propaganda among the workers.

The disunity of the workers' organizations and their geographical separation did not prevent the evolution of an increasingly hostile attitude among laborers toward capitalists and landowners. Shortly after the civil war of 1891, with the general strike of 1890 still fresh in mind, the leader of congressional forces and new Chilean president, Vice Admiral Jorge Montt proposed legislation outlawing strikes and other disruptions of economic activity. In justifying the legislation to Congress, its authors noted that "strikes promoted in the name of freedom to work are often the pretext adopted by demagogues to disturb order, cause injury or ruin to industry and misery to the workers." Significantly, the Congress did not pass this legislation, perhaps indicating an authentic commitment to freedom of association by certain parliamentary leaders, despite their abhorrence of movements menacing the flow of nitrate revenues or public order.

More important than legislative proposals, the Montt government moved to enlarge the army and intensify the German-oriented modernization begun before the civil war. In 1895 General Körner contracted thirty-six foreign officers (33 Germans, 2 Swedes, and 1 Dane) to serve as instructors in the Chilean army. Supported by calls from the most influential newspapers to expand the armed forces in the nitrate districts to convince the capitalists that the government would defend their property, as well as by the still more reactionary attacks on the very legitimacy of any political party representing lower-class interests, the Montt government acquired modern military hardware and made clear its commitment to law and order. If border disputes with Argentina or threats of renewed conflict with Peru and Bolivia were the main stimulus for modernizing the armed forces, in practice the Chilean labor movement became the principal target of military operations.

Successive governments through the first decade of the twentieth century maintained this commitment; by 1902 the permanent army had grown to 17,500, compared to its theoretical size of 2500 in 1879. The combination of a rapidly developing labor movement, the resistance by the government and ruling classes to acknowledge the legitimacy of such a movement, and a larger, modernizing military set the stage for a series of well-remembered tragedies that became symbols of struggle and forged a heritage of martyrdom for the modern Chilean labor movement. These include the maritime strike in Valparaíso in 1903, the dockworkers' strike in Antofogasta in 1906, and the massacre of workers at Santa María de Iquique in 1907. Both the army and the navy became instruments of repression of the labor movement.

Labor conflict and political crisis followed trends in the nitrate economy. Following the general strike of 1890 and the subsequent civil war, the cyclic depressions of the nitrate industry, upon which the Chilean state increasingly depended for revenues, led to the periodic unemployment of thousands of workers in the northern deserts. In turn, the nitrate recessions caused economic downturns throughout the Chilean economy. As the size of the nitrate work force and the level of production increased from decade to decade, so did the human misery occasioned by recessions. Table 5 illustrates

TABLE 5. WORKERS IN THE NITRATE INDUSTRY

Year	Workers Employed	Year	Workers Employed
1895	22,485	1923	41,099
1896	19,345	1924	59,649
1897	16,727	1925	60,785
1898	15,955	1926	38,118
		1927	35,788
1907	39,653		
1908	40,825	1928	59,963
1909	37,792	1929	58,493
1912	47,800	1930	44,464
1913	53,161	1931*	
1914	43,979	1932	8,535
1915	45,506	1933	8,486
		1934	14,133
1916	53,470		
1917	56,378		
1918	56,981		
1919	44,498		
1920	23,542		
1921	33,876		
1922	25,462		

* No data for 1931.

(Source: Laurence Stickell, "Migration and Mining: Labor in Northern Chile in the Nitrate Era, 1880-1930," unpublished Ph.D. dissertation, Indiana University, 1978.)

the cycles of boom and bust in the nitrate fields as reflected in the variations in the numbers of workers employed in the *oficinas*.

Until the disastrous depression of the 1930s, the nitrate industry expanded continually, with periodic depressions (1896-98, 1907, 1909, 1914-15, 1919-20, 1922, 1926-27) which inflicted unemployment upon the northern workers and forced them to migrate out of the nitrate camps to the ports and toward the central valley. Government commissions routinely documented the plight of the workers and urged reforms, but official action before 1924 consisted of minor social legislation—a workers' housing bill in 1906, a law establishing Sunday as a day of rest in 1907, and a law establishing a mandatory scheme for insuring against industrial accidents in 1917. Meanwhile the level of conflict, the strength of organized labor, and the spread of working-class militancy throughout the country turned the "social question" from the paternalistic concern of a select number of benevolent intellectuals into the most critical political issue confronting the country. Table 6 indicates the mounting participation of workers in strikes between 1911 and 1920, though official statistics clearly underestimate the size of the organized labor force and the number of strikes that occurred.

Not only the northern mining districts and urban centers experienced the effects of labor conflict. In 1911 the *Boletín de la Ofi-*

TABLE 6. STRIKES IN CHILE, 1911-20

Year	Strikes	Workers Involved
1911	10	4,762
1912	18	11,154
1913	17	10,490
1914	5	829
1915*		
1916	16	18,523
1917	26	11,408
1918	30	24,392
1919	66	23,529
1920	105	50,439

* No data reported for 1915.

(Source: *Boletín de la Oficina del Trabajo*, No. 18, 1922, p. 263.)

cina del Trabajo—the official organ of the Labor Office created in the first decade of the century to collect and publish labor statistics—recorded for the first time a strike in the countryside by forty rural workers. Earlier labor conflicts between landowners and rural workers had certainly occurred in the nineteenth century, but now an official government publication noted the emergence of class conflict in the rural sector. By 1921 the SNA was so concerned by the possibility of the organization of rural workers and *inquilinos* that it sent a letter to the Chilean president, Arturo Alessandri, urging him to take vigorous action to prevent further labor disturbances in the countryside and to protect private property.

In great part the extension of class conflict to the countryside responded to the efforts of the Chilean Workers' Federation, or Federación Obrera de Chile (FOCH). Indeed, the history of the Chilean labor movement to this day is heavily influenced by the origins, development, political alliances, and ideological orientation of FOCH prior to 1927. Founded in 1909 among the railway workers of Santiago under the aegis of a Conservative lawyer, FOCH gradually evolved into a radical, militantly anticapitalist, working-class organization. Under the influence of Luis Emilio Recabarren, who initially charged the organization with being an instrument of the bourgeoisie but helped to wrest it away from more moderate leadership, FOCH linked sympathizers of the Partido Demócrata and the Partido Obrero Socialista (POS), socialists, anarchists, and syndicalists.

Intra-organizational struggles for power eventually forced reformist elements to leave the movement; by 1921 FOCH had affiliated with the Red International of Labor Unions (RILU), and in 1922 the POS became the Chilean Communist Party. Overlapping membership and leadership between FOCH and the Communist party divided the labor movement as non-Communist Marxists, socialists, and reformers left both the POS and FOCH. Combined with the economic crisis of the early 1920s, these internal divisions reduced FOCH membership from 60,000 to perhaps 30,000 in 1922. Weaker in Santiago and Valparaíso than the anarchists, FOCH continued to be a major force among the nitrate, copper, and coal miners, as well as among the maritime workers, tramworkers, and rural labor in certain regions.

In addition to FOCH, anarchists and anarcho-syndicalists played a highly significant role among the Chilean work force through the mid-1920s. Especially influential on the docks, among artisans, and in the construction trades, the anarchists also competed for workers' loyalty in the coal mines, the nitrate fields, and other industries. Rejecting all compromise with the capitalist state, the anarchists identified government, church, and capital as the principal enemies. Viewed as an even more serious threat to established order than FOCH, the anarchists suffered serious repression at the hands of government and were a special target of the Ibáñez regime from 1927 to 1931. The anarchists emphasized direct action and rejected alliances with politicians or political parties—in marked contrast to FOCH. They also violently opposed the alliance between FOCH and the Communist party, arguing that the labor movement should not be dependent on any political party or any government. The anarchists' militancy and competition with FOCH or workers' groups supporting the Partido Demócrata occasionally led to physical confrontations and even murder within the labor movement. The coal mines of Lota, in particular, were the scene of bitter conflicts among opposing labor factions.

Unrelated to any of the larger labor organizations, there also developed a "socialist" movement in the far southern province of Magallanes among the workers of the enormous cattle and sheep ranches and meat-processing plants dominated by British capital. Here migrants from Argentina played an important role in the battle against employers, making the Punta Arenas labor organizations in part an extension of the Argentine socialists. Nevertheless, both the Radical party and the Partido Demócrata exercised a certain influence in Magallanes, as did FOCH and to a lesser extent the anarchists. With time the unions in Magallanes ranked among the most aggressive in the Chilean labor movement and were brutally repressed by British firms and Chilean authorities on more than one occasion in the decade 1910-20.

The evolution of a militant labor movement in the context of a political system catering to the aristocratic tastes of Santiago high society had produced an intolerable situation by the early 1920s. Congress repeatedly refused to adopt labor legislation or even to enact piecemeal reforms to ameliorate the worst abuses of labor contractors and unscrupulous employers. Meanwhile, the Chilean economy continued to depend upon export and import duties, particularly revenues from nitrate. Inheritance taxes, as well as taxes on land and capital had practically ceased to exist. A study published in the *Revista Chilena* by Alberto Edwards in 1917 concluded that taxes on land, capital, or income had declined from 18 percent of government revenue in 1880 to almost nothing in 1913.

The economic crisis precipitated by the outbreak of World War I led to reintroduction of a small "temporary" income tax on public employees and to an inheritance tax. These measures raised the proportion of government revenue derived from internal taxes to almost 10 percent. As soon as new economic relations with the Allies, especially the United States, produced an economic upswing in 1916, property tax rates declined, and Congress deleted the income tax on public employees; only 4 percent of government revenues came from internal taxes, while 89 percent originated in export taxes (61.5%) and import duties (27.1%). Five years after publication of Edwards' study, Raul Simón, later an Ibáñez adviser, concluded in an article entitled "Our Financial Situation" that "the war of [1879] gave us a military victory that subsequent governments converted into a diplomatic and financial defeat." Noting the debilitating inflation that devalued Chilean currency by more than 70 percent between 1880 and 1922, Simón called for new taxes on imports and proportionate increases in other taxes to replace the disproportionate dependence on export duties. But the Congress had no more intention of taxing landowners, industrialists, and property owners to finance the nation's development than it did of dealing effectively with the social question.

With the exception of a small number of progressive churchmen, the leadership of the Catholic Church reinforced the prejudices of conservative interests. In the first decade of the century the Chilean archbishop even attacked popular education and universal suffrage, while senators blamed the tide of labor protests upon "the campaign for compulsory public education that represents the wave of social-ism threatening to overwhelm us." These attitudes hardly portended great hope for the future in a country barely 38 percent literate and where, in the capital city, less than one-third of the population aged five to fifteen were enrolled in schools.

Despite the poverty and illiteracy of the masses, the physical mod-ernization and beautification of Santiago, Valparaíso, and other lead-ing cities allowed the well-to-do to immerse themselves in a charm-ing, comfortable, even pretentious lifestyle. The modernity and elegance of certain parts of Santiago, Valparaíso, or Viña del Mar contrasted markedly with the continued backwardness of much of the country and the squalor of urban slums, or *conventillos*. Social life for the wealthy centered in the aristocratic social clubs, the racing season, the opera, weekly or biweekly strolls along the Alameda be-tween Cochrane and Ejército streets, or outings in fancy carriages in the exclusive Parque Cousiño. In the words of one Chilean historian of the period, "These outings represented an imitation of the cus-toms of the times of the Spanish nobility in El Retiro, the French in the Bois de Boulogne or the wealthy bourgeoisie in Buenos Aires in the wide Avenida Alvear." For a theater-box (*palco*) at the *teatro municipal* the affluent paid 1000, 5000, even 20,000 pesos. These *palcos* served as meeting places of the political factions, for as much political activity went on at the theater, the opera, and the social clubs as in the Congress, which often simply formalized decisions made at social affairs.

The "good families" were few, and for them Santiago was a small world turning on the axis of the "high life." The society pages of the newspapers avidly reported the *vida social* of the elite and the goings and comings of the guests at the artistic or literary circles patronized by aristocratic women of the capital. Chile was governed by gentlemen who valued civility, tradition, and lineage—but who could also accept new blood and new money into their ranks when need be. Summer vacations at a country estate or near Valparaíso, trips to Europe where their sons and daughters were educated, and competition among the damsels to stay abreast of European fashions rounded out the good life for the masters of Chile. All this occurred in a country where more than half of all deaths recorded in 1913 were of infants and children under five years of age, and where the infant mortality rate more than tripled that of the United States or the United Kingdom, and significantly exceeded the rates in Egypt, Mauritius, Japan, Argentina, and even Mexico.

Notwithstanding an outpouring of literature on the social question and more than three decades of intellectual introspection on the causes of Chile's social and economic decline from the supposed greatness of the post-1879 period, the political system produced no solutions for the nation's ills. Social life for Santiago high society continued its whirl of *salones, tertulias,* operas, theaters, and summer vacations. But with the economic crisis following World War I, worker protests proved so threatening that the government declared a state of siege in the northern provinces in 1919; while in Magallanes, in mid-1920, troops shot down striking workers after first setting fire to their union building. Exacerbated by a lengthy strike in the coal fields, the political and economic situation seemed on the verge of breakdown. Congress could ill afford to put off any longer dealing with the social question.

The emergence of the social question as Chile's most pressing national problem coincided with truly dramatic demographic, technological, and economic changes in Chilean society. Population movements to the south and north and out of the rural areas into the cities intensified the trends initiated in the middle decades of the nineteenth century. From an essentially rural nation of 2 million people in 1880, Chile became an increasingly urban country of over

3.7 million in 1920 and of 4.2 million ten years later. Santiago's population mushroomed from 275,000 residents in 1900 to 700,000 by 1930, while Valparaíso reached a population of 200,000 in the same year. By 1930 almost one-fourth of Chile's population lived in Santiago or Valparaíso.

More important even than the advancing urbanization of the population, Chilean society and the economy became truly national with the extension of rail lines, telegraph networks, and steamship service and the evolution of a national labor market. Not only did the population of the provinces of Tarapacá and Antofogasta, which more than doubled between 1885 and 1920, become increasingly Chilean, —in 1885, 40 percent "foreign"; in 1920, 11 percent; in 1930, 8 percent—but the impressive mobility of labor also created a nationally integrated labor market. The periodic ups and downs of the nitrate industry, with the associated ebbs and flows of workers between the northern deserts, coastal towns, and southern provinces, contributed to increasing articulation between the country's regional economies. In a sense, though the patterns of trade characteristic of the mid-nineteenth century still prevailed, regionalism itself declined as a meaningful political force. In search of relief or work, workers shifted from southern agriculture to the northern mines or nitrate districts, then with recessions in the north, migrated to the ports of the *norte chico*, Valparaíso, Santiago, or into the central valley and beyond.

The longitudinal railroad that by 1915 connected Puerto Montt to Coquimbo linked the urban markets and the northern mineral districts to the central valley and southern producers. Steamship lines and the transverse, privately owned railroads of the nitrate regions made Chile's most dynamic economic sectors, along with the urban centers, the most important markets for Chilean agriculture and industry. With the exception of the northern railroads and the trans-Andean line, the Chilean state controlled the railroad system and deliberately extended it north and south with strategic and developmental, rather than commercial, objectives in mind. Cheap freight rates subsidized Chilean agriculture. In particular the railroad's penetration south allowed greatly expanded shipments of cattle, wheat, wine, lumber, and processed goods from the southern provinces to Santiago, Valparaíso, and north by ship to the nitrate and mining districts. This encouraged increased cultivation and modernization of southern agriculture, even as the seasonal competition for labor and hints of labor activism motivated southern landowners to mechanize the harvest.

The government also used the railroad, in times of recession, as a safety valve to funnel unemployed workers south or, in good times, to siphon labor north to nitrate and copper production centers. Fearing the concentration of unemployed workers in the northern ports, authorities issued free rail passes so that the unemployed could seek work or temporary quarters with relatives in other parts of the country. This policy somewhat ameliorated the immediate danger of a large-scale uprising, but it also spread throughout the entire country, in extremely visible, human terms, the effects of each nitrate recession. Creation of a government employment service (Servicio de Colocaciones), in response to the recession at the outset of World War I, further nationalized the labor market. In its efforts to place unemployed nitrate workers in agriculture, public works, or industry, the Servicio de Colocaciones soon found that landowners often rejected nitrate hands who, in any case, resisted the low wages and poor working conditions on the haciendas. Labor Department officials became accustomed to seeing complaints by landowners that nitrate workers placed in agriculture "stirred up" the *inquilinos*, refused to eat the food provided by the farm's administrator, or simply ate a meal and left. Thus, integration of the labor market began to erode the extensive traditional authority of the hacendados.

Unlike a true economic enclave, the nitrate economy spurred national economic integration. Though foreign investors remitted many of the industry's profits abroad, operation of the industry created markets for Chilean agriculture and lumber, coal, and processing industries and induced development of service and support activities. In turn, Chilean industries developed product lines intended as inputs for other domestic manufacturers as well as supplying consumer demands. Coastal shipping greatly expanded to provision the northern districts, while tax revenues from exports and imports yielded resources for extensive public works, modernization of the military, public education, and other government expenses. In addition, after 1900 Chilean capital made steady gains in the nitrate industry, and by 1920 national capital controlled over 50 percent of the nitrate sector.

If an enclave could be said to exist in the Chilean economy in the mid-1920s—in a political and social sense, only agriculture would qualify. The extreme concentration of good agricultural land, especially in the central valley, kept 60 to 75 percent of the region's rural labor force culturally isolated on the vast haciendas that dominated the countryside. In 1924 only 2,650 rural estates (2.7% of all farms) contained almost 80 percent of the agricultural land in the central valley. On these large estates the resident labor force remained at the mercy of the landowners for access to land, housing, and daily sustenance. Their votes belonged to the landowners who used them to install themselves in the Congress and to maintain the prevailing system of rural land tenure as well as to exert their influence more generally on Chilean national life. Congressmen from the provinces depended for their election upon landowners who mobilized their peons to vote and controlled the counting of ballots in the municipality. Frequently the most important landowners of a district virtually "owned" its congressional seat. In the 1920s the initial penetration by FOCH or political agents into the rural areas challenged this arrangement, but not until the 1950s and 1960s would political reforms destroy the hacienda as a political enclave that separated tenant labor from the national community.

In economic terms, however, the Chilean haciendas did not constitute an enclave but had participated in international commerce ever since the colonial era. The economic evolution of Chile from the late nineteenth century through the depression of the 1930s more completely incorporated agriculture into the national economy. Domestic markets became the primary consumers of the countryside's wheat, livestock, dairy products, lumber, fruits, and processed foodstuffs. This meant that domestic economic conditions, rather than

European, North American, or Australian markets, became the primary determinants of economic opportunities for Chile's agricultural interests. Rapid urbanization and the population growth in the northern provinces also pushed food prices upward. Higher food prices exacerbated the social question facing the country and created pressures for political regulation of the prices of food and basic necessities to mitigate the decline in real wages received by urban labor between 1890 and 1914. After 1932 efforts to retain the hacienda system and at the same time to pacify the urban labor force by regulating retail food prices would produce a curious "arrangement," (see Chapter 8) which ensured the continued exploitation of the rural labor force. Such efforts did nothing, however, to increase production and productivity in Chilean agriculture—the only real solution to feeding, at reasonable cost, a growing urban population.

National economic integration accompanied by political immobility and the intensifying social question concerned not only Chilean intellectuals but also leading Chilean military officers. The army's professionalization under Prussian leadership instilled in it a new sense of nationalism and a belief that its duty included regeneration of the country. Military writers like Carlos Soto Alvarez (1905) and Jorge Boonen Rivera (1917) emphasized the role of the armed forces in teaching patriotism and acting as agents of order and progress. Boonen Rivera went so far as to suggest that the army should be directly responsible for the revitalization of the nation. Two years later Captain Tobías Barros claimed that the army was the personification of the national ideal and that through active political intervention it must act to prevent further disintegration of the national situation. By 1921-22 some military leaders argued that the army should participate in all government policymaking. In 1922 an army captain published a speech delivered at the military club, in which he urged the army to exercise political influence to unify the diverse forces of the nation, to restore morality to public life, and to end the parliamentary chaos and immobility. According to this officer, the army alone of all Chilean institutions could rise above petty self-interest to save the nation.

The army had every reason to be concerned with Chile's social crisis. Political leaders had constantly called upon the armed forces to repress the mounting number of strikes and demonstrations during the first two decades of the twentieth century. A compulsory military service law (1900) brought large numbers of illiterate recruits to both army and navy, since the well-to-do generally managed to avoid the draft. Both services created primary schools to provide instruction to their personnel. Military service brought thousands of Chileans into a national institution, instructed them in the military's view of patriotism and national history, deployed them in regions far from their homes, and even provided training that could serve them when they left the service. Military schools for machinists, telegraphists, blacksmiths, construction workers, and miners as well as military participation in public works and disaster relief—for example, after the 1906 earthquake at Valparaíso—further engaged the army in "nonmilitary" projects.

Military dissatisfaction with the politics of the parliamentary period and with Chile's seeming economic decline manifested itself early in the twentieth century. In 1907 officers of the Santiago garrison established a "Liga Militar" as a lobby to secure better conditions and benefits for the army. Four years later leaders of the Liga Militar broached the subject of a military coup with Gonzalo Bulnes Pinto—son, grandson, and nephew of former presidents. Bulnes refused to go through with the plans for such a *golpe*, but not before the Liga Militar had expressed its opinions on matters ranging from government corruption, public education, crime, and economic policy to the need for increased benefits for the armed forces. Another abortive military movement in 1915, aimed at placing in power "a strong government able to end the political anarchy preventing the progress of the nation"; and in 1919 still another conspiracy among high-ranking officers to "avoid political chaos" and end the "dangers of communism" failed to end the parliamentary regime.

Especially disconcerting to the new generation of professional officers was the continual intervention by congressmen in the process of military promotions and assignments. Likewise, the apparent congressional favoritism of the more aristocratic, British-influenced navy over the middle-class officer corps of the army created interservice rivalries and frustrations. Gradually the military, and especially a group of professionally oriented army officers, resolved to end the regime of *politiquería* which they believed was debasing the army and weakening the fatherland.

World War I set in motion economic and political forces that doomed the parliamentary regime in Chile and ushered in the revival of copper as a principal source of foreign exchange and government revenues. It also shifted Chile's international economic orientation toward the United States and away from Britain and Germany. Between 1900 and 1914, American investments in Chile increased from approximately $5 million to almost $200 million—almost two-thirds the value of British investments in Chile. In particular, American investors acquired nitrate and mining properties, especially copper and iron. By the end of World War I (1918) American investors controlled over 87 percent by value of Chilean copper production, which increased fourfold from 31.4 million pesos to 132.8 million pesos during the course of the war. Modern technology, which allowed economic mining of low-copper content ore at El Teniente in Rancagua and the giant open-pit mine at Chuquicamata in Antofogasta province, along with other deposits in the environs of Copiapó and near Santiago, resulted in good profits from the Chilean mines for the Chile Exploration Company, American Smelting, Kennecott Copper, and Braden Copper Mining, among other companies. United States Steel and Bethlehem Steel also established themselves in Chile prior to World War I and expanded operations during the war. For the first time commerce with the United States exceeded 50 percent by value of Chilean foreign trade; by 1930 United States capital would account for some 70 percent of all foreign investment in Chile.

This fundamental reorientation of the Chilean economy toward the United States included large-scale introduction of American technicians, capital, machinery, and cultural influence into a country where North Americans had previously exerted little influence. Indeed, support by American diplomats for President Balmaceda during the civil war of 1891 and, earlier, Secretary of State Blaine's efforts to mediate the War of the Pacific had made Chile's relations with the United States less than cordial. Now the rapid "Americanization" of critical sectors of the economy, the intensified economic relations with the United States, and the latter's role in the termination of World War I meant the gradual replacement of British dominance of Chile's economy by that of the United States. It also brought a pervasive influx of North American consumer goods, popular culture, and prejudices.

The outbreak of the European war brought disaster to the Chilean economy, as it pitted Chile's two leading trading partners, England and Germany, against each other. Disruption of shipping lanes and diversion of British and German shipping to wartime duties drastically reduced nitrate exports in 1914 and early 1915. Thousands of workers lost their jobs; subsequently nitrate companies and the railroads cut wages between 10 and 15 percent. Government subsidies to finance stockpiling allowed continued production at a reduced level, and thus avoided a complete collapse. Nevertheless, nitrate production declined by 60 percent, and in Tarapacá alone over half of the 23,500 nitrate workers lost their jobs. In the city of Antofogasta *ollas del pobre*, the equivalent of soup lines, fed more than 4500 people a day. By late 1914 more than 48,000 people had left the nitrate region. Many Peruvians and Bolivians returned to Tacna or farther north to their native lands; Chileans dispersed southward. In the rest of Chile bankruptcies, runs on banks, and economic contraction resulted from the nitrate depression. In addition, the early war years led to shortages of consumer goods and raw materials for Chilean industries resulting in a reduction in economic activity and generalized price increases.

Quickly, however, Allied control of the seas permitted Chilean minerals to reach European and United States markets. Demand in the United States for Chilean nitrate and copper contributed to an economic upswing. American bankers followed United States investors. With official American entry into the war in 1917, demand for Chilean raw materials, especially nitrate, more than doubled from the 1915-16 levels. Though German development of synthetic nitrates during the war presaged even worse problems for Chile at the war's termination, a temporary boom permitted a renewed splurge of public works, road construction, port modernization, and the politics of patronage. Taking advantage of wartime demand, selected Chilean industries such as cement, textiles, and sugar refineries responded well to opportunities for import substitution. At the war's end, however, traditional industries still accounted for most of the value of industrial production, with food (44%), beverages (5.2%), textiles (4.7%), tobacco (4.7%), clothing and footwear (18.7%), and wood and wood products (6.5%) contributing over 80 percent by value of industrial output.

The temporary wartime boom ended almost as quickly as it began. German policymakers prohibited imports of Chilean nitrate to protect the manufacturers of synthetics. American and European markets found themselves with a temporary overstock—and a developing synthetic nitrate industry of their own. Though prices for copper remained high for another year, by 1919 the nitrate industry had entered another severe depression. For the second time in five years massive unemployment threatened the northern regions, and the economic side effects afflicted the rest of the country.

During the wartime prosperity Minister of Interior Eliodoro Yáñez decreed the creation of a *voluntary* conciliation and arbitration system to deal with labor conflict. With the authority of this decree the government intervened "informally" in several strikes to procure negotiated settlements between 1918 and 1920. The Yáñez decree represented an important recognition by the Chilean government of the necessity for establishing a system for managing industrial relations, but government authority remained quite limited due to the Congress' refusal to legislate in the field of industrial relations. As labor conflict intensified during 1919 and 1920, along with the post-war national depression, the social question became the major national issue before the presidential elections. With a paragon of the old elite opposing a self-declared reformer for the presidency, with strikes breaking out all over the country, and with electoral violence at a new peak, Chile appeared headed for another civil war—this time an explicit confrontation between the political and economic oligarchy and the supporters of reform. The events following the 1920 elections, however, made the frustrations and aspirations of the Chilean military, rather than the new President or the Congress, the real key to Chilean development in the next decade.

Amidst the post-World War I economic crisis, Chile faced a presidential election in which one of the candidates, Arturo Alessandri Palma, proclaimed "I want to be a threat to the reactionary spirits, a threat to those who resist all just and necessary reforms . . ."; and his opponent, Luis Barros Borgoño, represented the tradition of Santiago's political families. Alessandri, an upper-middle-class lawyer who had considerable political experience in the Congress and the Senate, carried his campaign to "the people." His incendiary speeches attacked the oligarchy and promised to alleviate the misery of the working classes. Accompanied by a high level of violence and intimidation, the election results proved so close that Congress turned the matter over to a "tribunal of honor" to sort out the charges of fraud and to verify the credentials of electors as well as vote totals. As Alessandri's supporters feared that Barros Borgoño might "steal" the election in Congress, they carried out demonstrations in Iquique, Antofagasta, Santiago, Valparaíso, and Concepción, despite Alessandri's agreement to accept the decision of the tribunal of honor.

Three weeks after the election the war minister Ladislao Errázuriz mobilized the armed forces and sent army and navy units north to meet a supposed threat from Bolivia. The mobilization itself proved to be a greater threat to the soldiers than the illusory Bolivian invasion. Disease spread among ill-fed troops who lacked munitions and other supplies. Rumor suggested that the war minister and his associates were profiteering in provisioning the troops. Others believed that the mobilization was a political move to attempt to divert national attention from the recent presidential elections or even to remove military officers who supported Alessandri from Santiago. Although the electoral tribunal gave the election and the presidency to Alessandri, anger over their role as political pawns further heightened the professional officers' discontent with parliamentary politics.

President Alessandri governed Chile from 1920 to 1924 in the face of hostility and obstructionism from the Congress. Ministerial changes, threats to delay budget and tax bills, and failures to authorize the military garrison to remain in Santiago—in short, all the now traditional parliamentary practices for the frustration of presidential programs—continued despite the economic crisis and the spread of labor conflicts. Congress refused to pass the paternalistic social laws sponsored by the Conservative party or those introduced by the Alessandri administration. And only forty days after assuming office, the President, notwithstanding his proclaimed commitment to reform and social justice, used troops to repress brutally workers' movements. At the nitrate *oficina* San Gregorio a massacre of workers in early 1921 added still another group of martyrs to the northern proletariat's struggle for decent treatment by the nitrate industry and recognition of labor rights by the Chilean state.

Even when the President managed to obtain a Liberal majority in the congressional elections of 1924, he could not unite his supposed supporters or persuade them to act on the critical legislation delayed for over four years. Alessandri's use of police and military at the polls to "maintain order" marred the legitimacy of the electoral victory in any case. At the same time it further involved the armed forces in immediate political questions. By mid-1924, with government salaries in arrears, a mounting budget deficit, rampant inflation, and failure to deliver on even the most modest of his campaign promises, Alessandri supported legislation to provide a salary for congressmen.

In August 1924 Congress dropped its consideration of urgent legislation for creation of a national bank, for social welfare laws, for military appropriations, and for other pressing matters, in order to deal with what many judged to be an unconstitutional proposal for it to vote its members a salary, or *dieta*. On an afternoon in early September when Congress appeared ready to approve the particulars of the salary measure, a group of more than fifty junior officers filed ominously into the gallery of the Congress. Newspapers in the capital the next day reported that the government intended to discipline the officers, though no regulation prohibited military personnel from attending congressional sessions. In support of their colleagues a larger group of officers attended an evening session of the Senate, where they heard legislators criticize their behavior and then were asked to leave the building by the minister of war.

Agitation within the army led high-ranking generals to inform President Alessandri that any disciplinary action taken against the junior officers might lead to a collective reaction by the army. Alessandri downplayed the incidents, draping them in the letter of the law that allowed military personnel to attend congressional sessions except when military matters were being debated. The matter could not be disposed of so easily. On September 4, 1924, some four hundred lieutenants and captains gathered at the Club Militar, to "strengthen the unity and comradeship among the elements of the army in these difficult times the armed forces are experiencing. . . ." The officers roundly attacked the minister of war, present at the meeting, and applauded General Luis Altimirano's words of support for the junior officers.

The next day high-ranking military officers presented a list of "petitions" to President Alessandri. These included action on the budget, social security laws, income tax legislation, social laws, payment of back salaries to public employees, and reformed pension, salary, and promotion schedules for the military. In addition the officers demanded the ouster of three ministers who had insulted them publicly in the Congress. According to one account, Alessandri had met the night before with certain officers and told them: "Request in writing the dispatch of specific projects [*de tales y cuales proyectos*]; I will sponsor them in Congress and close the Congress if they do not approve them." Alessandri's brother subsequently denied this account; but whatever the precise details, President Alessandri knew in advance about the military movement and had met with representatives of the protesting officers during the evening of September 4. On September 7, Alessandri vetoed the congressional salary bill and invited General Altamirano to head the cabinet; one day later Congress passed all the laws contained in the military petition. The military junta, though its petitions had been approved, refused to disband. A week later Alessandri resigned and left for Italy.

Prior to September 5, 1924, senior officers of the Chilean army and opposition politicians had seriously considered a coup against Alessandri who, according to the conspirators, had unconstitutionally intervened in the March 1924 elections, usurped power by dictatorial means, and dishonored the army. This conspiracy, organized by a secret society called TEA (tenacity, enthusiasm, abnegation), involved certain conservative elements of the armed forces in alliance with the opposition to Alessandri. When the movement of September 5, 1924, occurred, however, junior officers precipitated an essentially leaderless protest that evolved into a military coup. The more conservative, high-ranking officers—such as Luis Altamirano and Juan Pablo Bennett, who ultimately appeared as the leaders of the government junta—supported the junior officers in their professional demands such as for an improved salary schedule, for broadening of promotion opportunities, and for less political meddling in internal army affairs. They did not, however, support entirely the rest of the petitions on the list the younger officers presented to President Alessandri.

President Alessandri's resignation left the junta with no constitutional authority; the officers decided to request that Alessandri ask Congress for permission to absent himself from the country, and to accord him full presidential honors on his departure. When the President sought asylum in the American embassy, the junta faced the dilemma of devising an interim instrument for governing the country. Congress refused to accept Alessandri's resignation but voted him permission to leave the country for six months. The military junta then closed Congress and accepted Alessandri's resignation with the expectation of forming a provisional government. Behind the scenes, divisions within the armed forces made consolidation of the military government an impossibility. The junta announced a return to civilian politics and seemed to support the candidacy of Ladislao Errázuriz, the ultraconservative minister who had sent the armed forces on a wild goose chase to the northern deserts in 1920; but a group of officers headed by Ibáñez and Marmaduque Grove led a coup to "show . . . that the oligarchs are not masters of Chile." The *golpistas* called upon Alessandri to return and reassume the presidency. As a condition for his return, Alessandri demanded a return to civilian government, creation of a constituent assembly to consider constitutional reform, and return of the armed forces to their normal duties.

Alessandri returned to Santiago in March 1925 and resumed the duties of the presidency. Bowing to the influence of the armed forces and especially his war minister, Carlos Ibáñez, he failed to reconvene the Congress. In April, Alessandri named a commission to develop procedures for selecting members to a constitutional convention. When no satisfactory solution emerged, Alessandri commissioned a subcommittee to write a draft constitution for subsequent approval by plebiscite. From late May to July 22, the subcommittee worked on the constitutional proposal; in August a national plebiscite approved the new constitution under which Chile would be governed until 1973.

The new constitution shifted the balance of power from Congress to the executive. Included among its reforms were direct popular election of the president, an independent electoral tribunal to review election results, and prohibitions against congressmen serving as ministers or government employees. The presidential term was extended to six years with no immediate re-election permitted. Congress retained important budgetary authority and could override vetos, but it lost the traditional instruments used during the parliamentary era to immobilize executive policymaking—such as control over the cabinet, authority to prevent collection of taxes, and refusal to enact an annual budget.

Notwithstanding a shift of authority toward the executive, the new constitution officially recognized the role of political parties in national politics. By providing that the president and members of the House of Deputies and the Senate had overlapping and different terms of office, the constitution practically assured that no president could come into office in control of the legislative branch of government. Another provision in the constitution assigned the Congress the responsibility to choose the president "from among the citizens who have received the two highest relative numbers of votes"—if no candidate received a majority of the popular vote. In Chile's multiparty system, this provision gave Congress considerable leverage in "preconfirmation" bargaining with the two candidates who got the most votes in presidential elections. This leverage would prove significant time and time again in constraining or compromising the action of in-coming Chilean presidents. Thus while the 1925 constitution did decrease congressional authority and remove some of the traditional instruments whereby the Congress had controlled executive initiatives, it did not emasculate the Congress or eliminate its critical role in Chilean politics.

Shortly after Alessandri returned to Santiago, he presided over still another massacre of northern workers. At La Coruña, in June 1925, soldiers machine-gunned more than 1200 workers, destroyed their living quarters with field artillery, and brutally murdered a number of prisoners and wounded. A leading Socialist, historian, and politician, Alejandro Chelén Rojas, coldly notes that "San Gregorio in 1921 and Coruña in 1925 stamped with workers' blood the administration of the caudillo who [instead of] a 'threat to reactionary spirits' was [a threat] for the dispossessed that had so many hopes for his government." Other historians have noted that Alessandri attempted to prevent Ibáñez from using force against the workers, but Ibáñez ignored Alessandri's orders, just as he had rejected the President's order to resign his ministerial post before the presidential elections. When Ibáñez published a public letter to Alessandri on October 1, 1925, explaining his refusal to resign, including his role as "chief of the revolution," Alessandri resigned the presidency for the second time. Just before his resignation, he appointed Luis Barros Borgoño—his opponent in the presidential elections of 1920—minister of the interior, and thus Barros Borgoño was the Vice President after Alessandri's departure.

In the face of Alessandri's resignation, Ibáñez declared he would renounce his own candidacy if the major parties could agree upon a compromise candidate and avoid the spectacle of a complete return to politics as usual. The labor movement and leftist parties refused to comply, fomenting strikes and supporting their own candidate for the presidency, José Santos Salas. The traditional parties selected Emiliano Figueroa Larraín, a nondescript politician from a good family.

Figueroa Larraín easily won the election but failed to implement the spirit or the letter of the new constitution. Sensing his inability to deal with the realities facing the country or to control the minister of interior, Carlos Ibáñez, Figueroa Larraín requested permission to take a leave of absence from the country. This left affairs of state in the hands of Ibáñez. In May 1927, Figueroa Larraín officially resigned, whereupon Ibáñez had himself elected president in a carefully controlled election. Ibáñez obtained more than 222,000 of the slightly more than 230,000 votes cast.

Ibáñez's assumption of the presidency was blessed with far more auspicious economic developments than those confronting Alessandri in 1920. By 1924-25 international demand for nitrate had again strengthened. An all-time employment record, with more than 60,000 workers in the nitrate fields, brought renewed prosperity to the Chilean economy. Despite a recession in 1926-27 that briefly interrupted recovery, the final years of the decade saw a major boom in Chilean nitrates. Indeed, Ibáñez and his chief economic adviser, Pablo Ramírez, could take credit for the economic recovery that put most of the 70,000 unemployed in mid-1926 back to work by 1928. In the meantime, police monitored political and union activity and reported to Ibáñez and his ministers on the speeches or meetings of congressmen, politicians, and union leaders who seemed to oppose the regime. Reorganization of the national police (*carabineros*) under the minister of defense provided Ibáñez with a new, direct instrument for control of the opposition and a counterpoise to would-be challengers within the army.

Expanded production of copper added to the government's sources of revenue and to the economic recovery. So, too, did a large-scale influx of foreign capital in the form of private investment and loans. Total foreign investment in the country increased from $723 million in 1925 to more than $1 billion in 1930—exceeding domestic investment in both mining and industry. Taking advantage of increasing government revenues and the inflows of private foreign capital, the Ibáñez government embarked upon the largest public works program in Chilean history. Docks and port works, roads, sewage systems, water systems, and irrigation projects dotted the landscape from north to south. Construction of public buildings and paving of urban streets altered the faces of the nation's principal cities and employed thousands of workers. Dramatic expansion and reform of the educational system meant that in a decade Chile's schools had doubled their capacity. In an effort to encourage industry, the government pushed protective tariffs through Congress and founded the Institute for Industrial Credit. Previously the emphasis upon real estate as collateral for loans had seriously restricted access by domestic industrialists to investment capital. Industry responded to the new incentives with increased output and even some diversification.

This flurry of economic activity distracted most Chileans from the political repression of the Ibáñez regime. Also obscured was the growing indebtedness as a result of the large loans the government had contracted to finance the expansion of public sector activity. After years of sterile parliamentary debate and indifference, Ibáñez even managed to squeeze legislation on agricultural colonization and "land reform" out of the Congress in 1928. Establishment of the Caja de Colonización Agrícola as an agency to administer land purchases and subdivision of large estates marked an important first step, at least symbolically, in dealing with the structural defects of the Chilean agrarian economy. Despite the Caja's limited activity, even this innovation was rabidly denounced by leading Chilean land-owners.

In additional ways also the Ibáñez government represented a break with the parliamentary era. Technicians and middle-class professionals staffed growing ministries and public agencies previously manned overwhelmingly through political patronage by the traditional parties. In 1931 intellectuals and professional administrators in the Labor Department produced the Labor Code which incorporated the "social laws" of 1924 and created an elaborate framework for a modern industrial relations system. The Labor Code of 1931 served as the foundation for Chilean industrial relations for the next four decades.

Adoption of the "social laws" of 1924 regulating unionization, labor contracts, cooperatives, and social security had been followed by confusion. Following civil code tradition, all legislation required implementing provisions. These came slowly. Government officials and employers interpreted the laws pushed through Congress by the military coup quite differently from place to place. The Labor Code of 1931 consolidated existing legislation, including the "social laws" of 1924, and added regulations concerning agricultural workers and domestics, both of whom had been excluded from the earlier legislation. The code also established a national system of labor courts, as well as institutions to administer mandatory collective bargaining and arbitration (*juntas de conciliación*).

In general the Labor Code created a highly paternalistic and authoritarian system of government-worker relations. The code limited worker petitions and strikes to individual firms and restricted severely the activity of union federations. It gave authority to the government to order a "return to work" whenever a strike or lockout endangered public health or the economic or social life of the nation. Any labor conflict that failed to meet the rigorous requirements specified in the code could be declared illegal, and the unions were liable for any damages or losses under such circumstances. In practice these restrictive regulations meant that from 1932 on, illegal strikes outnumbered legal ones by a wide margin.

Notwithstanding the Labor Code's defects from the perspective of labor, it represented formal recognition by the Chilean state of the right of workers to organize, to petition employers for improved working conditions, to strike, and to have the work place regulated by an official agency—the Labor Department. Employers now had the obligation to enter into written contracts with workers, to bargain with unions, to obey labor legislation and social security laws and, more generally, to adopt a more limited view of the privileges of proprietorship. The Labor Code ended the classical liberal view of unrestricted property rights. The resistance of employer associations and landowners to the code's provisions testified to their awareness of its profound implications. Above all else, the Labor Code meant that the state recognized its role as an active agent in regulating class conflict and in institutionalizing procedures for managing the social question.

Ibáñez did not undertake these reforms out of benevolence or a desire to win the support of the labor movement. As with labor codes in Brazil under Vargas or later in Peronist Argentina, the Labor Code was seen as a means to control the labor movement, to subordinate it to the state, and to cleanse it of leftists and Marxists. Ibáñez used the police and army to persecute FOCH, the Communist party, and the anarchists. He also exiled leaders of the major political parties who objected to his restriction of civil liberties, to his intimidation of the press, his overt manipulation of Congress, and his disdain for the old politics. Many conservative Chileans, to whom the fascist-corporative governments of Primo de Rivera in Spain or Benito Mussolini in Italy seemed to offer a welcome relief from liberal democracy, fully supported Ibáñez's repression of popular movements and organizations. They applauded government officials who praised fascism in Italy and the ability of fascist regimes to direct economic growth and to curtail the corruption of liberal democracy. They also appreciated the regime's emphasis on work, order, and discipline. Ibáñez seemed to offer a version of the Portalian state adapted to the conditions of the twentieth century. Initially, many middle-class reformers also supported Ibáñez due to his emphasis on economic reforms, industrialization, agricultural colonization, and labor legislation.

An explicitly authoritarian, corporative orientation combined with a commitment to reform the apparatus of the Chilean state led both to significant policy innovations and lamentable abuses. Ibáñez transformed Congress into a captive, generally compliant assembly, thereby eliminating the central axis of traditional politics. He also created a government-controlled organization, the Republican Confederation for Civic Action, or CRAC, to replace existing labor organizations and the multiplicity of political parties of the pre-1927 period and thus sought to eliminate the influence of traditional and reformist political parties and to control the labor movement in an authoritarian style which later became common among the populist regimes in Latin America. In this effort Ibáñez ultimately failed, but there can be no question that his presidency represented a brief return to the ideals and methods of Portales—a swing of the pendulum away from liberalism and constitutional government. Eschewing "politics" and concentrating upon "cleansing" Chile by "cauterization," in both economic and political policies he established a precedent for another military dictatorship—much more brutal—in the mid-1970s. Like his successors in the 1970s, Ibáñez rejected liberal democracy, detested radicalism, and blamed politics for Chile's decadence.

If in many respects Ibáñez broke with the old order, the dependence of his government programs upon nitrate and copper revenues, along with increased levels of foreign investment and loans, made the regime as vulnerable to fluctuations in international markets as any Chilean administration since 1879. The stock market crash of 1929 soon paralyzed Chile's finances and wreaked havoc on the economy. Government efforts to form a new cartel called the Compañia de Salitre de Chile, or COSACH, in cooperation with the Guggenheim interests, brought criticism from economic nationalists and opponents of the government. It also failed to stem the effects of the depression. The value of copper and nitrate exports declined from over 200 million pesos in 1929 to 18.1 million in 1932; over 50,000 workers lost their jobs in the nitrate fields alone. Imports declined by over 75 percent in the same period, making Chile in this respect the country most seriously affected by the international depression. The government could not service outstanding loans or obtain new lines of credit. In February 1931, Congress extended Ibáñez's emergency powers to deal with the economic crisis; in May, Ibáñez declared he would maintain order by force of arms. Wage cuts for government personnel and the military followed, along with new income taxes, an increase in inheritance taxes, a moratorium on public works, and dismissals of public employees. These economy moves simply worsened the effects of the depression and added to unemployment. In July the government suspended service on the foreign debt in foreign currency—since the country's reserves were practically depleted. Poor harvests in 1931-32 added to the misery.

By late 1931 the government's program to disperse the northern unemployed in the agricultural regions or to shelter them in temporary barracks called *albergues* in the urban areas seemed a dreadful failure. The nation simply did not have the resources to provide relief for the thousands of unemployed and their families. Illustrative is the following excerpt from a report by the intendant of Talca to the minister of interior in January 1932:

> Apprised of government plans to begin shortly the distribution of 2000 families of unemployed workers throughout the central and southern provinces, I hasten, with all due respect, to make the following observations. . . .
>
> In Talca, without counting those unregistered by the Secretaria de Bienestar Social, there are more than 5000 unemployed, of which more than 700 along with their families are in the *albergues;* others are camped in emergency shelters along the roads and at the sites of public works, living off the small amount that good-hearted people can supply.
>
> In the countryside the poverty is much worse. The landowners have cut back their work to the minimum. . . . With the lack of capital, poor harvests, and drastic decline in prices, agriculture faces a total collapse. Many have no way to pay salaries, but they give their *inquilinos* milk in the morning and hot meals at noon, though they don't work.

. . . I visited nearby zones some days ago and saw tragedies
of hunger and misery that can't be described.

. . . For this reason it seems unlikely to me that the efforts by
the government to place the unemployed in agriculture will have
any success.

By the end of 1931 the director of the Labor Department reported to
the minister of social welfare that "The situation of the unemployed
is simply terrible in Iquique, Coquimbo, Ovalle, Calera, Santiago,
Talca, and Talcahuano. . . . The city of Santiago is so congested
with unemployed—that, with all the efforts we have made, there are
an enormous quantity of families that, as in the rest of the Republic,
have been violently evicted from their dwellings and live in unhealthy
makeshift shelters [ranchos]." In the same letter the director noted
that the government's cutbacks in public works and railroad activity
aggravated the crisis; the latter decision also negatively affected coal
production in the Lota region.

The concentration of unemployed in urban areas not only stretched
government relief efforts but also threatened public order. Intermittent attempts by the government to eradicate particular albergues
and disperse more workers into the rural regions met stiff resistance.
In turn, industrial and commercial interests in some cities petitioned
the government for more protection against "ill-intentioned individuals [maleantes] who sought to subvert public order."

Civilian and military opposition to the regime became bolder with
the government's apparent weakness. In late July 1931 a "general
strike" by professional associations, white-collar workers, and students demanded a return to constitutional government. As the cabinet decided to close all banks to prevent conversion of money into
foreign currency and to impose controls on foreign exchange, doctors
in Santiago went out on strike and vowed not to resume practice until Ibáñez resigned. Violence in the streets, resurgence of political opposition in all sectors including the military, and the insoluble economic dilemma forced Ibáñez to resign from office on July 26, 1931.

For the seventeen months following Ibáñez' resignation, the country suffered through several civilian and military governments of

varying political tendencies, including the famous "100 days" of a Chilean "Socialist Republic," under the alternating leadership of Marmaduque Grove, Carlos Dávila, and an alliance with the newly formed socialist movement called Nueva Acción Pública, or "New Public Action." International economic conditions put unmanageable strains on any national government, while lack of political consensus denied all the military and civilian-military coalitions sufficient support to impose order or to direct economic recovery. In September 1931 conservative civilian politicians and the commander of the Chilean armed forces requested military assistance from the United States in order to put down a naval mutiny supposedly inspired by "communistic" elements. In conversations with the American ambassador, the Chilean commander emphasized the serious nature of the "imminent danger of social war" and referred to the continental, rather than local, character of the communistic activities that he believed threatened the nation. Handcuffed by a 1922 treaty limiting transfer of naval armaments, the United States nevertheless expressed a willingness to supply other material should the Chilean government make a formal request. United States representatives also expressed their "appreciation of the desires of the Chilean government to maintain order and stable institutions and to protect American interests in Chile. . . ."

Using airpower to defeat the naval mutiny, the Chilean government withdrew its request for American military assistance but, according to the American ambassador, subsequently asked for "a specialist in communistic propaganda and activities in order to assist in ferreting out the ramifications and origins of the movement in Chile." The State Department replied that "this Government regrets that there is not available in the Government service a specialist whose services it could offer. . . ."

The confusion following Ibáñez's ouster ultimately produced a significant realignment of political forces on an explicitly Left-Right ideological continuum. Small socialist movements merged to form the Socialist party (1933); a split between Trotzkyists and Stalinists divided the Communist party; splinter groups from existing parties created the Radical Socialist party (ex-Radicals), the Democrat party, or, Partido Democrático (ex-members of the Partido Demó-crata), and the center-right Agrarian party (ex-Liberals and Radi-cals). These divisions and realignments introduced new personalities and new energy into Chilean politics while setting the stage for polit-ical struggle during the next four decades.

In the short term, however, six different governments "controlled" the country within a 101-day period in 1932. Seeking to end the cha-otic situation—and with much of the officer corps disillusioned with the military role in politics—General Bartolomé Blanche assumed provisional executive authority and scheduled the presidential elec-tion for October, 1932.

Contested among candidates representing the spectrum of politi-cal opinion, the presidential elections restored civilian government to Chile and returned Arturo Alessandri to the presidency. Alessandri obtained 184,754 of the 339,709 votes cast, while 20 percent of the electorate supported the socialist (Marmaduke Grove) or the Com-munist (Elías Lafertte) candidate. Subsequently the Left pressed Alessandri for social reforms, thereby restoring the social question to center stage in Chilean politics. In turn the Right sought restoration or reaffirmation of their status and privileges—which had been chal-lenged by certain policies of the Ibáñez administration as well as by the "Socialist Republic."

At the depths of the depression and in the midst of political uncer-tainty, no one could have forecast that for the next forty years Chile would be the only Latin American nation without illegal changes of government and with a system of formal democracy. Neither could anyone have predicted, despite increasing American economic inter-est in Chile, the major role United States policy would play in Chile's internal political development over the next four decades.

Chapter 8 • Chilean Democracy

Chile's political instability between 1920 and 1932 gave way to four decades of legally elected civilian governments. From 1932 until September 1973 Chile was the only Latin American nation in which competitive party politics, uninterrupted by coups, assassinations, or revolutions, determined the occupants of the presidency, Congress, and higher policymaking positions in the national bureaucracy. The same political parties competing at the national level also vied for control of local government institutions and for influence in national and regional student federations, labor unions, and other community or class organizations. Direct election of the president according to the provisions of the 1925 constitution made the selection of the chief executive a truly national event.

Incorporation of women (1949) and illiterates (1970) into the electoral registers increased by more than 300 percent the population eligible to vote. Improved literacy rates (50%, 1930; 75%, 1960), increased political awareness among working classes, and mandatory registration and voting did much to increase the number of voters in national elections. Important electoral reforms in 1958 and 1962 liberated the votes of rural workers from the control of landlords and reduced the possibility of vote buying and election fraud, thereby extending effective suffrage to practically the entire adult population. The Chilean political system during these years combined multiparty politics with presidential government. Unlike a parliamentary system, governments did not "fall." Presidents served six-year terms, and during these six years cabinet shifts could reflect new party alliances or an executive decision to govern with a "nonpolitical" cabinet of technical experts or even a cabinet of personal loyalists. But the extreme fragmentation of the party system made it difficult for presidents to control legislative action or even to maintain the total support of their own party. Despite the increased authority of the president under the 1925 constitution, the old tensions between the legislature and the executive characteristic of the parliamentary period still played an important role in national politics.

Political tension between the president and the Congress did not mean total stalemate, but it did impose a certain constraint on the ability of presidents to implement the electoral platform upon which they campaigned. Since presidential electoral platforms generally contained more "Left" or populist planks than the Congress would accept, the growing frustration among leftist members of presidential coalitions meant their eventual collapse, and a gradual drift of policy toward the Right during each president's term of office. Thus Congress allowed Conservatives, Liberals, moderate and traditional Radicals, and certain middle-class business interests to limit the reformist projects of presidential coalitions.

Control over the votes of rural labor assured the Conservative and the Liberal parties, along with some Radicals, of enough congressional seats to retain important veto power over presidential programs. The "stability" of Chilean formal democracy, therefore, depended upon the continued dominance of the landowners over the votes and the political activity of their farm work force. This dominance, in turn, depended upon maintenance of the hacienda system through the prevention of rural unionization and the exclusion of outside political influences.

Recurrent challenges to the hacienda system after 1930 threatened to upset Chile's political stability. The urban labor movement and Marxist political parties made periodic efforts to encourage agricultural unionism and to wrest control of rural votes from the landowners. Every national administration, however, relied upon a complex system of economic and political subsidies to the landowners, including the repression of the rural labor movement, in order to install and preserve Chilean formal democracy. And, much to their later, self-confessed distress, Communists and Socialists colluded in elaborating an "arrangement" that made maintenance of the hacienda system and exploitation of rural labor the cornerstone in the edifice of Chilean formal democracy.

The world depression of the early 1930s marked the beginning of a period in Chilean history when more than ever before internal developments responded to international economic and political movements. Disruption of foreign trade radically reduced the nation's import capabilities and stimulated a process of industrialization aimed at providing basic consumer goods and substitutes for other imported manufactured goods. Chilean manufacturers rejected liberal economic principles in regard to international trade and urged upon the government policies to encourage local production. Import quotas, licenses, tariff barriers, currency devaluation, and a complicated system of multiple exchange controls discriminated against foreign commodities. These measures limited the availability of foreign goods or made them prohibitively expensive, thereby forcing Chilean consumers to turn to newly established or expanding domestic firms. Import-substitution industrialization reduced manufactured goods from 50 percent of the value of Chilean imports in 1925 to only 16 percent in 1969—with imports in the latter year largely capital goods and high technology items.

In the years after 1930, utilizing imported foreign technology, capital goods, and primary or semiprocessed inputs for industry, Chile created a significant industrial sector, whose structure and composition altered as the predominance of agricultural-based firms (60 percent of total manufacturing income and 47 percent of employment in 1938) ended. Growth of the textile, chemical and petrochemicals, cement, and metal sectors—among other non-agricultural-based manufacturers—reduced the employment share of the agricultural-based firms to 35 percent in 1961. Overall, though the employment share of industry rose only from 17 percent in 1940 to approximately 20 percent in 1970, the absolute number of workers in industry almost doubled. By 1970 more than 560,000 Chileans earned their living in industrial employment, and this industrial labor force was becoming more significant in Chile's political life.

Government measures to stimulate industrialization led also to a significant increase in the size of the state bureaucracy. New credit institutions, exchange control commissions, and boards to regulate agricultural exports and establish retail price controls, added a network of governmental intervention in the national economy. Creation of a national development corporation (CORFO) in 1939 and the subsequent establishment of public and mixed-venture enterprises, as well as semi-autonomous "decentralized" public agencies in housing, school construction, agricultural extension, and social security entailed an even more significant amplification of the role of the state in defining the direction and character of national economic development.*

Not only did new state institutions indicate the changing role of national government in Chilean society, but they also created new employment opportunities for a growing group of salaried professionals and white-collar workers. The political implications of thousands of attractive government jobs were not lost on the political parties in their efforts to capture legislative majorities or to form government coalitions. By the early 1940s the public sector accounted for more than 50 percent of all internal investment capital, and in the years 1930-49 public employment more than doubled—a rate of increase twice that in mining or agriculture and 32 percent above even industry and construction. These developments provided the basis for the

---

* Between 1942 and 1952 these semi-autonomous, decentralized agencies gradually acquired their own legal identity and varying incomes derived from their own activities, apart from additional appropriations from the national budget.

consolidation of a bureaucratic "middle class" associated with an interventionist state. It would mean that a large proportion of the middle groups in Chilean society, both civilian and military, would support a further expansion of public activity in welfare, health care, education, and government-owned enterprises. If government activism meant marginal benefits for the working classes, it meant employment for the graduates of secondary schools, technical schools, and universities. Employment in the central administration more than tripled between 1925 and 1965, while national population barely doubled; this 300 percent increase in public employment did not include those holding positions in the semi-autonomous public enterprises such as the national airline (LAN) or national petroleum industry (ENAP).

In contrast to the aspirations and predictions of Chilean proponents of industrialization, however, significant industry did not mean

TABLE 7. GROWTH OF VOTER PARTICIPATION IN
PRESIDENTIAL ELECTIONS, 1925-70

Year	Total Votes Cast	Voters Registered	Percent of Population Registered to Vote	Total Population
1925	260,895	302,212	7.4	4,073,000
1927	233,103	302,142	7.2	4,188,000
1931	285,810	388,959	8.8	4,429,000
1932	343,892	429,772	9.0	4,495,000
1938	443,898	503,871	10.2	4,914,000
1942	466,507	581,486	11.1	5,244,000
1946	479,019	631,527	11.2	5,643,000
1952	955,102	1,105,029	17.6*	6,303,000
1958	1,250,437	1,521,272	20.8	7,316,000
1964	2,530,697	2,915,121	34.3	8,503,000
1970	2,954,799	3,539,747	37.0	9,566,000

* Including women for the first time in a presidential election.

(Source: Instituto Nacional de Estadísticas, Demografía, Chile, 1969; and Fernando Silva Sánchez, Los Partidos Políticos Chilenos, Viña del Mar, Chile: Imprenta Lourdes, 1972. After Edward W. Glab, Jr., "Christian Democracy, Marxism and Revolution in Chile: The Election and Overthrow of Salvador Allende," unpublished doctoral dissertation, Northern Illinois University, 1975, p. 148.)

increased economic independence. Wars in Europe, Korea, and Vietnam, international business cycles, and a complex, sophisticated network of multinational enterprises operating within a still more complicated international metals market limited Chilean economic performance. American, European, and multinational financial institutions determined the availability of credit and foreign investment for Chilean development.

Foreign corporations owned the principal enterprises that earned foreign exchange for the nation. Since intricate bargaining procedures among industrial consumers, the copper firms, and the United States government fixed the prices for these companies' copper output, production of increasing quantities of manufactured consumer goods did little to alter the historical reliance by Chile upon the export of one or several minerals. Indeed the combination of copper dependency and dependence upon foreign technology, capital goods, credit, investment funds, and technicians to carry out the process of industrialization made Chilean domestic development ever more vulnerable to external economic forces and to foreign manipulation.

Not only economic dependence increased in the period after 1930. International power struggles and ideological divisions conditioned Chilean politics. In the early 1930s a clear Left-Center-Right system of political cleavage replaced the old politics of factions, personalist cliques, and traditional party alignments. Marxism, liberalism, social Catholicism, and fascism all had supporters in Chile. The popular front, the Spanish Civil War, and nazism all influenced Chilean politics in the 1930s and 1940s. After World War II the so-called Cold

TABLE 8. EMPLOYMENT IN PUBLIC SECTOR, CENTRAL ADMINISTRATION

Year	Number
1925	32,877
1935	41,266
1945	59,645
1955	75,542
1965	109,699

(Source: Germán Urzua Valenzuela and Ana María García Barzelatto, *Diagnóstico de la burocracia Chilena 1818-1969*, Editorial Jurídica, Santiago, 1971.)

War drew United States agents and diplomats directly into Chilean politics in efforts to influence elections, manipulate labor organizations, disseminate American policy perspectives, and defend American investments. Likewise, the Soviet Union and Eastern European nations contributed funds and ideological orientation and direction for the country's Marxist parties and labor organizations. Although Soviet expenditures and influence in Chile never approximated that of the United States, the effects of Cold War rhetoric and the global confrontation between capitalist "free world" nations and the Soviet bloc gradually permeated Chilean society at all levels.

If the process of industrialization between 1932 and 1964 did not free Chile from dependence upon copper exports, foreign investment, or the fluctuations in the international economy, it did accelerate the trends toward urbanization and rural stagnation evident in the first decades of the twentieth century. Employment opportunities in industry attracted migrants from the countryside to major manufacturing centers in Santiago, Valparaíso, Concepción-Talcahuano, and other provincial centers such as Temuco and Talca. Even more than expanded economic opportunity in industry, however, the worsening conditions of labor in Chilean agriculture motivated rural workers and youths to flee the countryside. Real wages for rural workers declined by approximately 18 percent between 1940 and 1952 and by another 38 percent between 1953 and 1960. Tenant agricultural laborers (*inquilinos*) suffered a decrease in quantity and/or quality of land allotments and other non-cash perquisites such as rights to pasture animals, firewood, and food rations. Landlords supplied a lesser share of seed, fertilizer, or other inputs. In the period 1940/44–1950/54 the real earnings of sharecroppers and tenants declined by 27 percent, while landowners achieved a real gain in earnings of 33 percent. Indeed, the price of labor in agriculture declined relative to all other inputs between 1940 and 1960. Combined with the declining real income of agricultural labor, the rising real wages of blue-collar workers in manufacturing during the same period (1940/44–1950/54) accelerated the exodus from the countryside. Whereas total population approximately doubled from 1920 to 1960 (see Table 9), rural population increased by less than 18 percent. By 1960 more than half of all Chileans lived in cities of twenty thousand or more, well above the comparable figures for all major world areas except North America and Oceania.

Underlying these demographic and economic trends could be found a complex, contradictory set of political arrangements that permitted the most traditional social and economic institutions in the nation, the large rural estates, to survive intact through four decades of dramatic social change and economic modernization. To a great extent the survival of the hacienda system and its extensive subsidization by the state represented the trade-off between Marxists, reformers, and traditional political interests that permitted the establishment and maintenance of Chile's vaunted "stability" and "democracy." Whenever this trade-off was threatened, political toleration ended. When the large estates finally faced their demise in the period after 1964, so too did Chilean formal democracy.

Arturo Alessandri returned to the presidency in 1932 determined to implement the 1925 constitution, to establish the legitimate prerogatives of the presidency detailed in that document, and to carry out the main provisions of the Labor Code. In contrast to his earlier administration, Alessandri now eschewed incendiary rhetoric in favor of appeals to national unity. He appointed ministers without the

TABLE 9. DEMOGRAPHIC CHANGES IN CHILE, 1920-60

	1920	1930	1940	1950	1960
Total Population	3,785,000	4,365,000	5,063,000	6,295,000	7,628,136
Rural Population		2,185,800	2,421,300	2,530,400	2,650,500
Population in Cities, 20,000 plus, as percent of total population in Chile	28	32	35	43	51
Population in Cities, 20,000 plus, as percent of total population in Latin America	14	17	20	25	33

traditional overriding concern with party coalitions and managed to retain key ministers for four or five years of his six-year term—a feat almost unheard of in the days of parliamentary government. The emphasis on national unity, order, economic recovery, and constitutional rule gradually pushed the President into an ever more explicit alliance with the Right—the forces that had the most to gain from "law and order."

Faced with the depression-induced unemployment crisis, the continual threat of new military intervention, and the growing militance of socialist and communist movements, Alessandri allowed, even encouraged, the activity of white guards, called the "Republican Militia." According to the United States State Department files, in May 1933 President Alessandri personally reviewed a public parade of forty-two regiments of well-armed and equipped militiamen as it passed La Moneda, the presidential palace. As both a temporary counterbalance to the military and a threat to leftist movements, the militia played a significant role in polarizing Chilean politics until 1936 when the President ordered its dissolution. By then, the President's trusted military commander, General Oscar Novoa, had crushed an attempted coup in December 1933 and, through careful duty assignments and retirement of officers deemed too "political," had gradually brought the officer corps under presidential control.

Neutralizing the military threat eliminated one of the most difficult problems facing the administration. An upturn in the international economy and cautious domestic policy ameliorated the economic situation. Notwithstanding the government's extremely conservative fiscal policies, greater demand for copper and nitrates, the surge of industrial growth, and incentives to the private construction industry pulled the country out of the depths of the depression. Under the direction of arch-conservative Minister of Treasury Gustavo Ross, the administration reduced expenditures upon public works by almost 50 percent from 1932 to 1934; nevertheless official unemployment had practically disappeared by the end of 1935. In response to legislation passed at the end of 1933 allowing tax exemptions for a period of ten years on all buildings initiated before De-

TABLE 10. NUMBER OF UNEMPLOYED, DECEMBER 1932-DECEMBER 1937

1932	262,445
1933	132,642
1934	38,309
1935	13,601
1936	15,701
1937	15,829

(Source: *Legislación social y sindicatos legales en Chile*, Editorial Ginebra, Santiago n.d., CCCVI.)

cember 1935, construction increased by 40 percent in 1934 alone. This incentive not only balanced the deflationary effect of reduced public works but also renewed confidence in the private sector concerning the government's attitude toward private investment. Following on this legislation, a new public works program in 1936, focusing especially upon construction of roads, hospitals, and schools, accelerated economic recovery. Combined with construction in industry and the upturn in the export market, these projects alleviated most of the unemployment existing when Alessandri took office in 1932.

Inflation accompanied recovery. Price increases seemed to outpace salary gains, and a government freeze on salaries in the public sector alienated public employees. Failure of agriculture to provision adequately the urban centers and mining regions confronted the government with a dilemma that would underlie the contradictions in domestic political economy for the next forty years. With an ever more politicized and expanding urban labor movement, rising food prices spelled trouble for the incumbent government. Efforts to control food prices without a significant per capita increase in agricultural production required administrative controls on retail prices. Decree Law 520 of August 1932 created the General Commissariat of Subsistence and Prices, or Comisariato General de Subsistencia y Precios. Although this decree was promulgated during the brief reign of the "Socialist Republic," its major provisions remained in effect into the 1970s. It gave the General Commissariat authority to set prices for a wide range of goods considered of "basic necessity." It also extended authority to the General Commissariat to take charge of distribution

TABLE 11. LEGAL AND ILLEGAL STRIKES IN CHILE, 1932-57

Year	Legal Strikes	Personnel/ Workers Involved	Illegal Strikes	Personnel/ Workers Involved
1932	3	500*	3	100*
1933	7	648	3	100
1934	2	100	11	3,000
1935	10	1,197	20	4,236
1936	4	4,781	16	2,977
1937	4	460	17	2,569
1938	6	7,954	9	3,419
1939	20	5,674	6	5,249
1940	20	8,235	25	10,576
1941	15	2,041	16	890
1942	7	671	12	2,062
1943	26	1,897	101	46,832
1944	38	14,039	53	17,249
1945	36	32,334	112	66,612
1946	27	18,262	169	76,475
1947	37	17,887	127	51,652
1948	20	7,172	6	1,203
1949†	23	6,533	24	8,711
1950	28	12,058	164	41,833
1951	30	12,718	150	47,443
1952	45	28,073	156	89,566
1953	60	54,628	148	68,480
1954	61	25,009	247	49,687
1955	62	23,062	212	104,370
1956	25	5,138	122	95,300
1957	12	8,722	68	17,616

* Approximate figure.
† Year after implementation of Law for Permanent Defense of Democracy.

(Source: Chilean Labor Department, Annual Report 1948, and yearly, 1949-1958.)

of basic commodities, to expropriate or intervene in the administration of firms that refused to cooperate with government economic policies, to requisition production under specified conditions, and otherwise to regulate the operation of private firms. The more drastic provisions of this decree rarely were utilized from 1932 until the 1970s—when the Unidad Popular government, headed by President Salvador Allende, resorted to the terms of the 1932 decree to accelerate a program to transform Chile into a socialist society. From 1932 on, however, the government's authority to regulate the price of basic necessities created an expectation among the population that incumbent regimes would control the rate of inflation.

Along with the General Commissariat, the Junta de Exportación Agrícola was created to promote agricultural exports and otherwise to benefit producers; it also soon came under pressure from urban political forces. In times of rising prices and "food shortages" the labor movement and leftist political parties demanded restrictions on exports of agricultural commodities. In addition, the Junta de Exportación Agrícola, theoretically taking into account changing production costs, set floor prices for wheat. Inevitably, decisions on wheat prices were reflected in the price of bread—the basic food of the Chilean working classes. This made every price decision by the junta critical politically: it angered either producers or consumers.

Meanwhile, the increasing strength of the Socialist, Communist, and Radical parties and the growth of the labor movement during the second Alessandri administration made it politically impossible to ignore entirely pressures for price controls in urban areas. President Alessandri strongly favored the development of the *legal* union movement under the terms of the Labor Code, since he saw the code as a major result of his own zeal in the 1920s. Accordingly the administration supported efforts by the Labor Department to encourage the organization of legal unions. The unions in turn pressed for lower food prices. This meant a clash with agricultural interests.

Successful implementation of price controls and a restrictive agricultural export policy depended upon artificial depression of producer prices for agricultural commodities. Only gradually did succeeding administrations elaborate a complex array of direct and indirect subsidies to the landowners—including negative interest rates on credit, low freight rates on state railroads, exemption from import duties on farm machinery, export bounties, and exceedingly low tax rates on land and income. However, the most important trade-off in the arrangement that came to reconcile the conflicting interests of industrialists, urban workers, salaried middle-class groups, and landowners emerged quite soon after Alessandri assumed office.

Discrimination against the rural labor movement and repression of agricultural unionism would allow a superficial reconciliation of the contradictory interests of urban labor, reformist political movements, and the traditional landed elite.

From the end of 1932 until December 1938 the number of legal unions in Chile more than doubled, and membership rose from 54,000 to more than 125,000. At the same time, industrial relations gradually conformed to the provisions of the Labor Code as the technocrats of the Labor Department successfully channeled class conflict within the institutions established by the code. An exception to this trend, the predominance of illegal strikes over legal strikes, reflected the overly restrictive nature of the legislation regulating work stoppages; this exception did not prevent effective institutionalization of the procedures for labor disputes. Whereas prior to 1924 labor disputes represented a revolutionary challenge to the parliamentary system, the Alessandri administration (1932-38) most effectively established administrative capabilities for *routine* handling of worker-employer collective bargaining. The underlying revolutionary issues of the social question seemed to evaporate as unions and their political allies accepted the legitimacy of the *juntas de conciliación* and the labor courts.

Only in agriculture did employers *en masse* refuse to recognize the legitimacy of unionization and the very applicability of the Labor Code. In sharp contrast to his generalized commitment to implement the Labor Code, President Alessandri also discouraged agricultural unionization. Unfortunately for Alessandri, leading officials within the Labor Department, among them some who had helped to write the Labor Code, attempted to fulfill their duty by applying the terms of the code in the countryside. This included efforts to force landowners to introduce written contracts with all their workers, to pay social security taxes as the law required, and, most significant, to unionize agricultural labor.

The implications of a unionized agricultural labor force associated with reformist and Marxist political parties threatened not only the economic basis of Chilean agriculture but also the control of landowners over the votes of their agricultural tenants, sharecroppers, and resident laborers—votes that guaranteed the presence of rightist forces in the Congress.

The response to this threat by the Alessandri administration and the National Agricultural Society (SNA) provided the foundation for the political "solution" to the problems posed by rapid urbanization, industrialization, growth of the urban labor movement, and inflation. If rural labor could be forced to bear most of the costs of price controls discriminating against agriculture, and if landowners could be spared the inconvenience and cost of compliance with labor laws—while maintaining political control over the rural work force—then political "stability" could be maintained and the threat of discontent or violence in the cities could be reduced.

In response to initial unionization efforts in vineyards in Talca province and a small number of farms near Santiago in 1932 and 1933, the SNA protested to the Labor Department and to President Alessandri that the unionization provisions of the Labor Code did not apply to agriculture. Significantly, both the Labor Department and the Consejo de Defensa Fiscal, a kind of administrative supreme court, ruled against the landowners. The Labor Department concluded that "there is no doubt that the agricultural worker has the complete right to unionize." Taking its case directly to President Alessandri, however, the SNA secured a reversal of the Labor Department's decision in the form of an ambiguously worded telegram sent to all the department's offices:

> This Department, in conjunction with the government, is studying activities related to the unionization of workers in rural properties. Since there exist complex difficulties in carrying out these legal provisions, this Department orders you to refrain from assisting in the constitution of organizations of this type until you receive definite and precise instructions.

Since formation of a legal union required the presence of a labor inspector, this telegram effectively prevented organization of legal agricultural unions. No "definitive and precise" (or any other) instructions were forthcoming. True to the declarations made in his first presidential term (1920-24, 1925) when he noted the disadvantages of agricultural unionization, Alessandri's decision launched four decades of administrative, legislative, and physical repression of rural labor by successive national administrations. This repression served as the foundation of the political economy of Chilean formal democracy.

In June 1934—as if an omen of the future—*carabineros* massacred more than one hundred peasants protesting their eviction from their land in the frontier region of the upper Bío Bío. Rising in armed rebellion, the peasants of Ranquíl looted stores and threatened landowners before the national police murdered the movement's leaders and restored order. Shortly thereafter the Alessandri administration urgently requested Congress to approve new legislation on agricultural colonization, but the events at Ranquíl and the earlier action on rural unionization made clear the government's commitment to maintenance of the existing order in the countryside.

With the shift of the Alessandri government toward the Right, the most important reformist, middle-class party in Chile, the Radicals sought alliances with the Socialists and the Communists. At the urging of an agent of the Comintern, sent to Chile by the Soviets to influence the ideological orientation of the Chilean Communist party, the Chilean Communists adopted a popular front strategy. Comintern's new policy, enunciated in August 1935, told communist movements around the world that "the formation of a joint People's Front, providing for joint action with Social Democratic parties is a necessity. . . . Comrades, you will remember the ancient tale of the capture of Troy. The attacking army was unable to achieve victory until, with the aid of the Trojan Horse, it penetrated to the very heart of the enemy camp. We, revolutionary workers, should not be shy of using the same tactics."

In line with this new tactic Chilean Communists sought contacts with the ideologically divided Radical party, made efforts to reduce tension between themselves and the Socialists, and worked to form a united front against the Alessandri government. In December 1936, the Communists supported the formation of a unified national labor organization, the Confederación de Trabajadores de Chile (CTCH), headed by a Socialist secretary general, with a Communist serving as assistant secretary general. According to the agent sent by Moscow to Chile to direct the formation of the popular front movement, small favors and promises of support to selected leaders of the Radical party gradually created a nucleus of Radicals willing to include the Communists in a coalition aimed at capturing the presidency in 1938.

President Alessandri's hardening line toward the Left, his harsh repression of a railroad strike in 1936, and a growing willingness among leftist elements in the splintered Partido Demócrata, among Trotskyists, and other leftist fragments to oppose the government, produced a skeletal popular front executive committee in March 1936. Ideological diversity and the underlying distrust by Socialists and Radicals of the Communists dictated a mild declaration of objectives: restoration of democratic liberties, economic nationalism, socio-economic justice for the middle and working classes. Nevertheless, the alliance of organized labor with the popular front parties seriously threatened the political position of the Alessandri administration. One month later, by-elections for a vacant Senate seat from the provinces of Bío Bío, Malleco, and Cautín gave a surprising victory to the candidate of the Radical party.

Although the new senator was one of the wealthiest landowners in the region, national political analysts interpreted his victory as an initial indication of the viability of the popular front strategy. Despite continued reservations by more traditional leaders of the Radical party, including the party's eventual presidential candidate of 1938, Pedro Aguirre Cerda, most of the party's regional leaders sought to strengthen the popular front coalition. With upcoming congressional elections in March 1937, majority elements in the Radical party hoped through the popular front tactic to increase Radical influence. However, an intervening by-election in the northern provinces of Atacama and Coquimbo gave an unexpected victory to the Alessandrista candidate after a campaign that depicted the popular front as "a consortium organized by Moscow-bought Communists." Shortly thereafter, Radicals opposed to the popular front accepted ministerial posts in the Alessandri government.

The congressional elections of 1937 maintained rightist control in the legislature, though certain electoral trends encouraged supporters of the popular front. Both the Conservatives and the Liberals obtained higher vote totals than the Radicals, who again obtained approximately 19 percent of the ballots cast. The Communists polled only slightly more votes than the Chilean Nazi party. However, while the hold of the rightist parties over the rural districts combined with vote buying and coercion guaranteed their continued dominance in Congress, significant gains by the Socialist party helped persuade many Radicals to maintain the popular front for the up-coming presidential elections of 1938.

As the presidential election of 1938 approached, the Right chose as its standard bearer Alessandri's ex-treasury minister, Gustavo Ross Santa María. No doubts existed concerning Ross's ideological or political orientation; he represented the interests of the propertied classes. He was reputed to have answered an appeal for legislation to benefit the middle class with "for me there are but two classes, upper

TABLE 12. ELECTIONS, CHAMBER OF DEPUTIES, 1937

Party	Deputies Elected	Votes	Percent of Total Vote
Conservador	35	87,845	21.3
Liberal	35	85,515	20.8
Demócrata	7	20,026	4.9
Agrario	3	9,721	2.3
Socialista	19	46,050	11.2
Radical	29	76,941	18.7
Nacista	3	14,564	3.5
Democrático	5	18,676	4.5
Independientes	3	17,040	4.0
Acción Rep.	2	9,802	2.3
Comunista	6	17,162	4.2
Sin representación	—	9,217	2.3
Totals	147	412,812	100.0

(Source: Germán Urzua Valenzuela, Los Partidos Políticos Chilenos, Editorial Jurídica, Santiago, 1968, p. 81.)

and lower. To the first belong those who have gotten ahead in life; to the latter, those who, for whatever reason, have been failures." Ross's candidacy made clear the issues at stake in the 1938 election. An editorial in a leftist paper, *Claridad*, declared: "No one hates the people as he [Ross] does; no one is more likely to implement a 'strong' government, a government of hunger and the lash. . . . In choosing Ross, the Right has declared war on the Chilean masses." Not unexpectedly Ross's supporters compared him to Portales; the candidate's campaign slogan "Order and work" supported the historical parallel.

Divisions within the popular-front parties appeared to preclude their choosing a single candidate to contest the election against Ross. The Radical party claimed the "best right" to select a popular-front candidate; Socialists asked the front to support Marmaduque Grove, one of the leaders of the short-lived "Socialist Republic" of 1932. In a convention arranged through tough bargaining, each party nominated its candidate: Radicals, Pedro Aguirre Cerda; Socialists, Marmaduque Grove; Communists, Elías Lafferte; Demócratas, Juan Pradenas Muñoz. Six ballots later the convention appeared deadlocked. The next day, April 16, 1938, the Demócratas shifted their support to the Radical candidate; and early on April 17 the Socialists withdrew Grove, and the convention unanimously nominated Pedro Aguirre Cerda. A leader of the Radical party's anti-popular-front faction, ex-minister of interior under Alessandri in the 1920s, wealthy landowner, experienced politician—Aguirre Cerda now found himself the presidential candidate of the antifascist, popular-front movement he had originally opposed. His reluctance to accept Communist support consoled the moderate elements of the Radical party who hoped that his victory would allow them to increase their share of congressional representation and would give them access to public employment.

A bitter, violent, shrill electoral contest gave the popular-front candidate a narrow victory. Only when key military leaders informed Ross that he could not count on their support in preventing Aguirre Cerda's inauguration did the rightist candidate concede victory. The distribution of votes in the election revealed the basic sources of rightist political and economic power, as well as the critical role that continuation by the supposedly leftist government of the repression of rural labor would play in maintaining "social peace" during the next ten years. The rightist candidate defeated Aguirre Cerda overwhelmingly throughout the agricultural heartland of the central valley. Importantly, however, Communist and Socialist agents in the countryside broke enough votes away from the landlords to reduce the Right's expected margin of victory in Talca from 10,000 votes to less than 3000 and to achieve victory in Cautín. In the major cities and mining districts the popular-front candidate emerged victorious with the support of middle- and working-class voters. Radical party and Demócrata votes in parts of the frontier provinces and the lake

TABLE 13. PRESIDENTIAL ELECTION, 1938

Province	Aguirre Cerda	Ross Santa María
Tarapacá	6,164	4,162
Antofagasta	11,339	4,984
Atacama	4,834	2,580
Coquimbo	10,748	7,874
Aconcagua	4,001	7,474
Valparaíso	22,667	19,105
Santiago	64,297	50,998
O'Higgins	7,091	11,095
Colchagua	2,542	9,789
Curicó	1,950	4,805
Talca	5,717	8,485
Maule	1,934	4,817
Linares	3,592	8,764
Nuble	7,813	13,853
Concepción	17,417	9,734
Arauco	2,481	2,318
Bío Bío	6,054	6,797
Malleco	5,978	7,929
Cautín	13,125	12,228
Valdivia	12,982	10,811
Llanquihue	2,854	5,784
Aisén	412	440
Chiloé	2,513	3,257
Magallanes	4,215	526
Total	222,720	218,609

(Source: Germán Urzua Valenzuela, Los partidos políticos Chilenos, Editorial Jurídica, Santiago, 1968, p. 83.)

district provided a slim margin of victory for Aguirre Cerda or prevented a landslide for Ross. Significantly, the base of Radical power in the south consisted of landowners, industrialists, bureaucrats, and their clientele. Loss of these essentially conservative voters by the popular front, and others like them throughout the country, would have spelled defeat. To maintain their support the government would be forced to make important concessions in contradiction to his own populist rhetoric during the next three years.

Even more important, in the short run, the victory of Aguirre Cerda owed much to the unlikely last-minute support of Chilean Nazis and ex-dictator Carlos Ibáñez. In the 1938 presidential election Ibáñez again attempted to regain the presidency, railing against politicians and disorder. Supported by the Chilean Nazi party (Movimiento Nacional Socialista de Chile), Ibáñez never adopted Nazi rhetoric or uniform but could easily accept the Nazi vision of a strong state that ruled a disciplined people for the "common good." Among the Radicals and the Socialists, minority factions still remembered the Ibáñez presidency fondly. This meant that the popular-front candidate could lose enough votes to Ibáñez to permit the election of Ross.

Events leading up to the election produced an unlikely, indeed unique, alliance between the Nazis and the popular front. Disorders at the Congress when Alessandri read his last state of the union message were punctuated by shots fired toward the President by Nazi leader and deputy, González von Marées. When the government applied an internal security law against the Nazis and other demonstrators, the Ibáñez forces and the leftists united in attacking Alessandri and the Ross candidacy. Meanwhile, Ibáñez attempted to secure popular-front support for his candidacy and the withdrawal of Aguirre Cerda.

Unable to undermine Aguirre Cerda's candidacy and equally unable to muster widespread popular support for the Ibáñez candidacy, the Nazis decided to overthrow the Alessandri government with a coup. Nazi plans called for occupation of key buildings in Santiago, support from sympathetic army units, and the assassination of both rightist politicians, including Alessandri and Ross, and leaders of the popular front. Facing imprisonment by September 8, 1938, on conviction for his role in the shooting incident in Congress, the Nazi leader set September 5 as the day for the coup. Nazi youths occupied the university and seized the Social Security building.

Now after six years of constitutional government, Alessandri faced still another threat to his overriding objective: institutionalizing the 1925 constitution and maintaining political order. He responded harshly, authorizing the use of artillery against the occupants of the university. Soon after, the Nazi youths in the Social Security building surrendered to *carabineros*—who opened fire with submachine guns and small arms. More than sixty Nazi bodies were later removed from the building. A week later Alessandri requested authority from Congress to impose a state of siege for the remainder of his term. Ibáñez, who apparently had not actively participated in the coup attempt, surrendered almost immediately to army units and was jailed.

A week later Congress authorized President Alessandri to impose a state of siege and newspaper censorship and to employ other "extraordinary powers" to maintain public order. Prevented from carrying on his campaign, and promised influence in a popular-front government by Aguirre Cerda, Ibáñez withdrew his candidacy two weeks before the election. From his jail cell González von Marées endorsed the candidate of the popular front. Thus a popular front proclaiming its antifascist inspiration received part of its margin of victory from supporters of ex-dictator Carlos Ibáñez and from Chile's Nazi party.

The heterogenous electoral support that gave Aguirre Cerda the presidency, involved political contradictions incapable of resolution within the framework of formal democracy. Ibáñistas, Nazis, Communists, Socialists, and Radicals could not ultimately agree upon general policy or political methods.

President Aguirre Cerda faced several immediate crises shortly after assuming office. In January 1939 a disastrous earthquake in south-central Chile devastated Chillán, Concepción, and the neighboring provinces. Official reports counted over fifty thousand deaths and many times that number of casualties. Aguirre Cerda reacted quickly, declaring martial law in the affected provinces and organizing relief efforts. International assistance from Europe, the United States, and neighboring countries permitted quick restoration of basic services and transport. A week later, taking advantage of the urgent need to provide for reconstruction, the President presented Congress with a six-year plan for national development and reconstruction.

The enormous amount of money Aguirre Cerda indicated would be necessary to carry out the popular-front program along with the costs of reconstruction after the earthquake frightened the rightist majority in Congress. Conservatives and Liberals recognized the need to provide for reconstruction, but the remainder of Aguirre Cerda's ambitious program for national development, including large sums for low-cost housing and stimulation of industrial development, portended accelerated inflation, higher taxes, and expansion of the state bureaucracy. Congressional rejection of the development program, despite support for a massive reconstruction appropriation, sent Aguirre Cerda on a speaking tour to the devastated provinces to rally popular support.

In an effort to achieve a compromise, the President's minister of finance, Roberto Wachholtz, devised a new package for Congress, which proposed two separate agencies—the Relief and Reconstruction Corporation to deal with the immediate problems occasioned by the earthquake, and the National Development Corporation (CORFO) to carry out the longer-term economic objectives. In addition, the new proposal called for heavy reliance upon foreign loans instead of internal financing of the development projects. To prevent the popular-front parties from using CORFO for political advantage, its board of directors would represent producer groups as well as government officials; a single representative of the Chilean Workers Confederation (CTCH) would be included to make known labor's views.

This new plan angered many of the government's leftist supporters, particularly Socialists, whom the President mollified with promises of more patronage. In March 1939, after overcoming the rightist opposition through pressure on selected congressmen from the devastated provinces, Aguirre Cerda won a narrow victory for his development and reconstruction legislation. After further jockeying between the President and Congress, Law 6334 went into effect in late April 1939. This victory for Aguirre Cerda and the popular front would provide the basis for greatly expanded state intervention in national development. It also subordinated Chilean economic policy to the main sources of capital for CORFO—the United States Export-Import Bank (Exim Bank).

While Aguirre Cerda was fighting for approval of the reconstruction and development program, his popular-front allies, especially the Socialists and Communists, carried out a national campaign among urban and rural workers to mobilize support for the government. Labor conflicts, strikes, unionization efforts, and industrial violence created an atmosphere bordering on insurrection. For members of the President's own party, as well as for the Conservative-Liberal opposition, the most serious threat to maintenance of the fragile social order came from the massive wave of labor conflict and unionization in the countryside. An extension of the electoral campaign in the countryside directed by Communist functionaries, rural conflict and unionization in the first months of the popular front administration reached alarming levels. In 1939 the Labor Department officially registered 170 labor petitions from groups of rural laborers and *inquilinos*—compared to 6 in the previous year. During the same period campesinos organized more than 200 agricultural unions.

The National Agricultural Society and local groups of landowners appealed directly to President Aguirre Cerda to halt rural unionization and labor conflict in agriculture. In the middle of March 1939 some of the country's most influential landowners informed the President that they confronted "the initial elements of a state of revolution . . . produced under the pretext of the right of rural workers to organize." In agreement with all the parties of the popular front and the CTCH, President Aguirre Cerda illegally ordered suspension of rural unionization, using the same administrative device employed by President Alessandri in 1933. Despite the supposedly "temporary" nature of this suspension, it remained in effect until 1946.

Taking advantage of the vulnerability of agricultural workers, and of the willingness of popular-front parties to trade the welfare of the campesinos for "social peace" and support of the government's reconstruction and development legislation, landowners carried out a purge of union leaders and evicted large numbers of "troublemakers" from their tenancies. By the time the CTCH and the Communist party had repudiated this sacrifice of the rural work force to political expediency, Aguirre Cerda's new minister of interior, Arturo Olavarría Bravo, had already devised his system of "judgment day," or *juicio final*, to deal with rural militancy. As described by Olavarría himself,

> . . . A group of carabineros [police] would arrive at a farm accompanied by a convoy of trucks. When the inquilinos were assembled in the area, the carabinero officer would order those who wished to continue the strike to stand on his left. The officer would then order that the strikers gather their families, cats, dogs, chickens, and belongings and get in the trucks to be evicted. . . . This tactic I converted into a system. General Oscar Reeves Leiva, Director General of Carabineros, called it *el juicio final*, as the good ones went to the right and the bad ones to the left, as it is hoped will occur one day in the valley of Jehosaphat. Of course, I did not have to use the *juicio final* many times. . . .

Only the Trotskyists rejected Aguirre Cerda's sacrifice of the rural work force. In particular, Emilio Zapata, the leader and organizer of Chile's first national peasant league, Liga Nacional de Defensa de Campesinos Pobres ("National Poor Peasants League"), protested the government's acquiescence to landowner demands. Zapata delivered an angry critique of the government in the Congress and gradually broke with the popular-front coalition. Recalling the situation of 1939, Zapata remarked in 1971:

> What Aguirre Cerda had to do was tell the *patrones* that they couldn't use lockouts or sabotage production, and that they

couldn't throw people off the land in political reprisal. . . .
Neither Aguirre Cerda nor his ministers were responsive. They
were walls without ears. . . . Although they possessed the legal
means to prevent it, they did nothing while the landowners
threw the campesinos "into the streets" for the crime of voting
for Aguirre Cerda or for joining *ligas* or unions.

Rural workers had no means to resist landowner reprisals. The popular-front government provided police to enforce court orders for evic-
tions, to break the newly formed unions, and to allow the landowners
to retain control of the countryside. This was the price Aguirre Cerda
was willing to pay to gain support for the rest of his program in Congress and to maintain "social peace." Socialists, Communists, and
the CTCH likewise agreed to the terms of the bargain. In exchange,
legislation outlawing the Communists was rejected, the industrialization program emerged from Congress, and the Socialists occupied
high-level administrative posts.

Aguirre Cerda's concession to the landowners did not end the
Right's campaign against the government. Neither did it prevent
Emilio Zapata's National Peasant League from carrying out its "First
National Congress of Chilean Peasants" in Santiago in April 1939.
Rejecting the popular front's policies, leaders of the Trotskyist-
oriented organization called for intensification of class struggle and
the end of the latifundia. Two months later the Communists sponsored a highly visible "First National Congress of Rural Unions,"
preceding the National Congress of the CTCH. In the meantime
(late April) Socialist leaders called for a purge of the bureaucracy of
all "traitors," so that the public administration could be put completely at the service of the masses.

Tensions increased as rumors circulated that Socialist leader Marmaduque Grove had prepared a May Day speech calling for dissolution of Congress, recognition of the Socialist militia as an official
arm of the government, and other revolutionary measures. The rightist press, in a fashion remarkably similar to the campaign that would
later precede the military coup of September 1973, emphasized the
precarious nature of Chilean democracy, the growing Communist

threat, and alluded to the military role in preventing leftist extremists from destroying constitutional government. Aguirre Cerda responded by applying the internal security law against a leading rightist paper, El Diario Ilustrado, thereby preventing the paper's circulation outside of Santiago. Congress, in turn, censured the minister of the interior for violating freedom of the press in the El Diario Ilustrado case.

In the annual military parade honoring Arturo Prat, Chile's naval hero of the War of the Pacific, the Right found its military sympathizer when, according to the rightist press, General Ariosto Herrera Ramírez jumped from his horse to order removal of a Communist banner from a balcony of the presidential palace. In early July El Diario Ilustrado published a supposedly confidential circular detailing plans by the Socialists for an internal coup, or autogolpe, including provisions for formation of a red army, elimination of opposition politicians, and infiltration of the armed forces. (Again, we have a striking parallel with the "white paper" and the so-called plan zeta denounced by the Chilean Right and the military in 1973.)

In turn, the government announced discovery of a plot to oust the President. The rightist press made light of the government's claims, but investigations led Aguirre Cerda to request General Ariosto Herrera to resign. Herrera refused, and his military colleagues elected him president of the Club Militar in August 1939. Emerging as a hero of the Right, Herrera also supported the officers punished by the government for their supposed participation in the plot of early July. Ignoring orders from the minister of defense, he overtly insulted Aguirre Cerda with a decision to reinstate the officers in question. Thereupon the government relieved him of his command and asked him to resign his commission. On August 25, 1939, instigated by comrades of the second division he commanded and by the rightist press, General Herrera led an abortive coup attempt, in which the ever present hand of Carlos Ibáñez again was apparent. With the movement's quick collapse, Ibáñez sought asylum in the Paraguayan embassy.

The abortive coup passed the initiative back to the popular-front government. Congress allotted the President state of siege authority for a period of twenty days, during which time Aguirre Cerda purged the military of conspiratorial officers. Now, however, the latent divisions within the popular front itself surfaced with vengeance. Competition between Socialists and Communists to gain control of student movements and the CTCH exacerbated the traditional hostility between the country's two major Marxist parties. Internal divisions within the Socialist party, between those favoring the moderate policies of Aguirre Cerda and the more militant *inconformistas* and ex-Trotskyists, led to a party split and formation of the Socialist Workers party (PST) in 1941. Aguirre Cerda's own party remained divided between the would-be populists and the more conservative advocates of middle-class-oriented reform.

By the end of 1939 Congress passed only two major pieces of legislation, including the reconstruction-CORFO package; by early 1940 Aguirre Cerda reorganized the cabinet, relying upon wealthy, respected, personally loyal appointees rather than designees of the popular-front parties. In July 1940 the President publicly announced that labor conflicts in the countryside could not be tolerated, because they diminished agricultural production. A month later the minister of the interior instructed the *carabineros* to repress the activity of "professional agitators who provoke problems in the countryside and industrial centers." The President's effort to conciliate the rightist parties coincided with mounting conflict between Socialists and Communists, as well as with the internal split in the Socialist party. Communist attacks upon the Socialist minister of development, who negotiated for loans in the United States, drastically increased the level of conflict and precipitated a rupture in the coalition.

In January 1941, Socialists demanded the ouster of the Communists from the popular front; refusal by the popular-front executive committee to expel the Communists led to Socialist withdrawal. The CTCH, divided between Communists and Socialists, also voted by a narrow margin to leave the popular-front government. Finally, after an impressive victory of popular-front parties and Socialists in the congressional elections of 1941, the President's own Radical party withdrew its support from him when he refused to accept party dictates in regard to ministerial appointments and patronage. To embarrass the President, his party colleagues now opposed legislation that he sent to the Congress. This opposition destroyed Aguirre Cerda's power, and he died, a broken man, in late 1941. In his own words, "the Chilean working classes were just as poor . . . and just as miserable as when I became President."

Two Radical presidents and one interim president followed Aguirre Cerda. Juan Antonio Ríos, who had been a critic of Aguirre Cerda's cooperation with the Communists, served from 1942 to 1946, when he, too, died in office. Ríos renewed Radical contacts with Conservatives and some Liberals as the Right recognized the benefits of state support for *private* industrial enterprise. They also appreciated Ríos' anticommunist position and his decision to sustain the administrative order against rural unionization. Rapprochement between moderate Radical party factions and the Right coincided with a growing middle-class conservatism; at the same time the Radicals were trying to reconcile their own internal cleavages with the shifting trends in national politics. Positioned in the center of the political spectrum, the Radicals opportunistically entered in alliances with the Left or the Right, as expediency required, in order to retain their hold on the presidency and the patronage of a growing bureaucracy.

A new, most unlikely, coalition of Radicals, Communists, and Liberals brought Radical leader, Gabriel González Videla, to office in 1946. The policies of industrialization through CORFO loans to private investors and heavy borrowing from the Exim Bank continued. Shortly after González Videla assumed office, the Communist party unleashed a campaign of labor conflict and strikes even more extensive than the movement of the first years of Aguirre Cerda's presidency. During the 1946-47 harvest, rural workers engaged in more than 650 labor conflicts and formed more than 300 agricultural unions. Again, organization of rural labor threatened to destroy the underlying trade-off reconciling the socio-economic consequences of urbanization and industrialization and the political power of the landowners.

Fulfilling a campaign promise, González Videla rescinded the order issued by Aguirre Cerda in 1939 to restrict rural unionization. Quickly, however, the new President also fulfilled a bargain made with his rightist supporters in the Liberal party, and supported new legislation (Law 8811) that made agricultural unionization practically impossible. In contrast to the Labor Code regulating the majority of Chilean workers, the new law outlawed agricultural strikes and severely limited the rights of rural workers to present labor petitions and to engage in collective bargaining. Now, instead of an illegal administrative order, congressional legislation sanctified the arrangement whereby rural labor bore a disproportionate share of the costs of Chilean industrialization and continued to serve as "voting cattle" for the owners of the large rural estates. This legislation remained in effect until 1967.

In contrast to their performance in 1939, Communist leaders in 1946 and 1947 persisted in their unionization efforts and in their leadership of industrial conflicts despite the opposition of the President. From their ministerial positions in González Videla's government, the Communists refused to acquiesce in the renewed repression of rural labor. They carried the struggle to the mines and the cities, and thus incited fierce rightist opposition while also alienating themselves from the President. As landowners and industrialists called for cooperation with the President to "extirpate the Communist menace," Congress first extended González Videla's extraordinary powers to deal with subversion (Law 8837) and followed, in 1948, with the so-called Law for the Permanent Defense of Democracy (Law 8987). This legislation outlawed the Communist party, excluded its members from participation in the labor movement, and set up zones of banishment or "relegation" for subversives. This temporary elimination of the Communists from overt political activity and a "cleansing" of the labor movement restored political stability. It also reflected the integral relationship between the Cold War, American foreign policy, and Chilean domestic development.

American investment in Chile during the 1930s increased, as did Chilean awareness of the significant impact of foreign control over the copper and nitrates that provided most of the country's foreign exchange. Leftist political movements sought continually to undermine the position of United States firms, attacking the exploitation of Chilean resources by international monopolies and imperialism— already, by then, a synonym for the United States. The advent of a popular-front government with Marxist participation presented American interests with a delicate situation. To finance development projects the Chilean government needed resources; higher taxes on the copper industry appeared the most likely source of such capital. Further, the initial outline of the CORFO project, whether under Marxist or nationalist direction, threatened to expand significantly the state sector of the economy, to the detriment or even the elimination of American investments in oil, public utilities, mining, and basic industry.

The political compromise that had allowed the popular-front government to create CORFO shifted emphasis from internal to external financing for economic modernization and industrialization. Rather than greatly increased taxes on wealth and income in Chile, or taxes on the copper firms which would discourage further investment, moderate Radicals and industrial leaders opted for loans, credits, and foreign private investment as the source of risk capital. United States diplomats in Santiago and Washington, D.C., saw that it was possible to protect American interests through a careful lending policy and, at the same time, to support the anti-Marxist elements of the popular-front coalition; they developed a highly successful cooperative strategy for dealing with Aguirre Cerda's government. Despite Chile's hesitance to declare war against the Axis powers, the initial success of the policy American interests had elaborated gradually subordinated both Chilean economic policy and domestic political events to American needs during the Second World War and, in the aftermath, the Cold War.

Recognizing American credit policy's potential for influencing the popular front government, an embassy official made the following assessment of the alternatives open to United States policymakers:

> If we negotiate with Wachholtz [the moderate, Radical minister of finance in the first Aguirre Cerda cabinet] . . . we will strengthen the moderate elements in the popular front here; whereas if we deferred the negotiations in the expectation that the dissensions in the popular front here would come to a head we would be taking a long chance.

By the end of 1940 the United States Export-Import Bank had arranged credits totaling $17 million for CORFO—to be used exclusively to pay for materials, machinery, technical assistance, or consultants from the United States. During the next eight years Exim Bank and other American-dominated financial institutions continued to bankroll CORFO's large-scale investment program in housing, industry, agriculture, and commerce. Whereas CORFO's policies directly threatened the position of selected American firms, its overall effect was to greatly expand the market for imports of United States capital goods, in addition to placing Chilean policymakers in a vulnerable position vis-à-vis decisions made in Washington, D.C.

World War II raised international prices for copper. Practically all of Chile's copper, however, was marketed through subsidiaries of United States copper firms established in Chile—for whom the Allied governments fixed a ceiling price upon copper products during the course of the war. Different Chilean sources estimate that the loss Chile sustained by its "contribution" to the Allied war effort was between $100 million and $500 million. Further, Chilean dollar reserves accumulated from exports to the United States during the war were unfrozen at a time when postwar inflation substantially reduced their purchasing power. Moreover, in the United States recession of 1949-50 production by American copper firms in Chile was reduced after four years of deterioration in the terms of trade. When the outbreak of the Korean War quickly snapped the United States out of the recession, the American government and the copper companies reimposed price controls on copper.

American control of Chile's principal economic resources accompanied intensified involvement in Chilean politics. Cold War intrigue made post-World War II Chilean politics a confrontation zone for "Communism" and the "Free World." American policymakers considered the presence of Communist ministers in the González Videla government to be dangerous, and so allied with the Chilean Right in an active campaign to weaken, then destroy, Marxist political parties and the labor movement. Simultaneously the United States provided financial support for Socialist factions of the CTCH which opposed the rapidly increasing Communist influence. The United States gave badly needed financial assistance to the Chilean government on the condition that the Communist menace be eliminated. A split in the labor movement and the breakup of the CTCH were preliminary successes; a mounting anticommunist campaign by the rightist press and eventually by the González Videla government further heartened American diplomats and business interests.

Doubt still remained that González Videla would totally break his alliance with the Communists. Communist control of the labor movement, especially in copper and the coal mines, made any frontal offensive quite risky. Communist-inspired mobilization of rural labor and hundreds of agricultural labor conflicts in the 1946-47 harvest threatened the very foundation of the political arrangement elaborated by Aguirre Cerda and his Radical successors. Labor conflict in the northern provinces and a crippling coal strike panicked the Radical administration. In the meantime a representative of the Chilean government sought further economic assistance from the Exim Bank and the International Bank to bolster the Chilean economy. For, despite increased copper production, the declining terms of trade between Chile and the industrial nations significantly reduced the nation's import capabilities, even as the industrialization process necessitated greater quantities of capital goods, high technology, and raw materials.

Chile's suspension of foreign debt payments after the earthquake

TABLE 14. NET TERMS-OF-TRADE RELATIONS: PRICE INDEX FOR CHILE
(1938 = 100)

	Exports	Imports	Terms of Trade
1936	100.5	88.5	113.6
1937	129.7	96.9	133.8
1938	100.0	100.0	100.0
1939	107.5	94.7	113.5
1940	105.4	104.2	101.2
1941	109.2	113.1	96.6
1942	118.4	150.1	78.9
1943	120.9	168.7	71.7
1944	125.6	179.6	69.9
1945	129.7	183.2	70.8
1946	151.1	200.6	75.3
1947	201.1	245.4	81.9
1948	221.1	250.8	88.2
1949	220.3	246.1	89.5
1950	222.1	237.0	93.7
1951	279.4	276.9	100.9

(Source: Theodore H. Moran, *Multinational Corporations and the Politics of Dependence, Copper in Chile*, Princeton University Press, 1974, p. 71.)

of 1939, complaints by American businessmen that Chile's request for loans to finance hydroelectric development threatened American private interests, and rumors of nationalization of American oil and power companies, all delayed approval of the requests for new assistance. Despite the secret assurances by González Videla's special emissary to the State Department that the Chilean president did not favor communism and would oppose Argentine President Juan Perón's efforts to undermine American influence in the southern cone, no quick commitment on financial assistance was forthcoming. To the contrary, the State Department officials involved in the negotiations made clear the department's concern that Chile "adjust its debt situation" and improve the tax situation of the American copper companies.

Disappointed by the results of the economic mission to the United States, González Videla reportedly threatened the American ambassador with a deterioration in Chilean-American relations. In response, Ambassador Claude Bowers cabled a confidential message to the secretary of state, noting that "Chile is [a] key country in the struggle against Communism, and I feel that we should make every effort to overcome present impasse." As the Communist campaign of labor agitation mounted, so also did American concern with Chile as a Cold War battleground. Accounts of the rising Communist menace dominated correspondence from the American embassy in Santiago to Washington, D.C., from May 1947 on.

Anticipating a showdown with his ex-political allies, President Gonález Videla requested an emergency shipment of coal from the United States in case of Communist shutdowns of the coal mines. Ambassador Bowers recommended to the secretary of state, "I suggest situation set forth above [reference to a general strike scheduled for late June 1947] be taken into consideration in connection with Chile's request for coal stockpile in its struggle to combat Communism." In September 1947, Bowers reported to Washington that González Videla was gradually eliminating Communists from the administration, and on October 6, 1947, the ambassador cabled that "González Videla declared war on Communism as a result of what he claims is a Communist plot to overthrow the Government and obtain control of the production (in order to deprive the United States of the use in an emergency) of strategic raw materials, namely copper and nitrates." Despite heavy commitments to Europe and other Latin American nations, the United States assured the Chilean President that emergency coal shipments would be available. Three days later Ambassador Bowers cabled: "Our war with Communists is on two fronts, Europe and South America." After another four days had passed, the ambassador added: "The issue is clear as crystal —Communism or democracy."

With American assurances of coal shipments to break the coal miners' strike, the government moved in police and military units to restore order and terminate the labor conflict. Subsequently Chile broke off diplomatic relations with the Soviet Union, Yugoslavia, and Czechoslovakia, nations that the Chilean President accused of engineering political chaos through their domestic agents, the Chilean Communist party. The Law for the Permanent Defense of Democracy, passed in 1948, outlawed the Communist party, eliminated almost thirty thousand voters from the electoral registers, provided authority to purge the labor movement, and allowed the President to restore "democracy" to Chile. Implementation of Law 8811 on agricultural unionization, along with the Law for the Permanent Defense of Democracy, destroyed the impressive network of rural labor unions created from 1946 to 1947 and ended the threat to the hegemony of the political Right in the countryside. Thus the "arrangement" initiated by Alessandri and elaborated by the popular-front government could remain intact.

Appropriately, González Videla called upon Jorge Alessandri, the ex-President's son, to act as his finance minister. Anaconda announced plans for an additional $130 million investment in their copper properties at Chuquicamata. And despite the effects of the United States recession on a worsening Chilean economy, Exim Bank and the international lending agencies agreed to provide substantial economic assistance to the Chilean government. In the next four years Exim Bank not only financed the creation or expansion of a large number of Chilean industries, it also ensured, through its lending policies, that American machinery, technology, and patent holders participated in the process of industrialization. Exim Bank loans required the exclusive use of United States purchased capital goods for the Chilean industries receiving Bank credits and even that American carriers ship the goods to Chile. Further, whereas the Chilean government guaranteed the loans and even provided much of the capital, Exim Bank demanded that only private investors hold a majority of the industries' voting stock.

American influence in the development policies of the Chilean government benefited Chilean private investors as well as United States interests. Credit to agricultural and industrial interests from CORFO often entailed negative real interest rates; that is, inflation more than counterbalanced the interest rates, making credit a subsidy to debtors. Externally financed economic modernization was oriented toward importing capital goods for industry and labor-saving farm machinery and thereby strengthened the position of employers, especially in agriculture, vis-à-vis the labor force. Moreover, pri-

vate investors achieved a dominant voice in the three major industrial complexes originating from CORFO initiative—the Pacific Steel
Corporation (CAP), the National Petroleum Corporation (ENAP),
and the National Electric Corporation (ENDESA). Key stockhold-
ers included Kennecott Copper Corporation and influential members
of the National Society of Manufacturers. Even enterprises in which
CORFO had a majority interest acted more like private firms than
public enterprises, since entrepreneurs and bankers on the various
government policymaking agencies assured a favorable attitude toward private business.

The growing economic, political, and cultural influence of the
United States in Chile in the early post-World War II years did not
eliminate certain basic contradictions between Chilean national interest and the interests of American companies or foreign policies
dictated by the Cold War. Among some Chilean leaders and businessmen there developed a conscious awareness of the disadvantages
of subordinating Chilean copper policy, industrialization, and domestic politics to changes in United States policy. Efforts to establish particular industries through CORFO brought Chilean officials
and industrialists into direct conflict with U.S. corporations. Economic assistance conditioned with requirements to buy higher-priced
American products or to ship in costlier United States carriers provided obvious examples of differences in American and Chilean national interests. Most of all, the disparity between what copper exports might bring the nation and what they actually provided in
foreign exchange led groups on both the Right and the Left to re-
sent, if not attack openly, the American copper firms.

Notwithstanding increased taxation of the copper industry in the
early 1950s, pressures to exact greater benefits for Chile from the
country's most valuable natural resource increased gradually in that
decade and resulted, in the 1960s, in policies to nationalize the major
United States copper companies. The Chilean Right gratefully accepted American support for an anticommunist campaign, credits
for industrialization, cooperation in infiltrating the Chilean labor
movement with "responsible" unionists, and educational exchanges,

but they remained in their own way Chilean nationalists. This nationalism and their anger with American support for *agrarian reform* would ally them in the 1960s and early 1970s with middle-class and leftist political parties in efforts to eliminate American control over Chilean copper.

During three Radical administrations (1938-52), the combination of deficit-financing of industrialization, real salary gains for middle-class groups without proportional increases in internal taxation or government revenues, and the stagnation of agriculture heightened inflationary pressures. Despite government promises of progressive income redistribution and better educational opportunities, most urban workers along with the rural labor force actually lost ground in real income from 1938 to 1952, and more than one-third of the school-age children did not attend school. Worse, rather than gaining the "economic independence" promised by González Videla, the country had become increasingly dependent upon private foreign capital, loans, and marketing decisions made by the United States copper firms. Most strikingly, it had become more dependent upon imports of *food*. Domestic agricultural production did not keep pace with population growth and fell even further behind a rate of urbanization more than double that of population increase. Poor performance by agriculture necessitated a growing quantity of foreign exchange to feed Chile's people. It also meant further inflationary pressure added to currency emissions, deficit financing, and growth of the government bureaucracy.

Inflation meant frustration for the salaried middle classes and government employees even when periodic upward wage adjustments somewhat ameliorated the full impact of the price increases that caused suffering for most blue-collar workers and the rural labor force. By the 1952 presidential elections, with renewed labor agitation and González Videla's vacillating application of anticommunist and internal security legislation, Chile had a highly fragmented, weary, and frustrated electorate. Carlos Ibàñez took advantage of the population's exasperation with party politics and again emerged as an authoritarian, "above politics," antiparty candidate for president. Supported by a heterogenous coalition of Socialists, middle-class groups, dissident Radicals and Conservatives, and the ascendant Agrarian Labor party (*Partido Agrario Laborista*), Ibàñez swept into office with a broom as a symbol of his intentions to "clean house." Promising electoral reforms, an end to corruption, and eventual elimination of the anticommunist legislation, the ex-dictator overwhelmingly defeated the divided opposition.

As in the 1927-31 period, Carlos Ibàñez' lack of commitment to formal democracy or to the Chilean party system made his second administration highly personalistic, authoritarian, repressive—and in some ways quite innovative. Loyal to neither party nor ideology, Ibàñez filled government posts with upwardly mobile politicians from splinter parties or ethnic minorities, such as Arab-Chileans. Indifferent to the long-term strength of the traditional parties, the President cooperated with the Falange (later Christian Democrat) deputy, Jorge Rogers Sotomayor, in adopting a far-reaching electoral reform (1958) that would drastically curtail the power of the landlords in Chilean politics. Further, after using Law 8811 and the anticommunist legislation to repress agricultural unionism and the urban labor movement throughout his term of office, Ibáñez fulfilled his campaign promise to eliminate the Law for the Permanent Defense of Democracy prior to leaving office. This paved the way for consolidation of a new electoral coalition between Socialists and Communists, the Popular Action Front (FRAP), which almost captured the presidency in the 1958 elections.

The electoral reform of 1958 introduced an Australian ballot (a

TABLE 15. PRESIDENTIAL ELECTION, 1952

Candidate	Vote Totals
Carlos Ibáñez	446,439
Arturo Matte (Liberals & Conservatives)	297,357
Pedro E. Alfonso (Radicals & Falange)	190,360
Salvador Allende (Socialists & Communists)	51,975
Total	954,131

single official ballot) and increased penalties for electoral fraud and bribery. A public ballot meant that landowners could no longer effectively control the votes of rural workers through distribution of party ballots and monitoring of the polls to assure that workers voted "correctly." In addition, the new election law made voting compulsory and provided for jail terms or fines for nonvoters. This inducement to electoral participation combined with the official secret ballot ended the hegemony of the landowners in the rural districts. It also meant that the cornerstone of Chilean political stability, the hacienda system, would come under mounting pressure from 1958 on as the availability of rural votes sent Marxists, Christian Democrats, Radicals, and other smaller political parties into the countryside in search of rural votes.

If the eventual political consequences of the Ibàñez administration proved beneficial to rural workers and eroded the power of the Right, the immediate results of the administration's political and economic policies gravely affected the urban and rural poor throughout the nation. The end of the Korean War, and with it the plunging demand for Chilean copper, reduced Chile's import capabilities by almost 30 percent in 1953. At the same time, the country approached the limits of easy import-substitution industrialization. Investment as well as growth in economic output declined. In turn, government revenues decreased, but a system of automatic readjustment of salaries in response to inflation inhibited cutbacks in government expenditures. Stagflation that brought the annual inflation rate (86% in 1956) to the highest levels in Chilean history (before 1970-73) and international pressure on the government concerning debt payments moved the government to call in an American economic mission to design a program of stabilization. Hoping that the good relations between the Klein-Saks Mission and the International Monetary Fund would reopen international lines of support for the Chilean economy, the Ibáñez government attempted to implement the mission's recommendations.

The Klein-Saks recommendations conformed closely to what now is considered conventional, hard-line, antiflationary policies favored

by the International Monetary Fund: elimination of "excess demand" through wage controls, restrictions on credit, cutbacks on
government expenditures, elimination of subsidies by public services
such as water and transport, reduced currency emissions, replacement
of multiple exchange rates for a single "floating" rate, and removal
of price controls except for "essential commodities." This program
entailed suspension of automatic wage readjustments and efforts to
insure that wage increases did not exceed the rate of inflation. In
addition, the administration adopted a generally favorable attitude
toward development through incentives to private domestic investors
and the American copper companies. So-called New Deal, or *nuevo
trato*, legislation (1955), intended to attract further investment
through "profit stimulus," reduced effective tax rates on Anaconda
and Kennecott, as well as providing the companies with a number of
commercial, accounting, and exchange control benefits.

The Copper Department created as part of this legislation eventually gave the Chilean government much-needed technical capabilities to monitor the copper industry; but the immediate effect of the
nuevo trato was higher profits for Anaconda and Kennecott without
the desired further investments by the companies in Chile. Worse
still, from the Chilean perspective, Chile's share of the world market barely remained stable and the percentage of copper refined in
Chile by the companies actually declined from a high of 89 percent
in 1951 to merely 45 percent in 1958. In practice, the copper companies profited and private businesses adjusted to the inflationary
situation, while salaried and wage-earning Chileans bore the brunt of
the government's program. The administration imposed readjustments in remuneration substantially below the rate of inflation to
"depress demand." Workers and salaried employees consequently
found themselves with less money to spend on food, clothing, and
shelter. To carry through on the program, the Ibáñez government
was forced to deal harshly with the resultant labor agitation (1955-
57) and rioting in Santiago (1957); among other measures labor
leaders and "communists" were confined in detention camps under
the terms of the Law for the Permanent Defense of Democracy.

Inflation rates declined; so did the standard of living of the majority of Chileans. When restrictions on credit and subsidies to industrialists and landowners also angered the groups who, with the middle classes, had helped bring Ibáñez to power, the government lost the base of support it had briefly captured in the years from 1952 to 1955. As the 1958 presidential elections approached, unification of the leftist parties and total rejection of Ibáñez's policies by the mass of the Chilean electorate set the stage for another close contest in which the Socialist-Communist candidate, Salvador Allende, fell just short of victory.

TABLE 16. PRESIDENTIAL ELECTIONS, 1958

Province	Alessandri (supported by Liberals and Conservatives)	Bossay (Radical)	Zamorano ("leftist" priest)	Allende (FRAP)	Frei (Christian Democrat)
Tarapacá	3,558	3,859	529	8,299	4,922
Antofagasta	5,670	5,866	1,083	14,954	6,567
Atacama	2,533	5,423	247	6,167	3,621
Coquimbo	10,460	8,886	1,280	14,283	7,952
Aconcagua	10,018	4,233	1,530	7,290	5,953
Valparaíso	35,680	17,192	5,727	26,611	29,913
Santiago	151,797	51,984	11,194	121,452	91,305
O'Higgins	16,753	4,517	2,175	14,537	8,426
Colchagua	13,556	3,435	477	6,190	4,379
Curicó	6,509	2,458	704	6,067	3,107
Talca	9,763	4,163	7,206	8,584	6,377
Maule	5,823	4,551	830	2,749	3,375
Linares	10,674	4,044	4,156	7,927	5,912
Nuble	11,988	11,164	811	10,947	11,290
Concepción	17,418	13,091	624	34,594	18,154
Arauco	1,932	3,125	61	6,258	1,616
Bío Bío	7,660	4,670	200	7,360	3,611
Malleco	10,133	5,592	187	7,485	4,951
Cautín	21,228	8,979	920	11,921	12,587
Valdivia	12,387	6,791	637	11,559	7,545
Osorno	8,318	5,524	156	5,542	2,770
Llanquihue	7,430	4,304	219	4,056	6,075
Chiloé	6,146	4,621	157	3,689	1,559
Aisén	1,229	1,027	44	1,261	953
Magallanes	1,285	2,791	151	6,708	2,857
Total	389,948	192,110	41,305	356,499	255,777

The presidential elections of 1958 brought to office Jorge Alessandri, son of ex-President Arturo Alessandri and an experienced conservative economic minister. Having won the presidency with a scant plurality over Salvador Allende, Alessandri could not count upon a docile Congress or even the temporary popular base achieved by Ibáñez in 1952. A year after he took office, the Cuban Revolution injected a whole new concern into Chilean politics and American foreign policy. In an effort to counteract the appeal of the Cuban Revolution throughout the rest of Latin America, the United States proposed the Alliance for Progress, which included commitment to agrarian reform—the single policy most bitterly resisted by the Chilean Right during the previous thirty years. Although Alessandri attempted to maintain the essential administrative and legislative impediments to agricultural unionism and rural labor conflict, he found himself under rapidly mounting pressure from Marxist and Christian Democratic political activities among the rural labor force.

The electoral successes of the FRAP coalition in the countryside in the 1958 presidential election and the disappearance of the Law of the Permanent Defense for Democracy renewed interest among Socialists and Communists in political mobilization of rural workers. In addition, the growing strength of the Christian Democratic party in the early 1960s sent groups of Catholic organizers to rural areas to compete with the Marxists. Penetration of Marxist parties and Christian Democrats into the countryside, combined with the electoral reform of 1958, produced a fundamental alteration in Chilean politics in the 1961 congressional elections. For the first time in the twentieth century the Conservatives and the Liberals failed to gain one-third of the seats in Congress. FRAP obtained more votes than any other single party list and controlled 27.5 percent (40) of the seats in the Chamber of Deputies and elected thirteen senators (of a total of 45). The Christian Democrats, originally a small group that had broken away from the Conservative party in the late 1930s, for the first time polled more votes than the Conservatives.

The outcome of the 1961 congressional elections left the incumbent Alessandri administration dependent upon the Radical party.

TABLE 17. SUMMARY OVERVIEW OF LANDOWNER-GOVERNMENT RESPONSE TO RURAL LABOR ACTIVISM IN CHILE, 1932-57

Presidential Election	Landowner Reaction	Government Responses	Landowner Follow-up
1932-33 Presidential election (1932). First legally organized rural unions formed in Chile; several rural labor conflicts.	Pressure from SNA and other landowner associations on President Alessandri, claiming unionization in countryside not legal.	Circular 4060-4061 "temporarily" suspends rural unionization; remains in effect until 1937-38.	Workers involved in first legal unions around Molina (Talca Province) dismissed and evicted; workers presenting labor petitions (1934-35) arrested, dismissed, evicted.
1938-39 Popular-front candidate Pedro Aguirre Cerda elected. First large wave of rural unionization, labor conflicts.	Landowner associations publish numerous editorials railing against communist agitation; send letters to Pedro Aguirre Cerda. (Example: Landowners of Pirque claim: "Professional agitators have created discontent among workers and are forming unions, inciting social indiscipline. We have initial stages of a State of Revolution. Request that the government suspend for now all procedures leading to rural unionization.")	Ministerial Order 34[*] "temporarily suspends" rural unionization; remains in effect until 1946. [*] Clearly illegal, unconstitutional.	*Intendente of Curicó:* "Due to labor petitions presented by agricultural workers, the majority of affected landowners in this province are dismissing workers who participated. Workers whose families have lived on these farms for generations being forced to leave." *Intendente of Linares:* "Landowners have organized movement to evict on a massive scale rural workers from farms in this region."

1946-47 Gabriel González Videla elected President with Communist support. Communists occupy ministries; massive wave of rural (and urban-mining) labor conflicts, strikes, unionization.	Numerous editorials in SNA journal, *El Campesino*, denouncing agitations in the country. (Examples: November, December, 1946; March, 1947). Move in Congress to pass "special law" to regulate rural labor—with support of Gabriel González Videla.	Law 8811 (1947) restricts rural labor conflicts; outlaws strikes in agriculture; makes rural unionization almost impossible. Law 8987 (Law for the Permanent Defense of Democracy) outlaws Communists; "cleanses" labor movement—destroying most rural labor organizations.	Labor Department receives communications from all over the country reporting massive dismissals and evictions of rural workers—especially those active in labor conflicts or labor leaders.
1952-53 Carlos Ibáñez elected President with support of Socialists; campesino strike at Molina; march on Santiago; isolated conflicts elsewhere.	Calls for government intervention; application of Law 8987.	Application of Law 8987 against leaders of Molina strike; eventual negotiated settlement.	Dismissal of labor leaders in Molina farms—but during 1953-57 conflicts continue, in gradually reduced number.

The Radicals, hoping to win back the presidency in 1964, demanded ministerial participation in exchange for support of the government in the legislature. In addition, the Radicals now became advocates of "land reform." United States diplomats also put pressure on the Alessandri government to adopt a land reform program as a part of the Alliance for Progress.

Alessandri, a firm believer in the benefits of private enterprise and diminishing government "interference" in the economy, opposed the reformist elements that demanded sweeping social and economic changes in Chilean life. However, loss of congressional influence by Conservatives and Liberals, along with pressures from the Alliance for Progress and mounting Marxist/Christian Democratic political activity, forced certain changes upon the administration. In defense of their political base in the countryside, Conservatives and Liberals attacked the Alliance for Progress and argued that increased Chilean participation in the profits of the copper industry would do far more for the country than land reforms, tax reforms, or other redistributionist measures sponsored by the Alliance. In language that would become more familiar after the military coup of 1973, one Conservative senator cautioned that the potential for demagoguery in the Alliance for Progress threatened the basic values of the "Western and Christian world."

Attacked by both the Left and the Right, the American copper companies felt the impact of the first tentative measures that ultimately resulted in nationalization. Taxes on the industry increased by 10 to 15 percent, and a Conservative minister proposed a plan whereby the companies would be forced to raise production considerably as well as to increase drastically (to 90 percent) the amount of copper refined in Chile. Although this plan was blocked through cabinet reshuffles and negotiations between the companies and Alessandri, the political position of both the American copper companies and the Chilean landowners seemed ever less tenable.

The growing need to import food, inflation, and a mounting press campaign by leftist and reformist newspapers and intellectuals isolated the landowners politically and identified them in the public mind as the group largely responsible for Chile's social and economic backwardness. Intensified organizational activity by Marxists and Christian Democrats in the countryside reminded landowners of the labor crises and union struggles of 1939-41 and 1946-47. Once again editorials appeared in the major SNA publication warning of the threat of communism and anarchy if rural workers were allowed to unionize. Now, however, landowners lacked the political strength in Congress and the urban alliances necessary to prevent the first step toward transformation of the Chilean countryside.

In 1962, the year after the Right lost its veto power in Congress, and under pressure from Alliance for Progress officials who controlled the American "foreign aid" program, Chile adopted an agrarian reform law that began a decade-long assault upon the hacienda system. Law 15020 created three government agencies to administer programs of land reform, agricultural extension, and agricultural planning. Though under the Alessandri administration the government failed to carry out extensive agrarian reform, the legislation did provide a legal basis for more extensive transfers of land from large estates to small holders. In addition, two of the new government agencies—the Agrarian Reform Corporation (CORA) and the Institute for Agrarian and Livestock Development (INDAP)—would later play a revolutionary role in transforming Chilean agriculture and Chilean politics. In the short run (1962-64), the Alessandri government carried out what many Chileans called a "flower pot reform" (reforma de macetero), converting sixty thousand hectares of public lands and well-recompensed private estates into small and medium-size farms.

By the end of the Alessandri administration a three-way battle was shaping up for the 1964 presidential election. FRAP again supported the candidacy of Salvador Allende. The Christian Democrats, who obtained extensive financing from covert American sources, offered Eduardo Frei. The Right (Frente Democrático) presented Julio Durán, a member of the conservative wing of the Radical party. In March 1964 a congressional by-election to replace a popular Socialist congressman in Curicó was interpreted by the three contending forces as a barometer of electoral strength for the upcoming presidential elections. However accurately the Curicó by-election reflected national political sentiment, FRAP's decisive victory disheartened the Right which finished third behind the Christian Democrats. The Frente Democrático dissolved and, in an effort to prevent a "communist" victory, threw its support to Eduardo Frei.

In the presidential campaign that followed both the Christian Democrats and FRAP promised agrarian reform, rural unionization, and enforcement of labor law in the countryside. Both Marxists and Christian Democrats courted rural votes, supported rural strike committees, helped organize rural unions, and promised an end to the hacienda system. To the landowners the Christian Democrats were the lesser of two evils.

When the Christian Democrats won the presidential election, and found themselves in competition with the Marxists for rural votes in the upcoming congressional elections of 1965, the viability of the new government came to depend upon greatly increasing party representation in Congress. To achieve this, some Christian Democratic candidates adopted the most drastic tactics previously used by Marxists in the rural sector, including sponsorship of illegal agricultural strikes and land occupations. The rural votes that had guaranteed the political power of the hacendados in national politics now provided the impetus for a frontal attack on the hacienda system by the Christian Democratic administration, as well as by the Marxist opposition.

This attack on the hacienda system would first erode the political and economic arrangement that had held the Chilean party system together between 1932 and 1964, and would then intensify polarization of political conflict and so bring to an end Chile's vaunted political stability.

Chapter 9 • Christians and Marxists

Competition for the presidency in 1964 pitted against each other the Christian Democrats and the Marxist Frente de Acción Popular, both of which rejected the basic assumptions of capitalist liberal democracy. The Marxist-dominated FRAP coalition offered the ultimate prospect of creation of a socialist society in Chile. The Christian Democrats proclaimed that Chilean society required fundamental, even revolutionary, changes, but that these changes could be carried out through legal, peaceful means. To emphasize the difference between themselves and the Marxists, they adopted as the slogan of their program, "Revolution in Liberty."

The Christian Democrats criticized the evils of capitalism and materialistic socialism, offering in their stead a vaguely defined "communitarian" society or Christian socialism. Based upon writings of the French philosopher Jacques Maritain and upon Catholic social doctrine, a communitarian society would supposedly end class conflict through new types of "worker enterprises" that harmonize labor and capital. It would combine social pluralism and civil liberties with a just redistribution of wealth and income. But just as Marxist-Leninists lack any detailed description of the workings of a truly communist society, Christian Democrats had various visions of a communitarian society.

Marxist parties had played an active role in Chilean politics since the second decade of the twentieth century. Communists, Socialists, and Trotskyists could trace their ancestry to the labor movement of the late nineteenth century, the Partido Demócrata (1887), and the Partido Obrero Socialista (POS) led by Recabarren and his comrades after 1912. Although the Communist party dated only from 1922 and the Socialist party from the early 1930s, an indigenous Marxist movement linked to international Marxism had struggled for at least half a century to reform or destroy Chilean formal democracy.

In the labor movement the Marxists had created a firm base of popular support. Just as some families passed Catholicism from generation to generation, so other families transmitted loyalty to the Communist or the Socialist party. Party-oriented youth movements, retail shops, sports clubs, doctors, and even barber shops allowed most of such people's daily lives to go on within a network of party loyalists. Of course, not all party members or sympathizers so restricted their lives or committed themselves to party work, but both Communists and Socialists had established strong roots in Chilean soil.

The FRAP coalition's presidential candidate in 1964, Salvador Allende, was a savvy, well-known politician. During the popular-front years Dr. Allende served as minister of health and subsequently gained valuable political experience in the Congress. In 1952 and 1958, respectively, Allende lost presidential elections to Carlos Ibáñez and Jorge Alessandri. The slim margin of his loss to Alessandri in 1958 badly scared the traditional political parties, the Catholic Church, and policymakers in the United States.

In contrast to the Marxist parties, the Christian Democrats could trace their official existence back only to 1957. Prior to that time, however, the ideological and organizational evolution of Christian Democracy stemmed from Catholic social doctrine and from dissident and more progressive elements within the Chilean Conservative party. In particular, the papal encyclicals *Rerum Novarum* (1891) and *Quadragessimo Anno* (1931) established the foundations of official Catholic response to the dilemmas of industrial society and the international challenge of Marxism. Pope Leo XIII noted in *Rerum Novarum* that the process of industrialization and capitalist development concentrated production and wealth into the hands of "a small number of opulent and wealthy men and put upon the innumerable multitude of proletarians a yoke that differed little from slavery." Without organizations to defend them the workers found themselves "alone and defenseless . . . against the inhumanity of their masters." This critique of capitalist development did little immediately to influence the Latin American or Chilean Catholic hierarchy, but nonetheless provided doctrinal justification for initial efforts by progressive Catholic laypersons and clerics to improve the lot of the working classes.

Forty years later, at the depths of the world depression, Pope Pius XI reconfirmed the Church's concern for the plight of the working classes in a harsh attack on capitalism and international imperialism. Pius XI's *Quadragessimo Anno* went further than Leo XIII and specifically referred to the misery of the landless laborers of the countryside, indirectly placing the Church on the side of those advocating agrarian reform to bring about social justice.

These encyclicals and other doctrinal statements placed the Church in opposition to the economic and political liberalism upon which the institutions of Western capitalist democracy rested. Progressive Catholic social theorists rejected the legitimacy of labor market determination of wages, insisting upon a just wage sufficient to guarantee a decent standard of living for the worker and the worker's family. The Church also officially recognized the importance of workers' organizations—not as vehicles of class struggle, but as "instruments of concord and peace," guided by Christian principles in the solution of the social question. Despite this pacific orientation, *Rerum Novarum* recognized that harsh working conditions, long hours, and low pay sometimes justified workers in resorting to strikes or other forceful means to better their conditions.

In the first two decades of the twentieth century a small number of Catholic politicians and churchmen in Chile responded to the social question with proposals for reform inspired by the social doctrines elaborated in *Rerum Novarum*. Based in the Jesuit college of San Ignacio, Father Fernando Vives de Soler and Father Jorge Fernández Pradel influenced a group of future political leaders, priests, and bishops who later played a leading role in the development of Chilean Christian Democracy. By 1917 Father Vives and his colleagues had established a "Social Secretariat" and were engaged in unionization efforts among small numbers of workers in industry, transport, and commerce in Santiago. Objections by leading Conservative politicians undermined these first efforts and periodically forced the temporary European exile of controversial clerics.

Against the background of the post-World War I economic crisis in Chile, and the growing sentiment favoring separation of Church and State, the Chilean archbishop and prominent historian, Crescente Errázuriz, delivered a pastoral message entitled "On Social Action." Archbishop Errázuriz took note of the misery of many Chilean workers and, in particular, of the lamentable condition of the campesinos. Speaking several years before the military coup of 1924 forced the "social laws" upon a recalcitrant Chilean Congress, the archbishop accepted the necessity of workers' organizations in order "to obtain for the workers the benefits to which they have a right."

Coincident with the Church's increased concern with the plight of Chilean workers and campesinos after World War I, it also faced pressures for separation of Church and State. In June 1923 President Alessandri proposed legislation to Congress intended to protect religious freedom for all Chileans and to insulate the Catholic Church from its traditional role in partisan politics. Quoting Bishop Valdivieso (1859), the President pointed to the dangers associated with linking the "future of the Church, the most precious interests of religion, . . . to the fortunes of a [political] party." Negotiations between Church officials and the Alessandri administration assured the former title to its extensive property holdings, financial assistance, and the right to maintain or expand its role in education, public health, and charitable activities. Thus, when the Constitution of 1925 officially separated Church and State, the archbishop of Santiago could comment in his pastoral that "It is just to note that the authorities in Chile, in establishing this separation, have not been motivated by the spirit of persecution which characterizes other countries where Catholicism has been attacked. . . . The State is separated from the Church; but the Church is not separated from the State, and will always be ready to serve it."

Archbishop Errázuriz' effective leadership in the Church-State separation matter left the Church in a relatively unblemished political position. He averted direct confrontation between Liberals, Radicals, and Conservatives, thereby allowing these groups, along with the Church, to focus upon the threatening implications of the social question.

Pastoral messages and other doctrinal statements on the social question by leading intellectuals of the Chilean Church derived both from a real concern for the condition of the Chilean poor and also from the growing Marxist influence among the country's working classes. Catholic leaders, grounded in the Church's philosophical and theological rejection of "individualistic liberalism," attempted to forge a response to the social question that would be an alternative to the millenarian Marxist vision of a classless society. Indicative of this anti-Marxist motivation for part of the Church's concern with the social question, the bishop of Temuco in 1933 presented a paper at the Third Congress of Catholic Men entitled "A Study of the Practical Manner of Combatting Communism in Chile."

Anticommunism and sincere commitment to Catholic social doctrine provided the foundation of the education received at San Ignacio and Santiago's Catholic University by the generation of students in the late 1920s and early 1930s who would become the principal leaders of Chilean Christian Democracy. These young progressive Catholics—Bernardo Leighton, Manuel Garretón, Ignacio Palma, Radomiro Tomic, Eduardo Frei—served their political apprenticeship in the youth movement of the Conservative party. They became so active in carrying out the social doctrine of the Church that finally the Conservative party could not tolerate them, and in 1938 they broke away to form a new party, the Falange Nacional.

In the year that the Falange emerged as an independent political party, the Catholic Church created the Secretariado Nacional Económico Social (National Economic and Social Secretariat) in response to the social agitation associated with the growing strength of the Chilean popular front. Under the direction of Oscar Larson, who had previously worked with the Catholic Students Federation (ANEC), the Secretariat moved into direct social action, including organization of rural workers. Emilio Tagle, later the archbishop of Valparaíso, and Oscar Larson supported the formation of the Unión de Campesinos among rural workers in the region around Buin (Santiago province). By 1941 this Catholic rural labor union was reported to have three hundred members in twelve rural estates. It was hardly a massive organizational drive, especially when compared with the large-scale rural labor movement oriented by the Communists and Socialists (1939-41). Nevertheless this first Catholic support of rural workers' organizations infuriated the Conservative party, traditionally the Church's closest political ally.

In Fundo Huelquen, owned by a deputy of the Conservative party, a Falange lawyer and clerics assisted the workers in presentation of a labor petition to the landowner. The landowner attacked the clerics who participated in the workers' movement, suggesting that they leave determination of the workers' salaries to God and the conscience of the *patrón*. Subsequently the Conservative party demanded that the efforts of Larson, Tagle, and their colleagues be stopped and that the Unión de Campesinos be disbanded. The Church hierarchy acquiesced; Larson left for missions outside of Chile. Despite their immediate victory, the landowners recognized the threat of social movements inspired by Catholic social doctrine. They complained that "the *falangistas* are worse than the Communists, since we know how to defend ourselves against the Communists, but not so against the *falangistas*. . . ."

During the next decade the Falange remained a small, elitist social Christian party with a populist orientation. Occasionally Falange deputies made the critical difference in forging electoral or legislative coalitions or gave dramatic speeches in the Congress. For example, in 1947 Falange deputy Jorge Rogers Sotomayor bitterly denounced the rural unionization law (Law 8811) that reaffirmed the repression of rural workers. From time to time also, Falange leaders served in cabinet posts, beginning with Bernardo Leighton's brief stint as minister of labor (1938) in the second Alessandri administration. Progressive elements within the Church also continued with small-scale leadership-formation programs among workers and youth organizations. Neither in the political nor labor arena, however, did these progressive Catholics gain a mass following or exercise great national influence.

Complicating further the evolution of social Catholicism as a political force, new divisions within the Conservative party led to the foundation in the 1940s of the Partido Conservador Social Cristiano (Conservative Social Christian Party). Somewhat more conservative than the Falange, and led by more established ex-Conservative politicians, the Conservative Social Christian Party outpolled the Falange in national and local elections into the 1950s. The eventual dissolution in 1957 of the Partido Conservador Social Cristiano, however, united most progressive Catholics, along with ex-members of

TABLE 18. ELECTORAL EVOLUTION OF FALANGE NATIONAL, PARTIDO DEMÓCRATA CRISTIANA, CHAMBER OF DEPUTIES

Year	Total Votes	Percent of Electorate	Number of Deputies Elected
1941	15,553	3.5	3
1945	10,527	2.2	3
1949*	18,221	3.9	3
1953	22,353	2.8	3
1957	82,710	9.2	17
1961†	213,559	16.	23
1965	989,626	41.6	82

* In 1949 the Social Christian Party polled 2,018 votes without electing a deputy.
† Christian Democrats.

(Source: Adapted from Germán Urzua Valenzuela, *Los Partidos Políticos Chilenos*, Santiago, Editorial Jurídica, 1968, pp. 124-25.)

the Agrarian Labor party, into the Christian Democratic party (PDC) in anticipation of the 1958 presidential election.

After World War II a concern by the Holy See and the United States for the advance of Marxism in Chile gave new impetus and financial support to Catholic organizations among workers, students, women, and peasants. Middle-class reformers, professionals, and technicians, found in the Falange an alternative to the unmoving conservatism of the traditional parties and to the opportunism of the Radicals. With a heterogeneous base, the Falange developed as a multiclass movement under the continued direction of the generation of leaders who had founded it in the late 1930s. Slowly the Falange gained in national prestige and visibility, as it advocated extensive reforms consistent with the social doctrine of the Church.

Before 1953 the Falange was more active in urban areas and universities than in the countryside, but it would be the rural organizing activity of the Falange and Catholic labor leaders that did the most to boost the political credibility of the Catholic reformers. In 1952 a Falange politician, Emilio Lorenzini, began to organize rural labor around the town of Molina in Talca province with the Federación Sindical Cristiana de la Tierra. The vineyards of the Molina region had seen a number of rural labor conflicts between 1919 and 1952. As late as 1946-47 headline-making legal strikes occurred in the region's farms—before Law 8811 and the Law for the Permanent Defense of Democracy suppressed the rural labor movement. It was ironical that in applying the latter law the government had banished Communist leaders, such as José Campusano, to the Molina district. Tense cooperation in the fields between Falange and Communist cadres set the stage for fierce competition in later years.

Emilio Lorenzini affiliated the Federación Sindical Cristiana de la Tierra with the major Catholic labor organization, Acción Sindical y Ecónomico Chileno (ASICH). Formed in 1947 under the leadership of the Jesuit, Alberto Hurtado—after special authorization by the Jesuit general and Pope Pius XII—ASICH was a thorn in the side of both the Marxists and the traditional political parties in Chile. In the rural district around Molina, supported by Bishop Manuel Larraín (an early colleague of Father Hurtado in the awakening of the Catholic labor movement in the 1920s), ASICH and the Federación Sindical Cristiana de la Tierra provided campesinos with legal services, literacy and leadership training, and assistance in labor conflicts. In October 1953, Lorenzini organized the Primer Congreso Sindical de los Obreros Campesinos de Molina, where rural workers and union leaders drew up labor petitions to present in the vineyards of Molina in November (prior to the harvest). When the landowners refused to negotiate in good faith with the workers, the campesinos declared a strike. Illegal under the terms of Law 8811, the strike brought government repression. Lorenzini and other union leaders went to jail for offenses specified in the Law for the Permanent Defense of Democracy; the government dealt with progressive Catholics by applying legislation intended to control "communist" activities.

Unwilling to accept defeat, ASICH organized a march to Santiago by the Molina campesinos. The political effect of this march in the early days of the new Ibáñez administration forced the government to release Lorenzini and other union leaders as well as to pressure the landowners to negotiate with the farm workers—despite the fact that the strike was clearly illegal. For both the numbers of workers involved and its psychological impact on national politics, the Molina strike is generally cited as the most important rural labor conflict in Chile prior to 1964. More important in the long run, however, were the campesino leaders who emerged in the Molina region, and the spread of the Catholic rural labor movement throughout the central valley, which provided Falange and Catholic reformers with a growing base in the Chilean countryside. In addition, after years of sporadic Marxist political and labor activity in the rural districts, the Church, Falange politicians, and Catholic-oriented rural labor unions had carried out the most important agricultural strike in Chilean history. The Molina strike and the subsequent activism of Catholic rural organizations gave credibility to Falange claims that they favored land reform, social justice, rural unionization, and sweeping social change.

Only four years after the Federación Sindical de la Tierra emerged in Molina, the Jesuit general in Rome, at the request of the Chilean Church, sent to Chile the Belgian Jesuit and social scientist, Roger Vekemans. The Chilean Church wanted help in the battle against communism; Vekemans would spearhead the anticommunist offensive for the next decade. Vekemans recruited Belgian businessman J. N. A. Sierens to begin social research in Chile. Sierens put together a systematic survey of Chilean institutions, with special attention given to "communist penetration." Noting the slim defeat of Allende in the 1958 presidential elections, Sierens recommended coordinated action by the Church to prevent a potential Marxist victory in 1964.

Vekemans, at the head of the Centro Bellarmino, directed an intellectual, organizational, and political campaign under the aegis of a "research and development foundation," called by its acronym DESAL. Large grants from Western European governments, private foundations, and Christian Democratic parties, as well as funds from the United States Central Intelligence Agency, via the conduit of the International Development Foundation, funded DESAL and other Catholic intellectual and organizing efforts. Vekemans, along with Father Zañartu (affiliated with the University of Notre Dame in the United States) and other Jesuits, gave doctrinal direction to the campaign against Marxism in Chile. A thorough study of this international politico-religious penetration of Chilean politics by David E. Mutchler* documented an intricate web of financial arrangements and organizational ties emanating from Vekemans and his colleagues. In this web were entangled the mass media, labor, business, the American AID mission, CIA, Western European governments, political parties, and private foundations.

Complementing its research activities and elaboration of a new "development ideology," the Catholic Church's anti-Marxist offensive resulted in the creation of numerous neighborhood organizations, unions, farm committees, discussion groups, women's organizations, and quasi-political groups that could be mobilized for the

---

* *The Church as a Political Factor in Latin America* (New York: Praeger, 1971).

1964 election campaign. In the meantime, ASICH formed the Unión de Campesinos Cristianos in 1960 to unite isolated farm unions and worker's committees and to expand the rural labor movement. Moreover, parallel operations by Acción Católica Rural (Rural Catholic Action) and the Institute for Rural Education (IER)—also partially financed with American funds and partially staffed with Peace Corps volunteers—gave rise to the Asociación Nacional de Organizaciones Campesinas (ANOC), or the National Association of Campesino Organizations. After completing their training at the IER, ANOC leaders received salaries from the institute while they led rural labor conflicts, created Christian-inspired rural organizations, and opposed communism in the countryside.

These Catholic-oriented rural labor leaders mobilized thousands of Chilean campesinos into new organizations and inspired a growing rural activism. Though some leaders of the movement may have understood the international and the national political implications of their ties with IER, ACR, and the Christian Democrats, later events would demonstrate that many participants were more independent and more militant than their unknown patrons desired. Internal debates and conflicts over strategy and direction of the movement in the mid-1960s and after made clear that these campesino organizations were far more complex and less manipulable than their early directors had imagined. In the short term, however, these organizations proved an important resource in the campaign against Marxism in Chile.

As the political situation of the Alessandri government deteriorated after 1961, the rising Catholic rural labor movement, in alliance with the newly founded Christian Democratic party, represented a major alternative to the Marxist-dominated FRAP coalition of Communists, Socialists, and smaller reformist parties. The most prominent Christian Democratic leaders, including Eduardo Frei, had been schoolmates of important officials of Vekemans' Centro Bellarmino. Personal ties reinforced doctrinal and ideological connections between the Christian Democrats and the Jesuit intellectuals.

In 1962 the Chilean bishops entrusted Vekemans and Renato Poblete, an old schoolmate of Eduardo Frei, with preparation of a "pastoral plan" that would help Frei against Allende in the 1964 election. Also in 1962 the Chilean bishops initiated their own land reform experiments, anticipating the legislation passed by the Alessandri government later that year. Almost simultaneously the Church distributed a pastoral letter entitled "The Social and Political Duty." This pastoral made clear that "communism deprives man of his liberty, suppresses all dignity and morality of the human person; it denies to the individual all natural rights. . . . Communism destroys any bond between mother and child." During the 1964 election campaign Christian Democrats distributed thousands of copies of this pastoral letter and papered the walls of Chile with posters depicting the foreheads of Chilean children being branded with the hammer and sickle. The international Catholic offensive (1957-64) thus contributed to the domestic political campaign against the Marxists.

Meanwhile, Fidel Castro's sister, Juana Castro, came to Chile to tell the Chilean people, especially Chilean women, of the horrors of communism in Cuba. These developments combined with the psychological effect of the by-elections of Curicó—that prompted support by the Right for Frei's candidacy—and with millions of dollars in covert campaign contributions from American agents and European Christian Democrats, to give the Christian Democrats the presidency in 1964.

If anticommunism was the rationale for massive U.S., West German, and Church support for Chile's Christian Democrats, there existed within the Christian Democratic party many sincere reformers and even a small number of committed revolutionaries. President Frei's call for "Revolution in Liberty" was not empty rhetoric. The Christian Democrats intended to alter dramatically the very foundations of Chilean society, to redistribute income and wealth, to improve the living standards of, and to broaden opportunities for, the nation's workers and peasants, and to democratize the country's political and social life.

Faced with the many social and economic problems inherited from the process of economic development after 1930 and the historical legacy of a highly stratified class society, the Christian Democratic administration attempted to carry out a sweeping reform program encompassing every area of Chilean life. All the persistent problems of the Chilean economy received government attention—including efforts to control inflation, to improve the nation's balance of payments through stimulation of exports, to carry out large-scale agrarian reform, to enact meaningful tax reforms, and to make significant investments in public health, education and vocational training, and to expand the services of the Labor Department.

Almost every aspect of the government's program threatened either the political and economic privileges of the traditional elite or menaced leftist influence over organized labor and the urban and rural poor. No way existed for the Christian Democrats to implement their program without alienating the support of the rightist parties whose votes had elected President Frei. Similarly, no matter how successful the government was in implementing social and economic reforms, the FRAP parties could urge more rapid or more extensive changes in Chilean society; they could point to areas of policy failure and push working-class and peasant organizations into direct action that impelled the administration to move either faster than it desired or to use police to halt illegal land occupations or strikes.

Unfortunately for the Christian Democratic government, official policymakers clearly and precisely outlined the administration's short- and long-term goals in overly optimistic terms. Even with the Christian Democrats' stunning victory in the 1965 congressional elections, which gave them majority control of the House of Deputies, FRAP and rightist representatives in the Senate still managed to delay significantly passage of key legislation. Every major component of the government's program—"Chileanization" of the copper industry, agrarian reform/agricultural unionization, tax reform, wage-price stabilization, and proposals to stimulate industrial growth—faced the scrutiny and obstructionism of the opposition. This was, of course, merely a new version of the historical struggle between executive coalitions and Congress that had characterized Chilean politics in the parliamentary period and also after 1932—complicated now by the facts that a single party rather than a coalition controlled the executive and that traditional political forces considered some Christian Democrats *prepotentes*, or uncompromising.

Only in 1966-67, after considerable negotiation and compromise, did the copper legislation, agrarian reform, and agricultural unionization legislation clear the Congress. Predictably, the Marxists opposed any effort by the government to restrain inflation through limitations on wage readjustments. The Right, enraged at the government-sponsored mobilization of rural workers into unions and cooperatives as well as at the prospect of a real agrarian reform, held hostage the copper legislation in an effort to weaken the administration's agrarian program. The Right also exacerbated relations with the United States by joining the Marxists in a call for outright nationalization of the copper industry instead of the acquisition by the Chilean government of majority interest in the companies that the government called "Chileanization." Only half facetiously, leading Conservative and Liberal politicians suggested compensating the companies just as the United States-approved agrarian reform would compensate Chilean landowners for their expropriated holdings—with government bonds payable in thirty years.

The ambitious scope and the specificity with which the Christian Democrats set out their program made its effective implementation through legal means in a six-year period a practical impossibility. Notwithstanding greatly increased copper prices, due in part to the war in Vietnam, and substantial assistance from the Alliance for Progress, internal political opposition and the structural constraints of the Chilean socio-economic situation prevented total success. Thus, even the sometimes impressive accomplishments of the regime fell far short of its publicly announced objectives. Moreover, the severe drought of 1967-68 seriously disrupted agricultural production, thereby adding to the nation's economic difficulties. The discrepancy between stated objectives and actual attainment allowed both the rightist and the FRAP opposition to point to the failure of the Christian Democratic administration.

In one area especially, Christian Democratic policies led to dismal

TABLE 19. COMPARISON OF POLICY OBJECTIVES AND
PERFORMANCE OF "REVOLUTION IN LIBERTY"

Policy Objectives	Time Frame	Targeted Increase	Actual Increase
Retail prices	1965	25%	29%
Retail prices	1966	15%	23%
Retail prices	1967	10%	18%
Nonagricultural prices	1965	Less than 20%	28%
Money supply	1965	25%	65%
Real GNP	1964-70	23%	30%
Exports	1964-70	94%	94%
New farm ownerships	1964-70	100,000	28,000
New housing units	1964-70	360,000	260,000
Copper output	1964-70	90%	10%
Real GDP	1965-70	31%	18%
Per capita real GDP	1965-70	20%	5%
Gross investment	1965-70	70%	22% (through 1969)
Domestic saving	1965-70	100%	52% (through 1969)
Exports	1965-70	55%	68%
Copper exports	1965-70	70%	107%
Imports	1965-70	31%	63%

(Source: After Thomas L. Edwards, *Economic Development and Reform in Chile: Progress Under Frei, 1964-1970*, Latin American Studies Center, Michigan State University, 1972, p. 50.)

failure. Rather than decreasing Chile's economic dependence and reducing the influence of foreign capital on its economy, the Frei government created numerous incentives to attract foreign investors and subordinated public policy to conditions imposed by United States and international lending agencies. The incentives to foreign capital included generous profit-remittance arrangements and liberalized import regulations for firms establishing themselves in Chile. Promise of tax stability and exchange-control advantages also served to encourage foreign investment. In response to these incentives multinational enterprises substantially increased their investments in Chile, especially in the industrial sector. By 1970 over one hundred United States corporations had investments in Chile, among them twenty-four of the top United States-based multinationals.

Foreign investment brought with it high technology, capital-intensive production units that made little contribution to the government's efforts to reduce unemployment. Indeed, for the decade 1960-70, industry provided an average of only fifteen thousand new job opportunities per year—nowhere near enough to absorb the continuing tide of migrants from the countryside to the urban areas. This migration enlarged the rings of misery surrounding Santiago and other major cities, as the shantytowns and squatter settlements (*callampas*, or "mushroom towns") grew at alarming rates. In Santiago alone the *callampas* and squatter settlements sheltered nearly one-half million people, or 20 to 25 percent of the city's population.

Living conditions in these urban settlements varied from poor to deplorable. Most lacked basic urban services and amenities, including sewers and potable water. Unemployment levels ranged well above the official national figure of 8 percent, and underemployment disguised the desperate situation of families without any steady, dependable source of income. As in the rest of Latin America, these urban poor lacked meaningful unemployment insurance or welfare services that might guarantee even a "floor to misery." They endured a daily struggle for survival. Lacking also protection from unions or private charitable relief, thousands of slum dwellers and residents of the shantytowns of Santiago received the political messages of the "Revolution in Liberty" without obtaining the material benefits it promised.

When the government did respond to the physical needs of the urban poor with self-help housing projects (*operación sitio*), encouragement of *centros de madres* ("mothers' centers") or *juntas de vecinos* ("neighborhood councils"), construction of waterworks or installation of electric lines, there always remained those who felt left out. The admittedly partisan process that determined which groups of urban poor would benefit from government programs, whether because of party affiliation or the high visibility of political mobilization in particular settlements, further undermined the government's efforts. For every successful program there were more people left out than included. The backlog of need and poverty made even significant improvements in the living conditions of some groups of the urban poor a political defeat for the incumbent administration, just as

TABLE 20. DISTRIBUTION OF LABOR FORCE BY ECONOMIC SECTOR, 1960-1970 (1000S)

	1960	1961	1962	1963	1964	1965	1966	1967	1968	1969	1970	Percent
Agriculture	711.1	668.6	687.7	704.0	680.8	709.8	717.7	750.0	736.4	731.7	738.0	24.2
Mining	92.5	94.9	91.7	88.7	91.7	93.4	93.6	94.0	94.5	97.7	99.2	3.3
Industry	412.6	439.7	450.4	464.5	477.9	506.7	527.7	534.4	544.6	550.7	562.9	18.8
Construction	130.5	135.6	158.6	158.5	188.8	183.1	186.3	169.0	168.5	172.0	177.5	6.0
Electricity	10.8	11.0	11.1	11.8	12.3	12.5	11.9	11.9	11.8	11.8	11.8	0.3
Gas, and Water												
Commerce	260.3	265.5	279.0	294.1	311.1	330.0	351.0	375.0	404.2	428.5	451.5	15.1
Transport	121.2	126.0	135.0	139.0	143.8	148.0	149.5	156.2	161.8	167.4	175.6	5.9
Services	578.0	587.6	592.5	613.6	630.9	640.0	665.0	721.4	757.5	761.3	777.7	26.0
Total	2,317.0	2,348.9	2,406.0	2,474.2	2,546.3	2,623.5	2,702.7	2,811.9	2,879.3	2,921.1	2,994.2	100.0

(Source: Odeplan, Chilean Planning Agency.)

distribution of land to some thirty thousand campesinos alienated many times that number who did not receive land from the government program.

In part, the extremely favorable treatment afforded the multinationals by the Frei administration, and the constraints on the government's program of reform, stemmed from the negotiated "solution" to Chile's immediate balance of payments crisis facing the Christian Democrats when they came to office. Chile's accumulated international obligations in 1964, over $1 billion, required almost 40 percent of copper export earnings for debt service alone. To support the Frei government's "Revolution in Liberty," the United States and ten other creditor nations agreed to a "rollover" or credit relief plan of approximately $100 million for a two-year period and a grace period that allowed for a five-year repayment schedule beginning in 1968. Chile pledged in exchange to facilitate transfer of payments on the renegotiated debt and also to relax controls on foreign exchange for purchase of certain types of imports. In turn, AID provided large loans and other assistance to the Chilean administration; in 1964-65 AID accounted for almost 15 percent of Chile's national budget. Thus the financial feasibility of the Christian Democratic reforms depended not only upon the hope for better copper prices, but also upon the good will of U.S. policymakers and the cooperation of the multinational enterprises. Touting the "Revolution in Liberty" as a positive alternative to the Cuban revolutionary model, United States policymakers sought to buttress the Christian Democrats as well as to support American business interests in Chile. This strategy, reminiscent of the American decision to underwrite the initial CORFO projects in 1939 and 1940—only now on a much grander scale—entangled the Christian Democratic administration in the web of American foreign policy, including the war in Vietnam. It also exacerbated the internal divisions within the government party as the Christian Democratic youth movement and the more populist elements of the party rejected any identification with foreign capital, imperialism, the American embassy, or the Vietnam War.

Apart from its uneven record with respect to its announced social and economic objectives, the Christian Democratic government mobilized hundreds of thousands of women, students, workers, and campesinos into new unions, cooperatives, and community organizations. These organizations depended upon government encouragement or subsidies and came to expect continual economic benefits or expanded government services. Distribution of consumer goods, credit, agricultural inputs, and jobs through political agencies like Promoción Popular (Popular Promotion) and INDAP created a vast network of patronage and spoils tying bureaucrats, party hacks, slum dwellers, and campesinos to government pursestrings. Immediate benefits such as new sewing machines for a *centro de madres* or seed and fertilizer for a campesino cooperative helped convince the underclasses of the government's concern for their plight. Accompanied by promises of increasing material benefits by government enthusiasts who staffed the mushrooming public sector, these initial spoils of reform also created high expectations of rapid, often unobtainable, changes in lifestyle and of economic opportunities.

To a great extent the Christian Democratic program of political mobilization and deliberate "consciousness raising" (*concientización*) made impossible the attainment of its other major economic objectives such as control of inflation, increases in productivity, and higher levels of domestic savings and investment. With their hopes aroused by both the government's propaganda and the even more alluring Marxist vision in which redistribution of wealth and land would greatly improve the lot of the masses, Chilean workers and peasants could hardly be expected to accept government proposals for wage restraints, forced-savings plans, and moderation in labor disputes.

Moreover, as the government generally refused to use police or the military against slum dwellers, organized labor, or campesinos, illegal land occupations and even worker-declared "expropriation" of farms and factories occurred more frequently. Whereas the leftist press indignantly publicized the small number of cases in which the government did use force to halt labor conflicts or to remove trespassers—

TABLE 21. ILLEGAL STRIKES, URBAN LAND INVASIONS,
FACTORY SEIZURES, AND FARM SEIZURES (Tomas)

	1966	1967	1968	1969	1970
Urban land invasions		13	8	73	220
Factory tomas	n.d.	n.d.	5	24	133
Illegal strikes	936	878	901	771*	1,085
Farm tomas	36**	9	27	148	271

* First nine months only.
** 1960-1966.

(Source: Chilean Labor Department Annual Report for each year; Solon Barraclough and J. A. Fernández, *Diagnóstico de la reforma agraria Chilena*, Mexico, Siglo Veintiuno, 1974; Walden F. Bello, "The Roots and Dynamics of Revolution and Counterrevolution in Chile," unpublished doctoral dissertation, Princeton University, 1975.)

especially when workers died or were injured as in Puerto Montt in early March 1969—the political Right noted the government's reluctance to guarantee private property rights and organized white guards to defend its interests. No administrative decree or government policy could effectively limit popular mobilization once set in motion; only police or the military sufficed. With its unwillingness to adopt clearly repressive tactics, especially given the numerous divisions within the Christian Democratic party itself, the government found a lawful "Revolution in Liberty" to be illusory. If the government chose to uphold the law, it necessarily employed force against workers, peasants, and students acting illegally to accelerate the program of reform.

The Marxist parties, recognizing this dilemma, lost no opportunity to exacerbate it by proclaiming their support for land occupations, "farm seizures (tomas), and widespread illegal strikes. If in order to demonstrate its commitment to reform, the goverment invariably refused to halt these activities, then legal reform would have given way to an uncontrolled and uncontrollable revolutionary situation. Just as the leftists deliberately confronted the government with this choice between suppression of popular movements and chaos, so the rightists challenged the legality of the agrarian reform process and organized sometimes violent resistance to the government's legal reforms.

Complicating this situation, a minority element within the Christian Democratic party encouraged mass mobilization and political activism beyond the limits officially set by the Frei administration. In particular, Jacques Chonchol, director of INDAP, believed it necessary to go beyond the bounds of existing law in the unionization of rural labor and in support for agrarian reform. While the government sought to squeeze new legislation out of Congress (1964-67), Chonchol, via INDAP, promoted large numbers of agricultural labor conflicts and organized multifarm unions in direct violation of existing legislation. Not to be outdone, Communist and Socialist organizers competed with INDAP in the effort to mobilize the rural labor force against the landowners and to accelerate agrarian reform.

These efforts overwhelmed the Labor Department, which lacked sufficient personnel and resources to administer properly the mounting number of requests to form agricultural unions or to process efficiently the hundreds of agricultural labor disputes. After frequent appearances in its offices of INDAP organizers (*promotores*) representing campesino groups, the Labor Department ruled that INDAP officials "do not have the legal right to intervene in the presentation of labor petitions and in the process of negotiation of labor conflicts in the agricultural sector." In response, INDAP personnel received instructions to limit their intervention in rural labor conflicts to "informal" support or assistance. In addition, the new peasant organizations and even the Catholic rural labor movement, generated by ASICH and the Institute for Rural Education, pressured CORA, the agency responsible for implementing land reform, to speed up the expropriation and redistribution of agricultural land. Administrative inability to keep pace with the tide of popular mobilization and rising expectations made the government appear unwilling to fulfill its promises to the urban and the rural poor. It also made credible Marxist attacks on the government for failing to carry out completely its promised program. Added to criticism from the Right, united in the Partido Nacional after merger of Conservatives and Liberals in 1965, the dissident Christian Democrats and Marxists swamped the government reform program in sectarian politics and obstructionism.

The debate within the Christian Democratic party over the pace, character, and objectives of agrarian reform typified the basic contradictions that eventually proved fatal to the "Revolution in Liberty." The essential constraints on Chilean development could not be overcome without both improved distribution of wealth and income *and* increased production of goods and services. If redistribution occurred at the cost of current investment and reduced productivity, then any gains to the workers and peasants could only be temporary. Rising demands for goods and services without concomitant expansion of domestic production and export earnings could only lead to a renewal of the inflationary spiral. Under these conditions an ever more militant, politicized rural labor force became a serious obstacle to the government's overall economic program at the same time as it was a major social and political accomplishment of government policy.

More than any other aspect of the government program, official encouragement and often subsidization of the formation of thousands of organizations among Chile's urban and rural poor upset the equilibrium of Chilean society. It also created political forces that the government could not or would not control. Consistent with the ambiguity that characterized its reform program, the government sometimes did and sometimes did not call in police to squelch illegal rural labor conflicts, strikes in the cities or mines, or land occupations; sometimes it used a labor conflict as a pretext to place one of its representatives (*inteventor*) in the farm where the conflict was taking place and to organize the campesinos for eventual expropriation of the property.

Thus the "Revolution in Liberty" proved to be neither a revolution nor entirely lawful. It also failed to solve the fundamental economic problems the Christian Democrats themselves had identified in 1964: slow economic growth, instability of prices (inflation), dependence upon foreign markets and capital, and unequal distribution of wealth and income. Nevertheless, it did improve the living conditions of thousands of rural workers, tenants, and other beneficiaries of land reform; it did enact critical political and administrative reforms; it instituted a tax system that generated substantial internal revenues; and it spread the belief that the Chilean state could offer

TABLE 22. CHRISTIAN DEMOCRATIC AGRARIAN REFORM:
EXPROPRIATIONS, 1965–JULY 14, 1970

Year	Number of Properties*	Area in Hectares		Total Area
		Irrigated	Unirrigated	
1965	99	41,260.1	499,923.0	541,183.1
1966	265	57,877.4	468,326.0	526,203.4
1967	131	20,141.8	115,155.4	136,297.2
(Law 15.020)				
1967	86	30,443.1	119,285.4	149,728.5
(Law 16.640)				
1968	223	44,681.1	612,566.3	657,247.4
1969	314	54,478.8	807,361.8	861,840.6
1970	201	30,986.6	604,181.5	635,168.1†
(to July 14)				
Total	1,319	279,868.9	3,128,919.4	3,408,788.3

* Some *asentamientos* (land reform settlements) were formed by combining two or more properties.
† Error in original reads 535,163.1.
(Source: CORA, *Reforma agraria chilena*, 1965-1970, Santiago, CORA, 1970, p. 36.)

real hope for improvement of the lot of the poor. In the areas of education and public health the Frei government also made impressive gains. Primary school enrollment increased by 46 percent, university enrollments doubled, and matriculation in technical schools quadrupled. Public health programs that established numerous rural clinics and trained community health leaders cut Chile's atrocious infant mortality rate and also bettered other general health conditions.

The reformist legislation of the Frei years and the massive organizational drive encouraged by the Christian Democratic administration provided substantial leverage for further fundamental reforms in Chilean society. In this sense the Christian Democrats definitively destroyed the cornerstone of Chilean formal democracy as it had functioned since 1932, without providing anything but the vaguely conceived notion of a "communitarian" society to replace it.

As the 1970 presidential elections approached, the Unidad Popular coalition, with Salvador Allende as its presidential candidate, offered a "transition to socialism" as their answer to this dilemma. The Christian Democratic candidate, Radomiro Tomic, urged an inten-

TABLE 23. GROWTH OF CAMPESINO COOPERATIVE MOVEMENT, 1965-70

Year	Number	Members	Federa- tions	Coopera- tives Affiliated	Confed- erations	Federa- tions Affiliated
1964	24	1,718				
1965	43	3,204				
1966	84	7,802				
1967	123	11,452				
1968	171	18,456				
1969	222	30,034	7	51		
1970*	250	37,675	9†	81	1	9

* To October 22.
† Does not include five federations in- formation which would include 45 affiliated cooperatives.

(Source: INDAP, 1964/1970, n.p.)

TABLE 24. UNION MEMBERSHIP IN CHILE—1964 AND 1970

	1964		1970	
	Number	Members	Number	Members
Industrial or Plant Unions	632	142,958	1,437	197,651
Professional or Craft Unions	1,207	125,926	2,569	239,323
Agricultural Unions	24	1,863	510	114,112
Totals	1,863	270,542	4,006	551,086

(Source: Chilean Labor Department Annual Report for each year.)

TABLE 25. IMPROVEMENTS IN PUBLIC HEALTH DURING
THE FREI ADMINISTRATION

	1964	1969
General Mortality (per 1000)	11.1	8.9
Infant Mortality (per 1000 births)	102.9	79.0
Measles (per 100,000)	38.6	3.5
Typhoid Fever (per 100,000)	2.1	0.9
Tuberculosis (per 100,000)	48.8	29.6

(Source: Presidential message to the National Congress, Santiago, May 21, 1970; Sergio Molina, *El Proceso de Cambio en Chile*, Santiago, Editorial Universitaria, 1972, p. 89.)

sification of the "Revolution in Liberty." Jorge Alessandri, now an old man running as an "independent," appealed to the old elites and alienated middle-class sectors with the prospect of restoration of law and order.

From the perspective of the political Right the drastic nature of the Christian Democratic reforms between 1964 and 1970 prevented them from again supporting the Christian Democratic candidate as the lesser of two evils. In any case, most political analysts, including those in the American embassy in Santiago, predicted a victory for Alessandri. When Salvador Allende emerged with a slim plurality, Chile plunged into three years of dramatic change, punctuated by increasing polarization, political violence, and American intervention in Chilean politics. Christian Democracy's broad-front reformist projects proved to be both too much and too little of what Chile required to become a more Christian and more democratic society.

In the last year of the Christian Democratic administration political tension mounted. A "strike" (the so-called *tacnazo*, because it involved the Tacna regiment) among the officers and men of the Tacna and Yungay regiments of the army resulted in demands for the ouster of the minister of defense and for better pay and materiel for the armed services. Led by retired general Roberto Viaux, this military movement temporarily controlled the main arsenal, the noncommissioned officers' school, and the principal recruiting station; it reminded many Chileans of the events of 1924. Though the movement sputtered and dissolved after the resignation of the defense minister and government promises to attend to the military's economic demands, there was talk of a possible Viaux presidential candidacy after his incarceration—in striking parallel to the 1934 Senate campaign of Maramaduque Grove when the campaign slogan "From jail to the senate" inspired the Chilean Left. Members of the Socialist party took the opportunity to support military aspirations for improved pay and materiel despite their distrust of the reactionary tendencies of Viaux and his comrades.

Shortly thereafter the government pushed legislation through Congress to pacify the military. Even so, on November 19, 1969, the government felt compelled to issue an official declaration threatening severe sanctions against anyone seeking to subvert the discipline of the armed forces. The declaration also emphasized that the commanders of the armed forces and *carabineros* had reaffirmed their loyalty, discipline, and respect for democratic institutions. To confirm this, President Frei declared a "state of emergency" under the questionable authority granted to the executive in cases of "public calamity." This decree allowed the commander of the armed forces to take action to "prevent the commission of crimes or the occurrence of events affecting the security of the state."

At the same time that the Frei government was facing Chile's first serious overt breach of military discipline since the popular-front period, revolutionaries and pseudorevolutionaries incited an already highly politicized population to take matters of economic and social change into their own hands. The Movimiento de Izquierda Revolucionaria (MIR), or Left Revolutionary Movement, a relatively new revolutionary organization which rejected electoral politics, spread its inflammatory ideology among the Mapuche and the campesinos of southern Chile and into the *callampas* of the urban centers. Favoring direct action, MIR cadres, often university students from the University of Concepción, joined with the Mapuche in land "recuperation" movements that were met, not unexpectedly, by landowner resistance. Elements of the Socialist party and MAPU (a radical splinter group from the Christian Democratic party) and even certain Communists also turned to overt attacks on the rights of landed proprietors, industrial enterprises, and owners of urban land and housing projects.

Part of this mass mobilization owed its inspiration to the usual pre-presidential election rhetoric and vote seeking of the Marxist parties and the Christian Democrats. The Marxists, now in alliance with most of the Radical party and with a number of smaller parties, had again chosen Salvador Allende as their presidential candidate and formed a new version of the popular front called *unidad popular* (UP), or "popular unity." The popular unity electoral program called for revolutionary changes in Chile's political, economic, and social structure to overcome the exploitation and misery imposed upon the country by monopoly capitalism, imperialist exploitation, and class privilege. In the introduction to the UP electoral program, the parties of the coalition told the Chilean people that:

> Chile is a capitalist country, dependent on the imperialist nations and dominated by bourgeois groups who are structurally related to foreign capital and cannot resolve the country's fundamental problems—problems which are clearly the result of class privilege which will never be given up voluntarily.

The program criticized the Christian Democratic government as "nothing but a new government of the bourgeoisie, in the service of national and foreign capitalism, whose weak efforts to promote social change came to a sad end in economic stagnation, a rising cost of living, and violent repression of the people." According to the UP parties, the results of the Frei government demonstrated that reformism could not solve the problems of Chile's people.

To solve Chile's problems, the UP coalition proposed a peaceful transition to socialism. This required replacement of Chile's existing political institutions with a unicameral legislature, or people's assembly, to root out the evils of presidentialism and parliamentarism; reorganization of the judiciary and educational system; and greatly increased participation of workers and peasants through union and community organizations in national and local policymaking. Further, the program called for restructuring the economy by greatly increasing the scope of the "social" or public sector, by expropriating all agricultural estates of more than the equivalent of eighty hectares of irrigated land, and by nationalizing the financial system (banks and insurance companies) as well as "all those activities which have a strong influence on the nation's social and economic development." This last category seemed to open the door to a broad program of socialization of the means of production and of distribution channels. The UP indicated that with the dominant "social" sector of the economy there would coexist a "mixed" sector in which enterprises would combine public and private capital; and that, at least in the short run, small private firms could continue to operate. However, uncertainty among the country's small businesses concerning the eventual limits of the UP program, and the coalition's inability to reach internal agreement upon such limits, would produce serious political problems for the UP government (1970-73).

Opposing the UP coalition in the 1970 presidential election, the Christian Democrats chose as their candidate Radomiro Tomic. Tomic, ex-Chilean ambassador to the United States and one of the founders of the Falange, was considered an uncompromising leftist by the Chilean Right. Whereas other potential Christian Democratic candidates might have been able to reconstruct the alliance between the Partido Nacional, other conservative forces, and the Christian Democrats who elected Eduardo Frei in 1964, Tomic declared his unwillingness to cooperate with either the Right or the Radicals who refused to participate in the UP coalition. In a seeming attempt to appear even more revolutionary than Allende, Tomic highlighted his campaign with promises to complete agrarian reform by expropriating all the large rural estates "from the Andes to the sea" (*desde la cordillera hasta el mar*). Repeatedly Tomic emphasized that a victory in coalition with the Right was a victory *for* the Right. In contrast to his harsh attacks on the Partido Nacional and its candidate, Tomic's campaign speeches treated the possibility of an Allende victory as an alternative opportunity for progressive forces in Chile to unite and carry out fundamental social change.

If the Tomic candidacy, rather than that of a more moderate Christian Democrat, made rightist support for the Christian Democrats impossible, political polls showing ex-President Jorge Alessandri the likely victor in a three-way race for the presidency in 1970 whetted the appetite of the Chilean law-and-order forces for a return to "the stick" that Portales had once recommended to cure a nation's "bad habits." The combined support of the Partido Nacional, alienated middle-class groups, and a large number of urban and rural workers still attracted by the appeal of Alessandri's name, made his candidacy appear destined for success. Unfortunately for Alessandri and his supporters, his age and lack of vitality became embarrassingly evident in Chile's introduction to television politics. The image of a tired, inarticulate politician broadcast via television to many of the nation's voters reinforced the outhouse humor of UP election posters that caricatured Alessandri on a toilet with the caption "NICA or *Ni cagando*, politely translated as "No way!"

Alessandri's weakness as a campaigner and the Christian Democratic decision to go it alone split the vote three ways. Salvador Allende received a slim plurality. Notwithstanding the addition of Radicals and other small parties to the old FRAP coalition, the UP's share of the vote actually decreased slightly from that achieved by FRAP in the 1964 election. More than a mandate for Allende, the election clearly demonstrated the extreme political divisions within Chilean society in 1970, with the "centrist" candidate finishing last.

According to the Chilean constitution, when no presidential candidate received a majority of the votes, Congress could choose as president one of the two candidates with the highest vote total. Since the Christian Democrats controlled the deciding votes in Congress, Alessandri proposed to exchange an immediate resignation for congressional designation of him as president. This would have allowed Eduardo Frei, ineligible to succeed himself immediately, to enter new elections and refashion a Rightist-Christian Democratic alliance to prevent Allende from becoming president. While this plan attracted some Christian Democrats, most of the party's congres-

TABLE 26. PRESIDENTIAL ELECTIONS, 1964 AND 1970

Political Parties and Candidates	1964		1970	
	Total	Percentage	Total	Percentage
FRAP/UP (Salvador Allende)	977,902	39.5	1,070,334	36.3
Christian Democrats (Eduardo Frei, 1964 Radomiro Tomic, 1970)	1,409,102	55.5	821,801	27.8
Julio Duran*	125,233	5.0		
Jorge Alessandri			1,031,159	34.9

* Durán withdrew his candidacy before the election but still received 5% of the vote.

sional representatives and Radomiro Tomic opposed it firmly. Instead, they demanded passage of a package of constitutional guarantees with UP support prior to the congressional vote on Chile's next president: among these, guarantees of the multiparty system, maintenance of civil liberties and freedom of the press, access by all parties to government-controlled TV stations, protection for the armed forces against political purges or the creation of militia, continued existence of, and public subsidies for, the private educational system, autonomy of the university system, protection for public personnel—many added during the Frei administration—against dismissals or political persecution. In short, the Christian Democrats sought to buttress with constitutional amendments Chile's existing *political system* against the in-coming Allende administration's plans for a new institutional order. The Christian Democrats insisted that only approval of these amendments with the votes of UP deputies and senators would allow them to vote for Allende as president.

As the Christian Democrats bargained with the UP parties for constitutional amendments to limit the future course of an Allende government, Right-wing extremist groups, such as Patria y Libertad ("Fatherland and Freedom"), and United States business and diplomatic groups plotted to prevent Allende's inauguration. International Telephone and Telegraph, one of the largest American-based multinationals with interests in Chile, took the initiative in approaching the CIA with a plan to destabilize the Chilean economy through international economic pressure, delays, or cancellation of loans and credits, and by fomenting panic among Chile's private businesses. Covert efforts to bankrupt savings banks and to induce unemployment also figured in the American scheme to prevent Allende's confirmation by the Chilean Congress. Later, congressional hearings in the United States made clear that President Nixon and his closest foreign policy advisers, including Henry Kissinger, played an active role in this effort to subvert the work of Chile's Congress.

Despite the behind-the-scenes manipulations of ITT and American policymakers, the UP bargain with the Christian Democrats on the package of constitutional amendments seemed to assure an Allende victory in the congressional voting. Nevertheless, two days before the Congress was to decide on Chile's next president, extreme Right wing groups, allegedly with CIA backing, made a desperate effort to kidnap the commander-in-chief of the Chilean army. Apparently they hoped to cast the blame for the abduction on MIR or on the UP—and thereby change the Christian Democratic votes in the Congress or provoke military intervention. This ploy backfired. General Schneider resisted his assailants, and they mortally wounded him in an exchange of gunfire. Schneider died on October 25, 1970, the day after the Chilean Congress confirmed Salvador Allende as Chile's next president.

Proclaiming that with him the people (el pueblo) of Chile entered into the presidential palace, Salvador Allende received the presidential sash on November 3, 1970. Less than three years later Allende's body would be carried from La Moneda, testimony to his unsuccessful struggle to take Chile down the peaceful road to socialism.

Salvador Allende inherited the political mythology and constitutional legitimacy of a system no longer viable without substantial modifications. The increasing violence, including political terrorism and "expropriation" of money from banks by Miristas, as well as the challenge to civilian authority represented by the tacnazo in the last year of the Frei administration, reflected the decomposition of the political arrangements that had held together the old order. President Allende lacked a revolutionary army to carry out his will; he headed a precarious multiparty coalition lacking both internal cohesiveness and underlying agreement on the pace and character of change to be implemented by the unidad popular government. Like all reformist Chilean presidents in the twentieth century, President Allende faced a hostile Congress and entrenched bureaucracy. And he lacked even the popular mandate President Aguirre Cerda had achieved after the election won by the popular front in 1938.

Worse still, Allende was a Marxist whose program evoked the intense hostility of the majority of the Chilean electorate as well as the uncompromising and active opposition of the United States. From the outset, American foreign policy, both covert and diplomatic, sought to disrupt the Chilean economy, to cut off or stifle credit from international lending agencies, to provide financial and moral support for the regime's opponents—and to maintain friendly relations with the Chilean military. Viewed as a "test case" of the viability of elected Marxist governments not only in Latin America but also in Western Europe (especially France and Italy), the Allende government potentially threatened the integrity of the NATO alliance as well as the southern cone of South America. Friendly and expanding relations with Cuba and Eastern Europe, when added to the government's eventual expropriation of American copper companies and other foreign investments, persuaded hard-line American officials that every effort be made to "destabilize" the Chilean economy and oust the UP government. The concentration in Santiago of numerous leftist intellectuals and political exiles from other Latin American countries made the Chilean capital a center of revolutionary activity, closely scrutinized by secret police and military intelligence agents from Brazil, Bolivia, Uruguay, and Argentina.

Ironically, the very successes of certain of the UP government's programs, and the economic consequences of these successes, so polarized Chilean society that less than three years after Allende's inauguration (August 1973) the congressional opposition called upon the military to re-establish the "rule of the constitution and the law." In a setting quite different from the confrontation between President Balmaceda and Congress before the civil war of 1891, the confrontation between the UP coalition and the old order nevertheless adopted the familiar rhetoric and charges of Chilean politics: the President had violated his constitutional authority, and Congress sought to uphold its constitutional mandate, to assure respect for the constitution, and to prevent executive tyranny. Censure of government ministers and impeachment proceedings in Congress, so reminiscent of the structure of political conflict in the parliamentary period, now served as a reminder that the effort to implement socialism through legal means faced the challenge of the numerous checks and balances of liberal democracy inherent in the Chilean polity. Less than three weeks after Congress appealed to the armed forces to preserve Chilean democracy from presidential excesses, a military coup splattered the peaceful road to socialism with blood.

The popular unity government's short-term economic policies attempted to effect a massive income redistribution program through differential wage and salary readjustments to benefit the poorest sectors of Chilean society. In marked contrast to the stabilization schemes of the Ibáñez or Alessandri periods, the UP policymakers hoped to stimulate demand by providing significantly higher-than-inflation salary increments to the urban and rural poor. Added to increases in real income for the mass of Chilean workers, impressive increases in government expenditures and monetary expansion stimulated the stagnant economy. The administration's policymakers expected these measures to increase effective demand and, thereby, to convince Chilean entrepreneurs to utilize the excess capacity that idled numerous workers. Thus, through a combination of income redistribution, increase in effective demand, and reduction of unemployment, the UP government hoped to bring the country out of the economic recession inherited from the Frei government and to increase popular support for the Allende coalition.

Unfortunately for the government, the monopolistic structure of Chilean industry, rapidly expanding demands by workers for expropriation of farms and factories, and the corresponding distrust by private investors of the government's ultimate intentions toward private firms, all militated against substantial private investment programs. This meant that despite short-term improvements in industrial production and in worker consumption, the UP's programs of income redistribution in the context of a "transition to socialism"— with capitalist owners still making investment decisions—led inevitably to shortages, rising prices, and black markets. Instead of investing for the future, private entrepreneurs sold off their inventory at speculative prices or, in agriculture, disposed of farm machinery and cattle herds. They invested in dollars, German marks, or other hard currencies. Under these conditions rising demand, escalating emissions of currency, and deficit spending fueled an inflation of extraordinary magnitude. By mid-1973 the annual rate of inflation exceeded 300 percent and reduced the real income of workers and salaried employees to levels below those of late 1970 when the UP had taken office.

Every short-term success of government policy involved contradictions that led ever more rapidly to political and economic disaster. In part, this resulted from the disunity of the UP coalition. Acting as if the coalition were simply another executive-electoral alliance, each party demanded its share of the spoils. The government filled important administrative posts through an elaborate quota system which assigned personnel designated by the political parties to positions throughout the administration. Employment opportunities in the firms nationalized, "intervened," or requisitioned by the government became plums with which to reward party stalwarts or to combat unemployment. These difficulties led to precipitate declines in productivity throughout the economy.

In the rural sector, debate over the types of agricultural production units to establish on the expropriated farms created uncertainty among the campesinos and smallholders. Attacks on the *asentamiento* system introduced by the Christian Democrat administration alienated the beneficiaries of the Frei agrarian reform, while experiments with variations on collective farms, state farms, and regional production units resulted in virtual disorganization of the agricultural economy. After a good harvest in 1970-71, agricultural production declined seriously. As a result the government was forced to use scarce foreign exchange to import foodstuffs needed to meet the increased demand occasioned by higher worker incomes and to make up for the reduction in domestic production.

The government's methods for dealing with shortages, carrying out agrarian reform, and constructing the "social" or public sector of the economy exacerbated political tensions and intensified the economic crisis. In an attempt to minimize the problems of urban supply, the government organized public entities to compete with the private

TABLE 27. THE AGRARIAN SECTOR

Export of Goods and Agricultural Imports 1965-70
(yearly average), 1971 and 1972 (millions of dollars)

	1965-70	1971	1972
Total Exports	$939	$964	$836
Agricultural Exports	$ 24	$ 29	$ 19
Agricultural Imports	$184	$311	$468
Agricultural Imports as Percentage of Total Export Earnings	19.6%	32.2%	56.0%

(Source: Stefan de Vylder, *Allende's Chile*, Cambridge University Press, 1974, p. 202.)

sector in wholesale and retail distribution. DINAC, a public enterprise constituted by the amalgamation of several large distribution agencies acquired by CORFO, made efforts to gain control of wholesale distribution, while thousands of private supply and price committees *juntas de abastecimiento popular* (JAP) were organized to cooperate in local distribution of articles of consumption to urban neighborhoods. These JAP committees assisted inspectors from DIRINCO, the agency charged with enforcing price controls, in their efforts to prevent private retail merchants from evading such controls. Subsequently, the supply of "people's marketbaskets," or *canastos populares*, to the JAP for distribution to the people of the shantytowns and worker neighborhoods directly threatened the viability of Chile's more than 125,000 retail merchants and uncounted ambulatory vendors. The JAPs also served as a potential organizational mechanism for administering a direct, mandatory system of rationing as well as for monitoring the activities of opposition elements at the local level. None of these implications were lost upon the opposition which attacked the inefficiency, corruption, and "political criteria" with which the JAPs distributed the *canastas populares*.

Ideological and political fragmentation within the UP government heightened the economic uncertainty. Unable to control the activities of MIR, certain members of his own Socialist party, and the militant Mapucistas, President Allende failed to halt the acceleration

of farm and factory seizures and illegal strikes in which workers demanded nationalization or expropriation of the enterprises where
they were employed.

In the first eighteen months of the UP government, campesinos
temporarily or permanently occupied some 1700 rural properties. In
Article 171 of the agrarian reform law enacted by the Christian Democratic government, the Allende government found a legal mechanism to convert farm seizures or illegal strikes into de facto transfers
of managerial responsibility for rural estates. Article 171 provided
that "in case of lock-out or illegal work stoppage that, for any reason,
suspends exploitation of a rural enterprise, the President of the Republic can order resumption of labors [reanudación de faenas] with
the intervention of the civil authority . . . and the support of police
if necessary." The law gave the government official [interventor] assigned to "intervene" the farm "all the prerogatives necessary to continue operation of the enterprise." With this authority government
interventores could hire new personnel, incur new liabilities or pay
old debts, and decide what crops to plant or animals to sell. A short
period of intervention could easily bankrupt any farm or at least
make most owners quite willing to sell their farms to CORA on favorable terms. Thus, Article 171 of the agrarian reform law could be
used by the Popular Unity government as a flexible legal tool to
speed up the agrarian reform process—if only campesinos intensified
the process of illegal farm occupations or strikes. In practice this
tactic was used on so many farms that the administration soon ran
out of party loyalists in the agrarian bureaucracies to assign as interventores.

In the urban sector the government resorted to application of the
all-but-forgotten Decree Law 520, a vestige of the "Socialist Republic" of 1932. As indicated in Chapter 8, this decree law allowed the
government to requisition, intervene, or expropriate any private enterprise that failed to comply with laws regulating price controls,
speculation, stockpiling in anticipation of increases in official prices
for particular commodities, interruption of production, or refusal to
utilize efficiently installed capacity when the government decided

TABLE 28. REQUISITIONS AND INTERVENTIONS,
NOVEMBER 1970-NOVEMBER 1972

Period	Interventions	Requisitions	Total
November-December 1970	37	1	38
January-February 1971	23	—	23
March-April 1971	1	5	6
May-June 1971	12	12	24
July-August 1971	9	6	15
September-October 1971	24	7	31
November-December 1971	21	9	30
January-February 1972	13	6	19
March-April 1972	14	7	21
May-June 1972	16	3	19
July-August 1972	7	18	25
September-October 1972*	23	48	71
November 1972	2	4	6
Total	202	126	328

* During the October strike a large number of enterprises were subjected to intervention or requisition for participation in the general lockout. Most of these companies were later returned to their owners.

(Source: Based on Instituto de Economía, *La Economía Chilena en 1972*, pp. 116ff. After Stefan de Vylder, *Allende's Chile*, Cambridge University Press, 1974, p. 146.)

there existed a "shortage" of a particular commodity. Legislation against lockouts also gave the government leverage in labor conflicts. As in the agricultural sector, requisitions or interventions in industry could quickly bankrupt the legal owners and facilitate transfer of the affected industry to the public sector.

Under these conditions the predictions made in 1938 by Polish economist Oscar Lange proved entirely accurate. Indeed Lange's analysis is perhaps the most appropriate epitaph, as well as explanation, for the domestic economic failures of the UP government.

An economic system based on private enterprise and private property of the means of production can work only as long as the security of private property and of income derived from enterprise is maintained. The very existence of a government bent on introducing socialism is a constant threat to this security. Therefore, the capitalistic economy cannot function under a socialist government unless the government is socialist in name only.

TABLE 29. INDUSTRIAL ESTABLISHMENTS CONTROLLED BY THE CHILEAN STATE

Form of control	November 1970	December 1971	December 1972	May 1973
State ownership*	31	62	103	165
Under Intervention or Requisition	—	39	99	120
Total	31	101	202	285

* Both social and mixed areas and including six new industries that were created by the Chilean state after November 1970.

(Source: Stefan de Vylder, *Allende's Chile*, Cambridge University Press, 1974, p. 145.)

> . . . Owners threatened with expropriation have no induce-
> ment to make the necessary investments and to manage them
> efficiently. And no government supervision or administrative
> measures can cope effectively with the passive resistance and
> sabotage of the owners and managers.

No administrative device adopted by the government could cope with the resistance of the opposition. Black markets, shortages, and rampant inflation undermined confidence in the government and hardened the opposition forces against the de facto socialization of the economy. At the same time that the activities of MIR and the most radical members of the government coalition convinced the government's enemies that only violent resistance could halt consolidation of a new political reality, the Communists and Allende sought to negotiate a de-escalation of conflict with the Christian Democrats in exchange for clearly defined limits on the extent of socialization in industry and agriculture. Neither those who believed that socialism could be established only through force and popular mobilization, nor the Partido Nacional and the growing movement of economic and professional associations (*gremios*) committed to violent counterrevolution, gave any breathing room to the government's efforts to arrive at a pacific resolution of the crisis.

As the political and economic situation deteriorated, supply and distribution problems in the urban areas sent into the streets thousands of women from upper-, middle-, and even working-class homes, banging on pots and pans to symbolize the government's inability to resolve the economic crisis. In response, organized workers and their families facetiously offered to share their food with the *momios* (literally, "mummy," a term UP sympathizers applied to the supporters of the old order) if they were really unable to feed themselves. Moving their struggle against the government to the streets, leaders of the major trade associations and economic interest groups such as the SNA and the SFF allied themselves with extreme right-wing political organizations such as Patria y Libertad, PROTECO, and Soberania, Orden y Libertad (SOL). These recently organized movements established white guard vigilantes to resist farm and factory seizures and to recover occupied private property in *retomas*. By mid-1972 the opposition had united in a so-called *gremialista* movement. A massive strike in October of 1972 mobilized shopkeepers, professional and economic associations, bank clerks, students, and even certain working-class and campesino groups in an effort to shut down the Chilean economy. The strike was precipitated by the demand of the forty thousand members of the independent truckers' association that the government suspend its plans to create a state-owned trucking enterprise, but it quickly became openly political and directly challenged the UP government and its program.

Recognizing the critical political moment, ex-President Eduardo Frei personally influenced the Christian Democratic party to support the strike and mobilize its followers in opposition to the government. On October 15, 1972, the party's secretary general, Renán Fuentealba declared that the government was "acting openly in defiance of the constitution and the laws, as well as of fundamental human rights," and that this circumstance was "dangerous for all our citizens." In light of this danger, Fuentealba affirmed the Christian Democrats' adherence to the truckers' movement. Predictably, the Partido Nacional aggressively supported the strike, maintaining that only organized civil disobedience could overcome the government's effort to impose communism on Chile.

Faced with a situation bordering on insurrection, the UP government declared a partial state of emergency. This meant that military officers took over the responsibility for maintaining order, for enforcing temporary censorship on the opposition media, and, in effect, for shoring up the UP coalition's fragile position. By October 21, the newly created *comando gremial* confronted the government with a sweeping set of demands that, if accepted, would have amounted to abrogation of the UP program. Despite the serious economic effects of the strike (the government later estimated the loss to the country at almost $300 million), continued production in the factories and support by UP loyalists prevented a complete economic shutdown. The *gremialista* movement failed to win a definitive victory. In addition, the emergence of new working-class organizations, or *cordones industriales*, among the factory workers in Santiago's "industrial belts"—such as Los Cerrillos, Puente Alto, and Vicuña MacKenna— threatened the development of real popular militia and institutions of "parallel power." Pursuing a more revolutionary course than the leadership of the CUT, the Communist party, or President Allende, a nucleus of revolutionary workers in the *cordones industriales* began preparing for armed confrontation.

Coincident with the October strike, the opposition moved on the legislative front to impeach four of Allende's ministers. Faced with a loss of key advisers and the resurrection of the political tactic of censure and impeachment of ministers, President Allende made a critical political decision. He invited the army commander-in-chief, Carlos Prats, to serve as minister of interior while at the same time continuing in his army post. The President also included an air force general and an admiral in his new cabinet. Jacques Chonchol, the ex-Christian Democrat who served as Allende's minister of agriculture and was probably the member of the Allende ministerial team most hated by the opposition (because of his leadership in the agrarian reform process), left the cabinet.

Declaring their full confidence in General Prats, the leaders of the truckers' strike negotiated a settlement in early November that included promises by the government to return enterprises occupied by workers during the strike and also not to nationalize the transport and wholesale trade sectors of the economy. Although the government did not entirely fulfill these promises, the October strike had made the military the arbiter of the nation's political conflicts.

General Prats emphasized that the two most important tasks facing the new cabinet consisted of restoration of order and administration of peaceful, honest congressional elections in March 1973. In the aftermath of the truckers' strike, however, speculation abounded about the extent of American financial support and CIA involvement in the events of October. Meanwhile the opposition looked to the March 1973 elections as an opportunity to win the two-thirds majority in the Congress that would permit Allende's impeachment. The presence of General Prats in the interior ministry seemed to guarantee the integrity of the March elections, but it also inspired harsh condemnation from those on the left who proposed "getting on with the Revolution."

Concentrating their efforts on the upcoming elections, the Christian Democrats, the Partido Nacional, and other opposition forces forged an electoral alliance called CODE. The results of the March elections, however, proved a victory for no one. CODE obtained 55 percent of the votes but actually lost seats in the Congress to the UP coalition. The opposition *was* a majority, but it now faced three years of the Allende administration before the presidential elections scheduled for 1976. Notwithstanding the veracity of CODE's claims of electoral fraud and the abnormal delay in reporting the election returns, there could be no doubt that the UP coalition retained significant popular support. Despite the economic crisis, shortages of consumer goods, and the opposition's media offensive against the government, the UP coalition still could count on more than 40 percent of Chile's voters.

Between March 1973 and September 1973, intensified militancy by MIR and certain elements within the UP coalition, as well as public threats by Socialist leader Carlos Altamirano to infiltrate and subvert the armed forces, were juxtaposed to counterrevolutionary economic sabotage and terrorism. The galloping inflation rate increased the number of strikes, including an extremely costly work stoppage by the miners at the El Teniente copper mine in Rancagua. Workers who in the past had looked to Marxist union leaders now followed a Christian Democrat in a strike condemned by the UP government. Lasting more than two months, the strike drew support from thousands of university students and members of the Federation of Secondary Students in Santiago. It also directly pitted the UP government against an important group of organized workers—not against *momios*.

Amidst rampant inflation, political and economic crises, and the rising pitch of government and opposition rhetoric, unsuccessful negotiations between the government and the Christian Democrats continued—even after an abortive coup d'état by the second tank regiment in Santiago in June 1973. The quick defeat of this *tancazo* seemed to reaffirm General Prats's commitment to defense of the constitutional government. Gradually, however, Prats's apparent political ambitions, rumors that he would emerge as the UP presidential candidate in 1976, and an incident in which he reportedly threatened a woman driver with death for sticking out her tongue at him as he motored through Santiago, all combined to erode his support among fellow officers.

The political situation grew even worse in late July with new strikes by the truckers and the *gremialista* movement. After a temporary absence, representatives of the armed forces again returned to the cabinet to restore order (August 9, 1973). Now all three service commanders, as well as the commander of the national police force (*carabineros*), occupied ministries. Intensified implementation of the provisions of the gun control law, passed in 1972, sent military units to factories and shanty towns to disarm workers and forestall a popular insurrection. These searches for arms, or *allanamientos*, also served to collect intelligence on the quantity of arms available in the *cordones industriales*, and to train army units in tactics for confrontation with the civilian population at factory work sites, union halls, party offices, and in the *poblaciones*. The number of *allanamientos* increased gradually after early 1973. Less attention was given to the armed vigilantes organized by the *gremalista* and right-wing political movements. In July 1973, according to pro-*unidad popular* sources, only two of twenty-four *allanamientos* involved "groups of armed fascists"; all the rest were directed against factories, offices of *unidad popular* parties, government offices, or other supporters of the Allende government. By the first part of August, when the new military-based cabinet was organized, the *allanamientos* were coordinated operations of army, air force, and naval units moving against leftists throughout the nation.

In the meantime the *gremalista* strike movement continued, supported by the entire political opposition and students at the Catholic university. Unable to negotiate an end to the trucking strike and annoyed by obstacles put in his way by Allende's civilian supporters, air force General César Ruiz Danyau abruptly resigned from the cabinet only days after accepting the portfolio of transport and public works. President Allende's quick acceptance of Ruiz's resignation as minister *and as air force commander-in-chief* provoked a new political crisis, involving agitation among the general's air force colleagues.

Violence in the streets of Santiago, political terrorism by leftists and rightists, and an imminent state of political chaos elicited a call by the majority opposition in the Chilean Congress for the military to intervene to guarantee institutional stability, civil peace, security, and development. The same day, hundreds of wives of military officers gathered outside of General Prats's residence to demand his resignation. Prats resigned the next day and was followed by his military colleagues General Guillermo Pickering and Mario Sepúlveda (commander of the Santiago garrison). Now President Allende was at the mercy of General Augusto Pinochet Ugarte.

On September 11, 1973, General Pinochet and his fellow service commanders led a well-coordinated, brutal, and highly successful military movement that ended the UP government and resulted in the death of President Salvador Allende. According to the military, Salvador Allende committed suicide after surviving aerial bombardment of the presidential palace.

More has been written about Chile between 1970 and 1973 than about all the rest of Chilean history. The *unidad popular* experience raised important theoretical questions for socialist intellectuals and politicians concerning the viability and correct tactics of the "peaceful road to socialism." Those leftists who believe(d) in the possibility of such a process have sought to determine where the Allende government went wrong, how the process could have been salvaged, how European Communists and Socialists can prevent the "fascization" of the middle class which was the social base of the counterrevolution in Chile.

Although congressional investigations in the United States have made available incontrovertible evidence of extensive U.S. efforts to undermine the Allende government, many Marxists still insist that the "real" key to the failure of the UP administration was the activities of the "ultra-leftists." Typical in this respect, an important article in *World Marxist Review* (July 1974) noted that "the working class was gradually forced into isolation and the intermediate strata became, objectively, allies of the country's enemies. . . . The Chilean experience has reaffirmed anew that ultra-leftism is a boon for imperialism and reaction." In the year after the military coup, leaders of the Chilean Communist party who escaped the military intelligence's dragnet, still insisted that "at times of crisis we worked in alliance with the patriotic part of the Army faithful to the constitution and this played a decisive role in suppressing the October 1972 conspiracy [the truckers' strike]. This alliance could have developed were it not for the spread of ultraleftism."

In contrast, Trotskyists and other militant revolutionaries have seen in the Chilean experience new evidence that there can be no peaceful road to socialism. They argue that Allende should have armed and unleashed the workers and peasants in a violent revolutionary movement to destroy Chile's liberal democracy and the capitalist state. How the military would have reacted to such a move by President Allende in 1970 or 1971—and the inevitable massacre that would have occurred—is usually omitted from these "revolutionary" post-mortems.

For the Right and the Christian Democrats, of course, there is little interest in explaining why Allende failed to take Chile down the peaceful road to socialism. Like the Marxists and other UP supporters, however, they found soon enough that the military coup that ousted President Allende brought neither relief from economic crisis nor restoration of constitutional order. Instead, the Chilean military imposed a highly authoritarian, repressive political regime that effectively eliminated every basis of civil liberty and political freedom stipulated in the Chilean constitution of 1925.

The ultimate tragedy of *unidad popular*, then, was that President Allende lost the opportunity to carry out important social reforms while maintaining the political liberty that had evolved in Chile after 1932. United States diplomacy, economic pressure, and covert subversion of Chile's domestic politics played an important role in the failure of the UP coalition. However, American or other outside pressures could not by themselves have ensured this failure. Short of military intervention, the United States did not have enough leverage, even with the variety of economic and political screws it tightened, to guarantee Allende's failure. Whereas the Agency for International Development (AID), the Export-Import Bank, the Inter-American Development Bank, and the World Bank rejected Chile's requests for credit during 1971 and 1972, short-term credits from Western Europe, the Soviet Union, and the Socialist bloc more than made up for the withdrawal of financial support by the United States. A large foreign exchange surplus inherited from the Frei government even allowed temporary increases in imports to buttress the government's short-term emphasis on improved consumption for the working classes. This was so despite declines in copper prices that portended extreme balance-of-payment problems in 1971. By the end of 1971 the government's principal economic strategist, Pedro Vuskovic, alleged that lack of foreign exchange constituted the main constraint on further realization of the UP program. This constraint originated not in a net decrease in available foreign credits, but rather in circumstances occasioned by the government's own economic policies.

Whatever the full extent of United States complicity in the tragedy of September 1973, and whatever the impact of international economics, the most critical factor of all in the failure of the Allende administration was bad politics. Bad politics—the sprouting of revolutionary rhetoric without the force to impose a revolutionary program—produced a politico-economic crisis. Bad politics prevented conciliation and compromise with the Christian Democrats, the small shopkeepers, the truckers, the beneficiaries of the Frei agrarian reform—in short, with all the elements of the middle strata, working class, and peasantry who had nothing to lose and much to gain by an attack on economic monopolies and foreign corporations. President Allende failed because he lacked the power to impose a revolutionary socialist regime yet insisted on employing the rhetoric of revolution. He failed also because there is no peaceful road to the socialism envisaged by Marxist-Leninists in a liberal democratic polity. By pursuing an illusion that threatened the livelihood of broad sectors of the population, President Allende's *unidad popular* coalition set the stage for a counterrevolution that imposed upon Chile a regime of coercion, intolerance, and brutality unequaled since the era of conquest.

Chapter 10 • Epilogue

Not even the shrillest political rhetoric of leftists and rightists between 1970 and 1973 prepared Chileans for the ferocity of the military coup of September 11, 1973, or for the subsequent policies adopted by the military government. Accustomed as they were to the gross hyperbole of propaganda from all political parties and movements since the early 1930s, most Chileans did not really believe that a military putsch would occur; fewer still anticipated a military regime similar in orientation to the Brazilian dictatorship after 1964.

Called upon by opposition groups in the Congress to restore the constitution, the military leadership instead closed the legislature, curtailed activities by political parties, and outlawed the political organizations that had supported the *unidad popular* administration. Press censorship, suspension of civil liberties, and fierce repression of leading politicians, labor leaders, academics, and other supposed Marxist sympathizers merged into a "holy war" against what the military junta called the "Marxist cancer." After declaring a state of "internal war," the new regime charged military tribunals with trying officials of the ousted administration and others who opposed the military government.

349

Thousands of deaths in the first days after the coup were followed by systematic purges in which Allende supporters and other "subversives" were murdered or imprisoned. Accounts of torture in the improvised detention centers set up throughout the nation became so widespread as to be routine. General Pinochet justified the coup and the government's repressive measures by alleging that the Allende coalition had a plot (*plan zeta*) to murder military and civilian opposition leaders in order to impose communism definitively upon Chile. Moreover, the general maintained:

> The greatest possible enforcement and highest respect for Human Rights implies that these must not be exercised by those individuals who spread doctrines or commit acts which in fact seek to abolish them. This makes it necessary to apply restrictions as rigorous as the circumstances may require to those who defy the juridical norms in force. . . . Our attitude must necessarily remain inflexible for the good of Chile and its people.

In addition to justifying its violent extirpation of subversives, the Chilean junta pointed to the international significance of its victory over communism. Reminding Chileans of the glories of independence, General Pinochet declared that "Chile was one of the first countries in the world to abolish slavery. Now our country has broken the chains of totalitarian Marxism, the great Twentieth-Century Slavery, before which so many bow their heads without the courage to defeat it. We are thus once again pioneers in Humanity's fight for liberation."

The military pioneers in "Humanity's fight for liberation" did not limit their attacks to supporters of the Allende government. Once the initial campaign of terror and assassination had given way to gradual institutionalization of a military-police state, the regime's leaders made clear that they intended to write the final epitaph for Chilean formal democracy. Military rectors replaced academic administrators in the universities; Chilean higher education faced a thorough pogrom which practically wiped out departments and schools in the social sciences, philosophy, education, and other disciplines touched by liberal or Marxist influence. Social and ideological pluralism disappeared. In a fashion reminiscent of the military's heroes—Portales and Ibáñez—the junta declared its contempt for "old style" democracy and for politics. The junta rekindled the embers of the military movement of 1924 and Ibáñez' theme of antipolitics in 1952—but replaced Ibáñez's broom with torture and death—and promised to end forever the immorality, corruption, and ineptitude of civilian politics which had allowed the assumption of the *unidad popular* government.

In a declaration of principles published in March 1974, the junta announced that "guided by the inspiration of Portales, the government of Chile will energetically apply the principle of authority and drastically punish any outburst of disorder or anarchy." By 1975 the junta and its civilian collaborators were actively planning a "new institutional order" to replace the outmoded institutions of Chilean democracy. Four "constitutional" acts adopted between December 1975 and September 11, 1976, moved Chile in the direction of a constitutional military dictatorship.

The apparent contradiction of this three-word characterization will not surprise readers familiar with *Alice in Wonderland* or George Orwell's *1984*. Only by reading these constitutional acts can one appreciate fully the unintentional irony promulgated into law by Chile's military dictators. To illustrate, Constitutional Act Number 3 (September 4, 1976) stipulated, among other intriguing provisions:

> Article 1. Men are born free and equal in dignity. This constitutional act guarantees all individuals:
> 11. Liberty of conscience, and expression of all creeds and free exercise of all religions, as do not violate moral principles, good behavior or public order . . .
> 12. Freedom of opinion and information, in all ways and by all means, without prior censorship, notwithstanding responsibility under the law for offense or abuse as may be committed in use of these freedoms. However, the courts may prohibit publication or circulation of opinions or information affecting moral principles, public order, national security or the private life of individuals.
> . . . Individuals who may have been at any time convicted or

found guilty of threatening the institutional order of the Republic may not own, direct, or manage mass communications media,
nor may they in any way participate in functions connected
with the publication or broadcast of opinions or information.

Article 2. No individual may invoke any constitutional or legal
precept whatsoever to violate the rights or freedoms established
hereunder, or to threaten the integrity or operation of the state of
law or the established regime.

Any act of individuals or groups directed to disseminate doctrines which threaten the family, or which promote violence or
the concept of a society based on class struggle, or as may be
otherwise contrary to the established regime or the integrity or
operation of the state of law, is illicit and in violation of the institutional organization of the Republic.

If these sections read like a tongue-in-cheek Orwellian invention,
Constitutional Act Number 4 (promulgated at the same time as the
act above) seems to go further than even Orwell. To combat "latent
subversion" this act authorized the president of the republic to declare "a state of defense against subversion." Under such conditions
the president "may only restrict personal freedom, freedom of information, and the right of assembly." If the president declared a
state of "internal or external war" or a "state of internal commotion,"
his authority was still greater, including the power to deprive Chileans
of their citizenship and "to suspend or restrict all of the rights or
guarantees set forth in Constitutional Act Number 3. . . ."

By the end of 1976 the Chileans were living in a juridical Wonderland; but the enforcement mechanisms of the military junta could
hardly be characterized as a house of cards. And no Chilean could
merely wake up to escape the nightmare.

Of course not all Chileans opposed the military government. Initially many welcomed the end of economic and political chaos—and
also supported the vengeful persecution of Marxists, Allende supporters, labor leaders, and "uppity workers and peasants." The junta's
support for private enterprise and "law and order" appealed to rightist politicians, businessmen, and most of the professionals and white-
collar interests in the *gremialista* movement which had led the polit-

ical assault on the Allende government. With promises to combat inflation, restore security for private property, and "cleanse" the public administration, universities, and labor movement of Marxist influence, the junta struck a responsive chord among anti-Allende forces. By quickly outlawing the Marxist parties, destroying the CUT, and prohibiting labor conflicts and strikes, the military government gained the support of the country's business community. By selling off most of the firms added to the public sector between 1970 and 1973, the junta created an economic windfall for domestic and foreign investors. Chile's abrogation of the terms of the foreign investment code adopted by the Andean Pact nations gave foreign investors equal treatment with nationals.* New tax legislation provided further incentives for a renewed flow of foreign private capital into the Chilean economy.

Soon, however, reliance upon economic policies recommended by civilian advisers dominated by the conservative economics of the University of Chicago, alienated many business and professional groups. The policies adopted by the junta represented a radical departure from the import-substitution/protected-industrialization model prevalent since the 1930s. This decision destroyed numerous Chilean industries unable to compete with foreign imports, and also led to enormous increases in unemployment. Combined with a sharp price rise for most commodities, and with substantial reductions in the real income of Chilean workers, widespread unemployment meant hunger and despair for Chile's urban poor. Following an even more radical policy of stabilization than the ill-fated Klein-Saks program during the second Ibáñez presidency, the military government imposed misery upon hundreds of thousands of Chileans. Though cushioned somewhat by periodic wage adjustments in response to inflation, the decline in living conditions for the Chilean masses formed an integral part of government economic policy to stifle infla-

* The Andean Pact sought to regulate foreign investment and to reduce competition for investment capital among the Latin American signatories. The pact's terms imposed relatively stringent controls upon foreign investment in Chile and other member nations, Chile's new foreign investment legislation was incompatible with both the spirit and the letter of the Andean Pact agreement.

tion and to reorient production toward commodities in which Chile held comparative advantage. In addition, the government decreased public expenditures, reduced public personnel, eliminated subsidies on many basic consumer goods, and devalued Chilean currency. To encourage agricultural production, the junta returned many expropriated, requisitioned, or intervened farms to their former owners and gave thousands of land titles to campesinos by way of breaking up land-reform cooperatives, or *asentamientos*. In the industrial sector, the *cordones industriales* disappeared, as did most "workers' enterprises." Chile returned to an explicitly capitalist economic model that largely rejected even the protection of industries with tariff barriers or import quotas.

All in all, the government's economic policies were a profound attack on the very structure of the Chilean economy. The immediate result was a severe recession. A decline in copper prices worsened still further the economic situation. Not only the poor suffered from the junta's economic "shock treatment." Even as the inflation rate gradually declined, numerous small businesses unable to compete with imports faced bankruptcy. As early as January 1975 the ex-president of the SFF, Orlando Sáenz, called the military government's economic policies "one of the most resounding failures in our economic history." Notwithstanding erosion of support among influential business interests, the government remained firm in its determination to create a competitive private enterprise economy in Chile. A return to limited price regulation on basic commodities did not imply a diminished resolve to make Chile an efficient free market economy, to reduce inflation, and to rely upon a massive influx of private foreign capital to revitalize the economy.

While recognizing the social and human consequences of their economic policies, the military leadership and their civilian advisers pointed with pride to a number of signs of improved economic performance by the end of 1977. A reduced inflation rate, a favorable balance of trade, an upturn in industrial production and economic growth, decreases in the value of food imports, and a slightly reduced rate of unemployment, all led spokesmen for the government to take an optimistic look at 1978. Moreover, in mid-1977 the junta announced the dissolution of the secret police-intelligence agency (DINA) responsible for many of the worst abuses since 1973.

Despite the government's optimism, however, the great mass of the Chilean people lived in worse conditions than in the mid-1960s. The military dictatorship continued to exercise its power arbitrarily and unpredictably. In the decree that dissolved DINA, the regime created another agency, albeit with a different name, to take its place. Chilean exiles around the world continued to wonder if they could ever return to their homeland, or if Chile would ever again be free of military rectors in the universities, military censors over the media, military masters over a civilian population.

In the face of a United Nations charge of human rights violations in Chile, General Pinochet called a national referendum in the first week of 1978, in which Chilean citizens were asked to vote "no" or "yes" on the following resolution:

> In the face of the international aggression unleashed against the government of the fatherland, I support [General] Pinochet in his defense of the dignity of Chile, and I reaffirm the legitimate right of the republic to conduct the process of institutionalization in a manner benefiting its sovereignty.

With the opposition repressed and the mass media muffled, the government claimed that more than 75 percent of the electorate had expressed support for Pinochet. Based on this overwhelming "mandate," General Pinochet announced that there would be no further elections for a decade, and he told Chile's politicians, "It's finished for you."

In response to the consolidation of the regime's position as well as to apparent support reflected in the January 1978 plebiscite, General Pinochet lifted the "state of siege" in March and replaced it with the somewhat less restrictive "state of emergency." Under the "state of emergency," the military tribunals were theoretically subject to review by the Supreme Court, and civil liberties were partially restored. The following month (April 5, 1978) Pinochet announced an

amnesty for political prisoners and exiles. However, the amnesty decree contained enough exceptions—for example, it excluded those
guilty of misuse of public funds and other "economic crimes"—to
make it largely a public relations measure. Moreover, the official
translation of Pinochet's announcement distributed by the Chilean
embassy in Washington, D.C., made clear the general's firm intentions to prevent renewed political opposition:

> I wish to announce tonight that I have decided to pardon
> prison sentences or commute them to exile—that is, abandon-
> ment of the country—for all persons sentenced by military courts
> for crimes against the national security committed before or after
> September 11, 1973.
>
> Although it is entirely improper to refer to persons found
> guilty of a crime as political prisoners, now, as a result of the
> amnesty decree which is inspired by humanitarian motives, no
> one will be able to say that there are persons deprived of their
> freedom in Chile because of political happenings.
>
> I hope that this decision by my Government will be understood
> as a sign of pacification and not one of weakness, for anyone who
> falls into error in that respect runs the risk from now on of suffer-
> ing full application of the law.

By mid-1978 the military government had outlined a tentative plan
for transition to a "new institutionality." The details of this new
order remained unclear, but its general outline looked unmistakenly
authoritarian, antidemocratic, and corporative. According to government statements, under the new order political parties would serve
only as vehicles of communication—not as legal sources of opposition
or participants in policymaking for the nation. Old-style democracy
and party competition in the liberal democratic tradition remained
anathema to Chile's military rulers.

Whether General Pinochet's forecast that "it's finished" for
Chile's politicians—and Chilean democracy—proves accurate remains to be seen. Certainly the Chilean resistance will continue its
efforts to keep alive the memory of Chile's recent past as well as to
struggle for the destruction of what Pinochet called "authoritarian
democracy."

In Greece not long ago restoration of civilian government brought with it trials of military officers for crimes against humanity and for torture. The Greek tribunals convicted the ex-military rulers and sentenced them to prison or death. Knowledge of those proceedings makes it difficult for Chile's military rulers to relinquish power—even if they desired to do so. No regime of terror lasts forever; but as the last lines of this book were written, no early end to the Chilean dictatorship appeared likely.

Political Chronology

1534 King of Spain names Diego de Almagro governor of Neuva Toledo, extending approximately from Ica to just north of Tal Tal.

1535-36 Almagro expedition enters Chile and reconnoiters into the central valley. Finding no great source of wealth as in Peru, Almagro returns to Cuzco to contest the spoils of conquest with the Pizzaros.

1539 Pizzaro authorizes Pedro de Valdivia to lead expedition of conquest to Chile, which he baptizes Neuvo Extremo or Nueva Extremadura.

1540-41 Pedro de Valdivia's expedition arrives at the Mapocho river in December; Santiago founded February 12, 1541, and within the month Valdivia creates the first cabildo. September 11, 1541, local Indians attack the new town, practically destroying it and most of the settlers' provisions.

1540-53 Initial settlement and warfare with indigenous population under leadership of Valdivia. First towns founded: La Serena (1544); Concepción (1550); La Imperial, Valdivia, Villarrica (1552); Los Confines (1553).

1553 Battle of Tucapel, Valdivia killed by Indians led by cacique Lautaro—his ex-groom.

359

1553-57   Disputes among Valdivia's lieutenants over control of the colony. Continued warfare with Indians. Spanish defeated at Marigueñu (1554), settlements abandoned. Three years later Spanish destroy Lautaro's forces at Peteroa (1557).

1557-61   Viceroy at Lima names his son, García Hurtado de Mendoza, governor of Chile and sends an army financed out of the royal treasury to secure Chile. Alonso de Ercilla y Zuñiga, author of the epic poem, La Araucana, arrives with this expedition to Chile.

1557-59   Exploration of territory from Concepción to the south. Osorno founded (1558), and expedition under command of Juan Ladrillero penetrates to the Strait of Magellan. Fort at Tucapel reconstructed and Concepción resettled.

1559   Tasa de Santillán—ordinances seeking to regulate Indian labor and personal service to the Spanish—prohibits use of Indians as beasts of burden and require sufficient daily food for Indian workers. Ordinances largely ignored, despite application in mines at Quilacoya near Concepción.

1561-63   Administration of Governor Francisco de Villagra. Creation of Diocese of Santiago (1561). Bartolomé Rodrigo González Marmolejo appointed first Bishop. Fray Gil de González preaches "defensive war," unsuccessfully seeking to defend Indians.

1563-65   Interim administration of Pedro de Villagra. Pope Paul IV creates Diocese of La Imperial (1563). Philip II decrees establishment of Chile's first audiencia at Concepción (1565).

1565-67   Interim administration of Rodrigo de Quiroga. Audiencia installed at Concepción and town of Castro founded (1567) after expedition of exploration and conquest to island of Chiloé.

1567-75   Chile governed by Bravo de Saravia. Bishop of La Imperial advises king to suppress the audiencia (1570) because of its failure to help pacify the territory and deal firmly with abuses against the Indians. Despite continued efforts by the Bishop and royal decrees, encomenderos continue to evade regulations. Audiencia at Concepción abolished (1573).

1575-80   Rodrigo de Quiroga, one of the area's first conquistadors and lieutenant of Valdivia, assumes political leadership, supports encomenderos, and urges king to approve "personal service" of Indians to Spaniards. Carries out large expeditions of war against Indians in southern region. Prisoners are maimed to prevent their escape.

1580 Chillán founded.

1580-83 Interim administration of Ruíz de Gamboa, Quiroga's son-in-law. In effort to secure permanent appointment Gamboa cooperates with Bishop Medillín in promulgation of Tasa de Gamboa (1580) which sought to abolish "personal service." Gamboa fails to win decisive victory over Araucanians, and the Spanish king sends Alonso de Sotomayor, a veteran soldier, as governor of Chile.

1583-92 Administration of Alonso de Sotomayor. Gradual revocation of Gamboa's reforms; forced labor—personal service reinstated. Stimulation to mining economy in Quillota and Choapa valleys. Despite harsh campaigns against Araucanians, Indians remain unsubdued. Sotomayor's secret marriage to a Creole woman leads to his downfall.

1592-99 Administration of Martín García Oñez de Loyola, nephew of the viceroy of Peru and relative of Ignatius de Loyola, founder of the Society of Jesus (Jesuit order). Renewal of official concern with conditions of Indians. Outlaws sale of Indian captives or their transport from the south to northern mines or to Peru.

1598 Indian uprising under cacique Pelantaro. Oñez de Loyola is killed and decapitated in valley of Curalava. Nine years later his head is returned by Indians to Governor Alonso García Ramón. Philip II dies.

1599-1601 Several interim administrations. Abandonment of Spanish settlements in the south. Beginning of permanent royal subsidy (*situado real*) to finance war against Araucanians (1600).

1601-05 Administration of Alonso de Ribera. Permanent army is established in Chile (1603). Diocese of La Imperial moves to Concepción (1603). Indian offensive continues with Spanish defeats at Santa Cruz, Valdivia (1599), La Imperial and Angol (1600), Villarrica (1602), Osorno and Arauco (1604). Spanish respond with renewed sorties south. Southern economy totally disrupted.

1605-10   Administration of García Ramón. Accompanied to Chile by
           the Jesuit, Luis de Valdivia. Luis de Valdivia preaches "de-
           fensive warfare." García Ramón continues offensive against In-
           dians, suffering humiliating defeat in 1606. King authorizes
           perpetual slavery for captured Indian rebels (1608). Pope
           Paul V authorizes war against the Araucanians. Jesuit Luis de
           Valdivia arrives in Spain to seek official acceptance of "defen-
           sive warfare" (1609). In the same year a new audiencia estab-
           lished in Santiago.

1610-11   Interim administrations of Merlo de la Fuente and Jara
           Quemada. Luis de Valdivia's influence results in reappoint-
           ment of Alonso de Ribera as governor of Chile. Valdivia
           named as *visitador general*.

1612-17   Administration of Alonso de Ribera. Political intrigue be-
           tween governor and Luis de Valdivia. Murder of Jesuit mis-
           sionaries at Elicura provides pretext for renewed warfare
           (1614) despite official policy to the contrary.

1617-24   Interim administration of five different governors. Luis de
           Valdivia leaves Chile in 1619. "Defensive warfare" largely
           discredited. Tasa de Esquilache (1620) again seeks to regu-
           late Indian labor—generally unsuccessful.

1625-29   Administration of Fernández de Cordoba. King of Spain au-
           thorizes renewed warfare against Araucanians and slavery for
           captives. Governor allows branding of Indian captives. Span-
           iards suffer new military defeats, notably at Las Cangrejeras
           near Yumbel.

1629-39   Administration of Lazo de la Vega. Spanish defeat Arau-
           canians at La Albarrada (1631) and Philip IV officially
           abolishes "personal service" (1633). New regulations—Tasa
           de Lazo de la Vega (1635)—issued concerning Indian labor.
           Abolishes personal service but "allows" Indians to pay tribute
           in labor and "rent" their services. Widespread abuses.

1639-46   Administration of the Marquis de Baides. Governor attempts
           to negotiate with Araucanians. Pact of Quillín recognizes
           sovereignty of Araucanians. In exchange Indians agree to re-
           ceive missionaries. Peace treaty terms violated. Warfare re-
           sumes, though Indians help Spaniards repel invasion of south-
           ern Chile by Brouwer expedition (1643).

1646-49 Administration of Martín de Mujica. Earthquake destroys Santiago (1647). Followed by typhoid epidemic. Viceroy at Peru temporarily suspends certain taxes in Chile. Pact of Quillín renewed.

1650-56 Administration of Acuña y Cabrera. Cunco Indians kill crew of ship carrying situado to Valdivia (1651). Punitive expedition destroyed by Indians (1653). Nepotism and corruption weaken Spanish military. Indian uprising in 1655; vecinos of Concepción "depose" Acuña y Cabrera. Indians again push Spaniards out of southern settlements. Southern economy in shambles.

1656-63 Three interim administrations. King Philip IV prohibits future slave raids and military expeditions into hostile territory without prior approval. Viceroy at Lima appeals decisions to protect Peruvian labor supply.

1664-68 Administration of Francisco de Meneses. Governor in disputes with Church and audiencia. Corruption prevails as governor and supporters loot public administration, sell favors, and engage in slave raids (*malocas*) and trade. Peruvian viceroy, Count of Santistéban, supports continued enslavement of Araucanians.

1668-70 Two interim administrations succeed Meneses after he leaves Chile in disgrace.

1670-81 Administration of Juan Henríquez. Debate over treatment of Indians continues. Writings of Diego de Rosales gain influence. Queen Regent Mariana of Austria officially abolishes slavery in 1674. Henríquez and audiencia develop *depósito* system to circumvent abolition (1676). King Charles II reaffirms abolition decree of 1674 and orders freed Indians transported for their "care" to Peru (1679). King reverses his decree in response to Governor Henríquez's letters defending Chilean interests (1683). Pirates under Bartholomew Sharp sack La Serena (1680).

1682-92 Administration of José de Garro. Governor proposes massacre of Araucanian leaders. Viceroy and King reject Garro's proposal (1686). New pirate attacks at Coquimbo and La Serena (1686). Earthquake at Lima (1687) stimulates Chilean wheat production, increase in prices and temporary economic expansion.

1692-1700   Administration of Tomás Marín de Poveda. Royal decree of 1693 authorizes Indians to pay tribute in money or kind instead of personal service. Decree evaded as others in the past. Renewed efforts to pacify Araucanians through negotiations and missions—unsuccessful as in the past.

1700   Death of Charles II. Beginning of Bourbon era for Spanish America. Charles II leaves no successor. Throne is willed to Philip of Anjou (Philip V of Spain), grandson of Louis XIV of France.

1701-14   War of the Spanish Succession ended by the treaties of Utrecht and Rastadt. Philip V, King of Spain, renounces claim to French throne.

1713   England granted the *asiento* or monopoly on slave trade with Spain's colonies.

1701-08   Administration of Governor Francisco Ibáñez de Peralta. Corruption involving the situado. Civil war with rebels calling for ouster of governor. Rebellion suppressed. Increasing levels of contraband trade. Numerous complaints against governor lead to his removal by Philip V.

1709-16   Administration of Governor Juan Andrés de Ustáriz. Large scale commercial corruption involving French merchants after Ustáriz buys post of Chilean governorship for 24,000 pesos. Pirates under Captain Rogers find Alexander Selkirk ("Robinson Crusoe") on the island Más a Tierra in the Juan Fernández Archipelago.

1717-33   Administration of Governor Gabriel Cano de Aponte. Moderate policies pursued toward Mapuches. Period of relative peace with exception of rebellion in 1723. Earthquake provokes great damage to Santiago (1730) and affects seriously most of central Chile. Earthquake is followed by tidal wave at Valparaíso causing serious losses. Smallpox epidemic (1731).

1734-37   Interim administration of Manuel de Salamanca.

1737-45   Administration of Governor José Antonio Manso de Velasco. Founding of new towns in mining and agricultural districts, including San Felipe (1740), Los Angeles, Canquenes, San Fernando (1742), Melipilla, Rancagua, Curicó (1743). In recognition of his services, Manso de Velasco is made viceroy at Lima.

1745-55   Administration of Governor Domingo Ortiz de Rozas. Real Universidad de San Felipe inaugurated (1747) and La Moneda begins to function (1749). For his service in founding new settlements—Quirihue and Coelemu (1749), La Florida (1751), Casablanca and Petorca (1753), and Ligua (1754)—the king confers title upon Ortiz de Rozas. Ortiz de Rozas dies (1756) on return to Spain.

1751   Earthquake and tidal wave destroys Concepción.

1755-61   Administration of Governor Manuel de Amat y Junient. University of San Felipe begins operation (1757). Violent repression of prison rebellion in Santiago (1758). Amat y Junient becomes viceroy at Lima upon leaving Chilean post.

1761-68   Administration of Governor Antonio de Guill y Gonzaga. Foundation of Rere (1765), Yumbel (1766), and Tucapel el Nuevo (1765). Jesuits expelled from Chile (1767). Governor delegates much authority to corregidor Zañartu who imposes a reign of repression against criminals and indigents in Santiago. According to Francisco Encina, the slogan for Zañantu's program "By Reason or by Force" anticipated the slogan on the Chilean national escutcheon.

1768-73   After the death of Guill y Gonzaga, several interim administrations follow. New Indian uprisings and Spanish losses force negotiation of still another treaty (Paz de Negrete, 1770) in which Spanish give Indians compensation in money and cattle.

1773-80   Administration of Augustín de Jáuregui. Establishment of viceroyalty of Buenos Aires (1776), opening of direct commerce to Chile (1778), separation of Cuyo from Chile (1779). Governor introduces Draconian criminal legislation in efforts to curb violence, robberies, cattle rustling, and drunkeness. First significant census taken in Chile (1778). Like several of his predecessors, Jáuregui leaves Chile to become viceroy at Lima.

1780-87   Administration of Governor Ambrosio de Benavides. Administrative reorganization—introduction of intendant system

(1782) with Chile divided into two intendencies: Santiago and Concepción. Upon the death of Benavides, the Intendant of Concepción, Ambrosio de O'Higgins, becomes governor of Chile.

1783   Earth tremor and flooding in Santiago as Mapocho River rages through the city. Entire neighborhoods disappear.

1787-96   Administration of Governor Ambrosio de O'Higgins. Foundation of numerous new towns and mining centers. Public works, road construction, and beautification of Santiago. Encomiendas abolished (1791). New treaty with Indians in south (Parlamento of Negrete, 1793). Foundation of the *Consulado* (1795). O'Higgins becomes viceroy at Lima in 1796.

1796-1802   Administration of Governor Gabriel de Avilés y del Fierro and several interim administrations. Threat of war against England preoccupies the colony with preparations for defense against invasion. After brief tenure in Chile Avilés becomes viceroy at Buenos Aires and then at Lima. Interim governors follow until 1802.

1802-08   Administration of Governor Luis Muñoz de Guzmán. Continuation of public works programs in Santiago. Buenos Aires occupied by English (1806). Beginnings of political unrest in Chile. Vaccinations introduced in Chile (1805). Muñoz de Guzmán dies in 1808.

1808-10   Interim administration of Francisco Antonio García Carrasco. Unrest intensifies and governor is replaced by Mateo de Toro y Zambrano.

Sept. 18, 1810   Cabildo Abierto creates first junta, beginnings of Chilean independence movement.

1811-13   "Dictatorship" of José Miguel Carrera. Offspring of slaves born in Chile declared free (1811). Appearance of Chile's first newspaper, *La Aurora de Chile* (1812). Civil war in Chile.

1814   Treaty of Lircay. *Patria Vieja* ends after defeat of insurrectionists at Rancagua. Chilean forces retreat to Mendoza.

1814-17   *La Reconquista*—temporary restoration of Spanish authority as military expeditions from Peru defeat rebel forces.

1817   General San Martín and Bernardo O'Higgins lead army from

Argentina into Chile and defeat Spanish forces at Chacabuco (February 12, 1817).

1817-23   Dictatorship of Bernardo O'Higgins. Continued war against Spanish forces south of Santiago. Expeditionary force leaves Chile to liberate Peru (1820). Peruvian independence declared (1821) as San Martín occupies Lima. Titles of nobility abolished (1817).

1823-30   Period of chaos and political uncertainty dominated by liberal, federalist experiments and personality of Ramón Freire. Slavery abolished (1823). Federalist experiment (1826-28).

1828-30   Renewed civil war.

1830   Battle of Lircay (April 17, 1830). Conservative forces emerge victorious.

1831-41   Two five-year terms of President Joaquín Prieto. Constitution of 1833 adopted. Chile defeats Peru-Bolivia Confederation (1836-1839). Initiation of "Portalian State."

1842   University of Chile founded.

1849   Emergence of Liberal party.

1850   Sociedad de Igualdad established under leadership of Francisco Bilbao to contest election of Manuel Montt.

1841-51   Two five-year terms of President Manuel Bulnes, hero of the war against Bolivia and Peru. Civil War of 1851 mars succession, but Bulnes successfully defends his chosen successor, Manuel Montt.

1851-61   Two five-year terms of President Manuel Montt. Civil wars in 1851 and 1859 fragment ruling elite. Formation of Conservative party (1857). Economic boom as a consequence of gold strike in California. Expansion of Chilean commerce, mining and agriculture. Political challenge to clerical forces and old Conservative elite.

1861-71   Two five-year terms of President José Joaquín Pérez. Coalition governments incorporate Liberals and Conservatives into government as President breaks with party that elected him. Radical party formed in 1861 by Pedro León Gallo and the Matta brothers. Radical party becomes proponent of political reforms. "Theological Question" becomes a key issue in Chilean politics.

1871-75   Administration of President Federico Errázuriz Zañartu. Errázuriz dismisses Conservative members of coalition (1873) and forms cabinet entirely of Liberals, Radicals, and Nationals—the so-called Liberal Alliance. Religious question dominates domestic politics.

1876-81   Administration of President Aníbal Pinto. Severe economic crisis facing country "alleviated" by victory in the War of the Pacific (1879-1883). Chile acquires nitrate fields from Peru and Bolivia, increasing territory by more than one-third.

1881-86   Administration of President Domingo Santa María. Attempted renewal of political authoritarianism and anticlericalism. Suffrage extended to all males over 25 years of age.

1887   Formation of Partido Demócrata, Chile's first "populist" party. Election of first Partido Demócrata deputy in 1894.

1907   Massacre of workers at Santa María de Iquique.

1909   Gran Federación de Obreros de Chile founded. By 1917 becomes a militant labor organization (FOCH) and eventually affiliates with RILU.

1912   POS (Socialist Workers Party) founded by Luis Emilio Recabarren and supporters.

1919   Massacre of workers in Puerto Natales.

1920   Massacre of workers in Magallanes.

1920-24   First administration of President Arturo Alessandri. Allessandri, after populist campaign, is unable to move reforms through Congress. Military "coup" pushes social and labor legislation through Congress with a "rattling of sabers." Alessandri leaves the country.

1922   Establishment of Chilean Communist party.

1925   New Constitution approved. President Alessandri returns to Chile only to leave again after conflict with Defense Minister, Carlos Ibáñez.

1927-31   Ibáñez takes control of government after a period of "tutelage." Controlled elections provide a compliant congress. Massive public works program induces temporary prosperity as Ibáñez represses opposition. Stock market crash and depression bring Ibáñez's downfall.

1932-38   Arturo Alessandri returns to presidency after more than a year of juntas, insurrections, and uncertainty which includes the 100 days of a Chilean "Socialist Republic." Alessandri restores order, imposes the 1925 constitution, and utilizes fiscal conservatism to improve public finances. In departure from earlier (1920s) rhetoric, Alessandri presides over a Conservative regime.

1933   Creation of Socialist Party of Chile.

1934   Massacre of peasants at Ranquil.

1935-38   Formation of the Falange Nacional with splinter of Conservative youth group from Conservative party. Falange eventually (1957) becomes the Chilean Christian Democratic Party.

1936   Formation of Popular Front as prelude to 1938 presidential elections.

1938   Massacre of Nazis involved in protest movement (September 5) and incarceration of their leader, González Von Marées.

1938-41   Administration of Pedro Aguirre Cerda with support of Popular Front coalition. Reformist programs follow, including creation of Chilean Development Corporation (CORFO). Rural activism frightens political right; Popular Front parties agree to "suspend" rural unionization. Aguirre Cerda dies in 1941.

1942-46   Administration of President Juan Antonio Ríos. Popular Front dissolved but variety of coalitions follow. Communists and Socialists dominate labor movement but competition for control eventually divides leftist parties. President Ríos dies in 1946; new elections bring fellow Radical González Videla to the presidency.

1946-52   Administration of President Gabriel González Videla. Initial coalition of Radicals, Liberals, and Communists breaks up. González Videla, with support by the United States, moves against Communists. Communist party outlawed in 1948 and labor movements purged. Chile becomes Cold War battleground.

1947 New legislation restricts rights of rural labor. Conflicts in labor movement lead to divisions between Communist- and Socialist-led unions.

1948 Coal strikes and labor agitation. Law for the Permanent Defense of Democracy outlaws Communist party.

1952-58 Administration of President Carlos Ibáñez. Ibáñez elected on "anti-political" platform. Economic difficulties after the Korean War plague Ibáñez. High inflation rates and foreign advisers' stabilization programs undercut Ibáñez's popularity. Ibáñez approves electoral reform and relegalization of Communist party before leaving office.

1958-64 Administration of President Jorge Alessandri. After barely winning election over Salvador Allende, the candidate of the Leftist Coalition (FRAP), Alessandri presides over a conservative administration that introduced a number of minor reforms. Anti-inflation programs are relatively successful, but alienate workers, peasants, and part of the middle class. Under pressure from Alliance for Progress, a land reform law passes in 1962.

1964-70 Administration of President Eduardo Frei. Frei presides over the Christian Democratic "Revolution in Liberty" that dramatically alters Chilean politics and society. Mobilization of workers, peasants, slum-dwellers, and women destabilizes Chilean politics—and the government is unable to deliver on all its promises. Renewed inflation, economic stagnation, and seizures of farms, urban lots, and housing projects punctuate the last years of Christian Democratic government.

1970-73 Unidad Popular administration of President Salvador Allende. A program to put Chile on the peaceful road to socialism is met with bitter resistance by domestic and international opponents. Political polarization finally results in a bloody military coup, September 11, 1973.

1973-(79) Military dictatorship. Political parties are outlawed. Civil liberties restricted. Imprisonment and execution of political opponents rampant. Military proclaims they intend to establish a new institutional order devoid of "old style democracy." Junta reverses many reforms introduced by Unidad Popular government. Imposes conservative fiscal and economic policies. Encourages renewed foreign investment.

Selective Guide to
the Literature on Chile

This bibliography is intended as a starting point for the general reader in locating* materials on Chilean history and society. It is hoped that the specialist on Chile may also find in the topical bibliographic treatments a useful foundation for more intensive study of particular periods or themes in Chilean history. In general, the bibliography emphasizes published books. Manuscript sources, documents, and professional articles are listed in special cases or where I have relied upon particular works in the present volume.

In some respects Chilean historiography is extremely rich, detailed, and voluminous. For example, a comprehensive listing of works on colonial Chile, Chilean independence, or Chilean agriculture and rural society would require an extremely lengthy format merely for an alphabetical listing. Bibliography on the recent Unidad Popular period (1970-1973) has already reached massive proportions. In contrast, much remains to be done on pre-Hispanic Chile; no recent general history is available.

With this in mind, the bibliography that follows integrates chronological and thematic headings, beginning with a list of basic reference works and data sources, then moving to treatment of Chilean geography, population and natural resources, followed by studies on pre-Hispanic Chile through materials on the 1970s. In addition to suggestions for read-

* Place of publication for Chilean sources is Santiago, Chile, unless otherwise noted.

ing on particular topics or historical periods, an effort is also made to denote sources with especially helpful bibliographies of their own for those interested in specialized topics. Inasmuch as the present bibliography is *selective* rather than comprehensive, I have sought to cite sources for further research rather than to provide comprehensive lists of references for experts on specific themes or historical periods.

Even with this limited objective some readers will note the absence of a work they consider "basic" to the treatment of a particular topic or period, or even the absence of a topic they would have liked to have seen covered in the bibliography. While I hope these deficiencies will be minimal, I certainly welcome suggestions for additions to the selective bibliography for future editions of this history.

The following sources provide basic reference information on Chile. They include material on geographical features, census materials, statistical profiles, and biographical dictionaries.

Area Handbook for Chile, Washington, D.C., U.S. Govt. Printing Office, 1969;

Russell H. Bartley, *Latin America in Basic Historical Collections: A Working Guide*, Stanford, 1972 (information on manuscript holdings in libraries and collections);

M. L. Bohan and M. Pomerantz, *Investment in Chile: Basic Information for United States Businessmen*, U.S. Dept. of Commerce and Bureau of Foreign Commerce, 1960;

CORFO (Corporación de fomento de la producción), *Geografía económica de Chile*, texto refundido, 1967;

Lía Cortes and Jordi Fuentes, *Diccionario político de Chile: 1810-1966*, 1967;

Diccionario biográfico de Chile, 5th ed., 1944;

Pedro Pablo Figueroa, *Diccionario biográfico de Chile: 1550-1887*, 3 vols., 1897-1902; *Diccionario biográfico de extranjeros en Chile*, 1900;

Virgilio Figueroa, *Diccionario histórico, biográfico y bibliográfico de Chile: 1800-1931*, 5 vols., 1925-31;

Ronald Hilton (ed.), *Who's Who in Latin America Part IV: Bolivia, Chile, and Peru*, Stanford, 1947;

Instituto geográfico militar, *Atlas de la república de Chile*, 2nd ed., 1970;

Otto Neuberger, comp., *A Guide to Official Publication of the Other American Republics: Chile*, Washington, D.C., 1947 (entries arranged by name of Chilean government ministry);

Rosa Quintero Mesa, comp., *Latin American Serial Documents #7, Chile*, 1973 (titles of publications by Chilean government agencies in alphabetical order; also includes titles of numerous journals published in Chile);

Republic of Chile, Embassy in Washington, *Statistical Profile of Chile: 1967*, Washington, D.C., 1967 (mimeo);

República de Chile: *Dirección de estadística y censos* (census for 1940, 1952, 1960, 1970); *Dirección de estadística y censos: síntesis estadística*, 1968; *Dirección de estadística y censos: población total por provincias, Chile: 1885-1960*, 1964; and *Dirección general de estadística: estadística chilena* (Monthly 1960-70);

República de Chile, Oficina central de estadística, *Censo de 1854, 1865, 1875, 1895, 1907* (19th- and early 20th-century census reports);

Statistical Abstract of Latin America, Univ. of Calif., Los Angeles–Center for Latin American Studies;

El pasado republicano de Chile: o sea Colección de discursos pronunciados por los presidentes de la República ante el Congreso nacional al inaugurar cada año el período legislativo, Concepción, 1899 (collection of state of the nation addresses by presidents 1832-99).

BASIC GENERAL HISTORIOGRAPHICAL AND BIBLIOGRAPHICAL SOURCES

Fidel Araneda Bravo, "Los estudio históricos en Chile," *Atenea* 113, Nov.-Dec. 1953;

Horacio Aranguiz Dono, *Bibliografía histórica: 1959-1967*, 1970 (surveys of literature in 50 journals and books published between 1959 and 1967);

Ramón Briseño, *Estadística bibliográfica de la literatura chilena*, 2 vols., 1862-79 (includes a listing of newspapers by city and public documents arranged by presidential administration);

Herminia Elgueta de Ocsenius, *Suplemento y adiciones a la bibliografía de bibliografías chilenas*, 1930 (updates Laval's work (see below) to 1930, bringing total of titles reviewed to almost 600);

Guillermo Feliú Cruz, *Historia de las fuentes de la bibliografía chilena*, 3 vols., 1956-58 (evaluates contributions of all major bibliographers to 1958);

Hernán Godoy Urzúa, "El ensayo social: notas sobre la literatura sociológica en Chile," *Anales de la Universidad de Chile*, No. 120, Oct.-Dec. 1960;

Julio César Jobet, "Notas sobre la historiografía chilena," *Atenea* 291-292, Sept.-Oct. 1949;

Julio César Jobet, *Temas históricos chilenos*, 1973 (historiographical interpretation of selected themes in Chilean historical literature);

Ramón Laval, *Bibliografía de bibliografías chilenas*, 1915;

Luís Montt, *Bibliografía chilena*, 3 vols., 1904-21;

Robert Oppenheimer, *Chile: A Bibliography*, Los Angeles, 1977;

Nicholás Enrique Reyes and L. J. Silva Arriagada, *Ensayo de una bibliografía histórica y geográfica de Chile*, 1902 (lists works published to 1900; good source for locating local or regional studies);

William Sater, "A Survey of Recent Chilean Historiography 1965-1976," *LARR* (forthcoming) (an extensive overview and synthesis of recent scholarship on Chile);

Emilio Vaisse, *Bibliografía general de Chile*.

A number of anthologies and critical surveys offer introductions to Chilean art, literature, journalism, and music as well as biographical material on Chilean intellectuals and artists.

Fernándo Alegría, *Literatura chilena del siglo XX*, 2nd ed., 1962; and *La poesía chilena orígenes y desarrollo del siglo XVI al XIX*, Berkeley, 1954;

Homero Castillo and Raúl Silva Castro, *Historia bibliográfica de la novela chilena*, Charlottesville, 1961;

Samuel Claro and I. Urrutia, *Historia de la música en Chile*, 1973;

Luis E. Délano and Edmundo Palacios, *Antología de la poesia social de Chile*, 1962;

Julio Durán Cerda, *Panorama del teatro chileno: 1842-1959*, 1959;

Mario Godoy Quezada, *Historia del cine chileno*, 1966;

Mariano Latorre, *La literatura en Chile*, Buenos Aires, 1941;

Samuel A. Lillo, *Literatura chilena*, 7th ed., 1952 (official text on Chilean literature for secondary schools);

Eugenio Pereira Salas, *Historia de la música en Chile: 1850-1900*, 1957;

Antonio Romera, *Historia de la pintura chilena*, 1960;

Vicente Salas Viu, *La creación musical en Chile: 1900-1951*, 1951;

Raúl Silva Castro, *Panorama literario de Chile*, 1961; and *Prensa y periodismo en Chile: 1812-1956*, 1961;

Gaston Somoshegyi-Szokol, *Contemporary Chilean Literature in the University Library at Berkeley*, Berkeley, 1975 (partially annotated bibliography, and bibliographical guide to general anthologies and literary studies);

Arturo Torres Ríoseco and Raúl Silva Castro, *Ensayo de bibliografía de la literatura chilena*, Cambridge, Mass., 1935;

Fernando Uriarte, "La novela proletaria en Chile," *Mapocho* 4, 1965;

José Zamudio, *La novela histórica en Chile*, 1949.

GEOGRAPHY, POPULATION, AND NATURAL RESOURCES

From the time Pedro de Valdivia wrote to the Emperor Charles V in 1545 that, "this land is such that there is none better in the world for living in and settling," the role played by Chilean geography in shaping the territory's socio-economic and political development has been apparent to many writers on Chile. Early, now classic, accounts are Abbé Don J. Ignatious Molina, *The Geographical, Natural, and Civil History of Chile* (2 vols., trans. from the Italian with notes from the Spanish and French versions by the English editor, London, 1809) and Claudio Gay, *Historia física y política de Chile: documentos sobre la historia, estadística y la geografía* (26 vols., Paris, 1844-55). The best short summary of the relation between Chilean geography and historical development is Harold Blakemore, "Chile," in Harold Blakemore and Clifford T. Smith (eds.), *Latin America: Geographical Perspectives* (London, 1971). Other useful geographic and demographic summaries include *Area Handbook for Chile* (U.S. Govt. Printing Office, 1969); *Manual para invertir en Chile*, published by the Chile-California project, 1967 (see esp Chap. 1, "Visión general de Chile"); George Pendle, *The Land and the People of Chile* (London, 1964); Preston James, *Latin America* (4th ed., New York, 1964); Overseas Economic Surveys, *Chile* (London, 1958); Gilbert J. Butland, *Chile: An Outline of Its Geography, Economics and Politics* (London, 1956); Francis Maitland, *Chile: Its Land and People* (London, 1941); Benjamin Subercaseaux, *Chile: A Geographic Extravaganza* (trans. of *Chile: o una loca geografía*) New York, 1943. A much more detailed and technical summary also useful for its bibliography can be found in CORFO, *Geografía económica de Chile*, texto refundido (1967). Dated, but historically essential, is the classic by Enrique Espinosa, *Geografía descriptiva de la república de Chile*, 5th ed. (1903). Standard geographical treatments are provided in Elías Almeyda Arroyo, *Geografía de Chile* (1955); Sociedad Chilena de Historia, *Geografía de Chile: física, humana y economica* (1968); Pedro Cunill, *Geografía de Chile*, 2nd ed. (1970); Augusto Pinochet Ugarte, *Síntesis geográfica de Chile* (1963). Many descriptions of selected Chilean regions are also available. The most well known deal with the desert north, the central valley, and Antarctica: Isaiah Bowman, *Desert Trails of Atacama* (New York, 1924); W. J. Dennis, *Tacna and Arica* (New Haven, 1931); George McBride, *Chile: Land and Society*—the classic description of Chile's central valley agriculture and hacienda system—(New York, 1936); O. Pinochet de la Barra, *La antártica chilena* (1948). None of these last works is strictly speaking a geography, but all contain geographical information in addition to considerable historical, social and economic material. Two useful works that treat Chilean boundaries are: Jaime Eyzaguirre, *Breve historia de las fronteras de Chile*, 4th ed. (1973) and Robert D. Talbott, *A History of the Chilean Boundaries* (Ames, 1974).

INDIGENOUS PEOPLES

Although pre-Hispanic Chilean history is not thoroughly researched, a number of basic contributions in the field provide detailed and often conflicting information. Julio M. Montané's *Bibliografía selectiva de antropología chilena: Primera parte—Araucano, Pehuenches, Chiloé y territorios adyacentes; Segunda parte—generalidades: Zona norte y central*, 2 vols. (La Serena, 1963-64) contains approximately 400 references on Chilean Indians. Julian H. Steward (ed.), *Handbook on South American Indians*, Vol. II (New York, 1957), offers the best summary in English of Chilean indigenous civilizations. Other well-known studies are Augustín Edwards, *People of Old* (London, 1929); F. L. Cornely, *Cultura diaguita chilena y cultura de El Molle* (1956); Jorge Dowling, *Religión, chamanismo y mitología mapuches* (1973); René León Echaíz, *Prehistoria de Chile Central* (Talca, 1957); Tomás Guevara, *Historia de Chile prehispánico*, 2 vols. (1925-27); *Historia de la civilización de Araucania*, 7 vols. (1898-1913); Ricardo Latcham, *La prehistoria chilena* (1936) and *Organización social y creencias religiosas de los antiguos araucanos* (1924); Alejandro Lipschutz, *La comunidad indígena en América y en Chile* (1956); José T. Medina, *Los aborígenes de Chile* (1952); Greta Mostny, *Culturas precolombinas en Chile* (1960). Another very useful and readable overview of pre-Hispanic Chilean peoples appears in Francisco Esteve Barba, *Descubrimiento y conquista de Chile* (Madrid, 1946) along with a somewhat more extensive bibliography. As is the case with the study of pre-Columbian peoples in general, Julian Steward and Louis Faron, *Native Peoples of South America* (New York, 1959) offers a brief but helpful summary of knowledge on the natives of Chile, as does Wendell C. Bennett and Junius B. Bird, *Andean Culture History* (London, 1965). A more recent overview of pre-Columbian Chile by Osvaldo Silva appears in the first volume of a 4-volume (three in print) work edited by Sergio Villalobos, *Historia de Chile* (1974-76).

The Araucanian Indians' heroic resistance to the Spanish conquest inspired the first epic poem of Latin America, Alonso de Ercilla's *La Araucana*. Much of the historical work, chronicles, and other literature of the colonial period (see below) reflects this interest in the Araucanian people and their war against the Spanish. Several 19th-century descriptions of the Araucanians provide insight into the social and economic conditions prevalent after centuries of warfare: Ignacio Domeyko, *Araucania y sus habi-*

tantes (1st ed., 1845, 2nd ed., Buenos Aires, 1971); Pedro Ruís Aldea, *Los araucano i sus costumbres* (1st ed., 1856, Biblioteca de autores chilenos, Vol. 5, 1902); Edmund Reuel Smith, *The Araucanians, or Notes of a Tour among the Indian Tribes of Southern Chile* (London, 1855).

Recent scholarship on the Araucanians and Mapuche has been dominated by the work of Louis Faron: *Mapuche Social Structure* (Illinois, 1961); *Hawks of the Sun* (Pittsburgh, 1964); *The Mapuche Indians of Chile* (New York, 1968). All provide additional references. A mid-20th-century study by <u>Mischa Titien</u> *Araucanian Culture in Transition* (Ann Arbor, 1951) provides insight into the dilemma of Chile's Indians in the 20th century; Alejandro Saavedra's *La cuestión mapuche* (1971) presents a much more dismal picture twenty years later—with significant political implications.

TRAVEL ACCOUNTS

Observations of travelers provide information and insight often lacking in other sources. For an overview of travel accounts see Guillermo Feliú Cruz, *Notas para una bibliografía sobre viajeros relativos a Chile* (1965). Accounts by Chileans, North Americans, Latin Americans, and Europeans from the 17th century onward are both interesting reading and valuable resources for the historical study of Chile. Among the most useful are:

Henry Willis Baxley, *What I Saw on the West Coast of South and North America*, New York, 1865;

R. Nelson Boyd, *Chile: Sketches of Chile and the Chilians 1879-1880*, London, 1881;

Henry M. Brackenridge, *A Voyage to South America, performed by order of the American Government in the years 1817, and 1818, in the Frigate Congress*, 2 vols., Baltimore, 1819;

Alexander Caldcleugh, *Travels in South America during the Years 1819, 1820, 1821*, London, 1825;

Vicente Carvallo y Goyeneche, "Descripción histórica-geográfica del reino de Chile," *Colección de Historiadores* 10, 1879;

Richard J. Cleveland, *A Narrative of Voyages and Commercial Enterprises*, 2 vols., Cambridge, Mass., 1842;

Charles Darwin, *The Voyage of the Beagle*, Garden City, N.Y., 1962;

Thomas Cochrane Dundonald, *Narrative of Services in the Liberation of Chile, Peru and Brazil from Spanish and Portuguese Domination*, 2 vols., London, 1859;

George Alexander Findlay, *A Directory for the Navigation of the South Pacific Ocean*, London, 1863;

M. Frezier, *Relation du voyage de la mer du sud aux côtes du Chili et du Perou*, Paris, 1716;

Lt. J. Gilliss, *The U.S. Naval Astronomical Expedition to the Southern Hemisphere during the Years 1849-1852*, Washington, D.C., 1855, Vol. I (Chile);

María Graham, *Journal of a Residence in Chile during the Year of 1822*, London, 1824;

Thaddaeus Peregrinus Haenke, *Descripción del reyno de Chile*, 1942;

Samuel Haigh, *Sketches of Buenos Ayres and Chile*, London, 1829;

Basil Hall, *Extracts of a Journal Written on the Coasts of Chile, Peru, and Mexico in the Years 1820, 1821, 1822*, 2 vols., Edinburgh, 1826;

Adolph E. Howard, *A Handbook or Guide to British Shipmasters and Others Trading to the Coast of Chile*, Valparaíso, 1882;

Daniel J. Hunter, *A Sketch of Chile, expressly prepared for the use of emigrants from the United States and Europe to that country*, New York, 1866;

Samuel Burr Johnston, *Cartas escritas durante una residencia de tres años en Chile*, trans. by José Toribio Medina, 1917; and *Diario de un tipógrafo Yanquí en Chile y Peru durante la guerra de la independencia*, Madrid, 1919;

Gabriel Lafond de Lurcy, *Viaje a Chile*, 1970;

Mrs. C. B. Merwin, *Three Years in Chile*, New York, 1863;

John Miers, *Travels in Chile and La Plata*, 2 vols., London, 1826;

Fray Diego de Ocaña, "Relación del viaje a Chile: año de 1600," *Anales de la Universidad de Chile*, No. 120 (1960);

Vicente Perez Rosales, *Recuerdos del pasado*, trans. as *California Adventure*, San Francisco, 1947;

Eduardo Poeppig, *Un testigo en la alborada de Chile: 1826-1829*, 1960;

Ignacio Richard, *A Mining Journey Across the Great Andes*, London, 1863;

William S. W. Ruschenberger, *Three Years in the Pacific: 1831-1834*, Philadelphia, 1834;

W. H. Russell, *A Visit to Chile and the Nitrate Fields of Tarapacá*, London, 1890;

Domingo F. Sarmiento, *Chile: descripciones-viajes-episodios-costumbres*, Buenos Aires, 1961;

Peter Schmidtmeyer, *Travels into Chile over the Andes in the Years 1820-1821*, London, 1824;

Juan G. Serrato, *A través de Chile*, Buenos Aires, 1898;

William Bennet Stevenson, *A Historical and Descriptive Narrative of Twenty Years' Residence in South America*, 3 vols., London, 1825;

Thomas Sutcliffe, *Sixteen Years in Chile and Peru by the Retired Governor of Juan Fernández*, London, 1841;

Paul Truetler, *Andanzas de un alemán en Chile 1851-1863*, trans. by
Carlos Keller, 1958;
*Useful Information for Captains of Merchant Vessels and Others Trading
to the Port of Valparaíso*, Valparaíso, 1872;
George Vancouver, *A Voyage of Discovery to the North Pacific Ocean
and Round the World*, 3 vols., London, 1789;
Viajeros en Chile: 1817-1847, 1955 (Samuel Haigh, Alexander Cald-
cleugh, Max Radiguet).

CHILEAN HISTORY

Two historians, Diego Barros Arana and Francisco Encina, establish the
framework for Chilean historical studies. The foremost Liberal historian
of the 19th century, Diego Barros Arana produced the *Historia general de
Chile*, 16 vols. (1884-1902), the starting point for almost all Chilean historiography through 1833, including the conservative, revisionist *Historia
de Chile desde la prehistoria hasta 1891* by Francisco Encina, 20 vols.
(1940-52). A 3-volume summary of the Encina history by Leopoldo
Castedo—*Resúmen de la historia de Chile*—has gone through several editions and makes the Encina history somewhat more accessible to readers
unwilling to read or to acquire the 20-volume edition (1st ed., 1954).
Charles C. Griffin, "Francisco Encina and Revisionism in Chilean History," (*HAHR* 36, Feb. 1957) is an important critical review of the
Encina history. Ricardo Donoso's *Barros Arana: educador, historiador y
hombre público* (1931) provides an overwhelming bibliography of Barros
Arana's historical scholarship, including works on the independence movements and the Portalian period. A doctoral dissertation by Gertrude
Matyoka, *Diego Barros Arana and the Historia Jeneral de Chile* (Texas
Christian University, 1972) provides a more recent critical analysis of
Barros Arana's work as well as insight into 19th-century Chilean development. Also useful are Domingo Amunátegui Solar's 2-volume *Historia de
Chile* (1933)—intended as a secondary school textbook—and Jaime Eyzaguirre's *Historia de Chile*, 2 vols., 2nd ed. (1973), covering the period
from pre-Columbian times until 1861. Also of importance are Eyzaguirre's
earlier works, *Fisonomía histórica de Chile* (1948) and *Historia de Chile:
genesís de la nacionalidad* (1965). Luis Galdames, *Estudio de la historia
de Chile*, 8th ed. (1938), translated into English as *A History of Chile*
(Chapel Hill, 1941), is a one-volume survey ending shortly after the
Great Depression. An earlier narrative in English, A. U. Hancock, *History
of Chile* (Chicago, 1893), is largely a political history, ending with the
civil war of 1891. A brief narrative by Isaac Joslin Cox, "Chile" in
A. Curtis Wilgus's *Argentina, Brazil and Chile since Independence* (New
York, 1963), traces major events from 1808 until the mid-1930s. Ricardo

Donoso's *Breve historia de Chile* (Buenos Aires, 1963) is the briefest general history in Spanish. A secondary school text by Francisco Frías Valenzuela, based on the author's longer multivolume work, provides an important indication of what Chilean students learn of Chilean history, *Manual de historia de Chile*, 5th ed. (1960). Jay Kinsbruner's *Chile: A Historical Interpretation* (New York, 1973) is the closest thing in print to a recent English-language history of Chile, but the author makes it clear that this work is an interpretation of key developments in Chilean history rather than a history in the conventional sense.

In general, 20th-century history is not well developed in the available Chilean histories. However, one collection of articles edited by Hernán Godoy, *Estructura social de Chile* (1971), offers an excellent selection of materials on Chilean society, economy, and politics from the time of the conquest to the 1970s. In addition, this anthology contains an exceptionally good topical bibliography organized by historical period.

CONQUEST AND THE FORMATION OF CHILEAN SOCIETY

The single most important source of primary materials on the conquest of Chile is the series "Colección de historiadores de Chile y documentos relativos a la historia nacional (CH)," 51 vols. (1861-1953). This collection of chronicles, documents, and histories of the conquest has received priority from a number of Chile's most prominent historians and includes most of the key contributions to Chilean history in the early colonial period. Newer editions of some of the more salient works have been reissued recently in paperback in abbreviated form in a series called "Escritores coloniales de Chile," including Alonso de Góngora Marmolejo, *Historia de Chile desde su descubrimiento hasta el año 1575*; Alonso de Ovalle, *Histórica relación del reyno de Chile*; Alonso Gonzáles de Nájera, *Desengaño y reparo de la guerra de Chile*; Francisco Nuñez Pineda y Buscañan, *Cautiverio Feliz* (an account of life among the Araucanians by a captured Spaniard); and Diego de Rosales, *Historia general del reino de Chile*. Other key works in the "Colección de historiadores" are Vicente Carvallo Goyeneche, *Descripción histórico-geográfica del reino de Chile*; and Miguel de Olivares, *Historia militar, civil, y sagrada de Chile*. As in the rest of Spanish America many of these early writers on Chile were members of religious orders, especially the Society of Jesus (Jesuits).

A major figure in the creation of the "Colección de historiadores," José Toribio Medina, also made available large quantities of primary materials to scholars through his energetic archival research. Major published contributions include: *Cartas de Pedro de Valdivia que tratan del descubrimiento y conquista de Chile* (1953)—letters from Valdivia to Charles V;

Colección de documentos inéditos para la historia de Chile desde el viaje de Magallanes hasta la batalla de Maipo, 1518-1818, 30 vols. (1888-1902); and *Cosas de la Colonia* (1952). Other sources of primary materials include the *Archivo de la Capitania Jeneral; Archivo de la Real Audiencia; Archivo del Arzobispado de Santiago;* and the *Archivo Nacional de Chile.* In addition, the "Actas del cabildo de Santiago de 1541 a 1557 y de 1558 a 1577" can be found in the "Colección de historiadores," vols. 1 and 17.

Historical treatments of the period of conquest are numerous, ranging from biographies of Pedro de Valdivia and other conquistadores to comprehensive and detailed monographic studies. Among the most useful of the latter, Francisco Esteve Barba's *Descubrimiento y conquista de Chile* (Madrid, 1946) stands out as a reliable summary with helpful bibliography following each chapter. The set of histories from the Catholic point of view, by Catholic historian Crescente Errázuriz offers a comprehensive treatment of the period from the conquest to the late 16th century and an interpretation somewhat different than the Liberal orientation of Barros Arana, whose volumes—*Historia de Chile, Pedro de Valdivia*, 2 vols. (1911-21); *Historia de Chile sin gobernador 1554-1557* (1912); *Historia de Chile, Don García de Mendoza: 1557-1561* (1914); *Historia de Chile, Francisco de Villagra 1561-1563* (1915); *Historia de Chile, Pedro de Villagra 1563-1565* (1916); and *Seis años en la historia de Chile 1598-1605* (1908)—contain a wealth of detailed information. A recent doctoral dissertation at the University of Florida, Thomas Braman, *Land and Society in Early Colonial Santiago* (1975), synthesizes much of the older materials on the early years of conquest and includes a good working bibliography for this period.

On Pedro de Valdivia, his companions, and the conquest of Chile, a handful of well-known studies summarizes existing knowledge: Rosa Arcienega, *Don Pedro de Valdivia: Conquistador de Chile* (1943); Jaime Eyzaguirre, *Ventura de Pedro de Valdivia* (1963); Hugh R. S. Pocock, *The Conquest of Chile* (New York, 1967); Joaquín Santa Cruz, *Problemas históricos de la conquista de Chile* (1902); Luis Silva Lezaeta, *El conquistador Francisco de Aguirre* (1953); Ida W. Vernon, *Pedro de Valdivia: Conquistador of Chile* (New York, 1969). A sympathetic treatment of Valdivia's mistress, later wife of another Chilean governor, can be found in Stella B. May, *The Conqueror's Lady: Inéz de Suarez* (New York, 1930). Other historians have taken the biographies of major Indian chiefs as a point of departure, for example René León Echaíz, *El toqui lautaro* (1971).

The ongoing warfare between Spaniards and the Araucanians of Chile gave to Chilean colonial society a unique character, influencing settlement patterns, social and economic institutions, and the composition of its population. The best single volume interpreting the relationship between the frontier status of Chile and the evolution of Chilean society is Alvaro Jara's *Guerra y sociedad en Chile* (1971, translated from a French edition published ten years earlier). Jara's other work on colonial labor systems and Spanish-Indian relations complements the monograph and serves as a basis for colonial labor history: "Fuentes para la historia del trabajo en Chile" (*BACH* 54, 55, 58, 51, 1956-57, 1959); *El salario de los indios y los sesmos del oro en la Tasa de Santillán* (1961); *Los asientos del trabajo y la provisión de mano de obra para los no-encomenderos en la ciudad de Santiago: 1586-1600* (Estudios de historia económica americana, trabajo y salario en el período colonial, No. 1, 1959); "Salario en una economía caracterizada por las relaciones de dependencia personal," (*RCHG* 133, 1965). The only available interpretation of Spanish-Indian confrontation in English is Eugene H. Korth's, *Spanish Policy in Colonial Chile* (Stanford, 1968). Written from a Jesuit perspective Korth's study includes an admirable bibliography of primary sources as well as secondary treatments on the Spanish conquest and settlement of Chile. It is an essential starting point for any further work on this period of Chilean history. An earlier article by Louis de Armond, "Frontier Warfare in Colonial Chile," *Pacific Historical Review* (May 1954), is still an interesting introductory reading on the Chilean frontier.

Among the most valuable secondary sources on the Indian question and early colonial society are Domingo Amunátegui Solar, *Las encomiendas de indíjenas en Chile*, 2 vols. (1909); Miguel Luís Amunátegui, *Descubrimiento y conquista de Chile* (1862); Guillermo Feliú Cruz and Carlos Monje Alfaro, *Las encomiendas según tasas y ordenanzas* (Buenos Aires, 1941); Kalky Glauser R., "Orígenes del regímen de producción vigente en Chile," *CRN*, No. 8 (1971); Mario Góngora, *El estado en el derecho indiano, época de fundación: 1492-1570* (1951); "Vagabundaje y sociedad fronteriza en Chile: Siglo XVIII a XIX," *Cuadernos del Centro de Estudios Socioeconómicos*, No. 2 (1966); *Encomenderos y estancieros, estudios acerca de la constitución social aristocrática de Chile después de la conquista: 1580-1660* (1970); Nestor Meza Villalobos, *Políticas indígenas en los orígenes de la sociedad chilena* (1951); *La formación de la fortuna mobiliaria y el ritmo de la conquista* (1941); María Isabel Gónzales Pomes, "La encomienda indígena en Chile durante el siglo XVIII," *Historia* 5 (1966); Jorge Randolph, *Las guerras de Arauco y la esclavitud* (1966); Manuel Salvat Monguillot, "El régimen de encomiendas en los primeros tiempos de la conquista," *RCHG*, No. 132 (1964); Fernando Silva Vargas, *Tierras y pueblo de indios en el reino de Chile* (1962).

The most important Marxist contribution to conquest historiography is Luis Vitale, *Interpretación marxista de la historia de Chile*: Tomo 1: *Las culturas primitivas, la conquista español* (1957). One Chilean historian, Tomás Thayer Ojeda, has given special attention to the origins of the so-called "raza chilena" more generally. Major works include: *Elementos étnicos que han intervenido en la población de Chile* (1919); *Formación de la sociedad chilena y censos de la población de Chile entre los años 1540 a 1565, con datos estadísticos, biográficos, étnicos, y demográficos,* 3 vols. (1939-41); *Los conquistadores de Chile,* 2 vols. (1908); with Carlos J. Larraín, *Valdivia y sus compañeros* (1950).

COLONIAL SOCIETY AND CULTURE

Central to the development of Chilean society, as in the rest of Spanish America, the Catholic Church and its representatives played a critical role in conquest, social organization, education, and public policy. Eugene Korth's already mentioned study is a basic source in English for an overview of the role of the Church in shaping Spanish colonial policy in Chile. Among the numerous Spanish-language sources are: Diego Barros Arana, *Riquezas de los antiguos jesuitas de Chile* (1872); Francisco Enrich, *Historia de la compañia de Jesús en Chile,* 2 vols. (Barcelona, 1891); Crescente Errázuriz, *Los orígenes de la iglesia chilena: 1540-1603* (1873); José Ignacio Victor Eyzaguirre, *Historia eclesiastica, política y literaria de Chile,* 3 vols. (Valparaíso, 1950); Elías Lizana and Pablo Maulen (eds.), *Colección de documentos históricos recopilados del archivo del arzobispado de Santiago,* 4 vols. (1919-21); José Toribio Medina, *La inquisición en Chile,* 2 vols. (1890); Policarpo Gazulla, *Los primeros mercedarios en Chile: 1535-1600* (1918); Carlos Silva Cotapos, *Histoira eclesiástica de Chile* (1925).

Insight into colonial art, literature, and music in Chile can be found in Fernando Alegría, *La poesia chilena; orígenes y desarrollo del siglo XVI al XIX* (México, 1954); Luis Alvarez Urquieta, *La pintura en Chile durante el período colonial* (1933); Alfredo Benavides Rodríguez, *La arquitectura en el virreinato del Peru y en la capitania general de Chile,* 2nd ed. (1961); Alejandro Fuenzalida Grandón, *Historia del desarrollo intelectual de Chile: 1541-1810* (1903); *Historia de la literatura colonial,* 3 vols. (1878); Eugenio Pereira Salas, *Los orígenes del arte musical en Chile* (1941); *Historia del arte en el reino de Chile: 1541-1776* (1965); Luis Roa Urzua, *El arte en la época colonial de Chile* (1929); Tomás Thayer Ojeda, "Las bibliotecas coloniales en Chile," *Revista de bibliografía chilena y extranjera 1,* No. 11 (1943).

Colonial education and pastimes are treated in Miguel Luis and Gregorio Amunátegui, *De la instrucción pública en Chile* (1856); José Toribio Medina, *La instrucción pública en Chile desde sus orígenes hasta la fundación de la universidad de San Felipe de Santiago de Chile*, 2 vols. (1928); Eugenio Pereira Salas, *Juego y alegrías coloniales en Chile* (1947).

COLONIAL ECONOMY AND SOCIETY

Nineteenth-century treatments of the colonial economy of Chile reflect the struggle between liberalism and the Hispanic-Catholic tradition. More recent interpretations reflect the global confrontation between supporters of market economies, capitalism, and Marxism. The works by Alvaro Jara and Mario Góngora cited earlier provide the foundation for an understanding of Chile's colonial economy and economic institution. Eugene Korth's already mentioned work, *Spanish Policy in Colonial Chile* contains references to good primary sources. Articles on specialized themes on colonial society and economy as well as documents with commentary appear periodically in *RCHG*, *BACH*, and *Historia*.

Marxist interpretations of colonial society include José Cademartori, *La economía chilena* (1968) esp. chaps. 2 and 3; André Gunder Frank, *Capitalism and Underdevelopment in Latin America* (1969); Julio César Jobet, *Ensayo crítico del desarrollo económico-social de Chile* (1955); Hernán Ramírez Necochea, *Antecedentes económicos de la independencia de Chile* (1959); Marcelo Segall, *Desarrollo del capitalismo en Chile* (1953); "Las luchas de clases en las primeras décadas de la República de Chile," *Anales de la Universidad de Chile*, No. 125 (1962); Luis Vitale, *Interpretación marxista de la historia de Chile: La colonia y la revolución de 1810* (1969).

For an overview of historiography on the colonial period see Guillermo Feliú Cruz, *Historiografía colonial de Chile* (1957). Among the great number of works on colonial society and economy, including social and economic institutions and patterns of commerce, are the following basic studies:

Sergio Bagú, *Economía de la sociedad colonial*, Buenos Aires, 1949; and *Estructura social de la colonia*, Buenos Aires, 1952;

Marcello Carmagnani, *Les Mécanismes de la vie économique dans une société coloniale: le Chili* (1680-1830), Paris, 1973;

Miguel Cruchaga, *Estudio sobre la organización económica y la hacienda pública de Chile*;

Mario Góngora, "Los 'hombres ricos' de Santiago y La Serena a traves de las cuentas del quinto real," *RCHG*, No. 131, 1963;

Eugenio Pereira Salas, *Buques norteamericanos a fines de la era colonial: 1778-1810*, 1936;

Demetrio Ramos, *Trigo chileno, navieros del Callao y hacendados limeños*, Madrid, 1967;

Ruggiero Romano, *Una economía colonial: Chile en el siglo XVIII*, Buenos Aires, 1965;

Augustín Ross, *Reseña histórica sobre el comercio de Chile en la era colonial*, 1894;

Sergio Sepúlveda, *El trigo chileno en el mercado mundial*, 1959;

Sergio Villalobos, *El comerico y la crisis colonial: un mito de la independencia*, 1968, and *Comercio y contrabando en el Río de la Plata y Chile: 1700-1811*, Buenos Aires, 1965.

On mining in particular, the reader may consult:

J. Bruggen, *Bibliografía minera y jeologica de Chile*, 8 vols., 1919-27;

Alberto Herrmann, *La producción en Chile de los metales y minerales mas importantes de las soles naturales, del azufre y del guano desde la conquista hasta fines del año 1902*, 1903;

Augusto Orrego Cortés, *La industria del oro en Chile*, 1890;

Francisco San Ramón, *Reseña industrial e histórica de la minería y metalurgía de Chile*, 1899;

José Joaquín (Jotabeche) Vallejo, *Costumbres mineras*, date;

Benjamín Vicuña Mackenna, *El libro de la plata*, 1882; *El libro del cobre y del carbón de piedra*, 1883; and *La edad del oro en Chile*, 2 vols., 1932.

Studies on social themes in the colonial period, including the role of ethnic and cultural minorities in colonial Chile, are:

Domingo Amunátegui Solar, *Historia social de Chile*, 1936; and *La sociedad chilena del siglo XVIII: mayorazgos y títulos de castilla*, 3 vols., 1903-04;

Bunter Bohm, *Nuevas antecedentes para una historia de los judíos en Chile colonial*, 1963;

Marcello Carmagnani, "Colonial Latin American Demography: Growth of Chilean Population 1700-1830," *Journal of Social History*, No. 2, 1963; and *El salariado minero en Chile colonial, su desarrollo en una sociedad provincial: el norte Chico; 1690-1800*, 1963;

Guillermo de la Cuadra Gormaz, *Orígen de doscientos familias coloniales de Santiago*, 3 vols., 1941-47; *Orígen y desarrollo de las familias chilenas*, 1948-49; and "Censo de la capitania general de Chile en 1777," *BACH*, No. 12, 1940;

Enrique Eberhardt, *Historia de Santiago de Chile*, 1916;

Guillermo Feliú Cruz, *La abolición de la esclavitud en Chile*, 1942;

Alejandro Fuenzalida Grandón, *La evolución social de Chile: 1514-1810*, 1906;

Mario Góngora, *Orígen de los inquilinos de Chile Central*, 1960; and

"Urban Social Stratification in Colonial Chile," *HAHR* 55, 1975; with Jean Borde, *Evolución de la propiedad rural en el valle del Puange,* 2 vols., 1956;
Elías Lizana, *Colección de documentos historicos de archivo del arzobispado de Santiago,* 4 vols., 1919-21;
Rolando Mellafe, *La introducción de la esclavitud negra en Chile,* 1959;
Humberto Muñoz, *Los movimientos sociales en el Chile colonial,* 1945;
William F. Sater, "The Black Experience in Chile," *Slavery and Race Relations in Latin America,* R. Toplin (ed.), Westport, Conn., 1974;
Gonzalo Vial Correa, *El africano en el reino de Chile,* 1957.

On the cabildo and the effects of administrative reforms in the colonial period, see:

Julio Alemparte, *El cabildo en Chile colonial,* 1940;
Miguel Luis Amunátegui, *El cabildo de Santiago desde 1573 hasta 1581,* 3 vols., 1890-91;
Jacques Barbier, "Elite and Cadres in Bourbon Chile," *HAHR,* Aug. 1972 (clearly the most important recent revisionist work on the effects of the Bourbon reforms on colonial administration and society); *Imperial Reform and Colonial Politics: A Secret History of Late Bourbon Chile,* Ph.D. diss., Univ. of Connecticut, 1973;
David H. Edwards, *Economic Effects of the Intendency System in Chile: Captain General Ambiosio O'Higgins as Reformer,* Ph.D. diss., Univ. of Virginia, 1973;
Della M. Flusche, "The Cabildo and Public Health in Seventeenth Century Chile," *TA* 29, 1972; and "City Councilmen and the Church in Seventeenth Century Chile," *Records of American Catholic Historical Society of Philadelphia* 81, No. 3, 1970;
Carlos Ugarte, "El cabildo de Santiago y el comercio exterior del reino de Chile en el siglo XVIII," *Estudios de las Instituciones Políticas y Sociales,* Vol. I, 1967.

INDEPENDENCE AND THE AUTOCRATIC REPUBLIC

The exceptionally researched study, *Ideas and Politics of Chilean Independence: 1808-1833* by Simon Collier (Cambridge, Eng., 1967), is without a doubt the most important source in English on late 18th-century Chile, the independence movement, and the formation of the Portalian state. Collier's bibliography lists manuscript sources, contemporary newspapers and journals, as well as contemporary and modern scholarship on the period. I have relied heavily on Collier's work in my own discussion of this period in Chapter 4 and will not attempt here to replicate his bibliography. In addition, Collier's recent article "The Historiography of the Portalian Period 1830-1891 in Chile," *HAHR* (Nov. 1977) adds an important and systematic treatment of traditional and revisionist history on the independence period, formation of the Portalian state, and 19th-century Chilean historiography more generally.

Review of the historiography of the independence period is found in Gonzalo Vial, "Historiografía de la independencia de Chile," *Historia*, No. 4 (1965). Recent studies by American scholars have considerably expanded our knowledge of post-independence commercial affairs and the social composition of the Chilean oligarchy; S. F. Edwards, *Chilean Economic Policy Goals 1811-1829: A Study of Late Eighteenth Century Social Mercantilism and Early Nineteenth Century Economic Reality*, Ph.D. diss., Tulane Univ. (1971); and John Rector, *Merchants, Trade and Commercial Policy in Chile: 1810-1840*, Ph.D. diss., Indiana Univ. (1976); and "Transformaciones comerciales producidas por la independencia de Chile," *RCHG*, No. 143 (1975). The work of Roger Haigh, *The Formation of the Chilean Oligarchy: 1810-1821* (Salt Lake City, 1972) and of Mary Felstiner, *The Larraín Family in the Independence of Chile: 1789-1830*, Ph.D. diss., Stanford (1970), "Kinship Politics in the Chilean Independence Movement," *HAHR* 56 (Feb. 1976), offers insight into the nature and behavior of the Chilean oligarchy in the early 19th century. For accounts of the evolution of Chile's political elite in the 19th century see the classic work by Alberto Edwards Vives, *La fronda aristocrática* (1936) and the more recent study by Gabriel Marcella, *The Structure of Politics in Nineteenth Century Spanish America: The Chilean Oligarchy 1833-1891*, Ph.D. diss., Univ. of Notre Dame (1973).

The independence period and formation of the "Portalian" state have produced a voluminous literature. On the independence movement and its leaders see: Julio Alemparte, *Carrera y Feire* (1903); Miguel Luis Amunátegui, *La crónica de 1810*, 3 vols. (1876); *Don Manuel de Salas*, 3 vols. (1895); *Los precursores de la independencia de Chile*, 3 vols. (1919); with Benjamín Vicuña Mackenna, *La dictadura de O'Higgins* (Madrid, 1920); *La revolución de la independencia* (1945); and *Nacimiento de la república de Chile: 1808-1833* (1930); Stephen Clissold, *Bernardo O'Higgins and the Independence of Chile* (New York, 1969); Augustín Edwards, *The Dawn* (London, 1931); Francisco Antonio Encina, *Portales: Introducción a la historia de la época de Diego Portales: 1830-1891*, 2 vols. (1934); Fernando Errázuriz, *Chile bajo el imperio de la constitución de 1828* (1861); Jaime Eyzaguirre, *Ideario y ruta de la emancipación chilena* (1957); and *O'Higgins*, 3rd ed. (1950); Guillermo

Feliú Cruz, *El pensamiento de O'Higgins* (1954); Jay Kinsbruner, *Bernardo O'Higgins* (New York, 1968); William R. Manning (ed.), *Diplomatic Correspondence of the United States Concerning the Independence of Latin American Nations*, 3 vols. (New York, 1925); José Toribio Medina, *Actas del cabildo de Santiago de Chile durante el período llamado de la patria vieja: 1810-1814* (1910); Nestor Meza Villalobos, *La actividad política del reino de Chile entre 1806 a 1810* (1968); Bartolomé Mitre, *Historia de San Martín y de la emancipación sudamerica*, 3 vols. (Buenos Aires, 1887-88); Ricardo Montaner Bello, *Historia diplomática de la historia de Chile* (1961); Francisco José Moreno, *Legitimacy and Stability in Latin America: A Study of Chilean Political Culture* (New York, 1969) (the study by Moreno emphasizes the conflict between the "authoristic" tradition and the liberal principles espoused in the independence period and the 19th century); A. Orrego Luco, *La patria vieja*, 2 vols. (1935-57); Eugenio Orrego Vicuña, *O'Higgins: vida y tiempo* (Buenos Aires, 1946); Hernán Ramírez Necochea, *Antecedentes económicos de la independencia de Chile* (1959) (a Marxist interpretation of the independence movement); Raúl Silva Castro, *Engaña en la patria vieja* (1959); *Ideas y confesiones de Portales* (1954); and (ed.), *Escritos políticos de Camilo Henríquez* (1960); Benjamín Vicuña Mackenna, *El ostracismo de los Carrera* (1938); and *Tradición y reforma en 1810* (1961); Donald E. Worcester, *Sea Power and Chilean Independence* (Gainsville, 1962).

For post-1810 political development until the Constitution of 1833 the following sources are a good foundation: Benjamín Vicuña Mackenna, *Pipiolos y pelucones* (1939); Diego Barros Arana and Benjamín Vicuña Mackenna, et al., *Historia de la república de Chile: 1810-1830*, 5 vols. (1866-82); Ricardo Donoso, *Desarrollo político y social de Chile desde la constitución de 1833*, 2nd ed. (1942); *Las ideas políticas en Chile*, 2nd ed. (1967) (This last work is perhaps the most important statement by a Chilean author of the struggle between liberalism and Hispanic values as a constant issue in Chilean history.); Alberto Edwards, *La organización política de Chile: 1810-1833*, 2d ed. (1955); Jaime Eyzaguirre, "Las ideas políticas en Chile hasta 1833," *BACH* 1 (1933); Jay Kinsbruner, *Diego Portales: Interpretive Essays on the Man and Times* (The Hague, 1967); Daniel Martner, *Estudio de política comercial chilena y historia económica nacional*, 2 vols. (1923); Paul V. Shaw, *The Early Constitutions of Chile* (New York, 1930); Ramón Sotomayor Valdez, *Historia de Chile bajo el gobierno del general don Joaquín Prieto*, 4 vols. (1900-1903); Benjamín Vicuña Mackenna, *Don Diego Portales*, 2 vols. (Valparaíso, 1863); Carlos Walker Martínez, *Portales* (Paris, 1879); José Zapiola, *Recuerdos de treinta años: 1810-1840*, 5th ed. (1902).

NINETEENTH-CENTURY CHILE

Simon Collier's "The Historiography of the 'Portalian' Period: 1830-1891 in Chile," *HAHR* (Nov. 1977) must be consulted when treating this period of Chilean history. Allen Woll's doctoral dissertation, *A Functional Past: The Politics of History in Nineteenth Century Chile* (Univ. of Wisconsin, 1975), summarizes the ideological currents influencing 19th-century Chilean historiography and offers important insights into 19th-century Chilean society.

In general, historical studies on 19th-century development in Chile have come to rely less on the classical Chilean sources as American, British, Chilean, and European scholars produce monographs on particular themes, and Marxist historians and non-Marxist revisionists offer conflicting versions of socio-economic and political development in 19th-century Chile.

On Chilean social and economic development in the 19th century, Arnold J. Bauer, *Chilean Rural Society from the Spanish Conquest to 1930* (Cambridge, Eng., 1975) provides a useful overview along with a valuable bibliography. Harold Blakemore's *British Nitrates and Chilean Politics: 1886-1896* (London, 1974), a much broader work than its title suggests, offers a crucial interpretation of socio-economic development and Chilean politics, including a controversial treatment of the martyred president Balmaceda. For a radically different view, readers should consult Hernán Ramírez Necochea, *Historia del imperialismo en Chile* (1960); *La guerra civil de 1891: antecedentes económicas* (1953); and *Balmaceda y la contrarevolución de 1891*, 2nd ed. (1969). Frederick Pike's *Chile and the United States: 1880-1962* (Notre Dame, 1962) interprets much of 19th- and early 20th-century Chilean history and is probably the most readable overview available in English.

On 19th- and early 20th-century Chilean politics, Pike's work cited above is a useful summary. A more recent, revisionist view of post-1861 political developments is Julio Heise González, *Historia de Chile: el período parlamentario 1861-1925* (1974). This study is essential for understanding institutional evolution, the issues and myths surrounding the civil war of 1891, and early 20th-century political history. Heise's bibliography lists most of the important primary and secondary works on Chilean political and constitutional development from the early 19th century to the 1930s. In *Diagnóstico de la burocracia chilena: 1818-1969*, Germán Urzua Valenzuela and Anamaría Garcia Barzellatto provide the only available syntheses of the growth of the Chilean state apparatus since independence and the political implications of bureaucratic expansion, including developments in the 19th century. Ricardo Donoso's polemical *Desarrollo político y social de Chile desde la constitución de 1833* and *Las ideas políticas en Chile*, 2nd ed. (1967) are both among the key secondary works on the 19th century. For a Marxian interpretation, also the source of much revisionist history on the 19th century, see Julio César Jobet, *Ensayo crítico del desarrollo económico-social de Chile* (1955). Another important contribution to social history is Guillermo Feliú Cruz, "Un esquema de la evolución social de Chile en el siglo hasta 1891," in *Chile: visito a través de Augustín Ross* (1950).

In general, studies on the 19th century are much more specialized than those on earlier periods of Chilean history. As Chile was integrated into the web of expanding European and North American economies, it became itself a more complex and specialized society. Among the facets of this complexity examined by scholars are participation in the California and Australian gold rushes, growth of the mining and nitrate industry of the north, the beginnings of industrialization and intensified urbanization, immigration, transportation developments, war and military issues, diplomacy, intellectual development, and the emerging social question.

Such diversity makes topical categorization quite difficult. In the broad area of socio-economic evolution, including works on particular areas of the Chilean economy, social stratification and class conflict, the social question, technological change, and international economic relations, one school of historical scholarship has recently emphasized the "dependency" of Chilean development upon events in Europe and North America. Complementing more traditional Marxist treatments of Chilean socio-economic trends in the 19th century and Francisco Encina's earlier laments concerning the direction and character of Chilean development in *Nuestra inferioridad económica* (1955), the dependency theorists trace most problems facing Chile to this pattern of international exploitation in the past centuries. Key works in this tradition include Ramírez Necochea's already mentioned study, *Historia de imperialismo en Chile* (1960); Marta Harnecker and Gabriela Uribe, *Imperialismo y dependencia* (1972); and two doctoral dissertations Roger Burbach, *The Chilean Industrial Bourgeoisie and Foreign Capital 1920-1970* (Indiana Univ., 1975) and Charles G. Pregger Román, *Dependent Development in Nineteenth Century Chile* (Rutgers Univ., 1975). A related but more balanced approach is Aníbal Pinto Santa Cruz, *Chile: un caso de desarrollo frustrado* (1959).

Markos J. Mamalakis's conservative interpretation, *The Growth and Structure of the Chilean Economy: From Independence to Allende* (New Haven and London, 1976), stands in sharp contrast to the dependency theorists. Buttressed by data for the 19th century as well as the twentieth, along with thorough research in secondary sources, his conclusions con-

cerning the role and effect of foreign investment in Chile offer a significant counter to the dependency theorists. Notwithstanding these contributions, many of Mamalakis's conclusions must be read with caution,
as his technical focus sometimes glosses over the impact on the majority
of Chileans of selected policies and patterns of economic change.

For particular sectors or regions of the Chilean economy and economic
issues in the 19th century the following sources are of considerable value:
Marcello Carmagnani, *Sviluppo Industriale e Sotto-Sviluppo Económico:
il caso chileno 1860-1920* (Turin, 1971); C. W. Centner, "Great Britain
and Chilean Mining: 1830-1914," *Economic History Review*, No. 12
(1942); Henry William Kirsch, *The Industrialization of Chile: 1880-
1930*, Ph.D. diss. (Univ. of Florida, 1973); Santiago Machiavello Varas,
*El problema de la industria del cobre y sus proyecciones económicas y
sociales* (1923); Markos Mamalakis and Clark Reynolds, *Essays on the
Chilean Economy* (Homewood, Ill., 1965); Santiago Marín Vicuña, *Los
ferrocarriles en Chile* (1912); Max Nolff, "Industria manufacturera,"
CORFO, *Georgrafía económica de Chile* (1967); Robert B. Oppenheimer, *Chilean Transportation Development: The Railroads and Socio-
economic Change in the Central Valley*, Ph.D. diss. (Univ. of California,
Los Angeles, 1976); L. R. Pederson, *The Mining History of the Norte
Chico: Chile* (Evanston, 1966); John Whaley, *Transportation in Chile's
Bío Bío Region: 1850-1915*, Ph.D. diss. (Indiana Univ., 1974). Whaley's
work, an excellent economic history of the Bío Bío region, also discusses
primary sources and railroad statistics.

On nitrates, the most important sector of the economy in the late 19th
century, see in addition to the Blakemore work already mentioned, Oscar
Bermúdez, *Historia del salitre desde sus orígenes hasta la guerra del
Pacífico* (1963); G. Billinghurst, *Los capitales salitreros de Tarapacá*
(1889); Manuel Cruchaga, *Guano y salitre* (Madrid, 1929); J. R. Brown,
"Nitrate Crisis: Combinations and the Chilean Government in the
Nitrate Age," HAHR, No. 63. (1963); "The Chilean Nitrate Railways
Controversy," HAHR, No. 38 (1958); M. B. Donald, "History of the
Chile Nitrate Industry," *Annals of Science* 1 (Jan. 1936); and 2 (April
1936); Thomas O'Brien, *British Investors and the Decline of the Chilean
Nitrate Entrepreneurs: 1870-1890*, Ph.D. diss. (Univ. of Connecticut,
1975); J. F. Rippy, *British Investments in Latin America: 1822-1949*
(Hamden, Conn., 1966). A recently completed doctoral dissertation at
Indiana University (1978) by Laurence Stickell, *Migration and Mining:
Labor in Northern Chile in the Nitrate Era, 1880-1930*, will surely stand
as the most important social and labor history of the nitrate industry.

Each of the "major" events and international conflicts of Chile's 19th-
century history has occasioned its own historical literature. This includes,

of course, the war against the Peru-Bolivia confederation early in the century, participation in the gold rushes of California and Australia, the civil war of 1851 and 1859, the War of the Pacific, the civil war of 1891, and the effects of each economic boom or depression.

On the California gold rush's impact on Chile see Jay Monaghan, *Chile, Peru and the California Gold Rush of 1849* (Berkeley, 1973). A Marxist treatment of the civil wars of 1851 and 1859 is Luis Vitale's, *Las guerras civiles de 1851 y 1859 en Chile* (Concepción, 1971). Useful specialized studies on fiscal, financial, and public-sector performance include: Roberto Espinoza, *Cuestiones financieras de Chile* (1909); *La reforma bancaria y monetaria* (1913); Carlos T. Hamud, *El sector público chileno entre 1830-1930* (1969); and Augustín Ross, *Chile: 1851-1910: sesenta años de cuestiones monetarias y financieras y de problemas bancarios* (1911). Another ostensibly specialized study is Claudio Veliz, *Historia de la marina mercante de Chile* (1961), a work which goes well beyond history of the merchant marine, representing a basic source for Chilean economic history in the 19th century.

Immigration to Chile in the 19th century has also received limited, but careful attention in Carl Solberg, *Immigration and Nationalism: Argentina and Chile 1890-1914* (Austin, 1970); Jean Pierre Blancpain, *Les Allemands au Chili: 1816-1945* (Cologne, 1974)—a massive study of the German experience in Chile and their contribution to Chilean society; Mark Jefferson, *Recent Colonization in Chile* (New York, 1921); George Young, *The Germans in Chile: Immigration and Colonization 1849-1914* (New York, 1974).

For the most systematic and detailed discussion of Chile in world affairs in the 19th century, and the domestic impact of these events, see the award-winning volume by Robert N. Burr, *By Reason or Force: Chile and the Balancing of Power in South America 1830-1905* (Berkeley and Los Angeles, 1965). Burr's bibliography lists a wide range of official publications and other primary sources for Chilean international relations in the 19th century as well as materials on domestic development. An earlier but still useful look at Chilean diplomacy in the 19th century is Henry Clay Evans, *Chile and Its Relations with the United States* (Durham, N.C., 1927). Evans's book also surveys domestic socio-economic development in the 19th century. Other diplomatic studies include the classic by Mario Barros, *Historia diplomática de Chile 1541-1938* (Barcelona, 1970), which provides an overview from the colonial period to the Popular Front; William R. Sherman, *The Diplomatic and Commercial Relations of the United States and Chile: 1820-1914* (Boston, 1926). The war with Spain in the 1860s is treated in William Columbus Davis, *The Last Conquistadores* (Univ. of Georgia, 1950). Of great value for the War of the Pacific and late 19th-century Chile is William Sater's careful study, *The Heroic Image in Chile: Arturo Prat, Secular Saint* (Berkeley and Los Angeles, 1973). Sater's bibliography and notes contain numerous references to primary sources and government documents related to the War of the Pacific and Chilean economic and political development in the 19th century as well as newspaper and journal sources. Sater's article, "Chile during the First Months of the War of the Pacific," *Journal of Latin Studies* 5 (1973) is helpful for background on the Chilean situation as the country entered the War of the Pacific. Of related interest is Thomas Bader, *A Willingness To War: A Portrait of the Republic of Chile during the Years Preceding the War of the Pacific*, Ph.D. diss., Univ. of California at Los Angeles (1967).

The War of the Pacific and the subsequent diplomatic conflicts involving Chile, Peru, and Bolivia are the subjects of a large number of patriotic diatribes and some scholarly study. For varying interpretations of the war and polemical discussion of culpability the following list of sources may be consulted:

Pascual Ahumada Moreno, *Guerra del Pacífico*, 8 vols., Valparaíso, 1884-1891;

Jorge Basadre, *Historia de la república del Perú*, 6th ed., Lima, 1968 (Basadre is Peru's most eminent historian);

Gonzalo Bulnes, *Guerra del Pacífico*, 3 vols., Valparaíso, 1911;

Andrés A. Cáceres, *La Guerra del 79: sus campañas: redacción y notas por Julio C. Guerrero*, Lima, 1973 (the memoirs of Peru's leading general and hero of the War of the Pacific); and *La guerra entre el Perú y Chile: 1879-1883*, Buenos Aires, 1924;

Edmundo H. Civiti Bernesconi, *Guerra del Pacífico: 1879-1883*, 2 vols., Buenos Aires, 1946;

W. J. Dennis, *Tacna and Arica: An Account of the Chile-Peru Boundary Dispute and the Arbitration of the United States*, New Haven, 1931;

Francisco García Calderón, *Memorias del cautiverio: prólogo y notas de Ventura García Calderón*, Lima, 1949 (account of this Peruvian ex-president's capture and imprisonment by the Chileans after the occupation of Lima);

V. G. Kiernan, "Foreign Interest in the War of the Pacific," *HAHR* 35 (1955);

Francisco A. Marchuca, *Las cuatro campañas de la Guerra del Pacífico*, 4 vols., Valparaíso, 1926;

Sir Clements R. Markham, *The War between Peru and Chile: 1879-1882*, London, 1882;

Herbert Millington, *American Diplomacy and the War of the Pacific*, New York, 1948;

Mariano Felipe Paz-Soldán, *Narración histórica de la Guerra de Chile contra el Perú y Bolivia*, Buenos Aires, 1884.

The last decades of the 19th century brought the social question to Chile. In addition to the numerous contemporary accounts, political proclamations, and other writing, the following works are useful to the understanding of the social question and the labor movement in Chile: Robert Alexander, *Communism in Latin America* (New Brunswick, 1957); and *Labor Relations in Argentina, Brazil and Chile* (New York, 1962); Alan Angell, *Politics and the Labour Movement in Chile* (London, 1972); Jorge Barría Seron, *Breve historia del sindicalismo chileno* (1967); *Trayectoria y estructura del movimiento sindical chilena* (1963); and *El movimiento obrero en Chile* (1972); César A. DeLeon, "Las capas medias en la sociedad chilena del siglo XIX," *Anales de la Universidad de Chile*, No. 132 (1964); Julio César Jobet, *Recabarren, los orígenes del movimiento obrero y del socialismo chileno* (1956); Patricio Manns, *Breve síntesis del movimiento obrero* (1972); Michael Monteon, *The Nitrate Mines and the Origins of the Chilean Left: 1880-1925*, Ph.D. diss. (Harvard, 1974); James O. Morris, *Elites, Intellectuals, and Consensus: A Study of the Social Question and the Industrial Relations System in Chile* (Ithaca, N.Y., 1966)—this book provides the most complete list of references to newspaper, periodical and contemporary literature on the social question as well as secondary sources. It is the single most important reference source in English—; Hernán Ramírez Necochea, *Historia del movimiento obrero en Chile: siglo XIX* (1956); Alberto Varona, *Francisco Bilbao: revolucionario de América*, Buenos Aires (1973).

For a useful sample of contemporary sources on the social question and early labor histories see:

Juan Enrique Concha, *Cuestiones obreras*, 1899;

Luis Malaquías Concha S., *Sobre la dictación de u código del trabajo y de la previsión social*, 1907;

Javier Díaz Lira, *Observaciones sobre la cuestión social en Chile*, 1904;

Marcos Guitérrez Martínez, *La cuestión obrera i el derecho de propiedad*, 1904;

"Informes de los Señores Concha y Quezada," *Boletín de la sociedad de fomento fabril 20*, 1903;

Tulio Lagos V., *Bosquejo histórico del movimiento obrero en Chile*, 1947;

J. Lawrence Laughlin, "The Strike at Iquique," *The Journal of Political Economy* 17, 1909.

August Orrego Luco, "La cuestión social en Chile," *Anales de la Universidad de Chile* 119. Primero y segundo trimestre, 1961, No. 121 y 122;

Moisés Poblete Troncoso, *El derecho del trabajo y la seguridad social en Chile*, 1949;
J. Valdés Canje (pseudonym used by Alejandro Venegas), *Cartas al Excelentísmo Señor Don Pedro Montt*, Valparaíso, 1909;
Benjamín Vicuña Subercaseaux, *Socialismo revolucionario y la cuestión social en Europa y Chile*, 1908.

Political histories of Chile in the 19th century are numerous. Available to a lesser extent are summaries of the terms of individual presidents. Simon Collier's earlier cited article on the historiography of the Portalian period (*HAHR*, Nov. 1977) reviews the major work on this period while Harold Blakemore's "The Chilean Revolution of 1891 and Its Historiography," *HAHR* 45 (Aug. 1965) is the single most important review of sources on the civil war of 1891, Balmaceda, and Chilean society at the turn of the century.

Many of the Chilean histories of the 19th century represent Liberal attacks on Conservative or Portalian administrations or vice versa.

On individual presidential administrations see:

Juan Bautista Alberdi, *Biografía del general Don Manuel Bulnes: presidente de la República de Chile*, 1846;
José A. Alfonso, *Los partidos políticos en Chile*, 1902;
Alberto Edwards Vives, *El gobierno de don Manuel Montt: 1851-1861*, 1932;
Isidoro Errázuriz, *Historia de la administración Errázuriz*, 1935;
Jaime Eyzaguirre, *Chile durante el gobierno de Errázuriz Echaurren: 1896-1901*, 1957;
Germán Riesco, *Presidencia de Riesco*, 1950;
Ricardo Salas Edwards, *Balmaceda y el parlamentarismo en Chile*, 1914;
Ramón Sotomayor Valdés, *Historia de Chile durante los cuarenta años transcurridos desde 1831 hasta 1871*, 2 vols., 1875-76;
Benjamín Vicuña Mackenna, *Introducción a los diez años de la administración Montt, Don Diego Portales*. 2 vols., Valparaíso, 1863;
Cristian A. Zegers, *Aníbal Pinto: Historia política de us gobierno*, 1969.

The evolution of 19th-century political thought, parliamentary institutions, electoral reform, the crisis of the Balmaceda presidency, and the character of the Chilean oligarchy are treated in:

José A. Alfonso, *El parlamentarismo i la reforma política en Chile*, 1909;
Justo y Domingo Arteaga, *Los constituyentes de 1870*, 1910;
Abdon Cifuentes, *Un decenio de la historia de Chile*, 1905;
Malaquias Concha, *El programa de la democracia*, 1908;

Ricardo Donoso, *Alessandri, agitador y demoledor: cincuenta años de historia política de Chile*, 2 vols., 1952, 1954; and *Historia de las ideas políticas en Chile*, 1946;

Alberto Edwards Vives, *La fronda aristocrática*, 1936;

Rafael Egaña, *Historia de la dictadura y la revolución de 1891*, 1891;

Pedro Pablo Figueroa, *Historia de la revolución constituyente: 1858-1859*, 1889;

Maximiliano Ibáñez, *El régimen parlamentario en Chile*, 1908;

Abraham Konig, *La constitución de 1833 en 1913*, 1913;

José J. Larraín, *El derecho parlamentario chileno*, 2 vols., 1896-97;

José Victorino Lastarria, *La política constitución de la República de Chile comentada*, 1856;

José Maza, *Sistemas de sufragio i cuestión electoral*, 1913;

Hermógenes Perez de Arce, *El parlamentarismo*, 1901;

Paul Reinsch, "Parliamentary Government in Chile," *APSR*, June 1909.

Manuel Rivas Vicuña, *Historia política y parlamentaria de Chile*, 3 vols., 1964—a key figure in Chilean parliamentary politics provides valuable insight into the parliamentary era—;

Ramón V. Subercaseaux, *Memorias de ochenta años*, 1936.

The class basis of Chilean 19th-century politics is introduced in:

Frederick Pike, "Aspects of Class Relations in Chile, *HAHR*, Feb. 1963;

Luis Emilio Recabarren, *Los albores de la revolución social en Chile*, 1921—the author is the most well-known early leader of the Chilean labor movement—; and *Ricos y pobres a través de un siglo de vida republicana*, 1910.

THE CIVIL WAR OF 1891

The civil war of 1891, with its relationship to the nitrate economy, and also the symbol of President Balmaceda, has generated considerable historical literature. Harold Blakemore's, "The Chilean Revolution of 1891 and Its Historiography," *HAHR* 14 (1965) reviews this literature and offers the reader the benefit of Professor Blakemore's astute interpretation of the Balmaceda years. Blakemore's book, *British Nitrates and Chilean Politics: 1886-1896* (1974), is by far the most important recent work on the Balmaceda period, presenting much new material and a marked contrast to earlier work by Chilean nationalists and Marxists on the War of the Pacific, the role of British investors in Chilean politics, and on the policies of the Balmaceda administration. Among the most important treatments of the Balmaceda period and the civil war of 1891 are:

J. Bañados Espinosa, *Balmaceda: su gobierno y la revolución de 1891*, 2
    vols., Paris, 1894;
Aníbal Bravo Kendrick, *La revolución de 1891*, 1946;
J. Díaz Valderrama, *La guerra civil de 1891*, 2 vols., 1942;
O. Hardy, "British Nitrates and the Balmaceda Revolution," *Pacific His-
    torical Review* 17, 1948;
Maurice Kervey, *Dark Days in Chile*, London, 1891-92;
Michael Meeropol, *On the Origins of the Chilean Nitrate Enclave*, Ph.D.
    diss., Univ. of Wisconsin, 1973;
Cristótomo Pizarro, *La revolución de 1891*, Valparaíso, 1971;
Hernán Ramírez Necochea, *Balmaceda y la contrarevolución de 1891*,
    2nd ed., 1969 (a Marxist interpretation of the Civil War of 1891);
J. Rodríguez Bravo, *Balmaceda y el conflicto entre el congreso y el
    ejecutivo*, 2 vols., 1921, 1926;
Edwards R. Salas, *Balmaceda y el parlamentarismo en Chile*, 2 vols., 1914,
    1925;
J. Sears and B. W. Wells, *The Chilean Revolution of 1891*, Office of
    Naval Intelligence, Washington, D.C., 1893;
J. M. Yarrázaval, *El presidente Balmaceda*, 2 vols., 1940.

ECONOMY AND SOCIETY IN THE TWENTIETH CENTURY

It is very difficult to find a discussion of the Chilean economy that fails to
include discussion of Chilean politics. In an effort to provide a bibliographical overview of Chilean political economy in the 20th century, I have
compiled a list of works covering the economy to approximately 1970.
The works on this list include both general treatments and studies with a
more specialized focus. In addition, separate lists of references follow for
the agricultural sector, copper, and mining, due to the special importance
of these sectors of the Chilean economy both in strictly economic terms
and in regard to Chilean politics.

In addition to the recent work of Mamalakis (*The Growth and Structure of the Chilean Economy: From Independence to Allende*, 1976)
mentioned earlier, the best synthesis of Chilean political economy and
economic issues for the period 1952 to 1970 is Ricardo French Davis,
Políticas económicas en Chile: 1952-1970 (1973), which examines stabilization programs and economic policy from the time of the Klein-Saks
missions to 1970. It also includes extremely useful data series and an excellent bibliography of technical literature on the Chilean economy. For
general treatments of Chilean economic development and economic issues
see:

Jorge Alessandri, *La verdadera situación económica y social de Chile en la actualidad*, 1955;

Marco Ballesteros and Tom E. Davis, "The Growth of Output and Employment in Basic Sectors of the Chilean Economy," *Economic Development and Cultural Change* 11, 1963;

Jere R. Behrman, *Macroeconomic Policy in a Developing Country: The Chilean Experience*, Amsterdam, 1977;

José Cademártori, *La economía chilena: un enfoque marxista*, 1968;

Alvin Cohen, *Economic Change in Chile: 1929-1959*, Gainesville, 1960;

Luis Correa Prieto, *Nuestra economía y sus flaquezas: análisis no comprometido*, 1963;

ECLA (CEPAL), *Antecedentes sobre el desarrollo de la economía chilena: 1925-1952*, 1954;

P. T. Ellsworth, *Chile: An Economy in Transition*, New York, 1945;

Instituto de Economía de la Universidad de Chile, *Desarrollo económico de Chile: 1940-1956*, 1956; and *La economía de Chile: 1950-1963*, 2 vols., 1963;

Julio César Jobet, *Ensayo crítico del desarrollo económico social de Chile*, 1955;

Nicholas Kaldor, "Economic Problems of Chile," *Essays on Economic Policies* 2, London, 1964;

Santiago Machiavello Varas, *Política económica nacional antecedentes y directiva*, 2 vols., 1931;

Markos Mamalakis and Clark Reynolds, *Essays on the Chilean Economy*, Homewood, Ill., 1965 (includes special contributions on copper and agriculture);

Daniel Martner, *Estudio de política comercial chilena e historia económica nacional*, 2 vols., 1923;

Aníbal Pinto et al., *Chile hoy*, 1970; *Chile: una economía difícil*, 1964; *Tres ensayos sobre Chile y América Latina*, Buenos Aires, 1971; and *Hacia nuestra independencia económica*, 1963;

Universidad de Chile, *Desarrollo de Chile en la primera mitad del siglo XX*, I. 1953;

Stefan de Vylder, *From Colonialism to Dependence: An Introduction to Chile's Economic History*, Stockholm, 1977;

Mario Zañartu and John Kennedy (eds.), *The Overall Development of Chile*, Notre Dame, 1969.

Public finance, monetary issues, and the continuing debate over inflation and stabilization policy are discussed in:

Cesár Araneda Encina, *Veinte años de la historia monetaria de Chile: 1925-1945*, 1945;

Banco Central de Chile, *Evolución de las finanzas públicas de Chile: 1950-1960*, 1963;

Jorge Cauas, "Políticas de estabilización: el caso chileno," *Estudios monetarios* 2, 1970;

Tom E. Davis, "Eight Decades of Inflation in Chile: 1879-1959: A Political Interpretation," *Journal of Political Economy* 81, No. 4, 1963;

David Feliz, "An Alternative View of the 'Monetarist-Structuralist' Controversy," *Latin American Issues: Essays and Comments*. A. Hirschman (ed.), New York, 1961;

Frank Fetter, *Monetary Inflation in Chile*, Princeton, 1931;

Hermán Finer, *The Chilean Development Corporation*, Montreal, 1947;

Eduardo García, *Inflation in Chile: A Quantitative Analysis*, Ph.D. diss., M.I.T., 1964;

Joseph Grunwald, "The 'Structuralist' School in Price Stabilization and Economic Development: The Chilean Case," *Latin American Issues: Essays and Comments*, A. Hirschman (ed.), New York, 1961;

Albert O. Hirschman, "Inflation in Chile," *Journeys Toward Progress*, New York, 1963;

Klein-Saks Misión, *El programa de estabilización de la economía chilena y el trabajo de la Misión Klein-Saks*, 1958;

Rolf Luders, *A Monetary History of Chile 1925-1958*, Ph.D. diss., Univ. of Chicago, 1968;

Ministerio de Hacienda, *Cuentas fiscales de Chile: 1925-1957*, 1959;

Max Nolff and Felipe Herrera, *La inflación: naturaleza y problemas*, 1954;

OEDPLAN, *Cuentas nacionales: 1960-1970*, 1971;

Enrique Sierra, *Tres ensayos de estabilización en Chile*, 1970.

Sectoral development in industry, agriculture, mining, banking, and tax or exchange rate policy receive treatment in:

Pedro Aguirre Cerda, *El problema agraria*, Paris, 1929; and *El problema industrial*, 1933;

Oscar Alvarez Andrews, *Historia del desarrollo industrial de Chile*, 1936;

Sergio Aranda and Alberto Martinez, *Industria y agricultura en el desarrollo económico*, Instituto de Economía de la Universidad de Chile, 1970;

Eric Baklanoff, "Model for Economic Stagnation: The Chilean Experience with Multiple Exchange Rate," *Interamerican Economic Affairs* 13, Summer 1959;

Solon Barraclough, "Reforma agraria: historia y perspectiva," *Cuadernos de la Realidad Nacional*, No. 7, 1971;

Sergio Bitar, "Politica de desarrollo industrial," *Cuadernos de Economía*, No. 22, Dec. 1970;

Marcello Carmagnani and C. M. Hernández, "Evolución de la industria en Chile: 1860-1940," *Boletín del Centro de Estudios Socioeconómicos 1*, 1967;

CORFO, *Obreros industriales chilenos*, 1970;

F. Durán Bernales, *Población, alimentos y reforma agraria*, 1966;

Peter Gregory, *Industrial Wages in Chile*, Ithaca, N.Y., 1967;

Rodolfo Hoffman and F. Debuyst, *Chile: una industrialización desordenada*, 1966;

Instituto de Economía de la Universidad de Chile, *La tributación agrícola en Chile 1940-1958: algunas implicationes del sistema tributario chileno*, 1960;

Ricardo Lagos, *La industria en Chile antecedentes estructurales*, 1966;

Daniel Martner, *Estudio de política comercial chilena e historia económica nacional*, 2 vols., 1923;

Oscar Muñoz G., *Crecimiento industrial de Chile: 1940-1965*, 1968; and et al., *Proceso a la industrialización chilena*, 1972 (collection of articles considering development under conditions of dependence, and various aspects of industrial development in Chile);

Mariano Puga Vera, *El petroleo chileno*, 1964.

Concern with foreign investment and concentration of wealth and power in Chile are found in:

Jorge Ahumada, *En vez de la miseria*, 1958;

Genaro Arriabada, *La oligarquía patronal chilena*, 1970;

Sergio Bitar, "La inversión extranjera en la industria chilena," *Trimestre Económico 13*, No. 4, Oct.-Dec. 1971;

CORFO, *Análisis de las inversiones extranjeras en Chile: 1954-1969*, 1972; and *La inversión extranjera en la industria chilena*, 1970;

Fernando Galofré, *Entrepreneurial and Governmental Elites in Chilean Development*, Ph.D. diss., Tulane Univ., 1970;

Ricardo Lagos, *La concentración del poder económico, su teoria, realidad chilena*, 1961;

Maurice Zeitlin et al., "New Princes for Old? The Large Corporation and the Capitalist Class in Chile," *American Journal of Sociology 80*, July 1974.

CHILEAN AGRICULTURE, RURAL LIFE, AND AGRARIAN REFORM

Many writers have analyzed Chilean politics and society against the backdrop of the land tenure system, *inquilinaje*, deficient agricultural production, and the relationship between rural life and urban power. The literature on rural Chile is truly overwhelming. CIDA, *Chile: Tenencia de la tierra y desarrollo socio-económico del sector agrícola* (1966), and the annotated bibliography published by the Land Tenure Center at the University of Wisconsin at Madison—*Agrarian Reform in Latin America: An Annotated Bibliography* (1974)—are excellent sources of bibliographical references on agriculture, rural life, and agrarian reform in Chile. Key studies on rural Chile and the formation of the hacienda system include: Rafael Baraona et al., *Valle de Putaendo* (1960); Luis Correa Vergara, *Agricultura Chilena*, 2 vols. (1939); Ramón Domínguez, *Nuestro sistema de inquilinaje* (1867); M. Drouilly and Pedro Lucío Cuadra, "Ensayo sobre el estado económico de la agricultura en Chile," *BSNA* 10 (1878); Mario Góngora, *Encomenderos y estancieros* (1970); *Orígen de los "inquilinos" de Chile central* (1960) with Jean Border, *Evolución de la propiedad en el valle del Puange*, 2 vols. (1956); Silvia Hernández, "Transformaciones tecnológicas en la agricultura de Chile central: siglo XIX," *Cuadernos del centro de estudios socio-económicos*, No. 3 (1966); Gonzalo Izquierdo, *Un estudio de las ideologias chilenas: la sociedad de agricultura en el siglo XIX* (1968); Carlos Keller, *Una revolución en la agricultura* (1956); George McBride, *Chile: Land and Society* (Baltimore, 1936); Tancredo Pinochet Le-Brun, "Inquilinos en la hacienda de su excelencia," *Antología chilena de la tierra*, Antonio Corvalán, ed. (1970); Moisés Poblete Troncoso, *El problema de la producción agrícola y la política agraria nacional* (1919); Teodoro Schneider, *La agricultura chilena durante los últimos cincuenta años* (1904).

Significant recent contributions include the long list of works published at ICIRA in Santiago under the direction of Solon Barraclough prior to the military coup of 1973. Perhaps foremost on the list is Almino Affonso et al., *Movimiento campesino chileno*, 2 vols. (1970). Among others are: Andrés Pascal, *Relaciones de poder en una localidad rural*; Solon Barraclough, *Notas sobre tenencia de la tierra en América Latina*; Pablo Ramírez, *Cambios en las formas de pago a la mano de obre agrícola*; A. Corvalán et al., *Reforma agraria chilena: seis ensayos de interpretación*; Antonio Corvalán (ed.), *Antología chilena de la tierra*; Alejandro Saavedra, *La cuestión mapuche*; Hugo Zemelman, *El migrante rural*; Brian Loveman, *El campesino chileno le escribe a su excelencia*.

Other important studies include: F. Broughton, *Chile: Land Reform and Agricultural Development*, Ph.D. diss. (Univ. of Liverpool, Eng., 1970); Peter Dorner, ed., *Land Reform in Latin America: Issues and Cases* (Madison, Wisc., 1971); Roberto P. Echeverria, *The Effect of Agricultural Price Policies on Intersectoral Income Transfers*, Ph.D. diss. (Cornell Univ., 1969); Cristóbal Kay, *Comparative Development of the European Manorial System and the Latin American Hacienda System: An*

Approach to a Theory of Agrarian Change for Chile, Ph.D. diss. (Univ. of Sussex, Eng., 1971); Robert R. Kaufman, *The Politics of Land Reform in Chile* (Cambridge, Mass., 1972); Brian Loveman, *Struggle in the Countryside: Politics and Rural Labor in Chile 1919-1973* (Bloomington, Ind., 1976); Terry L. McCoy, *Agrarian Reform in Chile: 1962-1968*, Ph.D. diss. (Univ. of Wisconsin, 1969); Marvin Sternberg, *Chilean Land Tenure and Land Reform*, Ph.D. diss. (Univ. of California, Berkeley, 1962); Jeannine Swift, *Agrarian Reform in Chile: An Economic Study* (Lexington, Mass., 1971); William Thiesenhusen, *Chile's Experiments in Agrarian Reform* (Madison, Wisc., 1966).

COPPER

Since 1930 copper has dominated Chile's economy. At the mercy of international economic forces and controlled until 1971 by foreign firms, the copper industry was the source of perpetual political conflict. No other study has done so much to put the Chilean copper industry into an international perspective as Theodore Moran, *Multinational Corporations and the Politics of Dependence* (Princeton and London, 1974). Another study, less sympathetic to Chile and more sensitive to the interests of the American firms—but nonetheless extremely careful and well-researched— is Eric Baklanoff, *Expropriation of United States Investments in Cuba, Mexico, and Chile,* (New York, 1975). By far the most detailed recent work relating the Chilean copper industry to American investment is George Mason Ingram IV, *Nationalization of American Companies in South America: Peru, Bolivia, Chile,* 2 vols., Ph.D. diss. (Univ. of Michigan, 1973). Ingram's massive study includes an extensive bibliography on foreign investment in Chile, as well as Peru and Bolivia, along with sources on the Chilean copper industry in particular. Other valuable works on copper in the Chilean economy include:

Gregorio Amunátegui, "The Role of Copper in the Chilean Economy," *Latin America and the Caribbean: A Handbook*, Claudio Veliz (ed.), London, 1968;

Eric N. Baklanoff, "Taxation of United States-owned Copper Companies in Chile: Economic Myopia versus Long-run Self-interest," *National Tax Journal*, No. 14, March 1961;

"Contribution of Copper to Chilean Economic Development: 1920-1967," *Foreign Investment in the Petroleum and Mineral Industries: Case Studies of Investor-Host Country Relations*, Raymond F. Mikesell et al., Baltimore and London, 1971;

Norman Girvan, *Copper in Chile*, Univ. of West Indies, Jamaica, 1972;

Joseph Grunwald and Philip Musgrove, *Natural Resources in Latin Ameri-can Development*, Baltimore, 1970;

Markos Mamalakis, "The American Copper Companies and the Chilean Government, 1920-1967: Profile of a Foreign-owned Export Sector," *Foreign Investment in the Petroleum and Mineral Industries: Case Studies of Investor-Host Country Relations*, Raymond Mikesell et al., Baltimore, 1971;

Santiago Marín Vicuña, *La industria del cobre en Chile*, 1920;

Raymond Mikesell, "Conflict and Accommodation in Chilean Copper," *Foreign Investment in the Petroleum and Mineral Industries: Case Studies of Investor-Host Country Relations*, Raymond Mikesell et al., Baltimore, 1971;

Eduardo Novoa Monreal, *La nacionalización del cobre: comentarios y documentos*, 1972 (important source for copper policy under the Allende government);

C. W. Reynolds, "Chile and Copper," *Essays on the Chilean Economy*, M. Mamalakis and C. W. Reynolds (eds.), New Haven, 1966;

Thomas G. Sanders, "Chile and Its Copper," *AUFS West Coast South America Series 26*, No. 1, New York, 1969;

Mario Vera Valenzueal, *La política económica de cobre en Chile*, 1961.

REGIONAL AND LOCAL HISTORIES, URBANIZATION

From colonial times the formation and growth of urban centers has in-spired local and regional histories. In recent times rapid urbanization has become a most salient feature of Chilean life. Studies that focus on regional development or on Chilean urbanization more generally include: DESAL, *Poblaciones marginales y desarrollo urbano: el caso chileno* (1965); John Friedman and Thomas Lackington, "La hiperurbanización y el desarrollo nacional en Chile," *Estructura social de Chile*, H. Godoy, ed., (1971); Guillermo Geisse G., *Problemas del desarrollo urbano re-gional en Chile* (1968); Gabriel Guarda, "Influencia militar en las ciudades del reino de Chile," *BACH* 33, No. 75, (1966); and "El urbanismo imperial y las primitivas ciudades de Chile," *Finis Terrae*, No. 51, (1957) (these two articles describe the early urbanization in colonial Chile); Carlos Hurtado Ruiz-Tagle, *Concentración de población y desar-rollo económico* (1966); Bruce Herrick, *Urban Migration and Economic Development in Chile* (Cambridge, Mass., 1965); Fernando Marín G. and B. Salamón Roseblitt, *La vivienda colonial urbana* (1956); Mario Francisco Rothschild, *Regional Development and Sectoral Specialization: The Chilean Case*, Ph.D. diss. (Cornell Univ., 1973); Eduardo Secchi, *La casa chilena hasta el siglo XIX* (1952); Jorge Gustavo Silva, *La nueva era de las municipalidades de Chile recopilación histórica de la vida comunal del país* . . . (1931); Astolfo Tapia Moore, *Legislación urbanística de Chile: 1818-1959* (1961); Tomás Thayer Ojeda, *Las antiguas ciudades chilenas* . . . (1911); Frederick S. Weaver, Jr., *Regional Patterns of Economic Change in Chile: 1950-1964* (Cornell Univ. diss. series, 1968).

Numerous historical descriptions of the evolution of individual cities or towns also exist. For Santiago see: Guillermo Feliú Cruz, *Santiago a comienzos del siglo XIX: crónica de los viajeros* (1970) (excerpts from numerous travel accounts referring to physical environment, economy, and social life of Santiago in the early 19th century); Joseph Fichandler and Thomas O'Brien, "Santiago, Chile 1541-1581: A Case Study of Urban Stagnation," *TA* (1976); Vicente Grez, *La vida santiaguina* (1879). On the province of Valparaíso see: Roberto Hernández D., *Valparaíso en 1827* (Valparaíso, 1927); Carlos J. Larraín, *Viña del Mar* (1946); René M. Salinas, "Caracteres generales de la evolución demográfica de un centro urbano chileno: Valparaíso, 1685-1830," *Historia*, No. 10 (1971); *Población de Valparaíso en la segunda mitad del siglo XVIII* (Valparaíso, 1970); Benjamín Vicuña Mackenna, *Historia de Valparaíso*, 2 vols. (1936); and *Quintero: su estado actual y su provenir* (Valparaíso, 1874).

La Serena, Copiapó, Antofagasta, and other northern urban places are treated in: Domingo Amunátegui Solar, *El cabildo de la Serena: 1678-1800* (1928); Oscar Bermúdez, *Orígenes históricos de Antofogasta* (Antofagasta, 1966); and "Pica en el siglo XVIII; estructura económica y social," *RCHG* 3 (1973); Manuel Concha, *Crónica de la Serena desde su fundación hasta nuestro días: 1549-1870* (La Serena, 1971); Domingo Contreras Gómez, *La ciudad de Santa María de Los Angeles*, 2 vols. (1972-44); Bernardo Cruz, *San Felipe de Aconcagna*, 2 vols. (1949-50); Eugenio Chouteau, *Informe sobre la provincia de Coquimbo presentado al supremo gobierno* (1887); Julio Figueroa G., *Historia de San Felipe* (San Felipe, 1902); Martin I. Glassner, "Feeding a Desert City: Antofogasta, Chile," *Economic Geography*, No. 45 (1969); Carlos Keller, "Los orígenes de Quillota," *BACH*, No. 61 (1959); J. Larraín de Castro, "Los orígenes de Zapallar, contribución a la historia de la propiedad territorial," *BACH*, No. 12 (1940); Joaquín L. Morales O., *Historia del Huasco* (Valparaíso, 1896); Andrés Sabella, *Semblanza del norte chileno* (1955); C. M. Sayago, *Historia de Copiapó* (Copiapó, 1854).

Leonardo Mazzei, "Ensayo de un recuento bibliográfico relativo a la zona sur de Chile: Talca-Magallanes: 1812-1912," *HGFC*, provides a comprehensive bibliography of regional studies for the territory from Talca south. Illustrative studies for urban centers and their hinterlands from the Central Valley south include: Armando Braun Menéedez, *Pequeña his-*

toria Magallánica, 2nd ed. (Buenos Aires, 1954); Fernando Campos H., "Concepción y su historia," *BACH* (1970); Guillermo Cox y Méndez, *Historia de Concepción* (1822); Pedro Cunill, "Castro: centro urbano de Chiloé insular," *Antropología 2*, Primera semestre (1964); Gabriel Guarda, *La economía de Chile austral antes de la colonización alemana* (Valdivia, 1973); René León Echaíz, *Historia de Curicó*, 2 vols. (1975); S. Manuel Mesa, *Proyección histórica de la provincia de Linares* (Linares, 1965); Isabel P. Montt, *Breve historia de Valdivia* (Buenos Aires, 1971); Reinaldo Muñoz Olave, *Chillán: sus fundaciones y destrucciones: 1580-1835* (1921); Carlos Olguín B., *Instituciones políticas y administrativas de Chiloé en el siglo XVIII* (1971); S. Carlos Oliver, *El libro de oro de Concepción* (Concepción, 1950); Eduardo Pino Zapata, *Historia de Temuco* (Temuco, 1969); N. Alberto Recart, *El Laja un río creador* (1971); John H. Whaley, *Transportation in Chile's Bío Bío Region: 1850-1915*, Ph.D. diss. (Indiana Univ., 1974).

EDUCATION

The organization and role of education in Chilean society has received insufficient attention by historical researchers. Among the few significant contributions in this area, the following sources are foundations for future research:

Oscar Alvarez, "Aspectos sociólogicos del problema educacional en Chile," *Revista Méxicana de Sociología 20*, No. 3, 1958;

Miguel Luis Amunátegui, *Estudios sobre instrucción pública*, 3 vols., 1897-98;

Manuel Ballesterosa E., *Compilación de leyes y decretos vigentes en materia de instrucción pública*;

Manuel J. Barrera, "Trayectoria del movimiento de reforma universitaria en Chile," *Journal of Latin American Studies*, No. 10, 1968;

Rudolph C. Blitz, "Some Observations on the Chilean Educational System and its Relations to Economic Growth," *Education and Economic Development*, Chicago, 1965;

Fernando Campos Harriet, *150 años de desarrollo educational: 1810-1960*, 1960;

Raúl Cortes Pinto, *Bibliografía anotada de educación superior*, Universidad Técnica Federico, Santa María, 1967;

Ricardo Donoso, *Recopilación de leyes, reglamentos, y decretos relativos a los servicios de enseñanza pública*, 1937;

Clark C. Gill, *Education and Social Change in Chile*, Washington, D.C., U.S. Govt. Printing Office, 1966;

Amanda Labarca Hubertson, *Historia de la enseñanza en Chile*, 1939;

Ministerio de Educación Pública, *Bases generales para el planteamiento de la educación chilena*, 1961; and *Algunos antecedentes para el planteamiento integral de la educación chilena*, 1964;

Enrique Molina, *El liceo y la formación de la élite*, 1933;

Robert Munizata Aguirre, *El estado y la educación*, 1953;

Máximo Pacheco Gómez, *La universidad de Chile*, 1953;

Tancredo Pinochet, *Bases para una política educacional: al frente del libro de Amanda Labarca*, 1944;

Maximiliano Salas Marchant, *Reflexiones educaciones en torno a nuestro situación social*, 1942;

Gabriel Sanhueza, "Panorama de la evolución de las ciencias pedadógicas y la investigación educacional en Chile: 1900-1960," *Anales de la Universidad de Chile*, 120, No. 125, 1962;

Luis Terán, *Nuestra enseñanza secundaria: los problemas y las soluciones*, 1938;

Allen L. Woll, "For God and Country: Historical Textbooks and the Secularization of Chilean Society: 1840-1890," *Journal of Latin American Studies*, No. 7, 1975.

POLITICS—POLITICAL HISTORY, MEMOIRS, AND
GENERAL INTERPRETATIONS OF CHILEAN
POLITICS IN THE TWENTIETH CENTURY

Chilean politics in the 20th century has attracted considerable attention from Chilean authors and foreign observers alike. Before 1973, scholars routinely depicted Chile as a permanent exception to the common pattern of caudillismo and military government in Latin America. In practice, Chilean formal democracy did seem to depart from the "typical" Latin American political experience. Not surprisingly therefore, much of the literature on Chilean politics focuses upon constitutional history, elections, the party spectrum, and the various presidential administrations. For the English-language reader, the most important pre-1970 description and analysis of Chilean politics remains Federico Gil, *The Political System of Chile* (Boston, 1966). Other general works on Chilean politics, constitutional history, policy dilemmas, and class conflict range from the memoirs of Chilean presidents to careful studies of interest groups, the military or the Chilean legislature. Listed below are a number of books and articles of general interest to students of Chilean politics followed, in turn, by a list of works concerned particularly with elections, the political party system, and individual parties or movements:

Weston Agor, *The Chilean Senate: Internal Distribution of Influence*, Austin, 1971;

Jorge Ahumada, *La crisis integral de Chile*, 1966;

Arturo Alessandri, *Recuerdos de gobierno*, 3 vols., 1967;

Carlos Andrade Geywitz, *Elementos de derecho constitucional chileno*, 1963;

Mario Bernashcina, *Los constituyentes de 1925, 1945; Derecho municipal chileno*, 3 vols., 1952; and *Manual de derecho constitucional*, 1955;

H. E. Bicheno, "Antiparliamentary Themes in Chilean History: 1920-1970," *Allende's Chile*, Kenneth Medhurst (ed.), London, 1972;

Ricardo Boizard, *Cuatro retratos en profunidad: Ibáñez, Lafferte, Leighton, Walker*, 1950 (brief biographies of leading political figures);

Frank Bonilla and Myron Glaser (eds.), *Student Politics in Chile*, New York, 1970;

Claude G. Bowers, *Chile Through Embassy Windows: 1939-1953*, New York, 1958;

Ben Burnett, *Political Groups in Chile*, Austin, 1972;

Fernando Campos Harriet, *Historia constitucional de Chile*, 1956;

Peter Cleaves, *Bureaucratic Politics and Administration in Chile*, Berkeley, 1975;

Luis Correa, *El presidente Ibánez: la política y los políticos*, 1962;

Ricardo Cruz-Coke, *Geografía electoral de Chile*, 1952;

Francisco Cumplido C., "Constitución política de 1925: hoy crisis de las instituciones políticas chilenas," *Cuadernos de la Realidad Nacional*, No. 7, Sept. 1970;

Charles H. Daughtery (ed.), *Chile: Election Factbook*, Washington, D. C., 1963;

Ricardo Donoso, *Alessandri, agitador y demoledor: cincuenta años de historia política de Chile*, 2 vols., Mexico, 1952-54; and *Desarrollo político y social de Chile*, 1943;

Paul Drake, "The Political Responses of the Chilean Upper Class to the Great Depression and the Threat of Socialism: 1931-1933," *The Well Born and the Powerful*, F. C. Jaher (ed.), Urbana, Ill., 1973; and *Socialism and Populism in Chile, 1932-1952*, Univ. of Illinois, 1978;

Enzo Faletto, et al. (eds.), *Génesis histórico del proceso político chileno*, 1971;

Herman Finer, *The Chilean Development Corporation*, Montreal, 1947;

Jorge González von Marées, *El mal de Chile: sus causas y sus remedios*, 1940 (analysis of Chile's "problem" by Chilean Nazi leader);

José G. Guerra, *La constitución de 1925*, 1929;

Ernst Halperin, *Nationalism and Communism in Chile*, Cambridge, Mass., 1965;

Julio Heise González, *Historia constitucional de Chile*, 1954;

Phillip J. Houseman, *Chilean Nationalism: 1920-1952*, Ph.D. diss., Stanford Univ., 1960;

Eduardo Goddard Labarca, *Chile invadido: reportaje a la intromisión extranjera*, 1968;

Elías Lafferte, *Vida de un comunista*, 1957;

Norbert Lechner, *La democracia en Chile*, Buenos Aires, 1970;

Frank Marshall Lewis, *The Political Effects of a Multi-Party System upon the Presidential Form of Government in Chile*, Ph.D. diss. Univ. of Texas, 1955;

Armand Mattelart, et al., *La ideología de la dominación en una sociedad dependiente*, Buenos Aires, 1970;

Francisco José Moreno, *Legitimacy and Stability in Latin America: A Study of Chilean Political Culture*, New York, 1969;

Arturo Olavarría B., *Chile entre dos Alessandri*, 2 vols., 1962-65;

James Petras, *Politics and Social Forces in Chilean Development*, Berkeley and Los Angeles, 1969;

Frederick B. Pike, *Chile and the United States: 1880-1962*, Notre Dame, Ind., 1963;

Fernando Pinto, *Crónica política del siglo XX*, 1970;

Kalman Silvert, *The Chilean Development Corporation*, Ph.D. diss., Univ. of Pennsylvania, 1948; *Chile: Yesterday and Today*, New York, 1965; *The Conflict Society: Reaction and Revolution in Latin America*, New Orleans, 1961; "A Political-Economic Sketch of Chile," *AUFS Newsletter 4*, Jan. 1957; and "Some propositions on Chile," *AUFS West Coast South America Series 11*, No. 11 (Chile), New York, 1964;

Osvaldo Sunkel, "Change and Frustration in Chile," *Obstacles to Change in Latin America*, Claudio Veliz (ed.), New York and London, 1965;

Arturo Valenzuela, *Political Brokers in Chile: Local Government in a Centralized Polity*, Durham, N. C., 1977;

Thomas C. Wright, *The Sociedad Nacional de Agricultura in Chilean Politics: 1879-1938*, Ph.D. diss., Univ. of California, Berkeley, 1971;

Jordan Marten Young, *Chilean Parliamentary Government: 1891-1924*, Ph.D. diss., Princeton Univ., 1953;

Maurice Zeitlin, "The Social Determinants of Political Democracy in Chile," *Latin America*, J. Petras and M. Zeitlin (eds.), Fawcett, Conn., 1968.

POLITICS—ELECTIONS, POLITICAL PARTIES, AND POLITICAL MOVEMENTS

The evolution of Chilean political parties and the electoral system are treated in:

Roger Abbot, "The Role of Contemporary Political Parties in Chile," *APSR* 45, June 1951;

José Luis Castro, *El sistema electoral chileno*, 1941;

D. Corkhill, *From Dictatorship to Popular Front: Parties and Coalition Politics in Chile 1931-1941*, Ph.D. diss., Univ. of Essex, Eng., 1974;

Alberto Edwards, *Bosquejo histórico de los partidos políticos chilenos*, 1936;

Alberto Edwards and Eduardo Frei Montalva, *Historia de los partidos políticos chilenos*, 1949;

Federico Gil, *Genesis and Modernization of Political Parties in Chile*, Gainesville, 1962;

Sergio Guilsasti Tagle, *Partidos políticos chilenos*, 2nd ed., 1964;

René León Echaíz, *Evolución histórica de los partidos políticos chilenos*, 2nd ed., 1971;

Charles Parrish, Arpad Von Lazar, and Jorge Tapia Videla, *The Chilean Congressional Elections of March 7, 1965: An Analysis*, Washington, D.C., 1965;

Karen L. Remmer, "The Timing, Pace, and Consequence of Political Change in Chile: 1918-1925," *HAHR*, No. 57, May 1977;

Fernando S. Silva, *Los partidos políticos chilenos*, 1972;

Peter Snow, "The Political Party System in Chile," *South Atlantic Quarterly*, No. 62, Autumn 1963;

Arturo Valenzuela, "The Scope of the Chilean Party System," *Comparative Politics* 4, January 1972;

Karen Vincent-Smith (Remmer), *Party Competition and Public Policy in Chile and Argentina: 1890-1930*, Ph.D. diss., Univ. of Chicago, 1974.

On the Radical Party and the Popular Front period, in addition to the excellent study by Drake mentioned above; see:

Salvador Allende Gossens, "Pedro Aguirre Cerda," *Arauco*, Jan. 1964;

Alberto Baltra Cortés, *Pedro Aguirre Cerda*, 1960;

Francisco Barría Soto, *El partido radical: sus historia y sus obras*, 1957;

Florencio Duran Bernales, *El partido radical*, 1958;

Juan C. Fernández, *Pedro Aguirre Cerda y el frente popular chileno*, 1938;

Gabriel González Videla, *El partido radical y la evolución social de Chile*, Gainesville, 1962;

Luis Palma Zuñiga, *Historia del partido radical*, 1967; and *Pedro Aguirre Cerda: maestro-estadista-gobernante*, 1963;

Darío Poblete and Alfredo Bravo, *Historia del partido radical y del frente popular*, 1936;

Eudocio Ravines, *The Yenan Way*, 1951 (ex-Comintern agent in Latin

America recounts his role in formation of Chilean Popular Front and activities of Chilean Marxists);

Peter Snow, *El radicalismo chileno*, Buenos Aires, 1972;

John Reese Stevenson, *The Chilean Popular Front*, Philadelphia, 1942;

Richard R. Super, *The Chilean Popular Front Presidency of Pedro Aguirre Cerda: 1938-1941*, Ph.D. diss., Arizona State Univ. 1975;

M. Salvador Valdés, *Cinco años de gobierno de izquierda: 1939-1943: las instituciones y las finanzas*, Puente Alto, 1944;

Chilean socialism is discussed in:

Augustín Alvarez Villablanca, *Objetivos del socialismo en Chile*, 1946;

Fernando Casaneuva and Manuel Fernández C., *El partido socialista y la lucha de clases en Chile*, 1973;

Carlos Charlín, *Del avión rojo a la república socialista*, 1972 (excellent source of material on late 1920s and early 1930s);

Alejandro Chelén Rojas, *Trayectoria del socialismo*, Buenos Aires, 1967;

Salamón Corbalán, *El partido socialista*, 1957;

Mirian Hochwald, *Imagery in Politics: A Study of the Ideology of the Chilean Socialist Party*, Ph.D. diss., Univ. of California, Los Angeles, 1971;

Julio César Jobet, *El partido socialista de Chile*, 2 vols., 1971; and Alejandro Chelén R., *Pensamiento teórico y político del partido socialista*, 1972; *Socialismo y comunismo*, 1952; and *El socialismo chileno a través de sus congresos*, 1965;

Oscar Schnake Vergara, *Chile y la guerra: hacia una democracia dirigida*, 1941 (Political commentary by leading Chilean socialist);

Jack Ray Thomas, "The Evolution of a Chilean Socialist: Marmaduke Grove," *HAHR* 47, No. 1, 1967;

Oscar Waiss, *Presencia del socialismo en Chile*, 1952.

Key works for understanding the origins and growth of the Chilean Communist party include:

Carlos Contreras Labarca, *La conspiración de los enemigos del pueblo*, 1940; and *Por la paz, por nuevas victorias del frente popular*, 1939;

Jorge Jiles Pizarro, *Partido comunista de Chile*, 1957;

Hernán Ramírez Necochea, *Orígen y formación del partido comunista en Chile*, 1965.

The Conservative and Christian Democratic parties are studied by:

Ignacio Arteaga Undurraga, *Reseña histórica de las XVI convensiones del partido conservador*, 1947;

George Grayson, *El partido demócrata cristiano chileno*, Buenos Aires, 1968;

Frank Mazella, *Party-Building in a Modernizing Society: A Study of the Intermediate Leaders of the Chilean Christian Democratic Party*, 2 vols., Ph.D. diss., Indiana Univ., 1972;

Bartolomé Palacios and Héctor Rodríguez de la Sotta, *El partido conservador y la democracia cristiana*, 1933;

Marcial Sanfuentes C., *El partido conservador*, 1957.

Michael Potashnik treats the Chilean Nazi movement in *Nacismo: National Socialism in Chile:1932-1938*, Ph.D. diss. (Univ. of California, Los Angeles, 1974).

POLITICS—CATHOLIC CHURCH

The Catholic Church has played a significant but ambiguous role in recent Chilean history. With leading Church intellectuals and dignitaries associated with the Christian Democratic government and a sweeping anti-Marxist campaign after 1962, Church activity took on an overtly political character that contrasted markedly with its earlier linkage to the Conservative party. A number of studies captured this new reformist orientation of the Church; only David Mutchler, *The Church as a Political Factor in Latin America; with Particular Reference to Colombia and Chile*, New York (1971), details the role of Church policy and programs in the Cold War, the Alliance for Progress, and the domestic anti-Marxist movement in Chile. Mutchler's book is essential to the understanding of the recent role of the Chilean church in national life. Other important works on the "new" church in Chile and the Catholic reformers include:

Isidoro Alonso, Renato Poblete, and Garriso Ginés, *La iglesia en Chile: estructuras eclesiasticas*, Madrid, 1961;

William J. Coleman, *Latin American Catholicism: A Self Evaluation*, Maryknoll, N.Y., 1958;

John J. Considine (ed.), *The Church in the New Latin America*, Notre Dame, Ind., 1964;

William V. D'Antonio and Frederick B. Pike (eds.), *Religion, Revolution and Reform*, New York, 1964.

Oscar Domínguez, *El campesinado chileno y la acción católica rural*, Fribourg, FERES, 1961;

Henry Landsberger and Fernando Canitrot, *Iglesia, intelectuales y campesinos*, INSORA, 1967 (an excellent study of the role of progressive Catholics in the Chilean rural labor movement);

Alejandro Magnet, *El padro Hurtado*, 3rd ed., 1957;

J. Lloyd Mecham, *Church and State in Latin America*, Chapel Hill, 1966;

Frederick Pike, "Catholic Church and Modernization in Peru and Chile," *Journal of Interamerican Affairs* 20, No. 2, Mar. 1966;

Renato Poblete, *La iglesia en Chile*, Fribourg and Bogotá, FERES, 1962;

Thomas G. Sanders, "The Chilean Episcopate," *AUFS Newsletter*, July 1968;

Thomas G. Sanders and Brian H. Smith, "The Chilean Catholic Church During the Allende and Pinochet Regimes," *AUFS West Coast South America Series* 22, New York, 1975;

Secretariado General de Episcopado de Chile, *La iglesia y el problema del campesinado chileno*, 1962;

Ivan Vallier, *Catholicism, Social Control and Modernization in Latin America*, New York, 1970.

THE MILITARY IN CHILEAN POLITICS AND SOCIETY

Many Chilean sources, including government publications, deal with the history of the armed forces or particular military institutions such as the Escuela Militar. A doctoral dissertation by Tommie Hillmon, Jr., *A History of the Armed Forces of Chile from Independence to 1920*, Syracuse Univ. (1963), provides seventy pages of annotated bibliographical references to primary sources and secondary materials on the Chilean military and diplomatic relations with its neighbors as well as detailed studies of military campaigns in the independence period, Chile's 19th-century wars, and the civil wars of 1851, 1859, and 1891. Hillmon's bibliography also contains a very extensive list of travel accounts of Chile from the 17th century onward and could be profitably consulted by scholars reviewing travel literature for Chile and Latin America more generally. Frederick Nunn's *Chilean Politics: 1920-1931*, cited earlier, is a key source on the important role of the military in Chilean politics and society in the first three decades of the 20th century. Nunn's selective bibliography is extremely helpful for materials on the military and Chilean politics in this period. The same author's *The Military in Chilean History*, Albuquerque (1976), explores the role of the Chilean military from 1810 to the military coup of 1973. Nunn has also contributed a number of articles on the Chilean military from the 19th century to the 1940s. Other especially useful sources on the Chilean military in politics in the 20th century include:

Arturo Ahumada, *El ejército y la revolución del 5 de septiembre 1924: reminiscencias*, 1931;

R. Aldunate Phillips, *Ruido de sables*;

Pablo Baraona Urzua, et al., *Fuerzas armadas y seguridad nacional*, 1973;

General Juan Bennett, *La revolución del 5 septiembre*, 1925;

General Jorge Boonen Rivera, *Participación del ejército en el desarrollo y progreso del país*, 1917;

Estado mayor del ejército, *Historia militar de Chile*, 3 vols., 1969;

Roy Hansen, *Military Culture and Organizational Decline: A Study of the Chilean Army*, Ph.D. diss., Univ. of California, Los Angeles, 1967;

Alain Joxe, *Las fuerzas armadas en el sistema político chileno*, 1970;

Alberto Lara, *Los oficiales alemán en Chile*, 1969;

Carlos López V., *Historia de la marina de Chile*, 1929;

René Millar C., "Significado y antecedentes del movimiento militar de 1924," *Historia 2*, 1972-73;

Jorge Nef, "The Politics of Repression: The Social Pathology of the Chilean Military," *Latin American Perspectives* (*Chile: Blood on the Peaceful Road*), Summer 1974;

Lisa North, *Civil-Military Relations in Argentina, Chile and Peru*, Berkeley, 1966;

Alberto Polloni Roldán, *Las fuerzas armadas de Chile en la vida nacional*, 1972;

General Carlos Saez Morales, *Recuerdos de un soldado*, 3 vols., 1933-34 (good source for Chile's "Socialist Republic");

George Strawbridge, Jr., *Militarism and Nationalism in Chile: 1920-1932*, Ph.D. diss., Univ. of Pennsylvania, 1968;

Terrence S. Tarr, *Military Intervention and Civilian Reaction in Chile: 1924-1936*, Ph.D. diss., Univ. of Florida, 1960;

Augustín Toro Dávila, *Síntesis histórico-militar de Chile*, 2 vols., 1969.

CHRISTIAN DEMOCRACY

From 1964 to 1970 Christian Democratic ideology and leadership dominated Chilean society. For over three decades Christian Democratic intellectuals had proclaimed their doctrine, criticized Chilean society, and promised an alternative to capitalism and socialism. Key works of the Christian Democratic leaders provide some insight into their goals, values, and hopes for a new "communitarian" society in Chile:

Jaime Castillo, *Los caminos de la revolución*, 1972;

Jaime Castillo Velasco, *Las fuentes de la democracia cristiana*, 1963;

Jacques Chonchol and Julio Silva Solar, *Hacia un mundo comunitario: condiciones de una política social cristiana,* 1951;
Eduardo Frei Montalva, *Chile desconocido,* 1937; *La verdad tiene su hora,* 1955; *El social cristianismo,* 1951; *Pensamiento y acción,* 1958; *La política y el espíritu,* 1940; and *Aún es tiempo,* 1942;
Julio Silva and Bosco Parra, *Nociones para una política demócrata cristiana,* 1947;
William Thayer Arteaga, *Trabajo, empresa, y revolución,* 1968.

CHRISTIAN DEMOCRACY AND THE REVOLUTION IN LIBERTY

Despite the idealism of some Christian Democrats, the hard realities of Chilean politics and the historical legacy of the Chilean social question obstructed implementation of their reformist program. Supported heavily by United States policymakers with loans and "foreign aid" the Christian Democrats found themselves caught between the strong forces of the past and the calls for revolution from the political left. The hard road of political reform—the successes, failures, and the ultimate electoral defeat in 1970—are documented in a large and still growing literature. Key sources include:

Alan Angell, "Chile: The Difficulties of Democratic Reform," *International Journal,* No. 24, 1969; and "Christian Democracy in Chile," *Current History,* No. 58, 1970;
Richardo Boizard, *La democracia cristiana en Chile,* 1963.
Luis Corvalán L., *Chile hoy: la lucha de los comunistas chilenos en las condiciones del gobierno de Frei,* Buenos Aires, 1965 (analysis by leader of Chilean Communist party);
Thomas Edwards, *Economic Development and Reform in Chile,* Michigan State Univ., 1972;
Eduardo Frei, et al., *Reforma constitucional: 1970,* 1970;
Edward de Glab, Jr., *Christian Democracy, Marxism and Revolution in Chile: The Election and Overthrow of Allende,* Ph.D. diss., Northern Illinois Univ., 1975;
George W. Grayson, Jr., "Chile's Christian Democratic Party: Power Factions, and Ideology," *Review of Politics,* No. 31, Apr. 1969; and "Significance of the Frei Administration for Latin America," *Orbis,* No. 9, Fall 1965;
Leonard Gross, *The Last Best Hope: Eduardo Frei and Chilean Democracy,* New York, 1967;
David Lehman, "Political Incorporation versus Political Stability: The Case of the Chilean Agrarian Reform: 1965-1970," *Journal of Development Studies,* No. 7, July 1971;

Sidney Lens, "Chile's Revolution in Liberty," *Progressive*, No. 30, Oct. 1966;

Sergio Molina, *El proceso de cambio en Chile*, 1972;

Arturo Olavarría B., *Chile bajo la democracia-cristiana*, 6 vols., 1966-71;

James Petras, *Chilean Christian Democracy: Politics and Social Forces*, Berkeley, 1967;

Paul E. Sigmund, "Christian Democracy in Chile," *Journal of International Affairs*, No. 20, 1966;

Osvaldo Sunkel, "Change and Frustration in Chile," *Obstacles to Change in Latin America*, Claudio Veliz (ed.), New York and London, 1965;

William Thiesenhusen, "Grassroots Economic Pressures in Chile: An Enigma for Development Planners," *Economic Development and Cultural Change*, No. 16, April 1968;

J. Thome, "Expropriations in Chile Under the Frei Agrarian Reform," *American Journal of Comparative Law*, No. 10, Summer 1971;

Edward J. Williams, *Latin American Christian Democratic Parties*, Knoxville, Tenn., 1967;

Luis Vitale, *Esencia y apariencia de la democracia cristiana*, 1964;

Arpad Von Lazar and L. Quiros Videla, "Christian Democracy: Lessons in the Politics of Reform Management," *Interamerican Economic Affairs* 21, No. 4, Spring 1968;

Sergio Vuskovic, *Problemática demócrata-cristiana, propiedad, revolución, estado*, 1968.

UNIDAD POPULAR AND AFTER

Never has more been written about Chile than has appeared since 1970 with regard to the Popular Unity coalition and the subsequent military coup. The published literature is truly massive. Moreover, the number of books on non-political topics also mushroomed, creating a veritable wave of Chilean publications. Lee H. Williams, comp., *The Allende Years*, lists almost 3000 Chilean imprints held in selected North American libraries.

Existing materials on the Unidad Popular experience itself represent a mix of ideological and descriptive summaries of the events of the Allende years. A preliminary review of more than thirty of these analyses from differing ideological perspectives can be found in Arturo and J. Samuel Valenzuela, "Visions of Chile," in *Latin American Research Review 10* (Fall 1975). This review article is an excellent starting point for understanding the literature on the Unidad Popular years.

A Marxist-oriented review of the early literature after the coup is found in Ron Chilcote and Terry Dietz-Fee, "Assessing the Literature since the Coup," *Latin American Perspectives 1* (Summer 1974; a special issue,

Chile: Blood on the Peaceful Road). The same issue also includes articles on theoretical aspects of the Unidad Popular experience, the military, the upper classes, short-term effects of the military's economic policies, and agrarian reform from 1964 to September 1973.

To date, if forced to choose a single volume from among the hundreds of books, edited collections, and articles that analyze the Allende years, a good choice would be Stefan de Vylder's *Allende's Chile, The Political Economy of the Rise and Fall of the Unidad Popular* (Cambridge Univ., London and New York, 1974). This book is a careful and extremely well-developed analysis of the political, economic, and social context of the Allende experience and the factors leading up to the military coup of 1973.

An important source of materials for insight into the situation and position of the Catholic left, some Christian Democrats and others who left the party, during the Allende administration, is Jaime Ruiz-Tagle P., *Poder político y transición al socialismo: tres años de la unidad popular*. Published in September 1973, just before the coup, the volume includes a number of articles published in *Mensaje*, the Jesuit journal in Santiago, during the Unidad Popular years. In addition to offering a clear insight into the perceptions of the Catholic left during these years, its bibliography lists some 400 titles—most from Chilean journals, newspapers, magazines, and books from 1970 to 1973. Arrangement of titles by topic— transition to socialism, agrarian reform, the problem of power, classes and social groups, political parties and interest groups, etc.—facilitates use by researchers.

An extremely useful, edited collection on Chile in the 1960s and early 1970s is Arturo and J. Samuel Valenzuela, *Chile: Politics and Society* (New Brunswick, N. J., 1976), which includes an introductory assessment of the constraints upon the Allende government and articles treating electoral politics, public opinion, the labor movement, agrarian reform, foreign capital in the Chilean economy, and the "invisible blockade" by the United States against the Unidad Popular government. Walden F. Bello, *The Roots and Dynamics of Revolution and Counterrevolution in Chile*, Ph.D. diss. (Princeton Univ., 1975), provides a detailed political-historical analysis in the context of theories on economic development and class conflict. Bello's bibliography includes hundreds of periodical and journal articles on the Unidad Popular years. Paul Sigmund's *The Overthrow of Allende and the Politics of Chile, 1964-1976*, (Pittsburgh, 1977), offers an extremely readable analysis of Chilean politics from the mid-1960s through the Unidad Popular years, with brief treatment of the military regime.

Beyond these basic sources the following works offer a diversity of treatments of the Unidad Popular years:

Salvador Allende, *La lucha por la democracia económica y las libertades de difusión de la Presidencia de la República*, 1972; and *El mensaje del Presidente Allende ante el Congreso Peno*, Messages delivered May 21, 1971, 1972, 1973.

Juan E. Azcoaga, *El horizonte chileno*, Buenos Aires, 1973;

Pablo Baraona Urzua, *Chile: A Critical Survey*, 1972;

A. Bardon, et al., *Itinerario de una crisis política económica y transición al socialismo*, 1972;

Peter Camejo, *Allende's Chile: Is It Going Socialist?*, New York, 1971 (Trotzkyist assessment of Unidad Poplar program);

Gustavo Canihuante, *La revolución chilena*, 1971;

Fernando Castillo, et al., "Las masas, el estado y el problema del poder en Chile," *Cuadernos de la Realidad Nacional*, Apr. 1973;

Jacques Chonchol, "La reforma agraria en Chile: 1970-1973," *El Trimestre Económico*, No. 53, 1976;

Luis Corvalán, *Camino de la victoria*, 1971;

Regís Debray, *Conversations with Allende*, 1971;

Andres Echeverría and Luis Frei (eds.), 1970-1973: *la lucha por la juricidad en Chile*, 3 vols., 1974;

Les Evans (ed.), *Disaster in Chile*, New York, 1974 (Trotskyist view of 1970-73);

Richard E. Feinberg, *The Triumph of Allende: Chile's Legal Revolution*, New York, 1972;

Alejandro Foxley, et al., *Chile: busqueda de un nuevo socialismo*, 1971;

Joan Garcés, 1970: *la pugna política por la presidencia de Chile*, 1971; *El estado y los problemas tácticos en el gobierno de Allende*, Madrid, 1973 (analysis by Allende's political adviser); and (ed.), *Nuestro camino al socialismo—la vía chilena*, Buenos Aires, 1971 (excerpts from speeches and writings of Salvador Allende);

Federico Gil, Ricardo Lagos and Henry Landsberger (eds.), *Chile, 1970-1973: lecciones de una experiencia*, Madrid, 1977;

Instituto de Economía, *La economía chilena en 1971*, Universidad de Chile, 1972;

Sergio Onofre Jarpa, *Creo en Chile*, 1973 (analysis by right-wing político);

Dale C. Johnson (ed.), *The Chilean Road to Socialism*, New York, 1973;

Eduardo Labarca Goddard, *Chile al rojo*, 1971;

Gonzalo Martner (ed.), *El pensamiento económico del gobierno de Allende*, 1971;

Kenneth Medhurst (ed.), *Allende's Chile*, London, 1972;

Hernán Millas and Emilio Gilippi, *Chile 1970-1973: crónica de una experiencia*, 1974;

Orlando Millas, *Exposición sobre la política económica del gobierno y del estado de la hacienda pública*, Ministerio de Hacienda, Folleto No. 122, 1972;

Carlos Mistral, *Chile: del triunfo popular al golpe fascista*, Mexico, 1974;

Robert Moss, *Chile's Marxist Experiment*, Abbot Devon, Eng., 1973;

José Musalem, *Crónica de un fracaso*, 1973;

North American Congress on Latin America, "Chile: Facing the Blockade," *Latin America and Empire Report*, New York, 1973;

Claudio Orrago, *El paro nacional*, 1972;

Ian Roxborough, Phillip O'Brien, and Jackie Roddick, *Chile: The State and Revolution* (contains a very helpful "chronology of main events" 1969-September 11, 1973 and Marxist-oriented analysis of the Unidad Popular experience);

Unidad Popular, *Programa básico del gobierno de la Unidad Popular*, 1970;

Florencia Varas, *Conversaciones con Viaux*, 1972.

A variety of explanations for the failure of the Unidad Popular administration appear in:

Solon Barraclough, "The State of Chilean Agriculture before the Coup," *Land Tenure Center Newsletter*, No. 43, Jan.-Mar. 1974;

François Borricaud, "Chile: Why Allende Fell," *Dissent*, Summer 1974;

René Castillo, "Lessons and Prospects of the Revolution," *World Marxist Review*, No. 17, June 1974;

Pío García (ed.), *Las fuerzas armadas y el golpe de estado en Chile*, Mexico, 1974;

D. Holden, "Allende and the Myth Makers," *Encounter*, Jan. 1974;

Brian Loveman, "Allende's Chile: Political Economy of the Peaceful Road to Disaster," *New Scholar*, 1978;

Gary MacEoin, *No Peaceful Road: The Chilean Struggle for Dignity*, New York, 1974;

North American Congress on Latin America, "Chile: The Story Behind the Coup," *Latin America and Empire Report*, Oct. 1973;

David Plotke, "Coup in Chile," *Socialist Revolution*, No. 3, 1973;

Paul N. Rosenstein-Rodan, "Why Allende Failed," *Challenge*, May-June 1974;

Armando Uribe, *The Black Book of American Intervention in Chile*, Boston, 1975;

L. Whitehead, "Why Allende Fell," *World Today*, Nov. 1973.

Official explanations by the Chilean military of the rationale for the *golpe* and information on subsequent policies can be found in:

Chile, 11 de septiembre de 1975.
Chile, Junta de Gobierno, *Declaración de principios del gobierno de Chile*, 1974; *Algunos fundamentos de la intervención militar en Chile*, 2nd ed., 1974; and *Libro blanco del cambio de gobierno en Chile*, 1974;
Chilean Foreign Investment Law, 1976 (includes new investment code and analysis of special fishery policy);
Chilegram (monthly with "News from 'Chile'." Government propaganda and right wing views);
Constitutional Acts Proclaimed by the Government of Chile, Sept. 11, 1976;
Garardo Cortes Rencoret, "Introducción a la seguirdad nacional," *Cuadernos del instituto de ciencia política*, Universidad Católica de Chile, Feb. 1976;
Enrique Ortuzar Escobar, "La nueva institucionalidad chilena," *Cuadernos del instituto de ciencia política*, Universidad Católica de Chile, Jan. 1976;
"Primero de Mayo 1976," Speech by Minister Sergio Fernández on Labor Day, 1976 (includes decrees related to labor).

Accounts of repression by the military regime and the impact of their policies on the Chilean working classes are numerous. The following sources provide an overview of this literature:

Alan Angell, "Counter-revolution in Chile," *Current History*, Jan. 1974;
Chile: masacre de un pueblo, cristianos frente a los hechos, resistencia y solidaridad, Lima, 1974;
IDOC, *Chile Under Military Rule*, New York, 1974;
Phillipe Labreveux, *Chile bajo las botas-crónicas del terror*, Buenos Aires, 1973;
Ricardo Lagos and Oscar Rufatt, "Military Government and Real Wages in Chile," *LARR*, Summer 1975;
North American Congress on Latin America, "The United States Propping Up the Junta," *Latin America and Empire Report*, Oct. 1974;
Pablo Santillana, *Chile: análisis de un año de gobierno militar*, Buenos Aires, 1974;
"Terror in Chile," *New York Review of Books*, May 30, 1974;
Víctor Villanueva, *Modelo contrarevolucionario chileno*, Lima, 1976 (analysis by Peru's foremost expert on the military and politics);
Sergio Villegas, *Chile-El estadio: los crímenes de la junta militar*, Buenos Aires, 1974.

Index